Where to stay

in Northern Ireland

'Come on over in 1998 and see this beautiful place for yourself. Enjoy our great outdoors and experience our famous hospitality, and relax in the warmth of our welcome.'

Roy Bailie OBE
Chairman, Northern Ireland Tourist Board

Northern Ireland
Tourist Board

ISBN 1 86193 085 2

If you have any comments on listed establishments please write to:
Quality Assurance Manager
Northern Ireland Tourist Board
59 North Street, Belfast BT1 1NB

Pour tout commentaire relatif aux établissements répertoriés, écrire à:
Quality Assurance Manager
Northern Ireland Tourist Board
59 North Street, Belfast BT1 1NB

Wenn Sie Anmerkungen zu den aufgeführten Häusern haben, schreiben Sie bitte an:
Quality Assurance Manager
Northern Ireland Tourist Board
59 North Street, Belfast BT1 1NB

Front cover : Dufferin Arms Coaching Inn, Killyleagh, Co. Down

Printed by The Universities Press (Belfast) Ltd. 12m/11/97

Where to Stay
in Northern Ireland

Contents

How to use the guide 4

How to get to Northern Ireland
– air and sea links 10

Colour supplement 13

Special mentions in well known guidebooks 49
Getting around in Northern Ireland 51
Useful addresses and publications 52

Hotels, guesthouses, B&Bs
Belfast 53
County Antrim 63
County Armagh 107
County Down 113
County Fermanagh 143
County Londonderry 159
County Tyrone 179

Hostels 192

Self-catering accommodation 199

Camping and caravan parks 241

Index to hotels and guesthouses 264
Index to towns and villages 268
Key to symbols *back flap*
Map *inside back cover*

How to use this guide

The wide range, good quality and convenient location of accommodation for visitors to Northern Ireland are reflected in this guide. Prices and details of facilities are given for over 1,000 places to stay, in four main sections:

- All hotels, guesthouses and B&Bs (bed & breakfast). (Some also appear in the colour supplement).

- Hostels — youth hostels, independent hostels and other low-cost accommodation.

- Self-catering accommodation.

- Camping and caravan parks.

Hotels, guesthouses, B&Bs, hostels and self-catering accommodation are inspected annually by the Northern Ireland Tourist Board (NITB) and meet minimum standards. Hotels are classified by a star system and guesthouses are graded — explained on the page opposite. Self-catering accommodation is also classified by a star system. The section on camping and caravan parks, which are not subject to NITB inspection, has been compiled from information supplied by the operators.

PRICES

Always confirm prices when you book. Accommodation rates in the main listings are the *maximum* for 1998 and include VAT. There may be seasonal reductions or lower-priced rooms. Many places offer special rates for weekend or midweek guests and for families. The prices given for dinner relate to a typical 3-course meal with starter, main course, dessert, VAT and service. High tea is usually a lighter meal.

Prices in the colour supplement are the *lowest* room rates per person sharing, plus breakfast. Entries in this supplement have been placed by proprietors who wish to highlight their establishments.

ACCESS FOR WHEELCHAIR USERS

If you use a wheelchair or have limited mobility, look for entries with one of the new, national 'accessible' symbols indicating those hotels, guesthouses and B&Bs where the standard of access is suitable for wheelchair users:

- accessible to a wheelchair user travelling independently.
- accessible to a wheelchair user travelling with assistance.
- accessible to a person with limited mobility, but able to walk a few paces and up to a maximum of 3 steps.

The same information is not yet available for self-catering accommodation. However, self-catering units which may be suitable for wheelchair users are indicated — see page 199. Check essential details with the proprietor before you book the accommodation.

WALKING THE ULSTER WAY? 𝝹

Convenient places to stay, including campsites, are shown (𝝹). In areas where accommodation is less plentiful addresses may be off-route — check before you set off, and plan your schedule to take account of the availability of overnight accommodation.

Types of accommodation

The Northern Ireland Tourist Board has a statutory duty to inspect all accommodation units appearing in this guide. This ensures that they meet the minimum standards which apply to their category. The categories are hotels, guesthouses, bed & breakfast establishments, self-catering establishments and hostels.

Some hotels and self-catering establishments are listed as unclassified, and some guesthouses are ungraded (U). This is accommodation which has not been in operation long enough to be fully assessed or else the rating is being reviewed.

Hotels are classified by a star system

Five stars *****
Hotels of an international standard with luxurious and spacious guest accommodation including suites. High quality restaurants with table d'hôte and à la carte lunch and dinner menus.

Four stars ****
Large hotels with a high standard of comfort and service in well appointed premises. All bedrooms ensuite. Cuisine meet exacting standards. Comprehensive room service.

Three stars ***
Good facilities with a wide range of services. All bedrooms ensuite. Food available all day.

Two stars **
Good facilities with a reasonable standard of accommodation, food and services. Most bedrooms are ensuite.

One star *
Hotels with acceptable standards of accommodation and food. Some bedrooms have ensuite facilities.

Guesthouses are divided into grades A and B

Grade (A)
Comfortable establishments offering a range of facilities, including lounge and dining room for the exclusive use of guests. A choice of main course for evening meal is usually available. Washbasins are provided in all bedrooms and many have private bathrooms.

Grade (B)
Well furnished houses offering comfortable accommodation with a satisfactory standard of food and service. Most bedrooms have washbasins and some have ensuite facilities.

Bed & breakfast establishments

This category covers a variety of houses in both town and country areas, ranging from large period residences to modern bungalows. Evening meals are available in many of them.

Self-catering establishments

Self-catering establishments listed in this guide are professionally managed and are classified by a star system. The system is explained in the self-catering section (red pages).

Hostels

Hostels, which include youth hostels and boarding schools, provide clean, simple accommodation at a budget price.

Utilisation du guide

Ce guide reflète la variété et la qualité des possibilités d'hébergement proposées aux visiteurs en Irlande du Nord, ainsi que leur emplacement pratique. Il donne le prix et les détails des installations disponibles dans plus de 1 000 établissements en les divisant en quatre sections :

■ Tous les hôtels, pensions de famille et B&B (bed & breakfast). (Certains d'entre eux apparaissent également dans le supplément en couleur.)

■ Auberges — auberges de jeunesse, auberges indépendantes et autres possibilités d'hébergement à moindre coût.

■ Locations de vacances. Voir aussi le supplément en couleur.

■ Terrains de camping et de caravanes.

Les hôtels, pensions de famille, B&B et locations sont inspectés tous les ans par le Northern Ireland Tourist Board (NITB) et doivent se conformer à des normes minimum. Les hôtels sont classés selon un système d'étoiles et les pensions de famille reçoivent une classification — comme indiqué sur la page ci-contre. Les locations de vacances sont également classées selon un système d'étoiles. La section sur les terrains de camping et de caravanes, qui ne sont pas inspectés par le NITB, a été compilée à partir des informations fournies par leurs propriétaires.

PRIX

Demandez toujours confirmation du prix à la réservation. Les prix cités dans les listes représentent les tarifs maximum pour 1998 et comprennent la TVA. Les établissements pratiquent parfois des réductions saisonnières ou possèdent des chambres moins chères. De nombreux établissements proposent un tarif spécial pour les séjours individuels ou familiaux le week-end ou en milieu de semaine. Les prix indiqués pour le dîner comprennent généralement un repas typique de trois plats avec hors-d'oeuvre, plat de résistance et dessert, ainsi que le service et la TVA. Le 'high tea' est généralement un repas plus léger.

Les prix dans le supplément en couleur représentent le tarif minimum de la chambre par personne, plus le petit-déjeuner. Les entrées figurant dans ce supplément ont été demandées par les propriétaires qui souhaitent attirer l'attention sur leur établissement.

ACCÈS POUR FAUTEUILS ROULANTS

Si vous utilisez un fauteuil roulant, ou si vous ne disposez que d'une mobilité limitée, recherchez les entrées qui comprennent les nouveaux symboles nationaux 'accessible'. Ils indiquent les hôtels, les pensions de famille et les B&B accessibles en fauteuil roulant :

♿ Accessible aux personnes non accompagnées qui utilisent un fauteuil roulant.

♿ Accessible aux personnes accompagnées qui utilisent un fauteuil roulant.

♿ Accessible aux personnes ayant une mobilité limitée, mais qui sont en mesure de faire quelques pas et de monter jusqu'à trois marches.

Ces informations ne sont pas encore disponibles pour les locations de logements équipés. Pourtant, les locations permettant l'usage d'un fauteuil roulant sont signalées — voir la page 199. Il est toutefois nécessaire de vérifier les détails avec le propriétaire avant de réserver la location.

RANDONNÉES SUR LE SENTIER ULSTER WAY 🚶

Ce guide vous indique (🚶) des endroits pratiques où vous pourrez vous arrêter en chemin, y compris les terrains de camping. Dans les espaces où les possibilités d'hébergement sont plus limitées, il se peut que les établissements spécifiés ne se trouvent pas directement sur le chemin. Vérifiez avant de partir et planifiez vos étapes en fonction des possibilités d'hébergement.

Types d'hébergement

L'Office de Tourisme d'Irlande du Nord est dans l'obligation d'inspecter tous les établissements répertoriés dans ce guide, pour vérifier s'ils respectent les normes minimum applicables à leur catégorie. Les catégories sont les suivantes: hôtels, pensions, B&B (chambres d'hôte), locations de vacances et auberges.

Certains hôtels et locations de vacances sont répertoriés avec la mention 'Ungraded' (U), c'est-à-dire non-classés. Il s'agit-là d'établissements qui ne sont pas en activité depuis assez longtemps pour avoir été évalués pleinement ou bien des établissements dont le classement est actuellement en cours de révision.

Les hôtels sont classés par étoiles

Cinq étoiles *****
Hôtels de qualité internationale avec des chambres luxueuses et spacieuses, y compris des suites. Restaurants de grande classe avec menu table d'hôte et à la carte au déjeuner et au dîner.

Quatre étoiles ****
Grands hôtels avec un niveau de confort et de service élevé, dans des locaux bien aménagés. Toutes les chambres ont une salle de bains privée. La cuisine répond à des exigences très strictes. Service à l'étage très complet.

Trois étoiles ***
Bonnes installations avec un large éventail de services. Toutes les chambres ont une salle de bains privée. Repas disponibles toute la journée.

Deux étoiles **
Bonnes installations avec un niveau d'hébergement, de cuisine et de services raisonnable. La plupart des chambres ont une salle de bains privée.

Une étoile *
Hôtels offrant un niveau de confort et de restauration acceptable. Certaines chambres ont une salle de bains privée.

Les pensions sont divisées en catégories A et B

Catégorie (A)
Etablissements confortables offrant diverses installations y compris salon et salle à manger réservés exclusivement à la clientèle. Généralement, il y a un choix de plats principaux au repas du soir. Un lavabo est installé dans chaque chambre et beaucoup de chambres ont une salle de bains privée.

Catégorie (B)
Maisons bien meublées offrant un hébergement confortable avec un niveau de restauration et de service satisfaisant. La plupart des chambres ont un lavabo et certaines ont une salle de bains privée.

B&B

Cette catégorie comporte diverses maisons en ville et à la campagne, qui vont de grandes demeures anciennes à des villas modernes. Beaucoup offrent un repas du soir.

Locations de vacances

Les locations de vacances répertoriées dans ce guide sont gérées par des professionnels et sont classées selon un système d'étoiles. Ce système est expliqué dans la section 'locations de vacances' (pages rouges).

Auberges

Les auberges, qui couvrent auberges de vacances et pensions scolaires, offrent un hébergement simple et propre à des prix très avantageux.

Anleitung zu diesem Führer

Dieser Führer spiegelt die große Auswahl, die gehobene Qualität und günstige Lage der Unterkünfte für Besucher von Nordirland wider. Er enthält Preise und Angaben über die Einrichtungen von über 1000 Unterkünften in vier Abschnitten:

- Hotels, Pensionen und B&Bs (Übernachtung mit Frühstück). (Eine Anzahl sind in der Farbbeilage zu finden).

- Herbergen — Jugendherbergen, unabhängige Herbergen und andere preiswerte Unterkünfte .

- Unterkunft für Selbstversorger. (Eine Anzahl sind in der Farbbeilage zu finden).

- Zelt- und Wohnwagenplätze.

Hotels, Pensionen, B&Bs, Herbergen und Unterkünfte für Selbstversorger werden jährlich vom Northern Ireland Tourist Board (NITB) inspiziert und entsprechen dessen Mindestanforderungen. Die Klasse der Hotels wird mit Sternen angegeben und Pensionen werden eingestuft — Siehe Seite gegenüber. Unterkunft für Selbstversorger wird ebenfalls anhand von Sternen klassifiziert. Der Abschnitt über Zelt- und Wohnwagenplätze — diese werden nicht vom NITB inspiziert — wurde anhand der Angaben zusammengestellt, die von den Betrieben zur Verfügung gestellt wurden.

PREISE

Lassen Sie sich die Preise stets bei der Buchung bestätigen. Die Unterkunftspreise der aufgeführten Betriebe stellen die *Höchstpreise* für 1998 dar und gelten inklusive Mehrwertsteuer. Es werden unter Umständen saisonbedingte Preisermäßigungen oder

verbilligte Zimmer angeboten. Zahlreiche Betriebe bieten Gästen während des Wochenendes oder der Woche Sonderangebote. Die Preise für das Abendessen gelten für eine Mahlzeit mit drei Gängen mit einer Vorspeise, einem Hauptgericht und einer Nachspeise inklusive Mehrwertsteuer und Bedienung. 'High tea' ist gewöhnlich ein leichtere Mahlzeit.

Die Preise in der Farbbeilage stellen die *tiefsten* Zimmerpreise pro Person für zwei Personen, die ein Zimmer teilen, plus Frühstück dar. Eintragungen in diesem Abschnitt werden von Betrieben gemacht, die besonders auf sich aufmerksam machen möchten.

ZUGÄNGLICHKEIT FÜR ROLLSTUHLBENUTZER

Falls Sie einen Rollstuhl benutzen oder gehbehindert sind, halten Sie Ausschau nach Eintragungen mit einem der neuen, landesweiten 'Zugänglichkeits'-Symbole, die Hotels, Pensionen und B&Bs kennzeichnen, die für Rollstuhlbenutzer zugänglich sind.

- Zugänglich für Rollstuhlbenutzer ohne Begleitung.
- Zugänglich für Rollstuhlbenutzer mit Begleitung.
- Zugänglich für gehbehinderte Personen, die ein paar Schritte gehen und bis zu drei Stufen hochsteigen können.

Vergleichbare Informationen über Unterkünfte für Selbstversorger sind noch nicht verfügbar. Auf Unterkünfte für Selbstversorger, die für Rollstuhlbenutzer zugänglich sind, wird jedoch besonders hingewiesen, siehe Seite 199. Bitte lassen Sie sich die Angaben vor der Buchung vom Besitzer bestätigen.

UNTERWEGS ENTLANG DEM ULSTER WAY! 🚶

Günstig gelegene Unterkünfte, einschließlich Zeltplätze, werden aufgeführt (🚶). In Gegenden, wo das Angebot beschränkt ist, werden unter Umständen Adressen abseits der Route angegeben — vergewissern Sie sich daher vor dem Aufbruch und planen Sie Ihr Programm je nach Verfügbarkeit von Übernachtungsmöglichkeiten.

Unterkunftsarten

Das Northern Ireland Tourist Board ist gesetzlich verpflichtet, alle in diesem Führer aufgelisteten Unterkünfte zu überprüfen. Dies gewährleistet, daß sie den Mindestanforderungen der entsprechenden Kategorie genügen. Es wird zwischen folgenden Kategorien unterschieden: Hotels, Pensionen, Bed & Breakfast, Unterkunft für Selbstversorger und Herbergen.

Einige Hotels und Unterkünfte für Selbstversorger sind als 'nicht klassifiziert' und einige Pensionen als 'nicht eingestuft' (U) aufgeführt. Dabei handelt es sich um Unterkünfte, die erst seit kurzem geöffnet sind und daher noch nicht entsprechend beurteilt werden konnten, oder deren Einstufung überprüft wird.

Hotels unterstehen der Sterne-Klassifizierung

Fünf Sterne *****
Hotel von internationalem Standard mit luxuriösen und geräumigen Zimmern und Suiten. Erstklassiges Restaurant mit Table d'hôte und A la carte-Service.

Vier Sterne ****
Großes, gut eingerichtetes Hotel mit hohem Standard an Komfort und Service. Alle Zimmer mit Bad. Küche von höchstem Standard. Guter Zimmerservice.

Drei Sterne ***
Gute Einrichtungen mit einem großen Serviceangebot. Alle Zimmer mit Bad. Essen rund um die Uhr.

Zwei Sterne **
Gute Einrichtungen und Unterkunft, Küche und Service von angemessenem Standard. Die meisten Zimmer mit Bad.

Ein Stern *
Hotel von annehmbarem Standard bezüglich Unterkunft und Küche. Einige Zimmer mit Bad.

Bei Pensionen wird zwischen Klasse A und B unterschieden

Klasse A
Komfortabler Betrieb mit einer breiten Auswahl an Einrichtungen, einschließlich Aufenthaltsraum, Eßzimmer für Gäste. Gewöhnlich Auswahl beim Hauptgang des Abendessens. Waschbecken in allen Zimmern. Zahlreiche Zimmer mit Bad.

Klasse B
Gut eingerichtetes Haus mit komfortabler Unterkunft und zufriedenstellendem Standard von Küche und Service. Die meisten Zimmer mit Waschbecken und einige mit Bad.

Einige Pensionen, sie sind durch ein (U) nach dem Namen gekennzeichnet, sind noch nicht lange genug offen, um klassifiziert zu werden, oder es handelt sich um Betriebe, deren Klassifizierung überprüft wird.

Bed & Breakfast-Unterkunft

Diese Kategorie umfaßt Häuser in der Stadt und auf dem Land, von großen 'Period'-Häusern bis zu modernen Bungalows. Viele servieren Abendessen.

Unterkunft für Selbstversorger

In diesem Führer aufgelistete Unterkünfte für Selbstversorger stehen unter fachkundiger Leitung und werden gemäß einem Sterne-System klassifiziert. Das System wird im Abschnitt für Selbstversorger erklärt (rote Seiten).

Herbergen

Herbergen wie Jugendherbergen und Internate bieten saubere, einfache Unterkunft zu günstigen Preisen.

How to get to Northern Ireland – *by air*

Direct from	To	Airline	Reservations ☎
LONDON Heathrow	Belfast Int.	British Airways	0345 222111
LONDON Heathrow	Belfast Int.	British Midland	0345 554554
LONDON Gatwick	Belfast City	Jersey European	0990 676676
LONDON Luton	Belfast City	British Airways Express	0345 222111
LONDON Stansted	Belfast Int.	Jersey European	0990 676676
LONDON Stansted	Belfast Int.	Jersey European	0990 676676
NEW YORK	Belfast Int.	Aer Lingus	(800) 223-6537
NEW YORK	Belfast Int.	American Trans Air	(800) 382-5892
AMSTERDAM	Belfast Int.	Air UK	+44 1603 424288
Aberdeen	Belfast City	British Airways Express	0345 222111
Birmingham	Belfast Int.	British Airways	0345 222111
Birmingham	Belfast City	Jersey European	0990 676676
Blackpool	Belfast City	Jersey European	0990 676676
Bristol	Belfast City	Jersey European	0990 676676
Cardiff	Belfast City	British Airways Express	0345 222111
East Midlands	Belfast Int.	British Midland	0345 554554
Edinburgh	Belfast City	British Airways Express	0345 222111
Exeter	Belfast City	Jersey European	0990 676676
Glasgow	Belfast Int.	British Airways Express	0345 222111
Glasgow	Belfast City	British Airways Express	0345 222111
Glasgow	City of Derry	British Airways Express	0345 222111
Isle of Man	Belfast City	Jersey European	0990 676676
Jersey	Belfast Int.	British Midland	0345 554554
Jersey & Guernsey	Belfast City	Jersey European	0990 676676
Leeds/Bradford	Belfast City	Jersey European	0990 676676
Liverpool	Belfast City	British Airways Express	0345 222111
Manchester	Belfast Int.	British Airways Express	0345 222111
Manchester	Belfast City	British Airways Express	0345 222111
Manchester	City of Derry	British Airways Express	0345 222111
Newcastle-upon-Tyne	Belfast City	Gill Airways	0191-214 6666
Prestwick	Belfast City	Gill Airways	0191-214 6666
Shannon	Belfast Int.	Aer Lingus	(061) 451491
Southampton	Belfast City	British Airways Express	0345 222111

Ask your travel agent about other air services, including onward connections, charters and seasonal services

– and by sea

Ferry services from Britain and Europe to Ireland – North and South

From	To	Ferry company	Reservations ☎	Frequency, sailing time
SCOTLAND				
Cairnryan	Larne	P&O European Ferries	0990 980980	6 per day, 1 hr by Jetliner ship 3 per day, 2¼ hrs
Stranraer	Belfast	SeaCat	0345 523523	5 per day, 1½ hrs by SeaCat catamaran
Stranraer	Belfast	StenaLine	0990 707070	8 per day, 1¾ hrs by Stena HSS
Campbeltown	Ballycastle	Argyll & Antrim Steam Packet Company	0345 523523	2 per day, 3 hrs
WALES				
Holyhead	Dun Laoghaire	StenaLine	0990 707070	5 per day, 1¾ hrs by Stena HSS
Fishguard	Rosslare	StenaLine	0990 707070	3 per day, 1¾ hrs by catamaran 6 per day, 3½ hrs
Holyhead	Dublin	Irish Ferries	0990 171717	2 per day, 3¾ hrs
Pembroke	Rosslare	Irish Ferries	0990 171717	2 per day, 4 hrs
Swansea	Cork	Swansea-Cork	(01792) 456116	6 per week, 10 hrs
ENGLAND				
Liverpool	Belfast	Norse Irish Ferries	(01232) 779090	1 per day, 11 hrs
ISLE OF MAN				
Douglas	Belfast	Isle of Man Steam Packet Company	0345 523523	2 per week, May-Sept only, 2¾ hrs by SeaCat catamaran 5 hrs by ferry
FRANCE				
Le Havre	Rosslare	Irish Ferries	Le Havre 35 19 24 00	2-4 per week, 22 hrs
Le Havre	Cork	Irish Ferries	Le Havre 35 19 24 00	1 per week, 22hrs
Cherbourg	Rosslare	Irish Ferries	Cherbourg 33 23 44 44	2 per week, 17 hrs
Roscoff	Cork	Brittany Ferries	Roscoff 98 29 28 00	2 per week, March-Sept only, 15 hrs
Roscoff	Cork	Irish Ferries	Roscoff 98 61 17 17	1 per week, May-July only, 18 hrs

Note: hours of sailing are approximate

Rail and coach services from Dublin to Belfast

There are 8 trains each day (5 on Sunday) from Connolly St Station, Dublin, to Belfast. The Dublin-Belfast express train takes about 2 hours. Stops for ordinary trains include Newry, Portadown and Lisburn.
Rail information: ☎ Dublin 8366222/Belfast 899411.

The Dublin-Belfast express coach service runs 7 times a day (3 times on Sunday) and takes 3 hours.
Set-down points include Newry, Banbridge, Dromore, Hillsborough and Dublin airport.
Information: ☎ Dublin 8366111/Belfast 333000.

Where to Stay in Northern Ireland

1998 COLOUR SUPPLEMENT

Prices below are the *lowest* rate per person sharing for one night, plus breakfast

Belfast

Beechlawn House Hotel *
4 Dunmurry Lane
Belfast BT17 9RR
☎ **(01232) 612974 Fax 623601**

Family-owned and managed since 1965, the hotel has a country house atmosphere and is located within easy reach of all main roads and air/sea links. With two 18-hole golf courses and a riding school nearby, it makes a perfect holiday base.

Hotel open all year
B & B from £24

Laburnum Lodge
16 Deramore Park
Belfast BT9 5JU
☎ **(01232) 665183 Fax 681460**

Family-owned and managed. Set in a quiet residential area and within easy reach of Queen's University and city centre amenities. All rooms have private facilities and direct-dial telephones. Off-street parking and easy access via M1 motorway.

Guesthouse open all year ex Xmas
B & B from £25

Lisdara (A)
23 Derryvolgie Avenue, Malone Rd
Belfast BT9 6FN
☎ **& fax (01232) 681549**

A comfortable Victorian house in the quiet Malone area of south Belfast, convenient to the city centre, theatres and motorways. Home cooking. Private parking and beautiful gardens will help to make your stay relaxing and enjoyable. Fax is available.

Guesthouse open all year
B & B from £25

Oakdene Lodge (A)
16 Annadale Avenue
Belfast BT7 3JH
☎ **(01232) 492626 Fax 492070**

Large Victorian house set in its own grounds, 2½ miles from the city centre. We offer first class ensuite bedrooms with colour tv, direct-dial phone, hospitality tray, hairdryer, trouser press. Lift to all floors. Private carpark. There are several fine golf courses within easy reach.

Guesthouse open all year
B & B from £25

Old Rectory (A)
148 Malone Rd
Belfast BT9 5LH
☎ **(01232) 667882 Fax 683759**

Built in 1896 as the rectory for St John's Church, Malone, this family owned and run home in mature gardens is within easy reach of Queen's University and Belfast's best restaurants and theatres. All rooms have private facilities, colour tv and hospitality tray. Off-street parking.

Guesthouse open all year
B & B from £25

B & B prices are the *lowest* rate per person sharing for one night.

Roseleigh House (A)
19 Rosetta Park
Belfast BT6 0DL
☎ & fax (01232) 644414

Restored Victorian house in residential south Belfast, 10 minutes drive from city centre beside the main routes to the tourist areas of south Down and the Ards peninsula. Belvoir Park Golf Club is just 10 minutes walk. All rooms ensuite. Private parking.

Guesthouse open all year
B & B from £21

Hermitage Lodge
62 North Rd
Belfast BT5 5NJ
☎ & fax (01232) 203322

Luxuriously appointed town house in mature tree-lined gardens with off-road parking. Beautiful guest lounge and dining room. All bedrooms are ensuite. Close to the city centre, harbour airport and bus and rail stations. Suitable for non-smokers.

Bed-and-breakfast open all year
B & B from £35

Maranatha House
254 Ravenhill Rd
Belfast BT6 8GL
☎ & fax (01232) 460200

Large Victorian town house, 1½ miles from city centre, overlooking Ormeau Park. Convenient to Waterfront Hall, city airport, ferries, rail and bus stations. Eight ensuite rooms, one with disabled facilities. For business or pleasure. Warm welcome. Non-smoking.

Bed-and-breakfast open all year
B & B from £19.50

take a
walk
on the
wild
side

BELFAST
ZOO
Antrim Road
Belfast BT36 7PN
Tel: 01232 776277

Pine Lodge
42a Drumalig Rd, Carryduff
Belfast BT8 8EQ
☎ (01232) 814875

Pine Lodge is six miles from the city centre adjacent to Rockmount Golf Club where residents enjoy all facilities, including reduced green fees. We offer first-class ensuite accommodation with colour tv, radio, hospitality tray, hairdryer etc.

Bed-and-breakfast open all year
B & B from £20

Apartment 5 ***
Brooklands Court, 1-3 Annadale Avenue
Belfast BT7 3JH
☎ (01232) 660232 *or* (01846) 683131 *evening*

Very spacious 2nd-floor apartment in detached Victorian residence. Close to all amenities with views over the hills around Belfast. Two large bedrooms, shower room, study, cloakroom, kitchen and living room with dining area. Intercom, private payphone.

Self-catering apartment open all year
From £290 per week

L'Academie *****
14 College Gardens
Belfast BT9 5JQ
☎ & fax (01232) 666046

Two apartments in Victorian townhouse near Queen's University, each with one double bedroom. Equipped and furnished to a high standard. Secure garage in basement. Can be let as one unit via communicating door. Linen, towels and power included in rate.

Self-catering apartments open all year
From £350 per week

7 Musgrave Park Court ****
Balmoral
Belfast BT9 7HZ
☎ **& fax (01232) 666046**

Modern three-bedroom house close to King's Hall and Balmoral Conference Centre, ½ mile from M1. Sleeps four plus cot. Linen, two tvs, dishwasher, washer-drier, fridge-freezer, microwave, payphone. Rear garden. Parking. Electricity included in rate.

Self-catering house open all year
From £300 per week

Adair Arms Hotel ***
Ballymoney Rd
Ballymena BT43 5BS
☎ **(01266) 653674 Fax 40436**

Hotel comprising 40 ensuite bedrooms which have been recently refurbished. Grill bar. Town centre location. Close to the Glens of Antrim. We cater for the most discerning traveller.

Hotel open all year
B & B from £39

B & B prices are the *lowest* rate per person sharing for one night.

Bushmills Inn ***
25 Main St
Bushmills BT57 8QA
☎ (012657) 32339 Fax 32048

At the home of the world's oldest distillery, this award-winning hotel and restaurant has now recreated the Mill House, adding 22 spacious bedrooms overlooking the River Bush. Open peat fires and gas lights set the tone in this living museum of Ulster hospitality.

Hotel open all year
B & B from £39

Leighinmohr Hotel ***
Leighinmohr Avenue
Ballymena BT42 2AN
☎ (01266) 652313 Fax 656669

In a quiet location one mile from the town centre, ideal for both business and pleasure. Extensively refurbished rooms, all ensuite. Two rooms have spa bath. Restaurant, bar and function room. Facilities for the disabled. Home comforts at affordable prices.

Hotel open all year
B & B from £40

Templeton Hotel ***
882 Antrim Rd, Templepatrick
BT39 0AH ☎ (01849) 432984
Fax 433406

This tranquil lakeside hotel is in the easily accessible Antrim countryside. Rich in architectural detail, the prestigious Templeton has 24 luxurious bedrooms, an elegant à la carte restaurant, Upton grill room, function suite, lounge and Sam's Bar.

Hotel open all year ex 25, 26 Dec
B & B from £35

Causeway Hotel **
40 Causeway Rd
Giant's Causeway BT57 8SU
☎ (012657) 31210 Fax 32552

Splendidly situated at the entrance to the world famous Giant's Causeway, this old family hotel has been tastefully renovated to provide modern facilities while retaining its original grandeur and charm. The 28 ensuite bedrooms have tv and tea-making facilities.

Hotel open all year
B & B from £37.50

Highways Hotel *
Ballyloran, Larne
BT40 2SU
☎ (01574) 272272 Fax 275015

Set in four acres with well laid out gardens, beside the main Belfast-Larne dual carriageway, en route to the scenic Antrim coast. Larne ferry one mile, Belfast and Ballymena 20 miles. The hotel has 35 bedrooms and two conference rooms.

Hotel open all year
B & B from £47.50

The Beeches Country House (A)
10 Dunadry Rd
Antrim BT41 2RR
☎ & fax (01849) 433161

On A6 at Dunadry, near the International Airport, this secluded guesthouse in landscaped grounds offers quiet, rural accommodation and friendly atmosphere. Taste of Ulster member. Home-made soups a speciality. Golf, watersports, fishing nearby. Non-smoking.

Mrs Marigold Allen
Proprietor

Guesthouse open all year
B & B from £25

B & B prices are the *lowest* rate per person sharing for one night.

Caireal Manor (A)
90 Glenravel Rd, Martinstown
Cushendall BT43 6QQ
☎ (012667) 58465

Superior quality guesthouse on the A43 seven miles north of Ballymena. All bedrooms are ensuite. Relaxed rural surroundings. Golf, fishing and leisure facilities. Private carpark. We were pleased to receive an RAC Highly Acclaimed Award in 1996.

Guesthouse open all year
B & B from £25

Caldhame House (A)
104 Moira Rd
Crumlin BT29 4HG
☎ (01849) 422378

Guesthouse minutes from Belfast International Airport. All rooms executive-style ensuite finished to the highest specification, some with jacuzzi. Centrally located for touring. Convenient to Antrim, Belfast and M1. Near leisure amenities. Taxi available.

Guesthouse open all year
B & B from £18

Castle Erin Holiday & Conference Centre (B)
Castle Erin Rd
Portrush BT56 8DH
☎ (01265) 822744

Ideal situation on an elevated site overlooking the Atlantic ocean. A well established guesthouse with 49 rooms, 22 ensuite, Castle Erin has easy access to promenade, beach and shops. Warm, friendly atmosphere. There is a lift and a private carpark. Suitable for coach parties.

Guesthouse open all year
B & B from £17

Dan Campbell's (A)
2 Bridge St
Larne BT40 2ET
☎ **(01574) 277222**

A 100-year-old hostelry in Larne town, gateway to the famous Antrim coast. Three golf courses within six miles. Close to ferries, rail and bus stations, easy access to A8 dual carriageway. All rooms ensuite, tea/coffee, Sky Tv. Evening entertainment.

Guesthouse open all year
B & B from £25

Keef Halla Country House (A)
20 Tully Rd, Nutt's Corner
Crumlin BT29 4SW
☎ **& fax (01232) 825491**

Nearest guesthouse to Belfast International Airport. Perfect location for an overnight stay going to and from the airport. Collection service available. All bedrooms are ensuite with direct-dial telephone, tv and refreshments. Ideal base for touring. Convenient for Antrim, Belfast and Dundrod.

Guesthouse open all year
B & B from £20

Tullymore House (B)
2 Carnlough Rd, Broughshane
Ballymena BT43 7HF
☎ **(01266) 861233 Fax 862238**

Set in beautifully landscaped gardens on the edge of the award-winning village of Broughshane, Tullymore House has high quality standards that ensure you enjoy a highly personalised service where nothing is too much trouble.

Guesthouse open all year
B & B from £22.50

B & B prices are the *lowest* rate per person sharing for one night.

Windsor Guest House (B)
67 Main St
Portrush BT56 8BN
☎ (01265) 823793 Fax 824625

Family-run large period town house with a homely atmosphere. Very central for all amenities. Ideal for conferences and weekend groups. Some ground floor rooms available. Good home cooking. Two large residents' lounges with dining room seating 65.

Guesthouse open all year
B & B from £18

Ardenlee House
19 Kerr St
Portrush BT56 8DG
☎ (01265) 822639

Excellent hospitality in fine period house which retains its original pine and oak staircase and combines character with all modern comforts. Spacious ensuite rooms. Seafront location overlooking west strand and harbour with panoramic views of Donegal.

Bed-and-breakfast open March-Sept
B & B from £16

Cairnview
13 Croft Heights, Ballygalley
Larne BT40 2QS
☎ & fax (01574) 583269

Modern house in Ballygalley, four miles north of Larne. 'Guesthouse of the year' runner-up. Three ensuite bedrooms with Sky Tv, tea/coffee facilities. One ground-floor bedroom suitable for disabled guests. Private parking. Conservatory. Incredible views of glens.

Bed-and-breakfast open all year
B & B from £18

Craig Park
24 Carnbore Rd
Bushmills BT57 8YF
☎ **(012657) 32496 Fax 32479.** craig.park@dial.pipex.com

A very comfortable country house offering three superior quality large rooms, all ensuite with tv, tea/coffee facilities. Incredible views. Close to Bushmills and Causeway Coast and ideal for seaside, touring and golf holidays. One double family room and two twin rooms.

Bed-and-breakfast open all year
B & B from £25

Heagles Lodge
3 Heagles Rd, Ballybogey
Ballymoney BT53 6NZ
☎ **(012657) 41122 Fax 41001**

An attractive country home offering luxurious, spacious ensuite rooms with tv and tea/coffee facilities. Home-cooking and baking. Choice of breakfast menus. Convenient base for touring the north coast. Midweek and weekend discounts out of season.

Bed-and breakfast open all year
B & B from £16

Killen's
28 Ballyclough Rd
Bushmills BT57 8UZ
☎ **(012657) 41536 Fax 41070**

Secluded accommodation deep in the unspoilt Ulster countryside, the ideal place from which to explore the Antrim coast. Enjoy our indoor heated pool, sauna and sunbed, and exclusive restaurant before retiring to the Killen suite (right) or a comfortable double room.

Bed-and-breakfast open all year
B & B from £25

B & B prices are the *lowest* rate per person sharing for one night.

The Meadows
81 Coast Rd
Cushendall BT44 0QW
☎ (012667) 72020 Fax 71641

Modern house opposite boat slip on the A2. Ideal base for touring Glens and Causeway Coast. Boating, fishing, golf, beach, and shops within walking distance. Rooms are all ensuite, with tv, hospitality tray. One bedroom is suitable for disabled guests. Private parking and conservatory.

Bed-and-breakfast open all year
B & B from £17.50

Nine Glens
18 Toberwine St
Glenarm BT44 0AP
☎ (01574) 841590

Situated in the historical village of Glenarm, gateway to the Nine Glens. All rooms ensuite with tv, tea/coffee making facilities. Central heating. Private parking. Twelve miles from Larne harbour.

Bed-and-breakfast open all year
B & B from £15

Valley View
6A Ballyclough Rd
Bushmills BT57 8TU
☎ (012657) 41608/41319

Family-run country house in quiet location, ideal for exploring the north Antrim coast and Giant's Causeway. Tastefully decorated ensuite rooms with tv and tea/coffee facilities. We welcome you with tea and home-baking on arrival. Children welcome. Non-smoking.

Bed-and-breakfast open all year ex Xmas
B & B from £15

Whitehill
96 Gortgole Rd
Portglenone BT44 8AN
☎ (01266) 822124

Whitehill is pleasantly situated on a 70-acre farm. There are several good golf courses within five to seven miles. Boating and fishing nearby. Drive through the scenic Glens of Antrim, enjoy forest walks and visit the craft shop at the Cistercian Monastery.

Bed-and-breakfast open all year
B & B from £15

Apartment No 18 ****
The Links, Bushmills Rd
Portrush BT56 8SX
☎ (01265) 55842

Luxuriously furnished 2nd-floor penthouse with two bedrooms. Sky Tv, video, payphone, carpark. Superb views over Royal Portrush golf course and beach. Very convenient for golf, fine restaurants and Antrim coast walks and scenic drives.

Self-catering apartment open all year
From £225 per week

Craig-e-Brae ***
22 Tullynamullan Rd, Tannaghmore
Randalstown BT41 2JZ
☎ & fax (01266) 898030

Comfortable, secluded cottage convenient to all parts of Northern Ireland, restored in traditional style with modern kitchen and three bedrooms. VCR, satellite tv, dishwasher, fridge-freezer, microwave, coffee-maker. Fishing, golf and pony trekking nearby.

Self-catering cottage open all year
From £245 per week

B & B prices are the *lowest* rate per person sharing for one night.

Giant's Causeway Holiday Cottages ***
71 Causeway Rd
Bushmills BT57 8SX
☎ **(012657) 31673 Fax 32533**

Family-run business. Eight splendid three-bedroomed cottages in a superb coastal location, just ¼ mile from the Giant's Causeway. Central heating, open fires, laundry facilities, games room. Ideally situated for beaches, golf and fishing. Quality and service in relaxed surroundings.

Self-catering cottages open all year

From £190 per week

Island Cottage ***
Gobbins Rd
Islandmagee BT40 3TY
☎ **(01232) 241100 Fax 241198**

This beautifully restored cottage has stunning views of the sea and perfect privacy. Features include farmhouse kitchen, spacious living area with turf fire, central heating and all mod cons. Linen provided. One of 100 luxury cottages available through Rural Cottage Holidays Ltd.

Self-catering cottage open all year

From £250 per week

Jacaranda Apartments & Mermaid Cottages ***
58-60 Dhu Varren, Portrush BT56 8EW
☎ **& fax (012656) 41793** *evenings*

Luxury self-contained family accommodation in a quiet, residential area. All modern amenities, sea views. Five minutes' walk West Strand (safe rear path), 10 minutes to town centre and harbour. Patio, barbecue area. Private parking. Golf, rock fishing and restaurants nearby.

Self-catering – open June-Sept

From £145 per week

Seacrest ****
6 Bayhead Apartments
Portballintrae BT57 8RZ
☎ (01247) 852880

A newly built top floor apartment in owner-occupied building in the centre of the curve of Portballintrae Bay. Lounge and balcony overlook the picturesque harbour. Interior design and furnishings inspired by the work of Charles Rennie Mackintosh.

Self-catering apartment open all year
From £200 per week

County Down

Burrendale Hotel & Country Club ***
51 Castlewellan Rd
Newcastle BT33 0JY
☎ (013967) 22599 Fax 22328

Set in the Mournes, the Burrendale's good food, wine and relaxing atmosphere may be enjoyed in the à la carte Vine and Cottage Kitchen restaurants. The Country Club has a pool, jacuzzis, steam rooms, sauna, gym, health & beauty clinic. Riding, golf, fishing, walking.

Hotel open all year
B & B from £45

Old Inn ***
15 Main St
Crawfordsburn BT19 1JH
☎ (01247) 853255 Fax 852775

Charming thatched country inn, just three miles from Bangor and 10 miles from Belfast, ideal for both business and pleasure. Excellent accommodation, all ensuite, in relaxed rural surroundings. Award-winning garden. The highly acclaimed 1614 Restaurant is well worth a visit.

Hotel open all year
B & B from £35

B & B prices are the *lowest* rate per person sharing for one night.

Portaferry Hotel ***
10 The Strand
Portaferry BT22 1PE
☎ (012477) 28231 Fax 28999. Portafery@iol.ie

The Portaferry Hotel is a charming waterside village inn with well appointed ensuite bedrooms. Award winning seafood restaurant – 2 AA rosettes. Local places of interest include Mount Stewart, Castle Espie and the famous golf course of Royal County Down.

Hotel open all year
B & B from £45

White Horse Hotel *
High St
Ballynahinch BT24 8LN
☎ (01238) 562225 Fax 564141

Family-owned hotel in the town centre, 15 minutes from Belfast, ideal for business and pleasure. Excellent ensuite accommodation. Enjoy a wide choice of food in our dining room, lounge and coffee shop. Weekly entertainment, friendly atmosphere, private parking.

Hotel open all year
B & B from £25

Ardshane Country House (A)
5 Bangor Rd
Holywood BT18 0NU
☎ (01232) 422044 Fax 427506

Built at the turn of the 19th century, nestling amid mature gardens and glens, refined Ardshane is the ideal location for a relaxing stay. Spacious ensuite rooms. Our menus reflect our culinary expertise. Historical sites, the sea and a wide range of shops are nearby.

Miss Judith Caughey
General Manager

Guesthouse open all year
B & B from £30

Dufferin Arms Coaching Inn (A)
35 High St
Killyleagh BT30 9QF
☎ **(01396) 828229 Fax 828755**

The Inn stands in the shadow of Killyleagh Castle, close to Strangford Lough in an area of outstanding natural beauty (AONB). Three bars, rustic cellar restaurant and banqueting hall. Seven ensuite bedrooms (some with four-posters) and a separate residents' lounge.

Guesthouse open all year
B & B from £32.50

Beech Hill Country House
23 Ballymoney Rd, Craigantlet
Holywood BT23 4TG
☎ **& fax (01232) 425892**

Georgian-style house in the peaceful Holywood Hills. All rooms on ground floor, ensuite bathrooms, tv, coffee/tea facilities. Ulster Folk & Transport Museum, Bangor Marina, Strangford Lough, golf nearby. Easy access to Belfast City Airport and sea ferries.

Bed-and-breakfast open all year
B & B from £30

Cairn-Bay-Lodge
278 Seacliff Rd
Bangor BT20 5HS
☎ **(01247) 467636 Fax 457728**

Period house of great charm, set in extensive gardens overlooking Ballyholme Bay. Luxurious rooms all ensuite. Very suitable for commuting business executives. Easy access to ferry terminals and airports. Near excellent golf courses, fishing, sailing, and many places of interest.

Bed-and-breakfast open all year
B & B from £25

B & B prices are the *lowest* rate per person sharing for one night.

Drumgooland House
29 Dunnanew Rd
Seaforde BT30 8PJ
☎ (01396) 811956 Fax 811265

A large country house close
to the Mourne mountains on
60 acres of land. We have
ponies for trekking and a
small lake stocked with trout.
Ideal centre for golfing, and
pony and trap tours of the
local area. A very warm
welcome is extended to our
guests.

Bed-and-breakfast open all year
B & B from £19.50

Edenvale Country House
130 Portaferry Rd
Newtownards BT22 2AH
☎ (01247) 814881 Fax 826192

Beautifully restored Georgian
country house just two miles
from Newtownards in lovely
secluded area. Extensive
views of the Mournes over
Strangford Lough and
National Trust wildfowl
refuge. Sailboarding, golf,
birdwatching, riding nearby.
Stabling for horses, kennel.

Bed-and-breakfast open all year
B & B from £25

Forestbrook House
11 Forestbrook Rd
Rostrevor BT34 3BT
☎ (016937) 38105

Situated at the foot of Slieve
Martin and at the top of the
Fairy Glen. This detached
listed house, built in 1700, is
set in a healthy atmosphere
of pine, mountain and sea
air. A yacht club, golf club,
tennis courts, children's
playground and excellent
fishing facilities are nearby.

Bed-and-breakfast open all year
B & B from £17

Fortwilliam House
210 Ballynahinch Rd
Hillsborough BT26 6BH
☎ **(01846) 682255 Fax 689608**

A period residence on an
elevated site, surrounded by
mature trees, offering the
peace and tranquillity of the
country way of life. Centrally
located just off the main Dublin-
Belfast route, offering all the
facilities you expect from an
award-winning country house.

Bed-and-breakfast open all year
B & B from £25

Pheasants' Hill
37 Killyleagh Rd
Downpatrick BT30 9BL
☎ **& fax (01396) 617246**

Traditional country house in
a peaceful woodland setting.
Pretty ensuite rooms, comfy
beds, fresh flowers, log fires
and delicious food. Seven-
acre smallholding with
gardens, orchard, pond and
wild flowers. Surrounded by
nature reserve and on the
Ulster Way.

Bed-and-breakfast open all year
B & B from £21

Roadhouse Inn
157 Main St
Dundrum BT33 0LY
☎ **& fax (013967) 51209**

Refurbished coach-house in
picturesque Dundrum at the
foot of the Mournes, with
seven ensuite rooms.
Excellent restaurant, bars,
entertainment. Walking,
riding, climbing and golf.
Close to the popular resort of
Newcastle.

Bed-and-breakfast open all year
B & B from £25

B & B prices are the *lowest* rate per person sharing for one night.

'108'
108 Seacliff Rd
Bangor BT20 5EZ
☎ (01247) 461077

Charming listed terrace house on the coast road overlooking Belfast Lough. Close to all local amenities including sailing, golf, coastal walks, and good restaurants. 15 miles from Belfast. Not suitable for young children or smokers.

Bed-and-breakfast open all year
B & B from £20.50

The Hill Cottage ***
32 Jericho Rd, Killyleagh
Downpatrick BT30 6AF
☎ (01396) 828245

Delightful, well furnished 3-bedroom cottage with private sunny garden. Beautiful views over countryside. Ideal for relaxing family holiday. Children welcome. Golf, fishing, riding, sailing and birdwatching on Strangford Lough nearby.

Self-catering cottage open all year
From £200 per week

Killyleagh Castle Towers ****/***
Killyleagh Castle
Killyleagh BT30 9QA
☎ & fax (01396) 828261

Two 17th-century towers each with one double and one twin room. One 19th-century tower with two twin and one single. Studio-room (double with bathroom). Heated pool and tennis court in garden. Private parking in courtyard. Pubs, restaurants, shops nearby.

Self-catering apartments open all year
From £200 per week

Riverside Cottage ****
67 Forkhill Rd
Newry BT35 8QX
☎ (01693) 848273 Fax 65050

Cosy cottage with open fire beside the Ring of Gullion. Equipped to high standard with washer/dryer, dishwasher, microwave. Central heating, electricity and linen is all included. Golf, fishing, pony-trekking nearby. Convenient for pubs, shops. Newry three miles.

Self-catering cottage open all year
From £200 per week

Tory Bush Cottages ***
79 Tullyree Rd
Bryansford BT34 5LD
☎ (013967) 24348

A group of traditionally designed cottages in a beautiful rural setting, all with open fire, central heating, washing machine, dishwasher. Splendid views of the Mourne mountains. Mountain bike trails, Tollymore Forest Park and access to the Mournes.

Self-catering cottages open all year
From £220 per week

County Fermanagh

Killyhevlin Hotel ***
Dublin Rd
Enniskillen BT74 4AU
☎ (01365) 323481 Fax 324726

The Killyhevlin Hotel and chalets are situated on the shores of Lough Erne, in the heart of beautiful Fermanagh. Close to fishing, golf and water sports. Luxury rooms with ensuite facilities make this the ideal spot for weekend breaks, family holidays and touring by car.

Hotel open all year
B & B from £45

B & B prices are the *lowest* rate per person sharing for one night.

Mahon's Hotel **
Mill St
Irvinestown BT94 1GS
☎ (013656) 21656 Fax 28344

Family-run hotel established in 1883. Ensuite rooms with tv, radio, hairdryer, tea/coffee facilities. Games room, baby listening. Restaurant, coffee shop and entertainment at weekends. 'Bushmills Bar of the Year 1992'. Private carpark. Near Necarne Equestrian Centre.

Mr Joe Mahon
Proprietor

Hotel open all year
B & B from £32.50

Carrybridge Hotel
Carrybridge
Lisbellaw BT94 5NF
☎ (01365) 387148 Fax 387111

Beautifully situated family-run hotel on the shores of Upper Lough Erne. Twelve bedrooms, eight ensuite. Family rooms available. The ideal place for relaxing and exploring the lakes. Weekend entertainment. Eight miles from Enniskillen.

Hotel open all year
B & B from £22

The Cedars (A)
Drummal, Castle Archdale
Irvinestown BT94 1PG
☎ & fax (013656) 21493

This charming licensed country house is just around the corner from Castle Archdale Country Park, on the main Enniskillen-Kesh-Donegal road. All rooms are ensuite with tea/coffee making facilities and satellite tv. A very warm welcome awaits you.

Guesthouse open all year ex Xmas
B & B from £20

CAVAN COUNTY MUSEUM

Virginia Road, Ballyjamesduff, Co. Cavan, Ireland.
Tel: 353 49 44070 • Fax: 353 49 44332
E-mail: ccmuseum@tinet.ie

County Cavan Museum

The Cavan Sheela-na-Gig
(photo reproduced by kind permission of the National Museum of Ireland)

*T*he Museum houses the material culture of County Cavan and surrounding districts and tells the story of Cavan from Antiquity to the recent past, through beautiful and interesting artefacts, geological specimens, objets d'art and much more.

Selection from Costume Gallery

Facilities: coach/carpark; disabled access/toilets; tearoom; picnic areas; gardens/walkways; exhibition galleries covering archaeology, geology, natural environment, folklife, costume, audio-visual display and interactives.

Opening times: Tues-Sat 1000-1700
Sun 1400-1800 (June-Sept)
Mon-closed

Admission: Adults: £2; Children, Students & OAP's: £1
Groups by appointment
Guided tours on request

THIS PROJECT IS PART FINANCED BY THE EUROPEAN UNION European structural funds **- INTERREG** Programme

Corrigans Shore (B)
Clonatrig, Bellanaleck
Enniskillen BT92 2AR
☎ (01365) 348572

Newly-built guesthouse with three ensuite rooms, beside Upper Lough Erne, 50 yards from the shore. Evening meals, home baking. Packed lunches on request. Close to Marble Arch Caves, Florence Court House and Castle Coole. Enniskillen seven miles. Families welcome.

Guesthouse open all year
B & B from £15

Mullynaval Lodge
Boa Island
Kesh BT93 8AN
☎ (013656) 31995

Homely and relaxing atmosphere. This elegant residence has a new bedroom wing. All rooms are ensuite with CTV, tea/coffee making facilities. Two bedrooms are suitable for disabled guests. Sauna, snooker table. Sunny garden, private jetty, tennis.

Guesthouse open all year
B & B from £17.50

Tullyhona House (A)
59 Marble Arch Rd, Florencecourt
Enniskillen BT92 1DE
☎ (01365) 348452

Winner of six awards (includes Galtee Breakfast). Taste of Ulster member. Near Marble Arch Caves, Florence Court (National Trust). Ensuite rooms, with tv, hairdryer. A la carte menu, evening barbecue. Golf nearby. Calving tours in season. Children very welcome. Winter breaks.

Guesthouse open all year
B & B from £17

The Courtyard
Lusty Beg Island
Kesh BT93 8AD
☎ **(013656) 32032 Fax 32033**

Cottage-style houses on picturesque island on Lower Lough Erne. Ensuite rooms with satellite tv, tea/coffee. Simple, country-style furnishings, with restaurant, bar, live music. Indoor swimming pool, tennis court. Boats are available.

Bed-and-breakfast open all year
B & B from £27.50

Dromard House
Dromard, Tamlaght
Enniskillen BT74 4HR
☎ **(01365) 387250**

Beautifully situated, two miles from Enniskillen. Well appointed ensuite rooms with tv, hospitality tray. Ulster winner in Farm Tourism Awards. Take the woodland path to the lake shore of our conservation award winning farm. AA 4Q recommended. No smoking.

Bed-and-breakfast open all year
B & B from £17.50

Cygnet Lodge **
208 Newbridge Rd, Smith's Strand
Lisnaskea BT92 0EQ
☎ **(013657) 22122 (22240 *evening*) Fax 21893**

Luxury lakeshore lodge. Four bedrooms (3 ensuite). Linen and towels provided. Open fire in lounge, fuel supplied. Private spacious gardens. Canoeing, sailing and archery can be arranged, also use of indoor pool 200 yards away. Children and pets are welcome.

Self-catering lodge open all year
From £185 per week

B & B prices are the *lowest* rate per person sharing for one night.

Derryad Cottages ***
Derryad Quay
Lisnaskea BT92 0BX
☎ & fax 0181-5674487

On the tranquil shores of Lough Erne are Idlewild Villa (left, sleeps 8) and Innisfree Cottage (right, sleeps 5). Both have scenic views, lakeside gardens and private boat for superb fishing and sightseeing. Fully equipped: microwave, payphone, CTV. Free colour brochure.

Self-catering cottages open all year
From £160 per week

The Gate Lodge ***
Killyreagh, Tamlaght
Enniskillen BT74 4HA
☎ (01365) 387221 Fax 387122

Two bedrooms, sleeping six. Bath, shower and well equipped modern kitchen. Sitting room with open fire overlooks pretty garden. National Trust properties, Marble Arch caves nearby. Tennis court, fishing, boating and cycling. Small dog pen.

Self-catering lodge open all year
From £175 per week

Riverview Holiday Homes **
Tullyhommon
Kesh BT93 8BD
☎ (013656) 31224

Two cottages. Three and four bedrooms. Fully fitted kitchen has washing machine, tumble dryer. Open turf fire in living room, tv. Close to shops, post office, and restaurants. Water sports, fishing and pony riding nearby. Five-minute drive from Lough Erne.

Self-catering cottages open all year
From £175

Radisson Roe Park Hotel & Golf Resort ****
Roe Park
Limavady BT49 9LB
☎ (015047) 22222 Fax 22313

Radisson Roe Park offers unrivalled leisure facilities within an historic 155-acre country estate. The hotel offers a superb 18-hole championship parkland golf course, Fairways Leisure Club: indoor heated pool, O'Cahan's Bar, Courtyard Restaurant and Coach House Brasserie.

Hotel open all year
B & B from £45

Bohill Hotel & Country Club ***
69 Cloyfin Rd
Coleraine BT52 2NY
☎ (01265) 44406 Fax 52424

Our well appointed rooms, all ensuite, our excellent cuisine and superb leisure facilities including an indoor pool, make for a memorable stay on the Causeway Coast. On the inland road just five minutes from the resorts of Portrush and Portstewart. Conference facilities.

Hotel open all year
B & B from £40

Bushtown House Hotel & Country Club ***
283 Drumcroone Rd
Coleraine BT51 3QT
☎ (01265) 58367 Fax 320909

Country house hotel with 39 ensuite bedrooms and leisure complex which has a heated swimming pool. Open fires, two restaurants, superb hospitality, weekend entertainment. Conference facilities. Excellent sea-river fishing available, golf nearby.

Hotel open all year
B & B from £37.50

B & B prices are the *lowest* rate per person sharing for one night.

Lodge Hotel & Travelstop ***
Lodge Rd
Coleraine BT52 1NF
☎ (01265) 44848 Fax 54555

In private grounds, a short walk from the town centre, the hotel has 56 ensuite rooms and a comfortable dining room. Snacks and evening entertainment in Elliot's bistro and lounge. Seaside resorts, the Giant's Causeway and many more amenities nearby.

Hotel open all year
B & B from £27.50

Waterfoot Hotel & Country Club ***
Caw Roundabout, 14 Clooney Rd
Londonderry BT47 1TB
☎ (01504) 345500 Fax 311006

The hotel is of unique design. Its main public areas are circular and on several levels affording excellent views of the Foyle river and Donegal mountains. All ensuite rooms have tv and telephone. We also have extensive leisure facilities.

Hotel open all year
B & B from £39

Edgewater Hotel **
88 Strand Rd
Portstewart BT55 7LZ
☎ (01265) 833314 Fax 832224

Magnificently situated overlooking Portstewart Strand, the hotel has views of Donegal. With 31 ensuite rooms, sauna, jacuzzi, solarium and multi-gym, this is an ideal base for golfers and for exploring the Causeway Coast. Relaxed, friendly atmosphere.

Hotel open all year
B & B from £30

Golf Hotel *
17 Main St
Castlerock BT51 4RA
☎ (01265) 848204 Fax 848295

On the sandy shores of the North Atlantic with unrivalled views of the Donegal hills. All ensuite rooms have CTV, telephone, tea/coffee facilities. A la carte menu, grill, Sunday carvery. Entertainment weekends and nightly July-August. Beside 18-hole championship golf course.

Hotel open all year
B & B from £30

Lis-na-Rhin
6 Victoria Terrace
Portstewart BT55 7BA
☎ (01265) 833522

Guesthouse comprising eight bedrooms, six ensuite with one on the ground floor. Tea/coffee facilities. Sky Tv in residents' lounge. Convenient to all amenities. Private carpark. Breakfast and other meals are available for non-residents.

Guesthouse open all year
B & B from £15

The Poplars (B)
352 Seacoast Rd
Limavady BT49 0LA
☎ (015047) 50360

Six miles from Limavady, the Poplars is a modern house convenient for Benone Strand, golf courses, and the Ulster Gliding Club. Three rooms ensuite, two with showers. Tea/coffee facilities. Home cooking and baking a speciality. Entrance ramps for wheelchair use.

Guesthouse open all year
B & B from £16

B & B prices are the *lowest* rate per person sharing for one night.

Coolbeg
2e Grange Rd
Coleraine BT52 1NG
☎ **(01265) 44961**

Modern bungalow set in pleasant garden on the edge of town. All rooms have tv and tea/coffee facilities, and three are ensuite. Ideal for touring the north Antrim coast. Healthy Eating Circle member. Coolbeg is a Category One house, ideal for wheelchair users.

Bed-and-breakfast open all year ex Xmas
B & B from £17

Drumcovitt House
704 Feeny Rd, Feeny
Londonderry BT47 4SU
☎ **& fax (015047) 81224**

Historic listed house in established garden on upland farm in the foothills of the Sperrins. Many sites of archaeological interest within a five-mile radius. Fishing in Roe and Faughan rivers and golf at Limavady and Derry – which are all just a few miles away.

Bed-and-breakfast open all year
B & B from £16

Old Rectory
4 Duncrun Rd, Bellarena
Limavady BT49 0JD
☎ **(015047) 50477**

This former rectory, with ensuite rooms, built in 1774, nestles beneath magnificent Binevenagh mountain. Two-acre garden, with views of Lough Foyle. Gliding, fishing, watersports and golf nearby, and children's pool and bowling at Benone Beach Centre.

Bed-and-breakfast open Feb-Nov
B & B from £20

Raspberry Hill Health Farm
29 Bond's Glen Rd
Londonderry BT47 3ST
☎ & fax (01504) 398000

Set in beautiful rural surroundings in the foothills of the Sperrins. Facilities include swimming machine, sauna, steam cabinets, spa baths, tennis, walks, badminton, putting green. Full range of beauty and therapeutic treatments, weight/stress counselling.

Jennifer Nixon
Manager

Health farm open all year
3-day stay from £110

Strandeen
63 Strand Rd
Portstewart BT55 7LU
☎ & fax (01265) 833159

Enjoy peace and comfort overlooking the ocean. Views of the Atlantic from pretty ensuite rooms. Paintings, good books and log fire. Excellent breakfast. Beach, golf course and promenade minutes from doorstep. Safe parking. No smoking. '97 AA Award winner.

Bed-and-breakfast open all year
B & B from £20

Drumcovitt Barn ****
704 Feeny Rd, Feeny
Londonderry BT47 4SU
☎ & fax (015047) 81224.

Three luxury cottages, one with wheelchair access. Each has telephone and oil central heating, two have open fires. In quiet countryside three miles off A6, ideal base for touring Donegal, Giant's Causeway, Sperrins, Derry. Fax and email in office.
drumcovitt.feeny@btinternet.com

Self-catering cottages open all year
From £240 per week

B & B prices are the *lowest* rate per person sharing for one night.

King's Country Cottages ***/**/*
66 Ringrash Rd, Macosquin
Coleraine BT51 4LJ
☎ **(01265) 51367**

Three well equipped cottages each with central heating, open fire, washing machine and microwave. One cottage has wheelchair access. Close to Castlerock, Causeway Coast, good beaches. Convenient for golf, cycling, pony trekking and for walking the Ulster Way.

Self-catering cottages open all year
From £150

County Tyrone

Glenavon House Hotel ***
52 Drum Rd
Cookstown BT80 8JQ
☎ **(016487) 64949 Fax 64396**

In the centre of the province – the ideal base for your visit to Northern Ireland, with all the comforts of home. Facilities include a leisure centre, swimming pool, jacuzzi, steam room, fitness suite and gym. Conference facilities.

Hotel open all year
B & B from £47.50

Royal Hotel **
64 Coagh St
Cookstown BT80 8NG
☎ (016487) 62224 Fax 61932

Just two minutes' walk from the town centre, this lively family-run hotel offers ensuite bedrooms, with tv, direct-dial telephone, tea-making facilities. Grill, high tea and à la carte menus. Suitable for conferences, trade shows, wedding receptions.

Hotel open all year
B & B from £30

Silverbirch Hotel **
5 Gortin Rd
Omagh BT79 7DH
☎ (01662) 242520 Fax 249061

This pleasant hotel, with 46 ensuite rooms, on the outskirts of the busy market town of Omagh – gateway to the Sperrins – has excellent dining facilities. Near Gortin Glen Forest Park, Ulster-American Folk Park, Ulster History Park. Golf and fishing by arrangement.

Hotel open all year
B & B from £31.25

Derg Arms (B)
43 Main St
Castlederg BT81 7AS
☎ (016626) 71644 Fax 70202

This town centre guesthouse has six ensuite bedrooms with telephone and tv. The Derg river at the rear of the house is ideal for fishing. Fully licensed. Scenic Gortin Glen Forest Park and the Ulster-American Folk Park are nearby attractions.

Guesthouse open all year
B & B from £16

B & B prices are the *lowest* rate per person sharing for one night.

Stangmore Country House
65 Moy Rd
Dungannon BT71 7DT
☎ **(01868) 725600 Fax 726644**

This centrally heated nine-bedroom Georgian house is 1½ miles from Dungannon on the A29 towards junction 15 off the M1. Rooms all have tv, telephone, tea-making facilities and are tastefully decorated. We have a large drawing room and dining room, and a tv room.

Guesthouse open all year
B & B from £35

Romona's House
96 Circular Rd
Omagh BT79 7HA
☎ **& fax (01662) 245084**

Newly extended house, just a mile outside the town. Six ensuite bedrooms, each with telephone, tv, tea/coffee facilities and hairdryer. Disabled guests welcome. Five miles from Gortin Glen Forest Park, Ulster History Park and Ulster-American Folk Park. Golf nearby.

Bed-and-breakfast open all year
B & B from £18

Grange Court **/*****
21 Moyle Rd
Newtownstewart BT78 4AP
☎ **& fax (016626) 61877**

Purpose-built holiday complex with six self catering apartments, all furnished and equipped to a very high standard. Also on site is Aunt Jane's coffee shop and the Gateway visitor centre. A home-from-home base, ideal for touring holidays or activity breaks.

Self-catering apartments open all year
From £150 per week

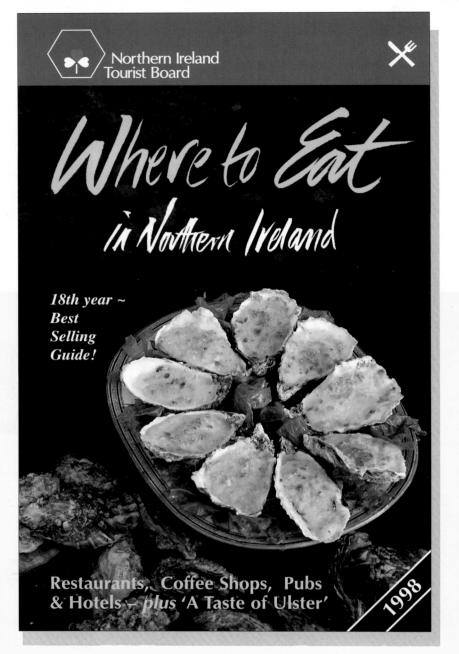

Northern Ireland Tourist Board

Where to Eat
in Northern Ireland

18th year ~ Best Selling Guide!

Restaurants, Coffee Shops, Pubs & Hotels – *plus* **'A Taste of Ulster'**

1998

Pocket-sized paperback for glove compartment! Comprehensive listing by town and village for over 1,600 eating places including all 'Taste of Ulster' restaurants, pubs and coffee shops. Opening times, price bands, brief description of food. Available from bookshops, newsagents, tourist information centres, airports, garage forecourts etc. throughout Britain and Ireland, price £2.99.

Special mentions - from the guidebooks

Northern Ireland hotels and guesthouses are winning more and more recognition in well known guides to tourist accommodation. Here is a list of places to stay which have been recommended in the most recent editions of the following well known guides: *Bridgestone 100 Best Places to Stay in Ireland, Bridgestone Irish Food Guide, Egon Ronay, Good Food Guide, Good Hotel Guide* and *Michelin*. Hotels and guesthouses which have attained Taste of Ulster membership, applied for under a voluntary registration scheme, are also indicated.

Belfast and area | page

Aldergrove Airport Hotel
Egon Ronay, Michelin — 53

Ash-Rowan Guesthouse
Bridgestone, Good Hotel Guide, Michelin — 55

The Cottage Michelin — 59

Culloden Hotel Egon Ronay, Michelin,
'A Taste of Ulster' member — 53

Dukes Hotel Egon Ronay, Michelin,
'A Taste of Ulster' member — 53

Europa Hotel Egon Ronay, Michelin — 53

Forte Posthouse Belfast
Egon Ronay, Michelin — 53

Holiday Inn Express Michelin — 53

Holiday Inn Garden Court
Egon Ronay, Michelin — 53

La Mon House Hotel Egon Ronay — 55

Malone Guesthouse
Bridgestone, Michelin — 57

Stormont Hotel Egon Ronay,
Michelin, 'A Taste of Ulster' member — 53

Stranmillis Lodge Michelin — 61

Wellington Park Hotel Egon Ronay — 54

County Antrim

Adair Arms Hotel, Ballymena
Egon Ronay — 18

Bayview Hotel, Portballintrae
Egon Ronay, Michelin — 93

The Beeches Guesthouse, Antrim
'A Taste of Ulster' member — 20

County Antrim continued | page

Bushmills Inn, Bushmills Bridgestone, Michelin,
'A Taste of Ulster' member — 19

Causeway Coast Hotel, Portrush
Egon Ronay, Michelin — 94

Country House Hotel, Ballymena Michelin — 69

Derrin House, Larne Michelin — 87

Dunadry Hotel, Dunadry Egon Ronay, Michelin — 84

Galgorm Manor, Ballymena Egon Ronay,
Michelin, 'A Taste of Ulster' member — 69

Glencroft Guesthouse, Portrush Michelin — 97

Laurel Inn, Lisburn 'A Taste of Ulster' member — 89

Londonderry Arms Hotel, Carnlough
Egon Ronay, 'A Taste of Ulster' member — 77

Maddybenny Farmhouse, Portrush
Bridgestone, Egon Ronay — 101

Magherabuoy House Hotel, Portrush
Michelin, 'A Taste of Ulster' member — 94

Magheramorne House Hotel, Larne Michelin — 87

Marine Hotel, Ballycastle
Egon Ronay, Michelin, 'A Taste of Ulster' member — 64

Quality Hotel, Carrickfergus
'A Taste of Ulster' member — 79

Royal Court Hotel, Portrush Egon Ronay — 94

Templeton Hotel, Templepatrick Egon Ronay,
Michelin, 'A Taste of Ulster' member — 19

Tullyglass House Hotel, Ballymena Egon Ronay — 70

County Down

Briers Country House, Newcastle Michelin — 133

Burrendale Hotel, Newcastle
Michelin, 'A Taste of Ulster' member — 28

Clandeboye Lodge Hotel, Bangor
Egon Ronay, Michelin — 117

Dufferin Arms Coaching Inn, Killyleagh
'A Taste of Ulster' member — 30

Glassdrumman Lodge, Annalong
Good Hotel Guide, Egon Ronay, Michelin — 113

Special mentions - from the guidebooks

County Down continued   page

Greenacres, Newtownards
'A Taste of Ulster' member   138

Hillyard House, Castlewellan
'A Taste of Ulster' member   194

Marine Court, Bangor Egon Ronay, Michelin   117

The Narrows, Portaferry Egon Ronay   140

Old Inn, Crawfordsburn Egon Ronay,
Michelin, 'A Taste of Ulster' member   28

Old Schoolhouse Inn, Comber
'A Taste of Ulster' member   123

Portaferry Hotel, Portaferry
Bridgestone, Egon Ronay, Good Hotel Guide,
Michelin, 'A Taste of Ulster' member   29

Rayanne House, Holywood
Michelin, 'A Taste of Ulster' member   128

Royal Hotel, Bangor
Michelin, 'A Taste of Ulster' member   117

Shelleven House, Bangor Michelin   118

Slieve Donard Hotel, Newcastle Egon Ronay   131

White Gables Hotel, Hillsborough
Egon Ronay, Michelin   127

Wyncrest Guesthouse, Kilkeel
'A Taste of Ulster' member   129

County Fermanagh

Courtyard, Lusty Beg Island, Kesh Egon Ronay   38

Drumshane Hotel, Lisnarick
'A Taste of Ulster' member   155

Jamestown House, Ballinamallard
Bridgestone, 'A Taste of Ulster' member   143

Killyhevlin Hotel, Enniskillen Good Hotel Guide   34

Lough Erne Hotel, Kesh Egon Ronay   152

Mahon's Hotel, Irvinestown Michelin   35

Manor House Country Hotel, Enniskillen
Michelin, 'A Taste of Ulster' member   145

Moohan's Fiddlestone, Belleek Michelin   144

Tempo Manor, Tempo
Bridgestone, Egon Ronay, Good Hotel Guide   158

Tullyhona House, Florencecourt
Bridgestone, 'A Taste of Ulster' member   37

County Londonderry   page

Ardtara Country House, Maghera
Egon Ronay, Good Hotel Guide, Michelin,
'A Taste of Ulster' member   174

Beech Hill Country House Hotel, Londonderry
Bridgestone, Egon Ronay, Good Food Guide,
Good Hotel Guide, Michelin,
'A Taste of Ulster' member   169

Brown Trout Golf & Country Inn, Aghadowey
Egon Ronay   159

Bushtown House Hotel, Coleraine Michelin   40

Camus House, Coleraine Michelin   163

Edgewater Hotel, Portstewart Michelin   41

Everglades Hotel, Londonderry
Egon Ronay, Michelin   170

Greenhill House, Coleraine
Michelin, Egon Ronay, 'A Taste of Ulster' member   161

Maritima House, Castlerock Michelin   160

Radisson Roe Park Hotel, Limavady
Egon Ronay, Michelin   40

Streeve Hill, Limavady Bridgestone, Egon Ronay   169

Waterfoot Hotel, Londonderry
Michelin, 'A Taste of Ulster' member   41

White Horse Hotel, Londonderry Michelin   170

County Tyrone

Blessingbourne, Fivemiletown Egon Ronay   185

Cohannon Inn Autolodge, Dungannon
Michelin   183

Fir Trees Hotel, Strabane Michelin   189

Grange Lodge, Dungannon
Bridgestone, Egon Ronay,
'A Taste of Ulster' member   184

Greenmount Lodge, Omagh
'A Taste of Ulster' member   187

Royal Arms Hotel, Omagh
'A Taste of Ulster' member   187

Tullylagan Country House Hotel, Cookstown
Egon Ronay, Michelin, 'A Taste of Ulster' member   181

Getting around in Northern Ireland

Driving

Throughout Britain and Ireland the rule is 'drive on the left and overtake on the right'. The speed limits are 30 mph (48 kph) in towns unless signs indicate otherwise; 60 mph (97 kph) on ordinary roads, and 70 mph (113 kph) on dual carriageways and motorways. Drivers and all passengers must wear seatbelts. Roads in Northern Ireland are well surfaced and signposted, and traffic volume is markedly lower than in Britain.

Driving licence

Your own driving licence is sufficient for short stays in Northern Ireland. Remember to carry it with you.

Parking

The universal blue 'P' sign shows a carpark or a layby at the roadside where you can park. You can usually park on the street if there is no yellow line at the kerb. On a single yellow line you may park except at the times shown on the small yellow signs on nearby posts. Do not park near pedestrian crossings.

Car rentals

Main international car rental firms are represented at the airports and can offer fly-drive deals: consult your travel agent. There are also many local firms: ask the tourist board for information bulletin 13 or consult the Yellow Pages.

The total cost of hiring a standard family car for a week, including insurance, unlimited mileage and tax, is £175-£255. A weekend rate (Fri-Mon) would be between £86-£100. Insurance and VAT may be added to the quoted price, so check what the total cost will be when you book. Most cars have manual gearshift, so ask in advance if you need automatic transmission. If you hire a car in the Irish Republic, you will find it cheaper to do a round trip and return the vehicle to the pick-up point.

If you break down

If the car is rented, contact the hire company. If you are a member of the Automobile Association, the Royal Automobile Club, or an affiliated organisation, you can use their 24-hour breakdown services. There are also plenty of commercial breakdown services to call on – unless a friendly Ulster driver stops to help you first.

Petrol (gas)

Prices fluctuate. At the time of going to press the approximate cost of unleaded petrol per litre was 65p and leaded fuel 70p.

Rail

There are four main rail routes from Belfast Central Station ☎ (01232) 899411 – north to Londonderry city via Ballymena and Coleraine, north-east to Larne (for Scotland), east to Bangor, and south to Dublin via Lisburn, Portadown and Newry.

Bus

Northern Ireland has an excellent bus network with regular services to towns not served by a rail link. Ulsterbus operates express buses from Belfast to Ulster's main towns and an express coach service to Dublin 7 times daily – 3 on Sunday. ☎ (01232) 333000.

 **Northern Ireland Tourist Board**

Northern Ireland Tourist Board Offices

Head Office
59 North Street, Belfast BT1 1NB.
☎ (01232) 231221 (administration),
fax (01232) 240960.

Dublin
16 Nassau Street, Dublin 2.
☎ Dublin 6791977, fax Dublin 6791863.
CallSave 1850 230230.

London
11 Berkeley Street, London W1X 5AD.
☎ 0541-555 250, fax 0171-409 0487.

Glasgow
135 Buchanan Street, Glasgow G1 2JA.
☎ 0141-204 4454, fax 0141-204 4033.

USA
551 Fifth Avenue, Suite 701, New York,
NY 10176.
☎ (212) 922 0101 or (800) 326-0036,
fax (212) 922 0099.
Email: info@northern-ireland.com

Canada
111 Avenue Road, Suite 450,
Toronto M5R 3J8.
☎ (416) 925 6368, fax (416) 961 2175.

Germany
Taunusstrasse 52-60, 60329 Frankfurt/Main.
☎ (069) 23 45 04, fax (069) 23 34 80.

France
Enquiries to Mailing Express, 189 rue d'Aubervilliers,
75886 Paris Cédex 18.
Minitel 3615 Nord Irlande.
☎ (1) 40 05 10 29.
Fax (1) 40 34 38 96.

Australia
Enquiries to All Ireland Tourism, 5th Level, 36
Carrington Street, Sydney, NSW 2000.
☎ (02) 9299 6177, fax (02) 9299 6323.

Passing through London?

Visit the All Ireland desk at the British Travel Centre,
12 Regent Street, Piccadilly Circus SW1. It is open
seven days a week.

Extra copies of this book are available from all
Northern Ireland Tourist Board offices, price
£3.99. Or you can order it, and any of the
publications listed below, direct by post from:

> Tourist Information Centre
> 59 North Street
> Belfast BT1 1NB
> ☎ (01232) 246609
> Minicom (01232) 233228

Where prices (sterling) are given, postage is
included. Some publications are free of charge.

Northern Ireland – an introduction in English,
French, German, Spanish, Italian or Dutch
– *specify language.*

Ireland North Holiday Map,
scale : ¼ inch to 1 mile (1: 250 000). £3.60.

Events 1998 – the year's major events.

Tourist Attractions Map – information guide
locating museums, castles, forests, stately homes,
ancient monuments, with telephone numbers and
opening times. 50p.

Where to Eat 1998 – pocket guide to over 1,600
restaurants, teashops, pubs. £2.99.

Gardens and historic demesnes. 50p.

Where to play golf. 50p.

Game fishing waters – salmon and trout. 50p.

Other information guides on a wide range of
subjects and activities, from tracing your roots to
birdwatching, sailing and walking, are available.
If you have a special interest and would like
further information please write to the Tourist
Information Centre at the address above.

Hotels

Culloden Hotel　*****
142 Bangor Rd, Holywood, BT18 0EX.
☎ (01232) 425223. Fax 426777.
B&B s£140 d£186. Rooms 80, ensuite 80.
Last orders 2130 hrs. Open all year ex Christmas.

Europa Hotel　****
Great Victoria St, BT2 7AP.
☎ (01232) 327000. Fax 327800.
B&B s£120 d£170. Rooms 184, ensuite 184.
High tea £8. Dinner £24.50.　Last orders 2400 hrs.
Open all year.

Stormont Hotel　****
587 Upper Newtownards Rd, BT4 3LP.
☎ (01232) 658621. Fax 480240.
B&B s£107 d£150. BB&M s£130.50 d£197.
Rooms 109, ensuite 109. Dinner £23.50.
Last orders 2200 hrs. Open all year.

Aldergrove Airport Hotel　***
BT29 4AB.
☎ (01849) 422033. Fax 423500.
s£82.50 d£90. Rooms 108, ensuite 108.
Dinner £16.50. Last orders 2200 hrs.
Open all year.

Beechlawn House Hotel　***
4 Dunmurry Lane, Dunmurry, BT17 9RR.
☎ (01232) 612974. Fax 623601.
B&B s£66 d£76. BB&M s£80 d£104. Rooms 34,
ensuite 34. High tea £7.50. Dinner £13.95.
Last orders 2130 hrs. Open all year.

Dukes Hotel　***
65 University St, BT7 1HL.
☎ (01232) 236666. Fax 237177.
B&B s£90 d£110. BB&M s£105 d£140. Rooms
21, ensuite 21. Dinner £15.
Last orders 2130 hrs. Open all year.

Forte Posthouse Belfast　***
300 Kingsway, Dunmurry, BT17 9ES.
☎ (01232) 612101. Fax 626546.
B&B s£88.95 d£88.95. BB&M s£104.95
d£120.95. Rooms 82, ensuite 82. High tea £10.
Dinner £16. Last orders 2215 hrs. Open all year.

Glenavna House Hotel　***
588 Shore Rd, Newtownabbey, BT37 0SN.
☎ (01232) 864461. Fax 862531.
B&B s£70 d£85. BB&M s£86.95 d£118.90.
Rooms 32, ensuite 32. High tea £10.95.
Dinner £16.95. Last orders 2200 hrs.
Open all year ex Christmas.

Holiday Inn Express　***
106 University St, BT7 1HP.
☎ (01232) 311909. Fax 311910.
B&B s£49.95. BB&M s£60 d£70. Rooms 114,
ensuite 114. Dinner £9.95. Last orders 2330 hrs.
Open all year.

Holiday Inn Garden Court　***
15 Brunswick St, BT2 7GE.
☎ (01232) 333555. Fax 232999.
B&B s£79 d£89. BB&M s£100 d£132. Rooms 76,
ensuite 76. High tea £8. Dinner £12.50.
Last orders 2215 hrs. Open all year.

Facilities are liable to change. Check prices when you book. Key to symbols is on the back flap.

Ivanhoe Inn & Hotel   ***
556 Saintfield Rd, Carryduff, BT8 8EU.
☎ (01232) 812240. Fax 815516.
B&B s£65 d£85. BB&M s£83.50 d£122.
Rooms 21, ensuite 21. High tea £12.
Dinner £18.50. Last orders 2130 hrs.
Open all year.

Jurys Belfast Inn   ***
Fisherwick Place, Great Victoria St, BT2 7AP.
☎ (01232) 533500. Fax 533511.
B&B s£65.50 d£72. BB&M s£81 d£103.
Rooms 190, ensuite 190. High tea £6.
Dinner £15.50. Last orders 2130 hrs.
Open all year ex Christmas.

Lansdowne Court Hotel   ***
657 Antrim Rd, BT15 4EF.
☎ (01232) 773317. Fax 370125.
B&B s£75 d£95. BB&M s£90.50 d£126.
Rooms 25, ensuite 25. High tea £12. Dinner £15.
Last orders 2115 hrs. Open all year.

Madison's Hotel   ***
Botanic Avenue, BT7 1JL.
☎ (01232) 330040. Fax 328007.
B&B s£40 d£55. Rooms 35, ensuite 35.
Dinner £15. Last orders 0100 hrs. Open all year.

Wellington Park Hotel   ***
21 Malone Rd, BT9 6RU.
☎ (01232) 381111. Fax 665410.
B&B s£87 d£126. BB&M s£105 d£162. Rooms
75, ensuite 75. Dinner £18.
Last orders 2230 hrs. Open all year.

Balmoral Hotel   **
Black's Rd, BT10 0ND.
☎ (01232) 301234. Fax 601455.
B&B s£45 d£65. BB&M s£57 d£89. Rooms 44,
ensuite 44. Dinner £12. Last orders 2200 hrs.
Open all year.

Malone Lodge Hotel **
60 Eglantine Avenue, BT9 6DY.
☎ (01232) 382409. Fax 382706.
B&B s£75 d£92. Rooms 33, ensuite 33.
Dinner £18.50. Last orders 2200 hrs.
Open all year.

Park Avenue Hotel   **
158 Holywood Rd, BT4 1PA.
☎ (01232) 656520. Fax 471417.
B&B s£59.50 d£79. Rooms 68, ensuite 35.
High tea £12. Dinner £17.
Last orders 2030 hrs. Open all year.

Regency Hotel   **
8 Lower Crescent, BT7 1RN.
☎ (01232) 323349. Fax 320646.
B&B s£55 d£70. Rooms 14, ensuite 14. Dinner
£15. Last orders 2300 hrs. Open all year.

B&B = bed and breakfast   s = single   d = double   BB&M = bed, breakfast & evening meal

La Mon House Hotel *
41 Gransha Rd, Castlereagh, BT23 5RF.
☎ (01232) 448631. Fax 448026.
B&B s£65 d£75. BB&M s£79 d£89. Rooms 38,
ensuite 38.   High tea £7.50. Dinner £14.
Last orders 2200 hrs. Open all year.

Renshaws Hotel *
75 University St, BT7 1HL.
☎ (01232) 333366. Fax 333399.
B&B s£55 d£75. BB&M s£64.50 d£84.50.
Rooms 22, ensuite 22. Dinner £9.50.
Last orders 2200 hrs. Open all year ex Christmas.

Unclassified Hotels
Parador Hotel, 473 Ormeau Rd, BT7 3GR.
☎ (01232) 491883.
Shaftesbury Plaza, 7-21 Bradbury Place, BT7 1RQ.
☎ (01232) 246161. (Opens early 1998).

Guesthouses

Ash-Rowan Guest House   (A)
12 Windsor Avenue, BT9 6EE.
☎ (01232) 661758. Fax 663227.
B&B s£46 d£66. BB&M s£69 d£112. Rooms 5,
ensuite 5. Dinner £23. Last orders 1900 hrs.
Open all year ex Christmas.

Bienvenue   (U)
8 Sans Souci Park, Malone Rd, BT9 5BZ.
☎ (01232) 681731. Fax 663021.
B&B s£42 d£55. Rooms 4, ensuite 4.
Open all year.

Blakely Lodge (U)
67 Malone Rd, BT9 6SB. ☎ (01232) 662985.
Fax 682246. B&B s£35 d£55. Rooms 3, ensuite 3.
Dinner £15. Last orders 17.30. Open all year.

Camera Guest House   (A)
44 Wellington Park, BT9 6DP.
☎ (01232) 660026. Fax 667856.
B&B s£40 d£60. Rooms 11, ensuite 11.
High tea £10. Dinner £16. Last orders 1200 hrs.
Open all year ex Christmas.

Eglantine Guest House   (B)
21 Eglantine Avenue, BT9 6DW. ☎ (01232) 667585.
B&B s£20 d£38. Rooms 7. Open all year.

Greenwood Guest House   (U)
25 Park Road, BT7 2FW.
☎ (01232) 202525. Fax 202530.
B&B s£32 d£48. BB&M s£47 d£78. Rooms 7,
ensuite 7. Dinner £15.
Open all year ex Christmas.

Kilnamar   (B)
174 Finaghy Rd South, Upper Malone, BT10 0DH.
☎ (01232) 611564. B&B s£30 d£50. BB&M s£40
d£70. Rooms 3, ensuite 3. High tea £8.50. Dinner
£10. Open all year.

Laburnum Lodge   (U)
16 Deramore Park, BT9 5JU. ☎ (01232) 665183.
Fax 681460. B&B s£36 d£57.
BB&M s£48.50 d£82. Rooms 6, ensuite 6.
Dinner £12.50. Last orders 2130 hrs.
Open all year.

Facilities are liable to change. Check prices when you book. Key to symbols is on the back flap.

Lisdara Guest House (A)
23 Derryvolgie Avenue, BT9 6FN.
☎ (01232) 681549.
B&B s£40 d£65. BB&M s£55 d£95.
Rooms 4, ensuite 4. Dinner £15. Open all year.

Liserin Guest House (B)
17 Eglantine Avenue, BT9 6DW.
☎ (01232) 660769/666235.
B&B s£19 d£38. Rooms 6, ensuite 4.
Open all year.

Lismore Lodge (A)
410 Ormeau Rd, BT7 3HY.
☎ & fax (01232) 641205.
B&B s£27 d£42. BB&M s£42 d£72.
Rooms 6, ensuite 6. High tea £12. Dinner £15.
Last orders 1900 hrs. Open all year.

Malone Guest House (A)
79 Malone Rd, BT9 6SH. ☎ (01232) 669565.
B&B s£35 d£50. Rooms 8, ensuite 8.
High tea £15. Dinner £20. Open all year.

Oakdene Lodge (A)
16 Annadale Avenue, BT7 3JH.
☎ (01232) 492626. Fax 492070.
B&B s£35 d£50. Rooms 17, ensuite 17.
Open all year.

Old Rectory (A)
148 Malone Rd, BT9 5LH.
☎ (01232) 667882. Fax 683759.
B&B s£40 d£60. BB&M s£55 d£90.
Rooms 4, ensuite 4.
Dinner £15. Last orders 1900 hrs. Open all year.

Pearl Court House (B)
11 Malone Rd, BT9 6RT.
☎ (01232) 666145. Fax 327344.
B&B s£29 d£45. Rooms 10, ensuite 6.
Open all year.

Roseleigh Guest House (A)
19 Rosetta Park, BT6 0DL.
☎ & fax (01232) 644414.
B&B s£34 d£47. BB&M s£46 d£71.
Rooms 9, ensuite 9. Dinner £12.
Last orders 2000 hrs. Open all year.

Windermere House (A)
60 Wellington Park, BT9 6DP.
☎ (01232) 662693.
B&B s£20 d£40. Rooms 8, ensuite 2. Dinner £12.
Last orders 1830 hrs. Open all year.

Bed & Breakfast

Aisling House
(Mrs D Devenny), 7 Taunton Avenue, Antrim Rd,
BT15 4AD.
☎ (01232) 771529.
B&B s£19 d£37. Rooms 3. Open all year.

Ashberry Cottage
(Mr S Mitchell), 19 Rosepark Central, Stormont,
BT5 7RN. ☎ (01232) 482441.
B&B s£17 d£32. Rooms 3. Open all year.

Facilities are liable to change. Check prices when you book. Key to symbols is on the back flap.

Ben Eadan

(Mrs C Rooney), 9 Thorburn Rd, Antrim Rd,
BT36 7HZ.
☎ (01232) 777764.
B&B s£18 d£32. Rooms 2, ensuite 1.
Open all year.

Botanic Lodge

(Mrs H Moore-Will), 87 Botanic Avenue, BT7 1JN.
☎ (01232) 327682.
B&B s£22 d£40. Rooms 17, ensuite 2.
Open all year.

Bowdens

(Mrs C Bowden), 17 Sandford Avenue,
off Cyprus Avenue, BT5 5NW.
☎ (01232) 652213.
B&B s£15 d£30. Rooms 3. Open all year.

The Cottage

(Mrs E Muldoon), 377 Comber Rd,
Dundonald, BT16 0XB.
☎ (01247) 878189.
B&B s£21 d£38. Rooms 2. Open all year.

Crecora

(Mrs C Gribben), 114 Upper Newtownards Rd,
BT4 3EN.
☎ (01232) 658257.
B&B s£17 d£34. Rooms 6, ensuite 2.
Open all year.

Drumragh

(Mrs S Cooper), 647 Antrim Rd, BT15 3EA.
☎ (01232) 773063.
B&B s£20 d£36. Rooms 2. Open all year.

The Eagles

(Mrs L McMichael), 131 Upper Newtownards Rd,
BT4 3HW.
☎ (01232) 673607.
B&B s£15 d£30. Rooms 4. Open all year.

East Sheen

(Mrs R Davidson), 81 Eglantine Avenue, BT9 6EW.
☎ (01232) 667149.
B&B s£18.50 d£37. Rooms 4.
Open Jan-Nov.

Enler Cottage

(Mrs J Dornan), 385 Comber Rd,
Dundonald, BT16 0XB.
☎ (01247) 873240.
B&B s£18 d£35. Rooms 2, ensuite 2.
Open all year.

The George

(Mrs C McGuinness), 9 Eglantine Avenue,
BT9 6DW.
☎ (01232) 683212.
B&B s£20 d£40. Rooms 6, ensuite 4.
Open all year.

Halcyon House

(Mrs M McQuaid), 68 Wellington Park, BT9 6DP.
☎ & fax (01232) 681648.
B&B s£25 d£40. Rooms 1. Open all year ex
Christmas.

Harveys

(Ms J Harvey), 192 Belmont Rd, BT4 2AT.
☎ (01232) 652320.
B&B s£17 d£34. Rooms 3. Open all year.

Facilities are liable to change. Check prices when you book. Key to symbols is on the back flap.

Helga Lodge
(Mr N Will), 7 Cromwell Rd, BT7 1JW.
☎ (01232) 324820. Fax 320653.
B&B s£22 d£40. Rooms 30, ensuite 8.
Open all year.

Hermitage Lodge
(Mr & Mrs Frew), 62 North Rd, BT5 5NJ.
☎ & fax (01232) 203322.
B&B s£35 d£55. Rooms 4, ensuite 4.
Open all year.

James House
(Mrs S Fleming), 55 Oakland Avenue, BT4 3BW.
☎ (01232) 650374.
B&B s£14 d£28. Rooms 5. Open all year.

Lucy's Lodge
(Mrs F McLean), 72 Salisbury Avenue, BT15 5EB.
☎ (01232) 776036.
B&B s£17.50 d£35. Rooms 4. Open all year.

Maranatha
(Mrs E McCrea), 254 Ravenhill Rd, BT6 8GL.
☎ & fax (01232) 460200.
B&B s£25 d£39. Rooms 9, ensuite 8.
Open all year.

Marine House
(Mrs Corrigan & Mrs Quinn), 30 Eglantine Avenue, BT9 6DX.
☎ (01232) 662828/381922. Fax 662828.
B&B s£19 d£38. Rooms 11, ensuite 4.
Open all year.

Pine Lodge
(Mr & Mrs O'Donnell), 42a Drumalig Rd, Carryduff, BT8 8EQ.
☎ (01232) 814875.
B&B s£25 d£40. Rooms 4, ensuite 4.
Open all year.

Queen's Elms
Queen's University, 78 Malone Rd, BT9 5BW.
☎ (01232) 381608. Fax 666680.
Bed only s£14 d£21.75. Rooms 300.
Open July-Sept.

Queen's University Common Room
1 College Gardens, University Rd, BT9 6BQ.
☎ (01232) 665938. Fax 681209.
B&B s£39.50 d£59.50. Rooms 25, ensuite 17.
Open all year.

Somerton House
(Ms Sharkey & Mr Scannell), 22 Lansdowne Rd, BT15 4DB.
☎ (01232) 370717.
B&B s£19 d£35. Rooms 7. Open all year.

Stranmillis College
Stranmillis Rd, BT9 5DY.
☎ (01232) 381271/384251. Fax 664423.
Groups only.
B&B s£18.50 BB&M s£27.50. High tea £5.
Dinner £9. Rooms 450. Open Easter & June-Sept.

Stranmillis Lodge

14 Chlorine Gardens, BT9 5DJ.
☎ (01232) 682009. Fax 683334.
B&B s£40 d£60. Rooms 6, ensuite 6.
Open all year.

The Warren House

(Ms M Hughes), 10 Thornhill Rd, Dunmurry,
BT17 9EJ.
☎ (01232) 611702.
B&B s£20 d£40. Rooms 2, ensuite 2.
Open all year.

White Lodge

(Mr & Mrs Cormacain), 11 Finaghy Park North,
BT10 0HQ.
☎ (01232) 619610.
B&B s£25 d£40. Rooms 2, ensuite 1.
Open all year.

YWCA Hostel

Queen Mary's Hall, 70 Fitzwilliam St,
Lisburn Rd, BT9 6AX.
☎ (01232) 240439.
B&B s£15 d£30. BB&M s£20.50. d£41.
Rooms 16. Dinner £5.50. Last orders 1500 hrs.
Open all year ex Easter & Christmas.

232 Duncairn Gardens

(Mrs B Sherry), BT15 2GP.
☎ (01232) 745550.
B&B s£18 d£30. Rooms 2. Dinner £7.
Open all year.

Facilities are liable to change. Check prices when you book. Key to symbols is on the back flap.

61

Tourist Information Centres open all year

Call in for an update on events and visitor attractions in Northern Ireland and to book your holiday accommodation.

ANTRIM
16 High St. ☎ (01849) 465156.

ARMAGH
40 English St. ☎ (01861) 521800.

BALLYCASTLE
7 Mary St. ☎ (012657) 62024.

BANBRIDGE
200 Newry Rd. ☎ (018206) 23322.

BANGOR
34 Quay Rd. ☎ (01247) 270069.

BELFAST
59 North St. ☎ (01232) 246609.

CARRICKFERGUS
Heritage Plaza, Antrim St.
☎ (01960) 366455.

COLERAINE
Railway Rd. ☎ (01265) 44723.

DOWNPATRICK
74 Market St. ☎ (01396) 612233.

DUNGANNON
Killymaddy, Ballygawley Rd.
☎ (01868) 767259.

ENNISKILLEN
Wellington Rd. ☎ (01365) 323110.

GIANT'S CAUSEWAY
Giant's Causeway Centre.
☎ (012657) 31855.

KILKEEL
6 Newcastle St. ☎ (016937) 62525.

LARNE
Narrow Gauge Rd. ☎ (01574) 260088.

LIMAVADY
7 Connell St. ☎ (015047) 22226.

LISBURN
Market Square. ☎ (01846) 660038.

LONDONDERRY
44 Foyle St. ☎ (01504) 267284.

NEWCASTLE
Central Promenade. ☎ (013967) 22222.

NEWTOWNARDS
31 Regent St. ☎ (01247) 826846.

OMAGH
Market Square. ☎ (01662) 247831.

County Antrim

ANTRIM

Hotel

Deerpark Hotel *
71 Dublin Rd, BT41 4PN.
☎ (01849) 462480. Fax 467126.
B&B s£30 d£50. Rooms 21, ensuite 21.
High tea £6. Dinner £10. Last orders 2130 hrs.
Open all year.

🄣 🄿 ♻ ❀ ♣ ☀ ❢ ☒ 🛏 🎠 🏛 ⛶ 🕯 🗡 ♪ ⌐ U
✓ ⌂ ✦ ☎ ⊡

Guesthouse

The Beeches (A)
10 Dunadry Rd, Muckamore, BT41 2RR.
☎ & fax (01849) 433161.
B&B s£40 d£65. BB&M s£55 d£95. Rooms 5,
ensuite 5. Dinner £15. Last orders 1830 hrs.
Open all year.

🄣 🄿 ❀ ♣ ☀ ☒ 🎠 🄪 🏛 ⛶ 🗡 ♪ ⌐
U ⌂ ✦ ⊡

Bed & Breakfast

Ashcroft
(Mrs R McKeown), 37 Thornhill Rd, BT41 2LH.
☎ (01849) 469117.
B&B s£16 d£35. Rooms 3. High tea £5.
Dinner £10. Open all year.

🄿 ❀ ♣ ☀ ☒ 🏛 ⛶ 🗡 ♪ ⌐ U ⌂ ✦

Ballyarnott House
(Mrs H McMinn), 7 Oldstone Hill, Muckamore,
BT41 4SB.
☎ (01849) 463292.
B&B s£15.50 d£31. Rooms 3. High tea £7.
Dinner £8. Open all year.

🄿 ❀ ♣ ☒ 🏛 🗡

Brograni
(Mrs M Marrs), 2 Steeple Green, BT41 1BP.
☎ (01849) 462484.
B&B s£15 d£30. BB&M s£22.50 d£45. Rooms 2.
High tea £6. Dinner £7.50. Open all year.

🄿 ♣ ☒ 🏛 ⛶ 🗡 ♪ ⌐ U ✓ ⌂ ✦

The Cottage
(Ms K Elder), 118 Belfast Rd, BT41 2BA.
☎ (01849) 464446.
B&B s£15 d£30. BB&M s£20 d£40. Rooms 3.
Dinner £5. Open Jan-Nov.

🄿 ❀ ♣ ☒ 🏛 🗡 ⌐ U ✦

The Croft
(Mrs E Hamilton), 18 Moylena Rd, BT41 4PA.
☎ (01849) 428242.
B&B s£15 d£30. BB&M s£22.50 d£45.
Rooms 1, ensuite 1. Dinner £7.50.
Last orders 2030 hrs. Open all year.

🄿 ❀ ☒ 🄪 🎠 🏛 ⛶ ⌐ U ✓ ⌂ ✦

The Lodge
(Mr & Mrs McIlvenna), 120 Belfast Rd, BT41 2BA.
☎ (01849) 467170. Mobile 0410 501802.
B&B s£16.50 d£33. Rooms 2. Open all year.

🄿 ❀ ♣ ☒ 🏛 ⛶ 🗡 ♪

Maranatha
(Mr & Mrs Steele), 69 Oldstone Rd, BT41 4SL.
☎ (01849) 463150.
B&B s£15 d£30. Rooms 3.
Open all year ex Christmas.

🄿 ❀ ♣ ☒ 🎠 🏛 ♪ ⌐ ⌂

The Stables
(Mr V McDonald), 96 Milltown Rd, BT41 2JJ.
☎ (01849) 466943.
B&B s£25 d£40. Rooms 9, ensuite 9.
Open all year.

🄿 ❀ ♣ ☀ ☒ 🏛 ⛶ 🗡 ♪ ⌐ U ⊡

Facilities are liable to change. Check prices when you book. Key to symbols is on inside back flap.

23 Thornhill Rd
(Mr & Mrs Dennison), BT41 2LH.
☎ (01849) 462964.
B&B s£16 d£32. Rooms 3. Open all year.

🅿 ※ 🐎 ▥. ⬗ ◔

Whitepark House
(Mr & Mrs Isles), 150 Whitepark Rd, BT54 6NH.
☎ (012657) 31482.
B&B s£26 d£45. Rooms 3. Open all year.

🅃 🅿 🏫 ❀ ♣ ※ ▥. ✂ ✦ ⬗ ∪ △ ⓩ ⚲

BALLINTOY

Guesthouse

Fullerton Arms (B)
22 Main St, BT54 6LX.
☎ & fax (012657) 69613.
B&B s£25 d£50. BB&M s£39 d£78. Rooms 6,
ensuite 6. Dinner £10. Last orders 2100 hrs.
Open all year.

🅿 🏫 ♣ ※ ☕ 🐎 ⒹⒶⓅ ▥. ✂ ✦ ⬗ ∪ ⚲ ⊞

Bed & Breakfast

Ballintoy House
(Mrs R McFall), 9 Main St, BT54 6LX.
☎ (012657) 62317.
B&B s£13 d£30. Rooms 3, ensuite 1. Open all year.

🅃 🅿 🏫 ❀ ♣ ※ 🐎 ⒹⒶⓅ 🐕 ▥. ✦ ⬗ ∪
✓ △ ⓩ ⚲

Glenside Farm
(Mr & Mrs McConaghy), 6 Craigalappin Rd,
BT54 6NJ.
☎ (012657) 31686.
B&B s£21 d£35. Rooms 2. Open June-Aug.

🅿 ♣ ※ ▥. ✂ ⚲

Knocksaughey House
(Mrs J McCaw), 122 Whitepark Rd, BT54 6LX.
☎ (012657) 62967.
B&B s£17.50 d£30. Rooms 2, ensuite 1.
Open all year.

🅿 ❀ ♣ ※ 🐎 ⒹⒶⓅ ▥. ▢ ✂ ✦ ⬗ ∪ ✓ △ ⓩ ⚲

BALLYCASTLE

Hotel

Marine Hotel ***
1 North St, BT54 6BN.
☎ (012657) 62222. Fax 69507.
B&B s£50 d£70. BB&M s£66 d£84. Rooms 32,
ensuite 32. High tea £12. Dinner £14.
Last orders 2100 hrs. Open all year.

🅃 🅿 ※ ! 🐎 🅶 ⒹⒶⓅ ▥. ▢ ℄ ✂ 🎵 ✦
⬗ ◔ ⚲ ⊞

Guesthouse

Glenluce (A)
42 Quay Rd, BT54 6BH.
☎ (012657) 62914.
B&B s£20 d£40. Rooms 8, ensuite 4.
Open all year.

🅿 🏫 ❀ ※ 🐎 ▥. ▢ ✂ ✦ ⬗ ∪ ✓ △ ⓩ ⚲

Bed & Breakfast

Ammiroy House
(Mrs M Crawford), 24 Quay Rd, BT54 6BH.
☎ (012657) 62621.
B&B s£20 d£32. Rooms 2. Open all year.

🅃 🅿 ❀ ※ ⒹⒶⓅ ▥. ▢ ⚲ ⊞

B&B = bed and breakfast   s = single   d = double   BB&M = bed, breakfast & evening meal

Antrim Arms

(Mr & Mrs Dobbin), 75 Castle St, BT54 6AR.
☎ (012657) 62284.
B&B s£17.50 d£35. Rooms 4, ensuite 1.
High tea £6. Dinner £8.
Last orders 2100 hrs. Open all year.

Ardmara

(Mr & Mrs Herron), 34 Whitepark Rd, BT54 6LJ.
☎ (012657) 69533.
B&B s£18 d£36. Rooms 3, ensuite 1.
Open April-Sept.

Beechwood

(Mrs A McHenry), 9 Beechwood Avenue, BT54 6BL.
☎ & fax (012657) 63697.
B&B s£15 d£30. Rooms 4, ensuite 2. Open all year.

Braemar

(Mrs B McIlroy), 72 Moyle Rd, BT54 6LG.
☎ (012657) 62529.
B&B s£14 d£28. Rooms 2. Open Jan-mid Nov.

Broughgammon

(Mrs F Chambers), 56 Straid Rd, BT54 6NP.
☎ (012657) 63260.
B&B d£30. Rooms 2. Open all year.

Broughinlea House

(Mrs A Hill), 59 Cushendall Rd, BT54 6QP.
☎ (012657) 62842.
B&B s£20 d£38. Rooms 3, ensuite 3.
Open all year.

Bushbane House

(Mr & Mrs McKiernan), 28 Whitepark Rd, BT54 6LJ.
☎ (012657) 63789.
B&B s£16 d£32. Rooms 4, ensuite 4.
Open all year.

Carneatly Lodge

(Mrs A McPherson), 48 Moyarget Rd, BT54 6HJ.
☎ (012657) 62150.
B&B s£18.50 d£37. Rooms 3, ensuite 3.
Open March-Nov.

Clare House

(Mrs P Black), 33 Whitepark Rd, BT54 6LL.
☎ (012657) 63889.
B&B s£15 d£30. Rooms 2. Open all year.

Colliers Hall

(Mrs M McCarry), 50 Cushendall Rd, BT54 6QR.
☎ (012657) 62531.
B&B s£18 d£36. Rooms 3, ensuite 3.
Open April-Sept.
On A2, 2m E of Ballycastle

Cúchulainn House

(Mrs M McMahon), 56 Quay Rd, BT54 6BH.
☎ (012657) 62252.
B&B s£15 d£37. Rooms 3, ensuite 2.
Open all year.

Cushleake House

(Mrs D Tompkin), 32 Quay Rd, BT54 6BH.
☎ & fax (012657) 63798.
B&B s£16 d£35. Rooms 2, ensuite 1.
Open all year.

Facilities are liable to change. Check prices when you book. Key to symbols is on inside back flap.

Fair Head View
(Mrs K Delargy), 26 North St, BT54 6BW.
☎ (012657) 62822.
B&B s£16 d£32. Rooms 3, ensuite 1.
Open all year.

Fragrens
(Mrs V Greene), 34 Quay Rd, BT54 6BH.
☎ (012657) 62168/62181.
B&B s£15 d£34. Rooms 8, ensuite 4.
Open Feb-Nov.

Glenfarg
(Mrs A Christie), 4a Moyarget Rd, BT54 6JA.
☎ (012657) 62404.
B&B s£16 d£32. Rooms 2. Open April-Oct.

Glenhaven
(Mrs A Gormley), 10 Beechwood Avenue,
BT54 6BL.
☎ (012657) 63612.
B&B s£15 d£30. Rooms 3. Open March-Oct.

Glenmore House
(Mrs V Brown), 94 Whitepark Rd, BT54 6LR.
☎ (012657) 63584.
B&B s£16 d£27. BB&M s£25 d£45.
Rooms 2, ensuite 1. Dinner £9.
Last orders 2100 hrs. Open all year.

Glenville
(Mr T Glass), 11 Market St, BT54 6DS.
☎ (012657) 63728.
B&B s£15 d£30. Rooms 2. Open April-Oct.

Gortconney House
(Mrs H Smyth), 52 Whitepark Rd, BT54 6LP.
☎ (012657) 62283.
B&B d£30. Rooms 3. Open May-Oct.

Hilsea
(Mr M Jameson), 28 Quay Hill, BT54 6BW.
☎ (012657) 62385.
B&B s£16 d£32. Rooms 17, ensuite 6.
Open March-Nov.

Kenmara House
(Mr E Shannon), 45 North St, BT54 6BP.
☎ (012657) 62600.
B&B s£20 d£40. Rooms 3, ensuite 1.
Open all year ex Christmas.

Kilmean Farm
(Mr & Mrs Kane), 4 Glenstaughey Rd,
BT54 6NE.
☎ (012657) 63305.
B&B s£15 d£30. Rooms 3. Open April-Oct.

Rathushard
(Mrs J Lynn), 3 Rathlin Rd, BT54 6DD.
☎ (012657) 62237.
B&B s£16.50 d£33. Rooms 3. Open all year.

Silversprings House
(Mrs M Mulholland), 20 Quay Rd, BT54 0BH.
☎ (012657) 62080.
B&B s£18.50 d£37. Rooms 3, ensuite 3.
Open March-Oct.

Facilities are liable to change. Check prices when you book. Key to symbols is on inside back flap.

Sunningdale
(Mr J Campbell), 28 Clare Rd, BT54 6DB.
☎ (012657) 63859.
B&B s£20 d£36. Rooms 2, ensuite 2.
Open March-Oct.

🅣 🅟 ✻ ⚘ ⊶ 🛋 ⌨ ✂ 🏃 å

Torr Brae
(Mrs O McHenry), 77 Torr Rd, BT54 6RQ.
☎ (012657) 69625.
B&B s£18 d£36. Rooms 3, ensuite 2.
Open all year.

🅟 ✻ ♠ ⚘ ⊶ 🐎 🏇 🛋 ✂ 🏃 ♪ 🖐 U ✓ ⚐ ⚘ å

Willeen
(Mrs E McAlister), 1 Church Rd, BT54 6EA.
☎ (012657) 63560.
B&B s£15 d£30. Rooms 1. Open all year.

🅟 ⌂ ✻ ♠ ⚘ ⊶ 🐎 ㎖ 🛋 ✂ 🏃 🖐 U ⚐ å

BALLYCLARE

Bed & Breakfast

Beechcroft
(Mrs B McKay), 43 Belfast Rd, Ballynure,
BT39 9TZ.
☎ & fax (01960) 352334.
B&B s£15 d£30. BB&M s£22 d£44.
Rooms 3, ensuite 2. High tea £5. Dinner £7.
Last orders 2000 hrs. Open all year.

🅟 ✻ ♠ ⚘ ⊶ 🐎 ㎖ 🛋 ✂ 🏃 ♪ 🖐 U ✓ ⚐ å ⊞

Bentra
(Mr & Mrs Minford), 16 Ballybentragh Rd, BT39 0DE.
☎ (01849) 433407.
B&B s£20 d£40. Rooms 2. Open all year.

🅟 ⌂ ✻ ♠ ⚘ ㎖ 🛋 ⌨ ✂ 🏃 🖐 ✓ ⚐ ⚘

Clannad Cottage
(Mrs A Burnison), 42 Ballygowan Rd, Ballynure,
BT39 9UP.
☎ (01960) 354516. Fax 322016.
B&B d£35. Rooms 1, ensuite 1. Open all year.

🅟 ✻ ♠ ⚘ ⊶ ㎖ 🛋 ⌨ ✂ 🏃 ♪ 🖐 U å

Fairways
(Mrs A Berry), 38 Orpinsmill Rd, BT39 0SX.
☎ (01960) 342419.
B&B s£23 d£36. Rooms 3, ensuite 1.
Open all year.

🅣 🅟 ✻ ♠ ⚘ ⊶ 🐎 🛋 ⌨ ♪ 🖐 U

Rockbank
(Mrs H Park), 40 Belfast Rd, Ballynure, BT39 9TZ.
☎ (01960) 352261.
B&B s£17.50 d£35. Rooms 3, ensuite 2.
Open all year.

🅣 🅟 ✻ ♠ ⚘ ⊶ 🐎 🏇 🛋 ⌨ ✂ 🏃 ♪ 🖐 å

Rua-Wai Farm
(Mrs A Hunter), 149 Templepatrick Rd, BT39 9RW.
☎ (01960) 352417.
B&B s£17.50 d£35. Rooms 3, ensuite 2.
Open all year.
On A57, 8m E of Airport

🅟 ✻ ♠ ⚘ ⊶ 🐎 ㎖ 🛋 ⌨ ✂ 🏃 ♪ 🖐 U ✓ ⚐ ⚘ ◎

Tildarg House
(Mrs J Thompson), 50 Collin Rd, BT39 9JS.
☎ (01960) 322367.
B&B s£20 d£35. Rooms 4, ensuite 1.
Open all year.

🅟 ⌂ ✻ ♠ ⚘ ⊶ 🐎 🛋 ✂ 🏃 ♪ 🖐

B&B = bed and breakfast   s = single   d = double   BB&M = bed, breakfast & evening meal

Woodbine Farm

(Mrs M Crawford), 98 Carrickfergus Rd, Ballynure,
BT39 9QP.
☎ (01960) 352092.
B&B s£17 d£30. BB&M s£25 d£50. Rooms 3,
ensuite 3. High tea £6. Dinner £9.
Last orders 2030 hrs. Open all year.
Off A2, 4m E of Ballyclare

P 🏠 ❀ ♣ 🌢 🐎 OAP ▥ ⚙ 🔌 🛈 ⌖ ∪ ⚓ ♞

Hotels

Ballygally Castle Hotel ***

274 Coast Rd, BT40 2RA.
☎ (01574) 583212. Fax 583681.
B&B s£50 d£76. BB&M s£65 d£105. Rooms 30,
ensuite 30. High tea £11. Dinner £14.95.
Last orders 2100 hrs. Open all year.

T P ❀ ♣ 🌢 ♗ ! 🐎 ▥ 🖵 ☏ ⚙ ⚘ 🛈 ⌖ ∪ ✓ ⚓ ⇄ ♈ ⊞

Halfway House Hotel **

352 Coast Rd, BT40 2RA.
☎ (01574) 583265. Fax 583510.
B&B s£33 d£55. Rooms 10, ensuite 10.
High tea £6.95. Dinner £12. Last orders 2045 hrs.
Open all year.

T P ❀ ♣ 🌢 ! 🐎 ▥ 🖵 ☏ ⚙ ⊞

Hotels

Galgorm Manor ****

136 Fenaghy Rd, Ballymena BT42 1EA.
☎ (01266) 881001. Fax 880080.
B&B s£95 d£115. BB&M s£119.50 d£164.
Rooms 23, ensuite 23. High tea £13. Dinner £24.50.
Last orders 2130 hrs. Open all year.

T P 🏠 ❀ ♣ 🌢 ! 🐎 ▥ 🖵 ☏ 🛈 ∪ ✓ ⚓ ♈ ⚘ ⊞

Adair Arms Hotel ***

Ballymoney Rd, BT43 5BS.
☎ (01266) 653674. Fax 40436.
B&B s£56 d£78. BB&M s£65 d£85. Rooms 40,
ensuite 40. High tea £8.95. Dinner £14.95.
Last orders 2200 hrs. Open all year ex Christmas.

P 🏠 ! ♗ 🐎 OAP ▥ 🖵 ☏ ⚙ ⚘ 🛈 ⌖ ∪ ✓ ⚓ ⇄ ♈ ⊞

Country House Hotel ***

20 Doagh Rd, Kells, BT42 3LZ.
☎ (01266) 891663. Fax 891477.
B&B s£70 d£80. Rooms 39, ensuite 39.
High tea £10. Dinner £16.
Last orders 2100 hrs. Open all year.

T P ❀ ♣ ! 🐎 OAP ▥ 🖵 ☏ ⚙ ⚘ ⚘ ⇄ 🔌 ⌖ ∪ ✓ ⚓ ⇄ ♈ ⊞

Leighinmohr Hotel ***

5 Leighinmohr Avenue, BT42 2AN.
☎ (01266) 652313. Fax 656669.
B&B s£42.50 d£63. BB&M s£55 d£88.
Rooms 20, ensuite 20. High tea £10. Dinner £15.
Last orders 2100 hrs. Open all year.

T P ❀ ! 🐎 OAP ▥ 🖵 ☏ 🔌 ⌖ ∪ ✓ ⚓ ⇄ ♈ ♞ ⊞

Facilities are liable to change. Check prices when you book. Key to symbols is on inside back flap.

Tullyglass House Hotel ***
178 Galgorm Rd, BT42 1HJ.
☎ (01266) 652639. Fax 46938.
B&B s£40 d£60. BB&M s£50 d£80.
Rooms 32, ensuite 29. High tea £7.50.
Dinner £15. Last orders 2145 hrs. Open all year.

Guesthouses

Beechfield   (U)
81 Galgorm Rd, BT42 1AA.
☎ (01266) 659709.
B&B s£25 d£40. BB&M s£35 d£60.
Rooms 8, ensuite 7. High tea £7. Dinner £9.
Last orders 1900 hrs. Open all year.

Tullymore House   (B)
2 Carnlough Rd, Broughshane, BT43 7HF.
☎ (01266) 861233. Fax 862238.
B&B s£35 d£60. BB&M s£45 d£80.
Rooms 8, ensuite 8. High tea £10. Dinner £12.
Last orders 2130 hrs. Open all year.

Bed & Breakfast

Beeches
(Mrs J Douglas), 46 Lisnafillan Rd, Gracehill,
BT42 1SA. ☎ (01266) 871660.
B&B s£19 d£34. Rooms 1.
High tea £5. Dinner £7.50. Open all year.

Ben Vista
(Mrs E Joyce), 79 Galgorm Rd, BT42 1AD.
☎ (01266) 46091.
B&B s£18 d£34. BB&M s£26.50 d£51.
Rooms 3, ensuite 2. Dinner £8.50.
Last orders 1800 hrs. Open all year ex Christmas.

Broadcroft
(Ms C Bailie), 94 Galgorm Rd, BT42 1AA.
☎ (01266) 45936.
B&B s£25 d£44. Rooms 3, ensuite 2.
Open all year.

Carnview
(Mr & Mrs McKeown), 5 Drumfin Rd, BT34 6TT.
☎ (01266) 685340.
B&B s£15.50 d£31. Rooms 3. Open all year.

Charmoor House
(Mrs C McNeill), 66 Craigadoo Rd, Moorfields,
BT42 4RD.
☎ (01266) 891872.
B&B d£20. Rooms 1, ensuite 1. Open all year.

Corner House
(Mrs L Kirkpatrick), 58 Knockahollet Rd, Dunloy,
BT44 9BA. ☎ (012656) 41332.
B&B s£15 d£30. Rooms 2. Open all year.

Crossview
(Mrs D Hanna), 146 Crankill Rd, Glarryford,
BT44 9EY.
☎ (01266) 685360.
B&B s£15 d£30. BB&M s£20 d£40. Rooms 2.
High tea £5. Last orders 2100 hrs. Open all year.

B&B = bed and breakfast   s = single   d = double   BB&M = bed, breakfast & evening meal

Dunaird House
(Mrs S Graham), 15 Buckna Rd, Broughshane,
BT42 4NJ.
☎ (01266) 862117.
B&B s£25 d£45. Rooms 3, ensuite 2.
Open all year.

The Firs
(Miss K Carson), 86 Duneoin Rd,
Glarryford, BT44 9HH.
☎ (01266) 685410.
B&B s£13 d£26. BB&M s£19 d£38. Rooms 1.
Dinner £6. Last orders 2100 hrs. Open all year.

Knockahollet
(Ms S Munnis), 84 Knockaholet Rd,
Dunloy, BT44 9BA.
☎ (012656) 41410.
B&B s£16 d£32. Rooms 3, ensuite 3. High tea £5.
Open all year.

Laurel Farm
(Ms M Buick), 8 Oldtown Rd, Ferniskey,
Kells, BT42 3NL.
☎ (01266) 891727.
B&B s£18 d£34. Rooms 1. Open July-Aug.

Meadow View
(Mrs H McDowell), 13 Redford Rd,
Cullybackey, BT43 5PR.
☎ (01266) 880738.
B&B s£20 d£32. BB&M s£30 d£52.
Dinner £10. Rooms 2, ensuite 2.
Open all year.

Neelsgrove Farm
(Mrs M Neely), 51 Carnearney Rd, Ahoghill,
BT42 2PL.
☎ (01266) 871225.
B&B s£16 d£37. BB&M s£26 d£57.
Rooms 3, ensuite 1. High tea £10.
Open Jan-Nov.

Quarrytown Lodge
(Mrs M Drennan), 15 Quarrytown Rd,
Broughshane, BT43 7LB.
☎ (01266) 862027.
B&B s£25 d£40. Rooms 4, ensuite 4.
Open all year.

Reekie Linn
(Ms G McDowell), 158 Galgorm Rd, BT42 1DE.
☎ (01266) 652143.
B&B s£20 d£40. BB&M s£30 d£60.
Rooms 2, ensuite 1. Open all year.

Roebury
(Mrs A Adams), 82 Granagh Rd, Cullybackey,
BT42 1DR.
☎ (01266) 880088.
B&B d£35. Rooms 1, ensuite 1. High tea £3.50.
Last orders 2100 hrs. Open Jan-Nov.

Shanleigh House
(Mrs M Hunter), 8 Shandon Park,
Grange Rd, Galgorm Rd, BT42 2ED.
☎ (01266) 44851.
B&B s£16 d£32. Rooms 3, ensuite 2.
Open all year ex Christmas.

Facilities are liable to change. Check prices when you book. Key to symbols is on inside back flap.

Slemish House

(Miss B Shaw), 51 Albert Place, BT43 6DY.
☎ (01266) 47383.
B&B s£23 d£32. Rooms 2. Open all year.

Slemish View

(Mr & Mrs Millar), 75 Cromkill Rd, BT42 2JR.
☎ (01266) 40355.
B&B s£15 d£26. BB&M s£23 d£42.
Rooms 2, ensuite 1. High tea £7. Dinner £8.
Last orders 2230 hrs. Open all year.

Springmount

(Mrs R Bell), 31 Ballygowan Rd, Kells, BT42 3PD.
☎ (01266) 891275.
B&B s£15 d£30. BB&M s£21 d£42. Rooms 2.
High tea £6. Dinner £8. Open all year.

Such Moor Stud

(Mrs R Robinson), 94 Crankill Rd, BT43 5NW.
☎ (01266) 880521.
B&B s£15 d£30. Rooms 2. Open all year.

Wilmaur

(Mrs M Caves), 83 Galgorm Rd, BT42 1AA.
☎ (01266) 41878.
B&B s£20 d£35. Rooms 4, ensuite 3.
Open all year.

BALLYMONEY

Hotel

Unclassified Hotel
Manor Hotel, 69 Main St, BT56 6AN.
☎ (012656) 63208.

Guesthouses

Athdara (A)

25 Portrush Rd, BT53 6BX.
☎ (012656) 65149.
B&B s£18.50 d£37. Rooms 3. Open all year.

Cooleen (A)

15 Coleraine Rd, BT53 6BP.
☎ (012656) 63037. Fax 63456.
B&B s£25 d£40. Rooms 6, ensuite 6.
Open Feb-Dec.
On B62, ½m N of Ballymoney

Hob Green Country House (B)

41 Kirk Rd, BT53 8HB.
☎ & fax (012656) 62620.
B&B s£20 d£37. BB&M s£28.50 d£54.
Rooms 4, ensuite 4. High tea £8.50. Open all year.

Seacon Hall (A)

40 Seacon Park, BT53 6QB.
☎ (012656) 62754.
B&B s£23 d£38. Rooms 4, ensuite 4.
Open Jan-Nov.

Bed & Breakfast

Arches

(Mr D McAllister), 51 Knock Rd, BT53 6LX.
☎ (012656) 64229.
B&B s£16 d£30. BB&M s£24 d£46.
Rooms 2, ensuite 1. High tea £8.
Last orders 2000 hrs. Open all year.

B&B = bed and breakfast   s = single   d = double   BB&M = bed, breakfast & evening meal

Ballyhivistock Country House

(Mrs M Ferguson), 129 Castlecatt Rd, Dervock,
BT53 8AD.
☎ (012657) 41077.
B&B s£16 d£32. Rooms 2, ensuite 2.
Open April-Oct.

Ballyrobin House

(Mr G Young), 142 Kirk Rd, Stranocum, BT53 8HT.
☎ (012657) 42077.
B&B s£20 d£30. Rooms 2, ensuite 1.
Open all year.

Carnglass Farmhouse

(Mr & Mrs Carson), 170 Ballybogy Rd, BT53 6PQ.
☎ & fax (012657) 41762.
B&B s£13.50 d£27. Rooms 2. Open all year.

Churchview House

(Mrs M McCracken), 151 Finvoy Rd, BT53 7JN.
☎ (012665) 71472.
B&B s£16 d£32. Rooms 3. Open all year.

Corvalley House

(Mr F Devlin), 88 Drumavoley Rd, Armoy,
BT53 8SB.
☎ (012657) 69746.
B&B s£15 d£30. Rooms 2, ensuite 1.
Open April-Sept.

Crossroads Farm

(Mrs S Adams), 99 Ballinlea Rd, Armoy,
BT53 8UQ.
☎ (012657) 51546.
B&B s£15 d£30. Rooms 2. Open all year.

Dun Gladey

(Mrs A Johnston), 6 Ballymena Rd, BT53 7AB.
☎ (012656) 63064.
B&B s£15 d£30. Rooms 2. High tea £6.
Dinner £8. Last orders 1200 hrs.
Open Jan-Nov.

Elm House

(Mrs McCrea), 60 Drumskea Rd, BT53 7ID.
☎ (012665) 63345.
B&B s£15 d£30. Rooms 1. Open all year.

Enagh Farm

(Mr & Mrs D Gilmour), 11 Drumskea Rd, BT53 7JB.
☎ (012656) 63169.
B&B s£15 d£30. Rooms 2. Open all year.

Glen Lodge

(Mrs B Kirkpatrick), 93a Frocess Rd, BT53 7EJ.
☎ (012656) 63800.
B&B s£18 d£35. Rooms 4, ensuite 4.
Open all year.

Heagles Lodge

(Mrs A Sharkey), 3 Heagles Rd, Ballybogey,
BT53 6NZ.
☎ (012657) 41122. Fax 41001.
B&B d£36. Rooms 2, ensuite 2. Open all year.

Facilities are liable to change. Check prices when you book. Key to symbols is on inside back flap.

Kenver Lodge
(Ms E Elliott), 26 Ballykenver Rd, Stranocum,
BT53 8PZ.
☎ (012657) 42142.
B&B s£16 d£32. BB&M s£24 d£48. Rooms 2.
High tea £6. Dinner £8. Last orders 2030 hrs.
Open all year.

Moore Lodge
(Sir Wm & Lady Moore), Vow Rd, BT53 7NT.
☎ (012665) 41043.
B&B s£50 d£100. Rooms 3, ensuite 2.
Open May-Aug.

Mountview House
(Mr & Mrs Getty), 23 Carrowcroey Rd, Armoy,
BT53 8UH.
☎ (012657) 51402.
B&B s£16 d£32. BB&M s£24 d£48. Rooms 5,
ensuite 5. Dinner £8. Open all year.

The Pines
(Mrs M Adams), 96 Bravallen Rd, BT53 7DU.
☎ (012656) 62893.
B&B s£15 d£30. Rooms 2. Open all year.

Sandelwood
(Mrs S Brown), 98 Knock Rd, BT53 6NQ.
☎ (012656) 62621.
B&B s£14 d£28. Rooms 3.
Open March-Oct.

The Sheddings
(Mrs K Hynds), 39 Macfin Rd, BT53 6QY.
☎ (012656) 65514.
B&B s£18 d£38. Rooms 4, ensuite 2.
Open all year.

Tearmann
(Miss N Diver), 121 Fivey Rd, Stranocum, BT53 8SB.
☎ (012657) 41039.
B&B s£22 d£44. Rooms 3, ensuite 2.
Open March-Oct.

Westwinds
(Mrs M McConaghie), 290a Moyarget Rd, Moss-side,
BT52 8EG.
☎ (012657) 41471.
B&B s£15 d£30. BB&M s£18 d£36.
Rooms 3, ensuite 2. Open all year.

38 Lisboy Rd
(Mrs W Skelton), BT53 8NG.
☎ (012656) 66423.
B&B s£13 d£26. Rooms 2.
Open April-Oct.

BROUGHSHANE

Bed & Breakfast

Dunaird House
(Mr & Mrs Graham), 15 Buckna Rd, BT42 4NJ.
☎ (01266) 862117.
B&B s£25 d£45.50. Rooms 4, ensuite 3.
Open all year.

Heather Lodge
(Ms L McCooke), 30 Knowhead Rd, BT43 7LF.
☎ (01266) 862060/862454.
B&B s£17.50 d£30. Rooms 2. Open all year.

B&B = bed and breakfast   s = single   d = double   BB&M = bed, breakfast & evening meal

BUSHMILLS

Hotel

Bushmills Inn   ***
25 Main St, BT57 8QA.
☎ (012657) 32339. Fax 32048.
B&B s£58 d£98. Rooms 30, ensuite 30.
High tea £9.95. Dinner £18.50.
Last orders 2130 hrs. Open all year.

Bed & Breakfast

Ahimsa
(Miss S Reynolds), 243 Whitepark Rd, BT57 8SP.
☎ (012657) 31383.
B&B s£18 d£30. BB&M s£26 d£46. Rooms 2.
Dinner £8. Last orders 2100 hrs.
Open all year. Vegetarian.

Ardeevin
(Mrs J Montgomery), 145 Main St, BT57 8QE.
☎ (012657) 31661.
B&B s£17 d£34. Rooms 3, ensuite 2.
Open all year.

Ballyholme Farm
(Mrs E Rankin), 198 Ballybogey Rd, BT57 8UH.
☎ (012657) 31793.
B&B s£15 d£30. Rooms 2. Open April-Sept.

Billy Old Rectory
(Mrs M Page), 5 Cabragh Rd, Castlecatt, BT57 8YH.
☎ (012657) 31208.
B&B s£20 d£40. Rooms 2, ensuite 2.
Open March-Oct.

Chris-Mull
(Mrs M McMullan), 4 Castlenagree Rd, BT57 8SW.
☎ (012657) 31154.
B&B s£15 d£30. Rooms 4. Open Jan-Nov.

Craig Park
(Mrs J Cheal), 24 Carnbore Rd, BT57 8YF.
☎ (012657) 32496. Fax 32479.
B&B s£25 d£50. Rooms 3, ensuite 3.
Open all year.

Danescroft
(Mrs O Rutherford), 171 Whitepark Rd, BT57 8SS.
☎ (012657) 31586.
B&B s£20 d£36. Rooms 3, ensuite 3.
Open Feb-Nov.
On A2, 5m NE of Bushmills

Fairview
(Mr & Mrs Barnes), 75 Ballyclough Rd, BT57 8UZ.
☎ (012657) 32007.
B&B s£18 d£36. Rooms 2. Open April-Sept.
On A2, 5m NE of Bushmills

Greenacres
(Mrs H McConaghy), 3 Isle Rd, Dunseverick,
BT57 8TD.
☎ (012657) 32084.
B&B s£16 d£32. Rooms 2, ensuite 2.
Open March-Oct.

Islands Farm
(Mrs P McLaughlin), 13 Islandranny Rd,
BT57 8YE.
☎ (012657) 31488.
B&B s£16 d£32. Rooms 2, ensuite 2.
Open April-Aug.

Facilities are liable to change. Check prices when you book. Key to symbols is on inside back flap.

Killen's

(Ms Killen & Mr Lafferty), 28 Ballyclough Rd,
BT57 8UZ.
☎ (012657) 41536. Fax 41070.
B&B s£30 d£40. BB&M s£45 d£70. High tea £10.
Dinner £17.50. Rooms 6, ensuite 6.
Last orders 2100 hrs. Open all year.

Kilmoyle Farmhouse

(Mrs R Carson), 11 Oldtown Rd, BT53 6PH.
☎ (012657) 41466.
B&B s£13.50 d£27. Rooms 2.
Open April-Oct.

Knocklayde View

(Mrs J Wylie), 90 Causeway Rd, BT57 8SX.
☎ (012657) 32099.
B&B s£15 d£30. Rooms 2. Open all year.

Montalto House

(Mrs D Taggart), 5 Craigaboney Rd, BT57 8XD.
☎ (012657) 31257.
B&B s£18 d£36. Rooms 4, ensuite 2.
Open March-Oct.
Off B17, W of Bushmills

North Winds

(Mrs L Ramage), 299 Whitepark Rd, BT57 8SN.
☎ (012657) 31374.
B&B s£16 d£32. Rooms 3. Open April-Sept.

Pineview

(Mrs M Simpson), 111 Castlecatt Rd,
BT53 8AP.
☎ (012657) 41527.
B&B s£17 d£32. Rooms 1, ensuite 1.
Open March-Sept.

Poachers Rest

(Ms S Kelly), 11 Cozies Rd, Castlecatt, BT57 8YG.
☎ (012657) 42125.
B&B s£15 d£30. Rooms 2. Open all year.

Revallagh

(Mrs A Rankin), 184 Ballybogy Rd, BT57 8UQ.
☎ (012657) 32295.
B&B s£16 d£32. Rooms 2. Open Jan-Oct.

Spring Farm

(Mr & Mrs Kerr), 15 Isle Rd, Dunseverick,
BT57 8TD.
☎ (012657) 31780.
B&B s£17 d£32. Rooms 3, ensuite 3.
Open all year.

Turfahun

(Mrs I Dobbin), 177 Straid Rd, BT57 8XW.
☎ (012657) 31918.
B&B s£17 d£34. Rooms 3, ensuite 3.
Open March-Oct.

Valley View

(Mrs V McFall), 6a Ballyclough Rd, BT57 8TU.
☎ (012657) 41608/41319.
B&B s£21 d£34. Rooms 6, ensuite 6.
Open all year ex Christmas.
On B67, 4m N of Ballymoney

B&B = bed and breakfast   s = single   d = double   BB&M = bed, breakfast & evening meal

6 Ballyclough Rd

(Mrs M McFall), BT57 8TU.
☎ (012657) 41319/41608.
B&B s£20 d£32. Rooms 3, ensuite 2.
Open all year.

167 Causeway Rd

(Mrs J Gregg), BT57 8SY.
☎ (012657) 31846.
B&B s£15 d£30. Rooms 2. Open April-Oct.

CARNLOUGH

Hotel

Londonderry Arms Hotel   ***

20 Harbour Rd, BT44 0EU.
☎ (01574) 885255. Fax 885263.
B&B s£45 d£75. BB&M s£60 d£105.
Rooms 35, ensuite 35. High tea £10. Dinner £15.
Last orders 2100 hrs. Open all year.

Guesthouses

Bethany House   (A)

5 Bay Rd, BT44 0HQ.
☎ (01574) 885667.
B&B s£16 d£32. BB&M s£20 d£40.
Rooms 7, ensuite 7. Last orders 1900 hrs.
Open all year.

Bridge Inn   (B)

2 Bridge St, BT44 0EH.
☎ (01574) 885669. Fax 885096.
B&B s£18 d£35. BB&M s£23.50 d£46. Rooms 5.
High tea £5.50. Dinner £7. Last orders 2100 hrs.
Open all year.

Bed & Breakfast

Glenview

(Mrs T McKay), 124 Ballymena Rd, BT44 0LA.
☎ (01574) 885546.
B&B s£16 d£32. Rooms 3, ensuite 1.
Open all year.

Harbour View

(Ms M McMullan), 50 Harbour Rd, BT44 0EU.
☎ (01574) 885335.
B&B s£15 d£30. Rooms 2. Open all year.

Shingle Cove

(Mrs J McAuley), 6 Shingle Cove, BT44 0EH.
☎ (01574) 885593.
B&B s£17.50 d£30. Rooms 3, ensuite 1.
Open all year.

7 Shingle Cove

(Mr & Mrs Rowan), BT44 0EH.
☎ (01574) 885638.
B&B s£15 d£30. Rooms 2, ensuite 2.
Open all year.

Facilities are liable to change. Check prices when you book. Key to symbols is on inside back flap.

77

CARRICKFERGUS

Hotels

Quality Hotel Carrickfergus ***
75 Belfast Rd, BT38 8PH.
☎ (01960) 364556. Fax 351620.
B&B s£75 d£75. Rooms 68, ensuite 68.
Dinner £15. Last orders 2045 hrs. Open all year.

Coast Road Hotel *
28 Scotch Quarter, BT38 7DP.
☎ & fax (01960) 351021.
B&B s£40 d£60. Rooms 21, ensuite 21.
High tea £5. Dinner £7. Last orders 2100 hrs.
Open all year.

Dobbins Inn Hotel *
6 High St, BT38 9HE.
☎ & fax (01960) 351905.
B&B s£44 d£64. BB&M s£54 d£76. Rooms 13,
ensuite 13. High tea £8. Dinner £12.
Last orders 2100 hrs. Open all year.

Bed & Breakfast

Beechgrove
(Mr & Mrs Barron), 412 Upper Rd, Trooperslane,
BT38 8PW.
☎ (01960) 363304.
B&B s£16 d£32. BB&M s£24 d£48. Rooms 6,
ensuite 4. Dinner £8. Last orders 1930 hrs.
Open all year.
Off A2, 1m S of Carrickfergus

Craigs Farm
(Mrs J Craig), 90 Hillhead Rd, Ballycarry, BT38 9JF.
☎ (01960) 353769.
B&B s£16 d£32. Rooms 3, ensuite 2.
Open all year.

Drumgart
(Mrs E Loughridge), 48 Hillhead Rd, Ballycarry,
BT38 9HE.
☎ & fax (01960) 353507.
B&B s£16 d£32. Rooms 3, ensuite 3.
Open all year.

Highlands
(Mrs S Hilditch), 34 Cairn Rd, BT38 9AP.
☎ (01960) 364773.
B&B s£15 d£30. Rooms 3. Open April-Sept.

Hillcrest
(Mr & Mrs Clarke), 66 Bellahill Rd, BT38 9LE.
☎ (01960) 367342.
B&B s£16.50 d£33. Rooms 2, ensuite 1.
Open all year.

Marina House
(Mr & Mrs Mulholland), 49 Irish Quarter South,
BT38 8BL.
☎ (01960) 364055.
B&B s£20 d£40. BB&M s£28 d£56.
Rooms 9, ensuite 2. Dinner £8.
Last orders 2100 hrs. Open all year.

Facilities are liable to change. Check prices when you book. Key to symbols is on inside back flap.

Parklands
(Mrs E Sherratt), 320 Upper Rd, Trooperslane, BT38 8PN.
☎ (01960) 362528.
B&B s£18 d£30. BB&M s£24 d£40. High tea £5.
Dinner £6. Last orders 2100 hrs.
Rooms 3, ensuite 1. Open all year.

Rose Cottage
(Mrs M Johnston), 287 Upper Rd, BT38 8PW.
☎ (01960) 360799.
B&B s£15 d£35. Rooms 3. Open all year.

Seaview
(Mr J Sutherland), 33 Larne Rd, BT38 7EE.
☎ (01960) 363170.
B&B s£15 d£30. BB&M s£21 d£42.
Rooms 3, ensuite 3. High tea £6. Dinner £7.50.
Last orders 2100 hrs. Open April-Oct.

Springbrook
(Mr I Beattie), 3 Island Rd, Ballycarry, BT38 9HB.
☎ (01960) 372329.
B&B s£19.50 d£35. Rooms 4, ensuite 2.
Open all year.

Tramway House
(Mrs V Reid), 95 Irish Quarter South, BT38 8BW.
☎ (01960) 355639.
B&B s£17 d£34. Rooms 2. Dinner £6. Open all year.

Whiteford Lodge
(Mr & Mrs Eakin), 75 Shore Rd, Greenisland, BT38 8TZ.
☎ (01232) 851704.
B&B s£16 d£32. Rooms 2. Open April-Sept.

CLOUGHMILLS

Bed & Breakfast

Dunauley
(Mrs C McAuley), 28 Ballycregagh Rd, BT42 9LB.
☎ (012656) 38779.
B&B s£17 d£32. BB&M s£26 d£50.
Rooms 3, ensuite 1. Dinner £9. Open all year.

CRUMLIN

Guesthouses

Caldhame House (A)
104 Moira Rd, BT29 4HG.
☎ & fax (01849) 422378.
B&B s£25 d£36. BB&M s£40 d£50.
Rooms 3, ensuite 3. High tea £12.50. Dinner £15.
Last orders 2000 hrs. Open all year.

Caldhame Lodge (A)
102 Moira Rd, BT29 4HG.
☎ & fax (01849) 423099.
B&B s£26 d£36. BB&M s£38 d£58.
Rooms 6, ensuite 6. High tea £10. Dinner £14.
Last orders 2000 hrs. Open all year.
5m from Airport

B&B = bed and breakfast   s = single   d = double   BB&M = bed, breakfast & evening meal

Keef Halla   (A)

20 Tully Rd, Nutts Corner, BT29 4SW.
☎ & fax (01232) 825491.
B&B s£25 d£40. BB&M s£40 d£70.
Rooms 7, ensuite 7. High tea £15. Dinner £15.
Last orders 1500 hrs. Open all year.

🅣 🅿 ❁ ♣ ⚒ 🐎 🎞 ♫ 🗄 🐘 🗓 ☂ 🛒 ⚓ 📚 🛡 U
✓ 🔺 ⚖ 🄴

Bed & Breakfast

Ashmore

(Mrs M McClure), 64 Main St, Glenavy, BT29 4LP.
☎ (01849) 422773.
B&B s£16 d£32. Rooms 2, ensuite 1.
Open all year.
On A26, S of Airport

🅿 ❁ ♣ ⚒ 🐎 🎞 ☂ 🌀

Clearsprings Farm

(Mrs E Duncan), 9 Belfast Rd, BT29 4FA.
☎ & fax (01232) 825275.
B&B s£17 d£30. Rooms 3, ensuite 1.
Open all year.
4m from Airport

🅿 ❁ ♣ ⚒ 🐎 OAP 🎞 🗓 ☂ ⚓ 🛡

The Croft

(Mrs S McCord), 2 Glen Rd, Glenavy, BT29 4LT.
☎ (01849) 422579.
B&B s£16 d£32. Rooms 2. Open all year.

🅿 ❁ ♣ 🐎 OAP 🎞 ☂ 🛡 U

Crossroads Country House

(Mr W Lorimer), 1 Largy Rd, BT29 4AH.
☎ (01849) 452491.
B&B s£17 d£34. BB&M s£27 d£44. Rooms 3.
Dinner £10. Last orders 2100 hrs. Open all year.
3m S of Airport

🅿 ❁ ♣ 🐎 🏇 🎞 🗓 ☂ ⚓ 🛡 U ✓ 🔺 ⚖

Dunore House

(Mrs A Hyde), 8 Crookedstone Rd, Aldergrove,
BT29 4EH.
☎ (01849) 452291.
B&B s£15 d£30. Rooms 3. Open all year.
½m from Airport

🅿 🎠 ❁ ♣ ⚒ 🐎 🎞 🗓 ☂ ⚓ 📚 U

Hillvale Farm

(Mrs J Duncan), 11 Largy Rd, BT29 4AH.
☎ (01849) 422768.
B&B s£16 d£32. Rooms 3. Open all year.
3m S of Airport

🅿 ❁ ♣ 🐎 🎞 ☂ ⚓ 🛡 U 🔺 ⚖

Mount Pleasant

(Mrs A Kennedy), 12a Carmavy Rd, Loanends,
BT29 4TF.
☎ (01849) 452346.
B&B s£20 d£32. Rooms 2, ensuite 1.
Open all year.
2m from Airport

🅣 🅿 ❁ ♣ ⚒ 🐎 🎞 🗓 ☂ ⚓ 📚 🔺 ⚖ 🌀

Seacash House

(Mrs I McIlwaine), 21 Killead Rd, BT29 4EL.
☎ (01849) 423207.
B&B s£15 d£30. Rooms 3. Open all year.

🅿 ❁ ♣ 🐎 🎞 🗓 ☂

Twin Oaks

(Mrs Y Biesty), 90 Cidercourt Rd, BT29 4RY.
☎ (01849) 452978.
B&B s£15 d£30. BB&M s£22 d£44. Rooms 2.
High tea £5. Dinner £7. Open all year.

🅿 ❁ ♣ ⚒ 🐎 🎞 🗓 ☂ ⚓ 🛡 U

Facilities are liable to change. Check prices when you book. Key to symbols is on inside back flap.

CUSHENDALL

Hotel

Thornlea Hotel *
6 Coast Rd, BT44 0RU.
☎ (012667) 71223. Fax 71362.
B&B s£35 d£55. Rooms 13, ensuite 13.
High tea £10. Dinner £13.50. Last orders 2100 hrs.
Open all year.

Guesthouse

Caireal Manor Guest House (A)
90 Glenravel Rd, Martinstown, BT43 6QQ.
☎ & fax (012667) 58465.
B&B s£25 d£50. BB&M s£40 d£75.
Rooms 5, ensuite 5. High tea £10. Dinner £15.
Last orders 2100 hrs. Open all year.

Bed & Breakfast

Ashlea
(Mrs M McCurry), 2 Tromra Rd, BT44 0SS.
☎ (012667) 71651.
B&B s£18 d£32. BB&M s£28 d£48. Rooms 3,
ensuite 2. High tea £8. Dinner £10.
Last orders 1700 hrs. Open April-Oct.

The Burn
(Mrs D McAuley), 63 Ballyeamon Rd, BT44 0SN.
☎ (012667) 71733 **or** (01266) 46111.
B&B s£18 d£32. BB&M s£29 d£54. Rooms 3,
ensuite 2. High tea £8. Dinner £11.
Last orders 2000 hrs. Open all year.

Coill Na Min
(Mrs C Donnelly), 12 Coast Rd, BT44 0RU.
☎ (012667) 71469.
B&B s£15 d£30. BB&M s£22 d£44.
Rooms 3, ensuite 2. Open all year.

Culbidagh House
(Mrs R Hamill), 115 Middlepark Rd, BT44 0SH.
☎ (012667) 71312.
B&B s£20 d£33. Rooms 2, ensuite 2.
Open April-Oct.

Cullentra House
(Mrs O McAuley), 16 Cloghs Rd, BT44 0SP.
☎ & fax (012667) 71762.
B&B s£20 d£33. Rooms 3, ensuite 2.
Open all year.

Garron View
(Mrs J McAuley), 14 Clogh Rd, BT44 0SP.
☎ (012667) 71018.
B&B s£16 d£32. Rooms 3, ensuite 3.
Open all year.

Glendale
(Mrs M O'Neill), 46 Coast Rd, BT44 0RX.
☎ (012667) 71495.
B&B s£16 d£32. Rooms 5, ensuite 5.
Open all year.

Irene
(Ms A Wilkinson), 8 Kilnadore Rd, BT44 0SG.
☎ (012667) 71898.
B&B s£15 d£30. Rooms 1.
Open April-Nov.

B&B = bed and breakfast   s = single   d = double   BB&M = bed, breakfast & evening meal

The Meadows
(Mrs A Carey), 81 Coast Rd, BT44 0QW.
☎ (012667) 72020. Fax 71641.
B&B s£20 d£40. Rooms 6, ensuite 6.
Open all year.

Mountain View
(Mrs B O'Neill), 1 Kilnadore Rd, BT44 0SG.
☎ (012667) 71246. Fax 71996.
B&B s£14 d£28. Rooms 3, ensuite 3.
Open all year.

Moyle View
(Mrs M Gaffney), 2 Ardmoyle Park, BT44 0QL.
☎ (012667) 71580.
B&B s£16 d£32. Rooms 3, ensuite 1.
Open all year.

Riverside
(Mr & Mrs McKeegan), 14 Mill St, BT44 0RR.
☎ & fax (012667) 71655.
B&B s£18 d£32. Rooms 3. Open all year.

Ryans
(Mrs M Lawlor), 9 Shore St, BT44 0NA.
☎ (012667) 71583.
B&B s£14 d£28. Rooms 2. Open all year.

Shramore
(Mrs K Quinn), 27 Chapel Rd, BT44 0RS.
☎ (012667) 71610.
B&B d£28. Rooms 2. Open May-Sept.

Tros-ben-villa
(Mr P Rowan), 8 Coast Rd, BT44 0RU.
☎ (012667) 71130.
B&B s£20 d£35. BB&M s£26 d£47.
Rooms 3, ensuite 3. High tea £6. Dinner £7.
Last orders 2100 hrs. Open all year.

CUSHENDUN

Hotel

Unclassified Hotel
Bay Hotel, 20 Strand View Park, BT44 0PL.
☎ (012667) 61267.

Guesthouses

The Cushendun   (B)
10 Strandview Park, BT44 0PL.
☎ (012667) 61266.
B&B s£20 d£40. BB&M s£30 d£60. Rooms 15.
Open July-Aug.

The Villa   (U)
185 Torr Rd, BT44 0PU.
☎ (012667) 61252.
B&B s£20 d£36. BB&M s£30 d£60.
Rooms 3, ensuite 2. High tea £9.50. Dinner £10.
Last orders 2000 hrs. Open April-Nov.

Bed & Breakfast

The Burns
(Mrs A McKendry), 116 Torr Rd, BT44 0PU.
☎ (012667) 61285.
B&B s£16 d£32. BB&M s£24.50 d£49. Rooms 2,
ensuite 2. High tea £8.50. Dinner £8.50.
Open all year.

Facilities are liable to change. Check prices when you book. Key to symbols is on inside back flap.

83

Drumkeerin
(Mrs M McFadden), 201a Torr Rd, BT44 0PU.
☎ (012667) 61554.
B&B s£20 d£40. Rooms 2, ensuite 2.
Open all year.

🅿 ❖ ♠ ⚘ ☏ 🎞 ▢ ✂ ♪

Sleepy Hollow
(Mrs W McKay), 107 Knocknacarry Rd, BT44 0NT.
☎ (012667) 61513.
B&B s£18 d£36. Rooms 2, ensuite 2.
Open all year.

🅿 ❖ ♠ ⚘ ☏ 🎞 ▢ ✂ ♪ ∪ ⚲

DERVOCK

Guesthouse

Knockanboy House
(Mrs A Liddle), Dervock, BT53 8AA.
☎ (012657) 41808. Fax 41023.
B&B s£30 d£60. Rooms 2. Open April-Nov.

🅿 ♨ ❖ ♠ ⚘ ☏ 🎞 ✂ ♪ ⌐ ∪ ✓ ⚇ ⇵ 🖼

DUNADRY

Hotel

Dunadry Hotel & Country Club ★★★★
2 Islandreagh Drive, BT41 2HA.
☎ (01849) 432474. Fax 433389.
B&B s£98.50 d£127. BB&M s£116.45 d£162.90.
Rooms 67, ensuite 67. Dinner £17.95.
Last orders 2145 hrs. Open all year.

Ⓣ 🅿 ♨ ❖ ♠ ⚘ 🍴 ☏ 🟢 🎞 ▢ ☎ ✂ ⚇ ⚲ ♪
⌐ ∪ ✓ ⚇ ⇵ 🍷 🖼

Bed & Breakfast

Wentworth Country House
(Mrs M Stewart), 30 Rathmore Rd, BT41 2HG.
☎ (01849) 432100. Mobile 0385 738964.
B&B s£17.50 d£35. Rooms 2, ensuite 2.
High tea £10. Dinner £12.50. Last orders 1800 hrs.
Open all year.

🅿 ❖ ♠ ⚘ ☏ 🎞 ▢ ♪ ⌐ ∪ ✓ ⚇ ⇵ 🕲 🖼

GIANT'S CAUSEWAY

Hotel

Causeway Hotel ★★
40 Causeway Rd, BT57 8SU.
☎ (012657) 31226/31210. Fax 32552.
B&B s£45 d£75. BB&M s£60 d£105.
Rooms 28, ensuite 28. High tea £9.50. Dinner £14.
Last orders 2100 hrs. Open all year.

🅿 ♨ ❖ ♠ ⚘ 🍴 ☏ 🎞 ▢ ☎ ✂ ♪ ⌐ ⚲ ⚇ 🖼

Guesthouse

Carnside Guest House (B)
23 Causeway Rd, BT57 8SU.
☎ (012657) 31337.
B&B s£18 d£36. BB&M s£28 d£56.
Rooms 8, ensuite 2. High tea £8. Dinner £10.
Last orders 1900 hrs. Open April-Oct.
On B146, 2m N of Bushmills

Ⓣ 🅿 ❖ ♠ ⚘ ☏ 🎞 ✂ ♪ ⌐ ∪ ⚇ ⇵ ⚲

B&B = bed and breakfast   s = single   d = double   BB&M = bed, breakfast & evening meal

Bed & Breakfast

Hillcrest Country House
(Mr K Laverty), 306 Whitepark Rd, BT57 8SN.
☎ & fax (012657) 31577.
B&B s£30 d£45. Rooms 3, ensuite 3.
High tea £9.50. Dinner £15. Last orders 2100 hrs.
Open Easter-Dec.

Kal-Mar
(Mrs M Mitchell), 64a Causeway Rd, BT57 8SU.
☎ & fax (012657) 31101.
B&B s£20 d£30. Rooms 2. Open all year.

Lochaber
(Mrs R Ramage), 107 Causeway Rd, BT57 8SX.
☎ (012657) 31385.
B&B s£13 d£26. Rooms 2. Open all year.

GLENARM

Hotel

Drumnagreagh Hotel **
408 Coast Rd, BT44 0BB.
☎ & fax (01574) 841651.
B&B s£40 d£60. BB&M s£50 d£80. Rooms 16,
ensuite 16. High tea £9. Dinner £15.
Last orders 2100 hrs. Open all year.

Bed & Breakfast

Black Bush Cottage
(Mrs E McAllister), 34 Dickeystown Rd, BT44 0BA.
☎ (01574) 841559.
B&B s£12.50 d£22.50. Rooms 1, ensuite 1.
Open all year.

Burnside Country House
(Mrs H Palmer), 37 Dickeystown Rd, BT44 0BA.
☎ (01574) 841331.
B&B s£16 d£32. Rooms 3, ensuite 1.
Open March-Oct.

Glen Davis
(Mrs B Davison), 36 Drumcrow Rd, BT44 0DX.
☎ (01574) 841361.
B&B s£15 d£30. Rooms 2. Open April-Sept.

Glen View
(Mrs G Ward), 43 Dickeystown Rd, BT44 0BA.
☎ (01574) 841698.
B&B s£15 d£30. BB&M s£25 d£50.
Rooms 2. High tea £8. Dinner £10.
Last orders 2100 hrs. Open all year.

Facilities are liable to change. Check prices when you book. Key to symbols is on inside back flap.

Margaret's House
(Mr J Morrow), 10 Altmore St, BT44 0AR.
☎ (01574) 841307.
B&B s£14 d£28. Rooms 5. Open all year.

P ♿ ♣ ☀ ☜ ▥ ☐ ✂ ☀

The Meadows
(Mrs F Watt), 53 Deerpark Rd, BT44 0DW.
☎ (01574) 841388.
B&B s£12.50 d£25. Rooms 1. Open April-Oct.

P ✿ ♣ ☀ ♥ ☜ OAP ▥ ✂

Nine Glens
(Mr & Mrs McLaughlin), 18 Toberwine St,
BT44 0AP.
☎ (01574) 841590.
B&B s£15 d£30. Rooms 3, ensuite 3.
Open all year.

T P ✿ ♣ ☀ ☜ OAP ▥ ☐ ✂ ☀ ☀

Town Brae House
(Mrs M McAllister), 6 Town Brae, BT44 0EE.
☎ (01574) 841043.
B&B s£15 d£30. Rooms 2. Open all year.

P ✿ ♣ ☀ ☜ ▥ ✂ ☺ ☀

35 The Cloney
(Mrs M Dempsey), BT44 0AD.
☎ (01574) 841640.
B&B s£17 d£34. Rooms 2, ensuite 2.
Open April-Sept.

P ✿ ☀ ☜ ▥ ☐ ☀

4 Toberwine St
(Mrs I Boyle), BT44 0AD.
☎ (01574) 841219.
B&B s£16 d£32. Rooms 2, ensuite 1.
Open April-Oct.

P ♿ ♣ ☀ ☜ ▥ ✂ ☀ ☀

Guesthouse

Millbay Inn   (U)
77 Millbay Rd, BT40 3RJ.
☎ (01960) 382436. Fax 382172.
B&B s£25 d£50. BB&M s£37.50 d£75.
High tea £10. Dinner £13.50. Rooms 3,
ensuite 3. Open all year.

P ✿ ♣ ☀ ♥ ☜ OAP ▥ ☐ ☏ ✂ ☀ ☀
☀ ☺ ☖ ⊞

Bed & Breakfast

Ashmore House
(Mrs A Mitchell), 135 Brown's Bay Rd, BT40 3TQ.
☎ (01960) 382276.
B&B s£16 d£32. BB&M s£24 d£48.
Rooms 3, ensuite 1. Dinner £8.
Open all year ex Christmas.

T P ✿ ♣ ☀ ☜ OAP ▥ ☐ ✂ ☀ ☺ ☖

The Farm
(Mr & Mrs Crawford), 69 Portmuck Rd, BT40 3TP.
☎ (01960) 382252.
B&B s£15 d£30. BB&M s£21 d£42.
Rooms 3, ensuite 1. High tea £4.50. Dinner £6.
Last orders 1930 hrs. Open Feb-Oct.

P ♿ ♣ ☀ ☜ ✂ ☀ ☀ ☺ ☖

Gobbins Lodge Health Spa
(Mrs S Meekin), 65 Gobbins Road, BT40 3TY.
☎ (01960) 353536. Fax 353600.
Rooms 6, ensuite 6. Inclusive courses
w/end/3 day/5 day. Open all year.

P ✿ ♣ ☀ ▥ ✂ ☙ ☀ ☀ ☀ ☺ ☖ ☀ ⊞

B&B = bed and breakfast   s = single   d = double   BB&M = bed, breakfast & evening meal

Hillview
(Mrs M Reid), 30 Middle Rd, BT40 3SL.
☎ (01960) 372581.
B&B s£18 d£34. Rooms 3, ensuite 2. High tea £8.
Dinner £10. Last orders 1700 hrs. Open Jan-Nov.
Off A2, 7m S of Larne

🛈 🅿 ❅ ♣ ⚶ ⛷ 🖩 ⛘ ⅍ ☂ ∪ ◍

Port O'Brien Cottage
(Mr & Mrs Hughes), Mullaghboy Road, BT40 3TR.
☎ & fax (01960) 382301.
B&B s£15 d£30. Rooms 2, ensuite 2. Dinner £5.
Open all year.

🅿 ♨ ❅ ♣ ⚶ ⛷ ⒟ 🖩 ⅍ ☄ ☂ ∪ ⬙

LARNE

Hotels

Magheramorne House Hotel   **
59 Shore Rd, BT40 3HW.
☎ (01574) 279444. Fax 260138.
B&B s£40 d£60. BB&M s£56 d£90. Rooms 40,
ensuite 40. High tea £11.50. Dinner £16.
Last orders 2100 hrs. Open all year.

🅿 ♨ ❅ ♣ ⚶ ⛛ ⛷ ⒟ ⚘ 🖩 ⛘ ☍ ☄ ☂ ∪ ⬙
⚡ ⛛ ◍ 🎟

Highways Hotel   *
Donaghy's Lane, Ballyloran BT40 2SU.
☎ (01574) 272272/3. Fax 275015.
B&B s£47.50 d£69. BB&M s£59.50 d£93.
Rooms 35, ensuite 35. High tea £18.50.
Dinner £17.50. Last orders 2100 hrs.
Open all year.

🛈 🅿 ❅ ♣ ⛛ ⛷ 🖩 ⛘ ☍ ⅍ ☄ ☂ ∪ ⅃
⬙ ⚡ ⛛ 🎟

Unclassified Hotels
Curran Court Hotel, 84 Curran Rd,
BT40 1BU. ☎ (01574) 275505.
Kilwaughter House Hotel, 61 Shane's Hill Rd,
BT40 2TQ. ☎ (01574) 272591.

Guesthouses

Dan Campbell's   (A)
2 Bridge St, BT40 2ET.
☎ (01574) 277222.
B&B s£30 d£40. BB&M s£45 d£75.
Rooms 12, ensuite 12. Dinner £15.
Last orders 2130 hrs. Open all year.

♨ ⛛ ⛷ ⒣ ⒟ 🖩 ⛘ ⅍ ☄ ☂ ∪ ⬙ 🎟

Derrin Guest House   (A)
2 Prince's Gardens, BT40 1RQ.
☎ (01574) 273269/273762. Fax 273269.
B&B s£25 d£36. Rooms 7, ensuite 4.
Open all year.

🛈 🅿 ⛷ ⚘ 🖩 ⛘ ☄ ☂ ∪ ⚡ 🎟

Manor Guest House   (A)
23 Olderfleet Rd, BT40 1AS.
☎ (01574) 273305.
B&B s£16 d£32. Rooms 8, ensuite 8.
Open all year.

🛈 🅿 ♨ ⚶ ⛷ ⚘ 🖩 ⛘ ⅍ 🎟

Seaview Guest House   (B)
156 Curran Rd, BT40 1BX.
☎ (01574) 272438/275397.
B&B s£20 d£36. Rooms 8, ensuite 5.
Open all year ex Christmas.

🅿 ♨ ⛷ ⚘ 🖩 ⛘ ⅍ ☂ 🎟

Facilities are liable to change. Check prices when you book. Key to symbols is on inside back flap.

Bed & Breakfast

Bellevue
(Mr & Mrs McKeen), 35 Olderfleet Rd, BT40 1AS.
☎ (01574) 270233.
B&B s£13.50 d£27. Rooms 3.
Open all year.

Cairnview
(Mrs J Lough), 13 Croft Heights, Ballygalley,
BT40 2QS.
☎ & fax (01574) 583269.
B&B s£18 d£36. Rooms 3, ensuite 3.
Open all year.

Chaine Park Villa
(Ms T Hall), 60 Glenarm Rd, BT40 1DS.
☎ (01574) 270910.
B&B s£17.50 d£35. BB&M s£27.50 d£55.
Rooms 3, ensuite 3. High tea £6.50. Dinner £10.
Last orders 2030 hrs. Open all year.

Clonlee
(Mrs E Gorman), 40 Glenarm Rd, BT40 1BP.
☎ (01574) 276159.
B&B s£14 d£28. Rooms 3. Open March-Oct.

Droagh Cottage
(Mrs M Porter), 175 Coast Rd, Droagh, BT40 2LF.
☎ (01574) 272932.
B&B s£25 d£50. Rooms 2. Open all year.

Drumahoe House
(Mrs R Wilson), 110 Drumahoe Rd, Millbrook,
BT40 2SN.
☎ (01574) 273397.
B&B s£14 d£28. Rooms 3. Open May-Sept.

Elmwood
(Mr & Mrs Weston), 69 Glenarm Rd, BT40 1DX.
☎ (01574) 276263.
B&B s£16 d£36. Rooms 3, ensuite 1.
Open May-Sept.

Estavel
(Mrs J Hynds), 64 Ballyhampton Rd, BT40 2SP.
☎ (01574) 272963.
B&B s£20 d£33. Rooms 2, ensuite 1.
Open all year.

Grassy Banks
(Mr & Mrs McMullan), 5 Cairnbeg Crescent,
BT40 1OH.
☎ (01574) 274394.
B&B s£15 d£30. Rooms 2. Open all year.

Harbour Inn
(Mr S Dempsey), 25 Olderfleet Rd, BT40 1AS.
☎ (01574) 272386.
B&B s£15 d£30. BB&M s£23 d£46. Rooms 4.
High tea £8. Dinner £8. Last orders 2130 hrs.
Open all year.

Hillview
(Mrs M Rainey), 36 Belfast Rd, BT40 2PH.
☎ (01574) 260584.
B&B s£18 d£32. Rooms 4, ensuite 3.
Open March-Oct.

B&B = bed and breakfast   s = single   d = double   BB&M = bed, breakfast & evening meal

Inverbann
(Mrs J Scott), 7 Glenarm Rd, BT40 1BN.
☎ (01574) 272524.
B&B s£18 d£32. Rooms 3, ensuite 3.
Open all year.

Killyneedan
(Mrs M McKane), 52 Bay Rd, BT40 1DG.
☎ (01574) 274943.
B&B s£14 d£28. Rooms 3, ensuite 1.
Open all year.

Loran House
(Ms Maxwell & Mr McAuley), 27 Curran Rd,
BT40 2BS.
☎ (01574) 277506.
B&B s£15 d£30. Rooms 2, ensuite 2.
Open all year.

Lynden
(Ms S Thompson), 65 Glenarm Rd, BT40 1DX.
☎ (01574) 272626.
B&B s£20 d£36. Rooms 2, ensuite 2.
Open all year.

Riverside Lodge
(Mrs D Turk), 20 Shanes Hill Rd, BT40 2PA.
☎ (01574) 272090.
B&B s£20 d£30. Rooms 1. Open April-Oct.

Roma
(Mr C Alexander), 146 Coast Rd, BT40 2LF.
☎ & fax (01574) 274748.
B&B s£17.50 d£35. Rooms 2. Open Feb-Nov.

Salama
(Mrs G Swan), 62 Curran Rd, BT40 1BU.
☎ (01574) 276813.
B&B s£15 d£30. Rooms 2, ensuite 1.
Open all year.

The Trees
(Mrs E Millar), 20 Ballywillan Rd, BT40 3LA.
☎ & fax (01574) 276633.
B&B s£15 d£30. BB&M s£20, d£40.
Rooms 2. Dinner £5. Open all year.

LISBURN

Guesthouses

Brook Lodge   (A)
79 Old Ballynahinch Rd, BT27 6TH.
☎ (01846) 638454.
B&B s£18 d£36. BB&M s£27, d£54.
Rooms 6, ensuite 4. High tea £5. Dinner £9.
Open all year.
5 ½ m NW of Ballynahinch

Laurel Inn   (U)
99 Carryduff Rd, Temple, BT27 6YL.
☎ (01846) 638422. Fax 638684.
B&B s£27.50 d£38.50. Rooms 6, ensuite 2.
High tea £6. Dinner £19.75. Last orders 2100 hrs.
Open all year.

Facilities are liable to change. Check prices when you book. Key to symbols is on inside back flap.

Bed & Breakfast

Ballinderry Country House
(Mr & Mrs Damaglou), 1c Old Rd, Upper
Ballinderry, BT28 2NJ.
☎ & fax (01846) 651653.
B&B s£32 d£50. BB&M s£43 d£72.
Rooms 5, ensuite 5. Dinner £11.
Open all year.

🅿 ❀ ♣ 🕮 ❑ ✄ ⟨ ⟩ ⌁ ↾ ∪ ⟋ △ ⇟ ▣

Braeside Farm
(Mrs G Finlay), 188 Comber Rd, BT27 6XQ.
☎ (01846) 638276.
B&B s£17 d£34. Rooms 1. Open April-Oct.

🅿 ❀ ♣ 〰 ♉ 🕮 ✄

Circular Lodge
(Miss D Price), 44 North Circular Rd, BT28 3AH.
☎ (01846) 665899.
B&B s£20 d£36. Rooms 2. Open all year.

🅿 ❀ ♉ 🐎 🕮 ❑ ✄ ⟨ ↾ ∪ ⟋ △ ⇟

Duneley House
(Ms P Duncan), 6 Moira Rd, Upper Ballinderry,
BT28 2HG.
☎ (01846) 651052. Fax 651822.
B&B s£20 d£30. Rooms 3. Open all year.

🅿 ❀ ♣ ♉ 🐎 🕮 ❑ ✄ ● ↾ ◔

Gil-Good Lodge
(Mr & Mrs Good), 13 Moira Rd, Upper Ballinderry,
BT28 2HQ.
☎ & fax (01846) 651534.
B&B s£22 d£40. BB&M s£35 d£66.
Rooms 5, ensuite 5. High tea £10. Dinner £13.
Last orders 2200 hrs. Open all year.

🅿 ❀ ♣ 〰 ♉ OAP 🕮 ❑ ✄ ⟨ ↾ ∪ ⟋ △ ⇟ ◔

Green Acres
(Mr & Mrs Reid), 115a Carryduff Rd, Temple,
Boardmills, BT27 6YL.
☎ (01846) 638631.
B&B s£20 d£36. Rooms 2, ensuite 2.
Open all year.
2m S of Carryduff Roundabout

🆃 🅿 ❀ ♣ 〰 ♉ 🕮 ❑ ✄ ⟨ ↾ ∪ ⇟

Hilltop
(Mr & Mrs McCarney), 60 Tullyard Rd, Drumbo,
BT27 5JW.
☎ (01232) 826356/526642.
B&B s£15 d£30. Rooms 2, ensuite 1.
Open all year.

🅿 ❀ ♣ 〰 ♉ 🕮 ❑ ↾ ∪ ◔

Hillview Farm
(Ms G Armstrong), 35 Stoneyford Rd, BT28 3RG.
☎ (01846) 648270.
B&B s£25 d£45. Rooms 2. Open all year.

🅿 ❀ ♣ 〰 ♉ 🕮 ❑ ✄ ⟨ ↾ ∪ ⟋ △ ⇟

Oakfield
(Mrs R Faloon), 9 Crumlin Rd,
Lower Ballinderry, BT28 2JU.
☎ (01846) 651307.
B&B s£18 d£36. BB&M s£28 d£45.
Rooms 6, ensuite 6. High tea £5. Dinner £10.
Open all year.

🅿 ❀ ♣ 〰 ♉ OAP 🕮 ❑ ✄ ● ⟨ ↾ ∪ ⟋ △ ⇟

Overdale House
(Mrs N McMullan), 150 Belsize Rd, BT27 4DR.
☎ & fax (01846) 672275.
B&B s£20 d£32. Rooms 3, ensuite 3.
Open all year.

🅿 🏠 ❀ ♣ 〰 ♉ 🐎 🕮 ❑ ☏ ✄ ⟨ ↾ ∪ △

Facilities are liable to change. Check prices when you book. Key to symbols is on inside back flap.

The Paddock
(Mrs N Gillespie), 36a Clontara Pk, Belsize Rd,
BT27 4LB.
☎ & fax (01846) 601507.
B&B s£16 d£32. Rooms 3. Open all year.

🅿 ✻ ♠ ⶅ ▥ ☐ ⵜ

Phenrey
(Mrs M Fulton), 7 Cockhill Rd, Maze, BT27 5RS.
☎ (01846) 621473.
B&B s£16 d£32. Rooms 2. Open all year.

🅿 ✻ ♠ ⶅ ▥ ☐ ⵜ ♪ ↾ ∪ ⟋

Strathearn House
(Mr & Mrs McKeown), 19 Antrim Rd, BT28 3ED.
☎ (01846) 601661.
B&B s£20 d£36. Rooms 3, ensuite 2.
Open all year.

🅿 ✻ ⶅ ▥ ☐ ⵜ ↾

NEWTOWNABBEY

Hotels

Chimney Corner Hotel ***
630 Antrim Rd, BT36 8RH.
☎ (01232) 844925/844851. Fax 844352.
B&B s£75 d£95. Rooms 63, ensuite 63.
High tea £6. Dinner £15.50.
Last orders 2130 hrs. Open all year.

📺 🅿 ♫ ✻ ♠ ▼ ⶅ ▥ ☐ ↺ ⵜ ♗ ♠ ⟍ ♪
↾ ▼ ◔ ⊞

Corr's Corner Hotel **
315 Ballyclare Rd, BT36 4TQ.
☎ (01232) 849221. Fax 832118.
B&B d£55. Rooms 30, ensuite 30. Dinner £13.50.
Open all year.

🅿 ♠ ▼ ▥ ☐ ↺ ⵜ ♪ ↾ ∪ ⟋ ▼ ◔ ⊞

Bed & Breakfast

Fairway View
(Mrs M Lennox), 178 Upper Rd, Greenisland,
BT38 8RW.
☎ (01232) 860433.
B&B s£20 d£40. Rooms 3.
Open all year ex Christmas.

🅿 ✻ ♠ ⵗ ⶅ ▥ ☐ ⵜ ↾

Iona
(Mrs P Kelly), 161 Antrim Rd, BT36 7QR.
☎ (01232) 842256.
B&B s£19 d£35. Rooms 4. Open all year.

🅿 ✻ ♠ ⵗ ⶅ [DAP] ▥ ☐ ⵜ ≟

Perpetua House
(Mrs D Robinson), 57 Collinbridge Park, BT36 7SY.
☎ (01232) 833041.
B&B s£20 d£38. Rooms 4, ensuite 1.
Open all year.

🅿 ✻ ⶅ [DAP] ⵏ ▥ ☐ ⵜ ≟

University of Ulster at Jordanstown
Shore Rd, Jordanstown, BT37 0QB.
☎ (01232) 366942. Fax 366862.
Groups only.
B&B s£18.70 d£37.40. Rooms 560, ensuite 12.
Open mid June-Sept.

🅿 ✻ ♠ ⵗ ⶅ ▥ ♠ ⌇ ⵠ ▼ ≟

109 Jordanstown Rd
(Mrs G McCabe), BT37 0NT.
☎ (01232) 864702.
B&B s£18 d£36. Rooms 3, ensuite 2.
Open all year.

🅿 ✻ ⶅ ▥ ☐ ↾ ⬠ ⵤ ≟

PORTBALLINTRAE

Hotels

Beach House Hotel ***
61 Beach Rd, BT57 8RT.
☎ (012657) 31214/31380. Fax 31664.
B&B s£42 d£64. BB&M s£55 d£90.
Rooms 32, ensuite 32. High tea £7. Dinner £13.
Last orders 2100 hrs. Open all year.

Bayview Hotel **
2 Bayhead Rd, BT57 8RZ.
☎ (012657) 31453. Fax 32360.
B&B s£45 d£75. BB&M s£55 d£95.
Rooms 16, ensuite 16. High tea £10.
Dinner £15. Last orders 2130 hrs.
Open all year.

Bed & Breakfast

Bayhead House
(Mr & Mrs Cooke), 8 Bayhead Rd, BT57 8RZ.
☎ (012657) 31441. Fax 31725.
B&B s£30 d£40. Rooms 6, ensuite 6.
Open all year.

Cedar Lodge
(Mrs M Wilson), 44 Ballaghmore Rd, BT57 8RL.
☎ (012657) 31763.
B&B s£17.50 d£30. Rooms 2.
Open all year ex Christmas.

Keeve-Na
(Mrs H Wilkinson), 62 Ballaghmore Rd, BT57 8RL.
☎ (012657) 32184.
B&B s£17 d£32. Rooms 3.
Open all year ex Christmas.

Kenbaan
(Mrs E Morgan), 55 Bayhead Rd, BT57 8SA.
☎ (012657) 31534.
B&B s£25 d£40. Rooms 4, ensuite 4.
Open all year.
½ m from Bushmills

Larkfield
(Mr & Mrs Wishart), 18 Ballaghmore Rd, BT57 8RH.
☎ (012657) 31726.
B&B d£20. Rooms 2, ensuite 2. Open Feb-Nov.

PORTGLENONE

Bed & Breakfast

Bannside Farmhouse
(Misses E & A Lowry), 268 Gortgole Rd, BT44 8AT.
☎ (01266) 821262.
B&B s£14 d£28. Rooms 3. Open all year.

Meadow Sweet
(Mrs J Shaw), 238 Gortgole Rd, BT44 8AT.
☎ (01266) 822014.
B&B s£15 d£30. Rooms 2. Open all year.

Facilities are liable to change. Check prices when you book. Key to symbols is on inside back flap.

93

Sprucebank
(Mrs T Sibbett), 41 Ballymacombs Rd, BT44 8NR.
☎ (01266) 822150. Fax 821422.
B&B s£17.50 d£35. Rooms 4, ensuite 1.
Open March-Oct.

🕻 🅿 ❀ ♣ ⚞ 🛋 ✂ 🎣 ↰ ∪

Whitehill
(Mr & Mrs O'Kane), 96 Gortgole Rd, BT44 8AN.
☎ (01266) 822124.
B&B s£15 d£30. Rooms 2. Open all year.

🅿 ❀ ♣ ⚟ ⚞ OAP 🐕 🛋 ✂ 🎣 ↰ ∪ ✓ ⚓ ⚘ 🔲

PORTRUSH

Hotels

Causeway Coast Hotel ***
36 Ballyreagh Rd, BT56 8LR.
☎ (01265) 822435. Fax 824495.
B&B s£58 d£80. BB&M s£70 d£100.
Rooms 21, ensuite 21. High tea £9.50. Dinner £14.
Last orders 2100 hrs. Open all year.

🕻 🅿 ❀ ⚟ 🍴 ⚞ 🛋 🖵 📞 ● 🎣 ↰ ∪ ✓ ⚓
⚘ 🍸 🐾 🔲

Magherabuoy House Hotel ***
41 Magheraboy Rd, BT56 8NX.
☎ (01265) 823507. Fax 824687.
B&B s£50 d£80. Rooms 38, ensuite 38.
Dinner £15. Last orders 2130 hrs. Open all year.

🕻 🅿 🎠 ♣ ⚟ 🍴 ⚞ OAP 🛋 🖵 📞 ✂ ⚟ 🎣 ↰ ∪
⚓ ⚘ 🍸 🐾 🔲

Royal Court Hotel ***
233 Ballybogey Rd, BT56 8NF.
☎ (01265) 822236. Fax 823176.
B&B s£55 d£95. Rooms 18, ensuite 18.
Dinner £15. Last orders 2100 hrs.
Open all year.

🕻 🅿 ⚟ 🍴 ⚞ 🛋 🖵 📞 🐾 🔲

Eglinton Hotel **
49 Eglinton St, BT56 8DZ.
☎ (01265) 822371. Fax 823155.
B&B s£49 d£70. BB&M s£60 d£90.
Rooms 29, ensuite 29. High tea £8. Dinner £15.
Last orders 2130 hrs. Open all year.

🕻 🅿 ⚟ 🍴 ⚞ OAP 🐕 🛋 🖵 📞 ✂ ⚟ 🎣 ↰ ∪ ✓
⚓ ⚘ 🍸 🐾 🔲

Port Hotel *
53 Main St, BT56 8BN.
☎ (01265) 825353. Fax 824862.
B&B s£35 d£54. BB&M s£42 d£67.
Rooms 15, ensuite 15. High tea £7.50. Dinner £10.
Last orders 2100 hrs. Open all year.

🕻 ⚟ 🍴 ⚞ OAP 🛋 🖵 📞 ✂ ● 🎣 ↰ ∪ ✓ ⚓
⚘ 🍸 🐾 🔲

Unclassified Hotel
Golf Links Hotel, Bushmills Rd, BT56 8JQ.
☎ (01265) 823539.

Guesthouses

Abbeydean (B)
9 Ramore Avenue, BT56 8BB.
☎ (01265) 822645.
B&B s£15 d£30. Rooms 12, ensuite 3.
Open March-Sept.

🕻 ⚟ ⚞ OAP 🛋 ✂ 🎣 ↰ ∪ ✓ ⚓ ⚘ 🐾

B&B = bed and breakfast s = single d = double BB&M = bed, breakfast & evening meal

Alexandra (B)
11 Lansdowne Crescent, BT56 8AY.
☎ (01265) 822284.
B&B s£20 d£36. BB&M s£30 d£56.
Rooms 6, ensuite 1. Dinner £10.
Last orders 2000 hrs. Open all year.

Anvershiel (A)
16 Coleraine Rd, BT56 8EA.
☎ (01265) 823861.
B&B s£17.50 d£35. BB&M s£40 d£50.
Rooms 5, ensuite 5. High tea £12. Dinner £15.
Open all year.

Asher Cottage (U)
63 Ballyhome Rd, BT56 8NG.
☎ (01265) 823015.
B&B s£20 d£40. BB&M s£28 d£56.
Rooms 3, ensuite 3. Dinner £8.
Last orders 1730 hrs. Open all year.

Ballymagarry Country House (A)
46 Leeke Rd, BT56 8NH.
☎ (01265) 823737. Fax 822542.
B&B s£40 d£50. Rooms 4, ensuite 4.
Open April-Sept.

Belvedere Town House (B)
15 Lansdowne Crescent, BT56 8AY.
☎ (01265) 822771.
B&B s£18 d£32. Rooms 15, ensuite 5.
Open all year.

Brookvale Guest House (A)
61 Coleraine Rd, BT56 8HR.
☎ (01265) 823678.
B&B s£25 d£38. BB&M s£33 d£54.
Rooms 10, ensuite 10. Dinner £8.
Open all year.

Brown's Country House (A)
174 Ballybogey Rd, Ballywatt, BT52 2LP.
☎ (012657) 31627/32777. Fax 31627.
B&B s£25 d£40. BB&M s£36 d£62.
Rooms 8, ensuite 8. Dinner £11.
Last orders 12 noon. Open all year ex Christmas.
Off B62, 5m NE of Ballymoney

Carrick-Dhu Guest House (A)
6 Ballyreagh Rd, BT56 8LP.
☎ (01265) 823666. Fax 825271.
B&B s£25 d£50. BB&M s£35 d£70.
Rooms 6, ensuite 6. High tea £10.50.
Dinner £15. Last orders 1000 hrs.
Open April-Oct.

Casa-A-La-Mar (B)
21 Kerr St, BT56 8DG.
☎ & fax (01265) 822617.
B&B s£16 d£32. BB&M s£22 d£44. Rooms 7,
ensuite 2. Dinner £6. Last orders 1800 hrs.
Open all year.

Castle Erin (B)
Castle Erin Rd, BT56 8DH.
☎ (01265) 822744.
B&B s£29 d£46. BB&M s£36 d£60.
Rooms 49, ensuite 22. High tea £7.50.
Dinner £9. Open all year.

Facilities are liable to change. Check prices when you book. Key to symbols is on inside back flap.

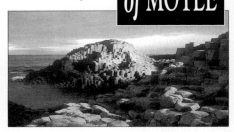

Clarmont (B)
10 Lansdowne Crescent, BT56 8AY.
☎ & fax (01265) 822397.
B&B s£25 d£45. Rooms 10, ensuite 10.
Open Jan-Nov.

Glencroft (B)
95 Coleraine Rd, BT56 8HN.
☎ (01265) 822902.
B&B s£25 d£38. BB&M s£37 d£62. Rooms 5,
ensuite 2. Dinner £12. Last orders 1900 hrs.
Open all year ex Christmas.

Glenkeen Guest House (A)
59 Coleraine Rd, BT56 8HR.
☎ (01265) 822279.
B&B s£25 d£40. BB&M s£33.50 d£57.
Rooms 10, ensuite 10. High tea £7. Dinner £8.50.
Last orders 1630 hrs. Open all year.

Hayesbank/Kantara (A)
5 Ramore Avenue, BT56 8BB.
☎ (01265) 823823. Fax 822741.
B&B s£18 d£36. BB&M s£26 d£52.
Rooms 36, ensuite 5. Dinner £8.
Last orders 1630 hrs. Open all year.

Ma-Ring Guest House (B)
17 Kerr St, BT56 8OT.
☎ (01265) 822765.
B&B s£25 d£35. BB&M s£35 d£55.
Rooms 14, ensuite 10. Dinner £10.
Last orders 1900 hrs. Open all year.

Mount Royal (B)
2 Eglinton St, BT56 8DX.
☎ & fax (01265) 823342.
B&B s£21 d£36. BB&M s£29 d£52. Rooms 6,
ensuite 1. High tea £6. Dinner £8.
Last orders 1400 hrs. Open all year.

Old Manse (B)
3 Main St, BT56 8BL.
☎ (01265) 824118.
B&B s£21 d£40. BB&M s£30 d£58.
Rooms 5, ensuite 2. Dinner £9. Last orders 1930 hrs.
Open all year.

Prospect House (B)
20 Lansdowne Crescent, BT56 8AY.
☎ (01265) 822299.
B&B s£16 d£32. BB&M s£21 d£42.
Rooms 12, ensuite 6. Dinner £5. Open all year.

West Bay View (B)
48 Mark St, BT56 8BU.
☎ (01265) 823375/823035.
B&B s£22 d£40. BB&M s£28 d£50.
Rooms 39, ensuite 14. Dinner £8.
Last orders 1830 hrs. Open all year.

West Strand Guest House (B)
18 Kerr St, BT56 8DG.
☎ (01265) 822270.
B&B s£17.50 d£30. BB&M s£23 d£46.
Rooms 15. High tea £5.50. Dinner £7.50.
Last orders 1830 hrs. Open April-Oct.

Facilities are liable to change. Check prices when you book. Key to symbols is on inside back flap.

Windsor Guest House   (B)

67 Main St, BT56 8BN.
☎ (01265) 823793. Fax 824625.
B&B s£24 d£40. BB&M s£31 d£54.
Rooms 27, ensuite 6. High tea £5. Dinner £7.
Open all year.

Bed & Breakfast

Aarondale

(Mr Shields & Miss Duff), 21 Coleraine Rd,
BT56 8EA.
☎ (01265) 824289.
B&B s£18 d£30. Rooms 4. Open all year.

Abercorn House

(Mrs L Paul), 57 Coleraine Rd, BT56 8HR.
☎ (01265) 825014/825136.
B&B s£22 d£36. Rooms 9, ensuite 9. High tea £5.
Dinner £7.50. Last orders 2030 hrs. Open all year.

Aghalun

(Mrs A Ebbitt), 2 Caldwell Park, BT56 8LZ.
☎ (01265) 823166.
B&B d£40. Rooms 3, ensuite 2.
Open March-Nov.

Alexander House

(Mrs T McDiarmid), 23 Kerr St, BT56 8DG.
☎ (01265) 824566/824996.
B&B s£16, d£28. Rooms 5. Open all year.

An Avarest House

(Mr & Mrs Pollock), 64 Mark St, BT56 8BU.
☎ (01265) 823121.
B&B s£23 d£36. Rooms 10, ensuite 2. High tea £6.
Dinner £8. Open all year.

An Uladh

(Mrs M Mair), 73 Eglinton St, Golf Terrace,
BT56 8DZ.
☎ (01265) 822221.
B&B d£38. Rooms 8, ensuite 6.
Open all year.

Ardenlee House

(Mr & Mrs Walker), 19 Kerr St, BT56 8DG.
☎ (01265) 822639.
B&B s£20 d£40. Rooms 3, ensuite 3.
Open Feb-Nov.

Ashlea House

(Mrs G Hunt), 52 Kerr St, BT56 8DQ.
☎ (01265) 823094.
B&B s£15 d£28. Rooms 2.
Open April-Sept.

Atlantic View

(Mr C McIntyre), 103 Eglinton St, BT56 8DZ.
☎ (01265) 823647. Fax 825394.
B&B s£18 d£30. Rooms 8, ensuite 2.
Open all year.

B&B = bed and breakfast   s = single   d = double   BB&M = bed, breakfast & evening meal

Atlantis
(Mr & Mrs Torrens), 10 Ramore Avenue,
BT56 8BB.
☎ (01265) 824583.
B&B s£16 d£28. BB&M s£21 d£38.
Rooms 14, ensuite 3. Dinner £5.
Open all year ex Christmas.

Ballymacrea House
(Mrs L McKenzie), 220 Ballybogy Rd, BT56 8NE.
☎ (01265) 824507.
B&B s£22.50 d£45. Rooms 1. Open all year.

Ballywillan Farm
(Mrs F Nevin), 201 Ballywillan Rd, BT56 8NT.
☎ (01265) 823291.
B&B s£16 d£32. Rooms 3. Open April-Oct.

Bayview House
(Mr & Mrs Young), 20 Kerr St, BT56 8DG.
☎ (01265) 822050.
B&B s£15 d£30. Rooms 2, ensuite 2.
Open all year.
On A2, 1m E of Portrush

Bethel
(Mr & Mrs Graham), 7 Lansdowne Crescent,
BT56 8AY.
☎ (01265) 822354.
B&B s£20 d£42. BB&M s£20 d£58.
Rooms 14, ensuite 4. High tea £6. Dinner £9.
Last orders 1600 hrs. Open all year.

Beulah House
(Mr & Mrs Anderson), 16 Causeway St, BT56 8AB.
☎ (01265) 822413.
B&B s£16 d£32. BB&M s£23 d£46. Rooms 10.
Dinner £7. Last orders 1400 hrs. Open all year.

Bonita Vista
(Mrs E Allen), 5 Strand Avenue, Whiterocks,
BT56 8ND.
☎ (01265) 823411.
B&B s£16 d£32. Rooms 3, ensuite 1.
Open June-Aug.
On A2, 1m E of Portrush

Borelands
(Mrs J Boreland), 48 Causeway St, BT56 8AD.
☎ (01265) 822399.
B&B s£15 d£30. Rooms 3. Open June-Sept.

Brae-Mar
(Mr A Torrens), 28 Kerr St, BT56 8DK.
☎ (01265) 824054 **or** 825224.
B&B s£17.50 d£34. Rooms 5, ensuite 1.
Open all year.

Brookhaven
(Mrs E Goligher), 99 Coleraine Rd, BT56 8HN.
☎ (01265) 824164.
B&B s£16.50 d£33. Rooms 3, ensuite 1.
Open all year.

Facilities are liable to change. Check prices when you book. Key to symbols is on inside back flap.

Causeway House
(Mr D Devenney), 26 Kerr St, BT56 8DG.
☎ (01265) 824847.
B&B s£25 d£40. Rooms 6, ensuite 5.
Open April-Nov.

🆃 ✳ 🌿 🛏 🐎 🏛 ◻ ✂ 🎵 🏌 ∪ 🐕 💷

Clontara
(Mrs H Hamill), 8 Ballyreagh Rd, BT56 8LP.
☎ (01265) 824030.
B&B s £25 d£36. Rooms 3, ensuite 1.
Open April-Oct.

🅿 ✳ ♣ 🌿 🐎 🏛 ✂ 🐕

Craigdorragh
(Ms S Jamieson), 15 Morrison Park, BT56 8HZ.
☎ (01265) 823920.
B&B s£16 d£28. BB&M s£21 d£40. Rooms 1.
High tea £6.50. Open April-Sept.

🅿 ✳ 🐎 🏛 ✂ 🎵 🏌 ∪ 🛆 🏊 🐕

Drumlee
(Mr & Mrs Torrens), 50 Mark St, BT56 8BU.
☎ (01265) 823133.
B&B s£15 d£30. BB&M s£20 d£40.
Rooms 27, ensuite 2. Last orders 1730 hrs.
Open all year.

🆃 🌿 🐎 🅾🅰🅿 🏛 ✂ 🎵 🏌 ∪ 🐕

Ellensville
(Mrs M Davison), 130 Coleraine Rd, BT56 8HN.
☎ (01265) 823245.
B&B s£17 d£30. Rooms 3. Open all year.

🅿 ✳ ♣ 🐎 🏛 ✂ 🐕

Galgorm House
(Mr & Mrs Semple), 117 Eglinton St, BT56 8DZ.
☎ (01265) 823787.
B&B s£20 d£40. Rooms 11, ensuite 6.
Open all year.

🌿 🐎 🅾🅰🅿 🏛 ◻ 🎵 🏌 ∪ 🛆 🐕 💷

Glenshane
(Mrs M McCorriston), 113 Eglinton St, BT56 8DZ.
☎ (01265) 824839.
B&B s£12.50 d£37. Rooms 5, ensuite 4.
Open all year.

🅿 🌿 🐎 🅾🅰🅿 🛏 🏛 ◻ ✂ 🎵 🏌 ∪ 🛆 🏊 🐕

Gracefield
(Mrs F Hume), 13 Magheramenagh Drive,
BT56 8SP.
☎ (01265) 822089.
B&B d£36. Rooms 1, ensuite 1.
Open April-Sept.

🅿 ✳ 🐎 🅾🅰🅿 🏛 ✂ 🌐 🐕

Harbour House
(Ms M McGuckian), 36 Kerr St, BT56 8DQ.
☎ (01265) 822130.
B&B s£25 d£45. Rooms 9, ensuite 5.
Open April-Oct.

🆃 🅿 🎠 🌿 🅾🅰🅿 🏛 ◻ 🎵 🏌 ∪ ✓ 🛆 🏊 🐕

Hillrise
(Ms Moore & Mrs Snodden), 24 Dhu Varren,
BT56 8EN.
☎ (01265) 822450.
B&B s£25 d£40. Rooms 5, ensuite 5.
Open all year.

🅿 ✳ 🌿 🐎 🏛 ◻ ✂ 🎵 🏌 ∪ 🛆 🏊 🐕

Hoylake House
(Mrs D Colgan), 10 Victoria St, BT56 8DL.
☎ (01265) 824374.
B&B s£20 d£40. Rooms 5. Dinner £10.
Open all year.

🅿 🎠 🌿 🐎 🅾🅰🅿 🏛 ◻ ✂ 🏌 ∪ 🏊 🐕

B&B = bed and breakfast   s = single   d = double   BB&M = bed, breakfast & evening meal

Islay-View
(Mrs E Smith), 36 Leeke Rd, BT56 8NH.
☎ (01265) 823220.
B&B s£25 d£36. Rooms 3, ensuite 3.
Open March-Sept.
Off B62, 2½m from Portrush

Leander House
(Mr & Mrs Quinn), 6 Bath Rd, BT56 8AP.
☎ (01265) 822142.
B&B s£16 d£37. Rooms 9, ensuite 2.
Open all year.

Loguestown Farm
(Mrs M Adams), 58 Loguestown Rd, BT56 8NY.
☎ (01265) 822742.
B&B s£24 d£35. Rooms 4, ensuite 1.
Open all year.
Off A29, 1m S of Portrush

Maddybenny Farm House
(Mrs R White), 18 Maddybenny Park,
Loguestown Rd, BT52 2PT.
☎ & fax (01265) 823394.
B&B s£30 d£50. Rooms 3, ensuite 3.
Open all year ex Christmas & New Year.
Off A29, 2m S of Portrush

Malvern House
(Mrs J Hassin), 36 Mark St, BT56 8BT.
☎ (01265) 823435.
B&B s£17.50 d£35. BB&M s£23.50 d£47.
Rooms 9, ensuite 3. Open all year.

Mill Strand House
(Mrs J Steele), 27 Kerr St, BT56 8DQ.
☎ (01265) 824868.
B&B s£15 d£30. Rooms 2. Open all year.

NI Hotel & Catering College
Ballywillan Rd, BT56 8JL.
☎ (01265) 823768. Fax 826200.
B&B s£18 d£36. Rooms 84, ensuite 31.
Last orders 2100 hrs. Open June-Aug.

Number 25
(Mrs E McAuley), 25 Coleraine Rd, BT56 8EA.
☎ (01265) 824508.
B&B s£17.50 d£35. Rooms 3, ensuite 1.
Open all year ex Christmas.

Oakdene
(Mrs J Collins), 6 Lansdowne Crescent, BT56 8AY.
☎ & fax (01265) 824629.
B&B s£18 d£36. Rooms 16, ensuite 7.
Open all year.

The Pink House
(Mr & Mrs King), 122 Atlantic Rd,
Island Flackey, BT56 8PA.
☎ (01265) 824499. Fax 822765.
B&B s£25 d£40. BB&M s£35 d£60.
Rooms 3, ensuite 3. Dinner £10.
Last orders 2100 hrs. Open all year.

Facilities are liable to change. Check prices when you book. Key to symbols is on inside back flap.

101

Port-Na-Glas
(Mr & Mrs Singleton), 111 Eglinton St, BT56 8DZ.
☎ (01265) 824352.
B&B s£18.50 d£37.
Rooms 13, ensuite 5. Dinner £5.
Open June-Sept.

Port O Call
(Mr & Mrs Moffatt), 28 Dhu Varren,
BT56 8EN.
☎ (01265) 822570.
B&B s£13.50 d£27. Rooms 5.
Open Jan-Nov.

Ramona
(Mr & Mrs McKibbin), 8 Ramore Avenue,
BT56 8BB.
☎ (01265) 824734.
B&B s£17 d£30. BB&M s£23 d£42.
Rooms 11. High tea £6. Dinner £6. Open all year.

Rathlin House
(Mr & Mrs Davidson), 2 Ramore Avenue,
BT56 8BB.
☎ (01265) 824834.
B&B s£15 d£30. BB&M s£22 d£44.
Rooms 11. High tea £5.50. Dinner £7.
Last orders 1930 hrs. Open all year.

Rochester
(Mr & Mrs Barr), 6 Mount Royal,
Eglinton St, BT56 8DZ.
☎ (01265) 822778.
B&B s£14.50 d£29. Rooms 8. Open all year.

Shangarry
(Mr & Mrs Morgan), 4 Causeway St, BT56 8AB.
☎ (01265) 822362.
B&B s£16 d£30. BB&M s£20 d£37.
Rooms 8. Dinner £4.50. Last orders 2030 hrs.
Open April-Oct.

Summer-Island House
(Mrs A Armstrong), 14 Coleraine Rd, BT56 8EA.
☎ (01265) 824640.
B&B s£25 d£40. Rooms 4, ensuite 3.
Open Jan-Nov.

Sunnyside House
(Mr N Lerwill), 45 Causeway St, BT56 8AB.
☎ (01265) 825465.
B&B s£18 d£36. Rooms 3. Open all year.

RANDALSTOWN

Guesthouse

Creeve House Country Guest Inn (B)
115 Staffordstown Rd, BT41 3LH.
☎ (01849) 472547. Fax 479494.
B&B s£20 d£30. Rooms 8, ensuite 8.
Open all year.

Bed & Breakfast

The Beeches
(Mrs S Ross), 10 Ballynafey Rd, BT41 3HZ.
☎ (01648) 50262.
B&B s£17.50 d£27. BB&M s£20 d£40.
Rooms 11, ensuite 4. Dinner £6.50.
Last orders 2100 hrs. Open all year.

B&B = bed and breakfast   s = single   d = double   BB&M = bed, breakfast & evening meal

Lurgan West Lodge
(Mrs S McLaughlin), 15a Old Staffordstown Rd,
BT41 3LD.
☎ (01849) 479691.
B&B s£20 d£30. Rooms 3, ensuite 2.
Open all year.

RATHLIN ISLAND

Guesthouse

Rathlin Guest House   (B)
The Quay, BT54 6RT.
☎ (012657) 63917.
B&B s£16 d£30. BB&M s£25.50 d£39.50.
Rooms 4. Dinner £9.50. Last orders 1900 hrs.
Open March-Sept.

TEMPLEPATRICK

Hotel

Templeton Hotel   ***
882 Antrim Rd, BT39 0AH.
☎ (01849) 432984. Fax 433406.
B&B s£95 d£120. BB&M s£113.95 d£157.95.
Rooms 24, ensuite 24. High tea £11.80.
Dinner £18.95. Last orders 2145 hrs.
Open all year ex Christmas.

Bed & Breakfast

Moat Inn
(Mr R Thompson), Donegore, BT43 7DP.
☎ (01849) 433659.
B&B s£25 d£50. Rooms 2, ensuite 2. Dinner £12.
Open Easter, July & Aug.

Toberagnee Dairy Farm
(Mr & Mrs Hyde), 54 Lylehill Rd, BT39 0ES.
☎ (01849) 432389.
B&B s£15 d£30. Rooms 2. Open all year.

TOOMEBRIDGE

Hotel

O'Neill Arms Hotel   *
20 Main St, BT41 3TQ.
☎ (01648) 50202/50885. Fax 50970.
B&B s£25 d£40. BB&M s£35 d£60.
Rooms 11, ensuite 5. High tea £10. Dinner £14.
Last orders 2200 hrs. Open all year.

Bed & Breakfast

Ardnaglass House
(Mr E Stinson), 39 Grange Rd, BT41 3QB.
☎ (01648) 50694. Fax 59511.
B&B s£16 d£32. Rooms 2.
Open all year.

Facilities are liable to change. Check prices when you book. Key to symbols is on inside back flap.

Rose Cottage

(Mr I McBride), 140a Crosskeys Rd, BT41 3PY.
☎ (01648) 50563. Fax 50338.
B&B s£15. High tea £2.50. Dinner £8.50.
Last orders 1700 hrs. Open all year.

WATERFOOT (or GLENARIFF)

Bed & Breakfast

The Bay

(Mrs A Colligan), 204 Garron Rd, BT44 0RB.
☎ (012667) 71858.
B&B s£14 d£28. Rooms 3. Open April-Sept.

Dieskirt Farm

(Mrs K McHenry), 104 Glen Rd, BT44 0RG.
☎ (012667) 71308/71796. Fax 71308.
B&B s£17.50 d£33. BB&M s£27.50 d£53.
Rooms 3, ensuite 2. Open April-Dec.

Lasata

(Mrs B Leech), 72 Glen Rd, BT44 0RG.
☎ (012667) 71578.
B&B s£25 d£40. Rooms 3, ensuite 2.
Open all year.

B&B = bed and breakfast   s = single   d = double   BB&M = bed, breakfast & evening meal

Lurig View
(Mrs C Ward), 4 Lurig View, BT44 0RD.
☎ (012667) 71618.
B&B s£16 d£28. Rooms 2. Open all year.

Sanda
(Ms E O'Loan), 29 Kilmore Rd, BT44 0RQ.
☎ (012667) 71785.
B&B d£34. Rooms 2, ensuite 2.
Open all year.

Tamlagh House
(Mr H Harvey), 43 Glen Rd, BT44 0RF.
☎ (012667) 72002.
B&B s£15 d£30. Rooms 2, ensuite 2.
Open April-Sept.

Teach-na-tra
(Mr & Mrs Wheeler), 201 Garron Rd,
BT44 0RA.
☎ (012667) 71236.
B&B d£30. Rooms 1, ensuite 1.
Open July-Aug.

Wilmar House
(Mrs M McAllister), 26 Kilmore Rd, BT44 0RQ.
☎ (012667) 71653/71700.
B&B s£14 d£28. Rooms 2.
Open March-Sept.

WHITEHEAD

Bed & Breakfast

Crestbank
(Mrs K Todd), 13 Marine Parade, BT38 9QP.
☎ (01960) 372338.
B&B s£17 d£34. Rooms 2. Open all year.

Grasmere
(Mrs E Wilson), 22 Brooklands Park, BT38 9SN.
☎ (01960) 372330.
B&B s£16 d£32. Rooms 2. Open all year.

Green Acres
(Mrs H Kirk), 3 Slaughterford Rd, BT38 9TG.
☎ (01960) 373257.
B&B s£15 d£30. Rooms 3. Open all year.

The Moorings
(Mrs H Wilson), 25 Marine Parade, BT38 9QP.
☎ (01960) 372545.
B&B s£15 d£30. Rooms 3. Open all year.

Seascape Country House
(Mrs M Purdy), 59a Quay Lane, BT38 9SS.
☎ (01960) 378283.
B&B s£15 d£34. Rooms 5, ensuite 2.
Open all year.

Seaview
(Mrs R Craig), 19 Beach Rd, BT38 9QS.
☎ (01960) 378524.
B&B s£16 d£32. Rooms 2. Open all year.

Facilities are liable to change. Check prices when you book. Key to symbols is on inside back flap.

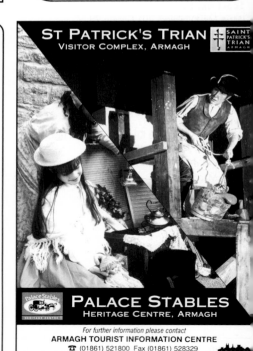

County Armagh

Hotels

Charlemont Arms Hotel *
63 Lower English St, BT61 7LB.
☎ (01861) 522028/522719. Fax 526979.
B&B s£29 d£54. Rooms 11, ensuite 9.
High tea £15. Dinner £18. Last orders 2100 hrs.
Open all year ex Christmas.

🛈 🅿 ♨ ❋ 🐾 ♞ 🖳 ⬚ 🖳 ⬚ 🕻 ⚷ 🎵 ⌐ ∪
⬙ ⚡ 🎣 🖼

Drumsill Hotel *
35 Moy Rd, BT61 8DL.
☎ (01861) 522009. Fax 525624.
B&B s£49.50 d£74. BB&M s£62 d£99.
Rooms 10, ensuite 10. Dinner £12.50.
Last orders 2200 hrs. Open all year.

🛈 🅿 ❋ ♣ 🕊 ♨ 🐾 🖳 🖼 🐴 🖳 ⬚ 🕻 🎵 ⌐ ⚶ ∪
⚓ ⬙ ⚡ 🖼

Guesthouse

De-Averell Guest House (A)
No 3 Seven Houses,
47 Upper English St, BT61 8DW.
☎ (01861) 511213. Fax 511221.
B&B s£32.50 d£59. BB&M s£39.50 d£75.
Rooms 4. High tea £10.95. Dinner £15.
Last orders 2130 hrs. Open all year.

🅿 🏠 ♨ 🐾 🖳 ⬚ 🕻 ⚷ 🎵 ⌐ ⚶ ∪ ⚓
⬙ ⚡ ⚶ 🖼

Bed & Breakfast

Dean's Hill ·
(Mrs J Armstrong), College Hill, BT61 9DF.
☎ (01861) 524923.
B&B s£25 d£50. Rooms 3, ensuite 2.
Open all year.

🅿 🏠 ❋ ♣ 🕊 🐾 🖳 🧦 ⌐ ∪ ⬙ ⚡

Desart
(Mrs S McRoberts), 99 Cathedral Rd, BT61 8AE.
☎ (01861) 522387.
B&B s£15 d£30. BB&M s£25 d£50. Rooms 5.
High tea £10. Open all year.

🅿 🏠 ❋ ♣ 🐾 🖳 ⬚ ⚷ 🎵 ⌐ ∪ ⚶ ⬙ ⚡

Hillview Lodge
(Mr & Mrs McBride), 33 Newtownhamilton Rd,
BT60 2PL.
☎ (01861) 522000. Fax 528276.
B&B s£25 d£40. Rooms 6. Open all year.

🛈 🅿 ❋ ♣ 🕊 🐾 🖳 ⬚ ⚷ 🎵 ⌐ ∪ ⚶ 🍃 🖼

Mountnorris House
(Mrs L Walker), 41 Main St,
Mountnorris, BT60 2TS.
☎ (01861) 507543.
B&B d£34. Rooms 3. Open all year.

🅿 🏠 ❋ ♣ 🕊 🐾 🖳 ⚷ 🎵 ⌐

Ni Eoghain Lodge
(Mr N McGeown), 32 Ennislare Rd, BT60 2AX.
☎ (01861) 525633.
B&B s£14 d£28. Rooms 3, ensuite 3. High tea £6.
Open all year.

🅿 ❋ ♣ 🕊 🐾 🖳 🎵 ⌐ ⚶

Padua House
(Mrs K O'Hagan), 63 Cathedral Rd, BT61 4OX.
☎ (01861) 522039 **or** 528888.
B&B s£12 d£24. Rooms 2. Open all year.

🅿 ❋ 🕊 🐾 🖼 🖳 ⬚ ⚷ ⌐

Facilities are liable to change. Check prices when you book. Key to symbols is on inside back flap.

St Michael's
(Mrs J McParland), 1 Mullinure Lane, BT61 7RT.
☎ (01861) 527958.
B&B s£18 d£36. Rooms 3, ensuite 3.
Open all year.

🌐 🅿 ❄ ⚶ ⌛ ▥ ⌷ ⅄ ♪ ⌐ ∪ ♤ ⚡

CRAIGAVON
(See also Lurgan and Portadown)

Hotel

Silverwood Hotel *
Kiln Rd, Silverwood, Lurgan, BT66 6NF.
☎ (01762) 327722. Fax 325290.
B&B s£55 d£70. BB&M s£70 d£100.
Rooms 27, ensuite 27. High tea £10. Dinner £15.
Last orders 2115 hrs.
Open all year ex Christmas.

🌐 🅿 ❄ ♣ ⚐ ⌛ ▥ ⌷ ⌕ ♪ ⌐ ♤ ⚡ ⚑ 🆔

CROSSMAGLEN

Bed & Breakfast

Lima Country House
(Mrs E Ryan), 16 Drumalt Rd, Ummericam,
Silverbridge, BT35 9LQ.
☎ (01693) 861944.
B&B s£16 d£32. BB&M s£24 d£48.
Rooms 4, ensuite 3. High tea £8. Dinner £8.
Last orders 2100 hrs. Open all year.

🅿 ❄ ♣ ⚶ ⌛ 🐴 ▥ ⌷ ☎ ⅄ ♪
⌐ ∪ ✓ ♤

Cnoc Mhuire
(Mr & Mrs McShane), 40 Annaghmare Rd,
BT35 9BG.
☎ (01693) 861896.
B&B s£14.50 d£25. BB&M s£22.50 d£41.
Rooms 2. High tea £6. Dinner £8.
Last orders 2130 hrs. Open April-Oct.

🅿 ❄ ♣ ⚶ ⌛ ▥ ⅄ ♪ ⌐ ∪ ♤ ⚡

Murtagh's Bar & Lounge
13 North St, BT35 9HB.
☎ (01693) 861378.
B&B s£20 d£32. BB&M s£28 d£48.
Rooms 3, ensuite 1. High tea £8. Dinner £8.
Open all year.

⚐ ⌛ 🆔 ▥ ⌷ ⅄ ♪ ⌐ ∪ ♤ ⚡ 🆔

22 Ballyfannahan Rd
(Ms J McCavitt), Cullyhanna, BT35 0LZ.
☎ (01693) 868864.
B&B s£15 d£30. Rooms 3, ensuite 2.
Open all year.

🅿 ❄ ♣ ⚶ ▥ ⅄ ♪ ⌐

KEADY

Hotel

Unclassified Hotel
Carnwood Lodge Hotel, 121 Castleblaney Rd,
BT60 3HT. ☎ *(01861) 538935.*

KILLYLEA

Bed & Breakfast

Heimat
(Mr & Mrs McLoughlin), 6 Polnagh Rd, BT60 3AY.
☎ (01861) 568661.
B&B s£15 d£30. Rooms 3, ensuite 1.
Open all year.

🅿 ❄ ♣ ⚐ ▥ ⅄

B&B = bed and breakfast   s = single   d = double   BB&M = bed, breakfast & evening meal

The Hollow
(Mrs R Gillespie), 23 Lisagally Rd, BT60 4LY.
☎ (01861) 568625.
B&B s£15 d£28. Rooms 2. Open May-Sept.

P ❁ ♣ ⚶ ⌂ OAP ▥ ⤢ ♪ ↑ ∪ ✓

LOUGHGALL

Bed & Breakfast

Ashtree Hollows
(Mr & Mrs Wright), Lissheffield Rd, BT61 8QB.
☎ (01762) 891165.
B&B s£18 d£36. Rooms 2, ensuite 2. Open all year.

P ❁ ♣ ⌂ OAP ▥ ⎁ ⤢ ♪ ↑ ∪ ✓

Greenhall Country House
(Mrs A Lavery), 123 Cloveneden Rd, BT61 8LE.
☎ (01868) 784218.
B&B s£14 d£28. Rooms 3. Open all year.

T P ❁ ♣ ⚶ ⌂ ⌖ ▥ ↑ ∪ ⌂ ⇄ ⊞

LURGAN
(See also Craigavon)

Hotel

Ashburn Hotel *
81 William St, BT66 6JB.
☎ (01762) 325711. Fax 347194.
B&B s£32.50 d£52. BB&M s£41 d£69.
Rooms 12, ensuite 12. Dinner £15.
Last orders 2115 hrs. Open all year.

P ❢ ⌂ ▥ ⎁ ↻ ♪ ↑ ✓ ⌂ ⇄ ❢ ⊞

MARKETHILL

Hotel

Unclassified Hotel
Gosford House Hotel, Main St, BT60 1PU.
☎ (01861) 551676. Fax 551810.

NEWTOWNHAMILTON

Bed & Breakfast

The Commons
(Ms T Mackin), 5 The Commons, BT35 0DP.
☎ (01693) 878854.
B&B s£14 d£28. Rooms 2. Open all year.

P ♣ ⌂ ▥ ⎁ ⤢ ♪ ↑ ✓ ⌂ ⇄

PORTADOWN
(See also Craigavon)

Hotels

Carngrove Hotel **
2 Charlestown Rd, BT63 5PW.
☎ (01762) 339222. Fax 332899.
B&B s£47.25 d£68.50. BB&M s£59.25 d£92.50.
Rooms 35, ensuite 35. High tea £10. Dinner £14.
Open all year.

P ❁ ♣ ❢ ⌂ OAP ▥ ⎁ ↻ ⤢ ♪ ↑ ∪ ✓ ⇄ ❢ ⌖ ⊞

Seagoe Hotel **
Upper Church Lane, BT63 5JE.
☎ (01762) 333076. Fax 350210.
B&B s£52.75 d£69.75. BB&M s£68.75 d£85.75.
Rooms 37, ensuite 37.
High tea £13. Dinner £17. Last orders 2130 hrs.
Open all year ex Christmas Day.

T P ❁ ♣ ❢ ⌂ ▥ ⎁ ↻ ⤢ ♪ ↑ ⌂ ⇄ ❢ ⏚ ⌖ ⊞

Facilities are liable to change. Check prices when you book. Key to symbols is on inside back flap.

Guesthouse

Drumcree House (B)
38 Ashgrove Rd, BT62 1PA.
☎ (01762) 338655.
B&B s£19 d£38. BB&M s£30 d£60.
Rooms 4, ensuite 2. High tea £10. Dinner £12.
Last orders 1900 hrs. Open all year.

Bed & Breakfast

Avonbawn
(Mrs M Hughes), 140 Thomas St, BT62 3AN.
☎ (01762) 339030.
B&B s£17 d£30. BB&M s£30 d£56. Rooms 3.
Dinner £13. Open all year.

Bannview Squash Club
60 Portmore St, BT62 3NF.
☎ (01762) 336666.
B&B s£24 d£40. Rooms 10, ensuite 10.
High tea £7.50. Dinner £9.50.
Last orders 2030 hrs. Open all year.

The Cottage
(Mr & Mrs Turkington), 17 Gallrock Rd, Birches,
BT62 1NP.
☎ (01762) 852189.
B&B s£27.50 d£45. Rooms 4. High tea £10.
Dinner £12. Open all year.

Redbrick Country House
(Mrs M Stephenson), Corbrackey Lane, BT62 1PQ.
☎ (01762) 335268.
B&B s£16 d£32. Rooms 3. Open all year.

Slantry House
(Mr & Mrs McKeever), 113 Charlestown Rd,
BT63 5PR.
☎ (01762) 333391.
B&B s£19 d£36. BB&M s£29 d£56. Rooms 3.
High tea £8. Dinner £10. Last orders 2000 hrs.
Open all year.

125 Summerisland Rd
(Mrs E Neville), Ardress, BT62 1SJ.
☎ (01762) 851437.
B&B s£14 d£24. Rooms 3. High tea £5.
Open all year.

RICHHILL

Guesthouse

Ballinahinch House (B)
47 Ballygroobany Rd, BT61 9NA.
☎ & fax (01762) 870081.
B&B s£16 d£30. Rooms 3. Open April-Sept.
Off A3, SW of Portadown (B131 Richhill)

Bed & Breakfast

Course Lodge
(Mr & Mrs McNally), 38 Annareagh Rd, BT61 9JT.
☎ (01762) 871258.
B&B d£20. Rooms 3, ensuite 1. Open all year.

B&B = bed and breakfast   s = single   d = double   BB&M = bed, breakfast & evening meal

WARINGSTOWN

Guesthouse

Planters Tavern   (A)
4 Banbridge Rd, BT66 7QA.
☎ (01762) 881510. Fax 882371.
B&B s£45 d£66. Rooms 12.
High tea £10. Dinner £12.50. Open all year.

▨ ▥ ✦ ▮ ➤ ▦ ◻ ◟ ✂ ◢ ▶ ∪ ✓
◭ ⇗ ☂ ⊞

Bed & Breakfast

The Curatage
(Mrs E Turkington), 6 Banbridge Rd, BT66 7QA.
☎ (01762) 882285.
B&B s£19 d£35. Rooms 4, ensuite 4.
Open all year.

▨ ✸ ✦ ➤ ▦ ◻ ✂ ◢ ▶ ⊞

Ivanhoe
(Mrs F Dewart), 10 Valley Lane, BT66 7SR.
☎ (01762) 881287.
B&B s£16 d£28. Rooms 3. Open all year.

▨ ✦ ➤ ▦ ✂

Facilities are liable to change. Check prices when you book. Key to symbols is on inside back flap.

Making Northern Ireland More Accessible.

Northern Ireland is truly a unique place. That's why it exerts such an attraction on visitors from around the globe. They come time and time again to experience the wide variety of destinations and activities. The towering Mourne Mountains. Antrim's breathtaking coast with its cliffs and bays. The city of Armagh set in lush countryside. County Tyrone's moors and forests, nestling in the shadow of the Sperrin Mountains. Fermanagh's famed lakeland and the historic city of Derry. And, of course, the natural wonder that is the Giant's Causeway.

Whatever your interests ... cultural, outdoor pursuits, enjoying the scenery, or just taking that well earned rest, Northern Ireland has something for you.

And, if you're a wheelchair user or have limited mobility, you'll be pleasantly surprised at just how accessible everything is.

Our guide gives you specific details on where to stay. We can also help with a range of advice designed to make your visit as pleasant as possible, such as how to travel to Northern Ireland, transport facilities once you're here, and which of the many tourist attractions are accessible to you.

For your copy of our booklet detailing accessible serviced accommodation, or any other advice you may need, contact the Northern Ireland Tourist Board at any of the telephone numbers below.

Northern Ireland may be a new experience for you, but we're sure it's one you'll enjoy.

Northern Ireland Tourist Board

11 Berkeley Street, London W1X 5AD Tel: 0541-555 250 • 135 Buchanan Street (first floor), Glasgow G1 2JA Tel: (0141) 204 4454
St. Anne's Court, 59 North Street, Belfast BT1 1NB Tel: (01232) 246609 Minicom (01232) 233228 • 16 Nassau Street Dublin 2 Tel: (003531) 6791977

County Down

Guesthouse

Glassdrumman Lodge   (A)
85 Mill Rd, BT34 4RH.
☎ (013967) 68451. Fax 67041.
B&B s£85 d£110. BB&M s£112.50 d£165.
Rooms 10, ensuite 10. Dinner £27.50.
Last orders 2000 hrs. Open all year.

🇹 🅿 ❁ ♣ ☀ ⏃ 🛏 □ ⚲ ⚞ ✂ ✈ ↰ ∪ ⬥ ⚡ 🄵

Bed & Breakfast

Dairy Farm
(Mrs C Gordon), 52a Majors Hill, BT34 4QR.
☎ (013967) 68433.
B&B s£18.50 d£34. Rooms 2, ensuite 2.
Open all year.

🇹 🅿 ❁ ♣ ☀ ⏃ 🄳 🛏 □ ✂ ✈ ↰ ∪ ⬥

Fair Haven
(Mrs I Jardine), 16 Moneydarragh Rd, BT34 4TY.
☎ (013967) 68153.
B&B s£17 d£32. BB&M s£25 d£48.
Rooms 3, ensuite 2. High tea £7.50. Dinner £8.
Open all year.

🅿 ❁ ♣ ☀ ⏃ 🛏 ✂

Four Winds
(Mrs D Stevenson), 237 Kilkeel Rd, BT34 4TW.
☎ (013967) 68345.
B&B s£16 d£32. Rooms 3, ensuite 2.
Open all year.

🇹 🅿 ❁ ♣ ☀ ⏃ 🐎 🛏 □ ✂ ✈ ∪ ⬥ ◐

Heathdene
(Mrs A Chambers), 76 Mill Rd, BT34 4RH.
☎ (016937) 68822.
B&B s£15 d£34. Rooms 2, ensuite 2.
Open all year.

🅿 ❁ ♣ ☀ ⏃ 🛏 ✂ ↰ ∪

Heathermount
(Mr & Mrs Rodgers), 48 Old Rd, Glassdrumman,
BT34 4RD.
☎ (013967) 67019.
B&B s£15 d£30. Rooms 3, ensuite 1.
Open April-Oct.

🅿 ❁ ♣ ☀ ⏃ 🄳 🛏 ✈ ↰ ∪ ✂ ⬥ ⚡ 🄵

Kamara
(Mrs J Gordon), 106a Kilkeel Rd, BT34 4TJ.
☎ (013967) 68072.
B&B s£14 d£28. Rooms 2, ensuite 1.
Open all year.

🅿 ❁ ♣ ☀ ⏃ 🛏 □ ✂ ⚫ ✈ ↰ ⬥

Montevideo
(Ms M Marks), 260a Head Rd, BT34 4RL.
☎ (013967) 68870.
B&B s£18 d£30. Rooms 3. Open April-Oct.

🅿 ❁ ♣ ☀ ⏃ 🛏 ✂

Oldtown Lodge
(Mrs I McMath), 46 Oldtown Rd, BT34 4RN.
☎ & fax (013967) 68350.
B&B s£16 d£30. Rooms 2, ensuite 2.
Open April-Sept.

🅿 ❁ ♣ ☀ ⏃ 🛏 ✂ ✈ ↰

Sycamores
(Mrs A McKee), 52 Majors Hill, BT34 4QR.
☎ (013967) 68279.
B&B s£23 d£36. BB&M s£35.50 d£61.
Rooms 3, ensuite 3. Dinner £12.50. Open all year.

🇹 🅿 ❁ ♣ ☀ ⏃ 🄳 🛏 □ ✂ ✈ ↰ ∪ ⬥ ⚡

32 Majors Hill
(Mrs N Gordon), BT34 4QR.
☎ (013967) 68348.
B&B s£16 d£28. Rooms 2. Open all year.

🅿 ❁ ☀ ⏃ 🄳 🛏 ✂

Facilities are liable to change. Check prices when you book. Key to symbols is on inside back flap.

ARDGLASS

Guesthouse

Burford Lodge (U)
30 Quay St, BT30 7SA.
☎ (01396) 841141.
B&B s£16 d£30. BB&M s£21.50 d£43.
Rooms 6, ensuite 6. Dinner £5.50.
Last orders 2000 hrs. Open all year.

Bed & Breakfast

Ardglass Bungalow
(Mr & Mrs Convery), 11 High Green, BT30 7UU.
☎ (01396) 841721.
B&B s£16 d£30. Rooms 2. Open all year.

The Cottage
(Mrs B O'Shea), 9 Castle Place, BT30 7TP.
☎ (01396) 841080.
B&B s£17 d£32. Rooms 4, ensuite 2.
Open all year.

Strand Farm
(Mrs M Donnan), 231 Ardglass Rd, BT30 7UL.
☎ (01396) 841446.
B&B s£16 d£30. Rooms 3, ensuite 1.
Open April-Oct.
On B1, 1½m NW of Ardglass

BALLYHALBERT

Bed & Breakfast

Bayview
(Mrs E Patton), 187 Harbour Rd, BT22 1BP.
☎ (012477) 58908.
B&B s£13 d£25. Rooms 3. Open all year.

Glastry House
(Mrs B McFerran), 18 Victoria Rd, BT22 1DG.
☎ (012477) 38555.
B&B s£15 d£30. Rooms 2. Open March-Sept.

BALLYNAHINCH

Hotels

Millbrook Lodge Hotel *
5 Drumaness Rd, BT24 8LS.
☎ (01238) 562828. Fax 565405.
B&B s£32.50 d£49. BB&M s£42.50 d£69.
Rooms 16, ensuite 16. High tea £7.50. Dinner £15.
Last orders 2100 hrs. Open all year.

White Horse Hotel *
17 High St, BT24 8LN.
☎ (01238) 562225. Fax 564141.
B&B s£32.50 d£55. BB&M s£42.50 d£75.
Rooms 11, ensuite 9. High tea £10. Dinner £15.
Last orders 2130 hrs. Open all year.

B&B = bed and breakfast   s = single   d = double   BB&M = bed, breakfast & evening meal

Bed & Breakfast

Ballycreen Manor
(Mrs M Cahoon), 15 Laurel Rd, BT24 8TP.
☎ (01238) 563794.
B&B s£25 d£38. Rooms 3. Open all year.

Bushymead Country House
(Mrs S Murphy), 86 Drumaness Rd, BT24 8LT.
☎ (01238) 561171.
B&B s£20 d£40. BB&M s£33 d£66.
Rooms 6, ensuite 5. High tea £7. Dinner £9.
Last orders 2100 hrs. Open all year.

Dairy Lake House
(Mrs V Hawthorne), 172 Old Belfast Rd, BT24 8YJ.
☎ (01238) 561543.
B&B s£15 d£30. BB&M s£26 d£52.
Rooms 3, ensuite 2. High tea £10. Dinner £12.
Last orders 2100 hrs. Open all year.

Edenavaddy House
(Mrs M Reid), 6 Edenavaddy Rd, BT24 8JJ.
☎ (01238) 562962.
B&B s£13 d£26. Rooms 3. Dinner £5.
Open all year.

Glen View
(Mrs E Skelly), 40 Ballymaglave Rd, Spa,
BT24 8QB.
☎ (01238) 562684.
B&B s£15 d£26. Rooms 2. Open Feb-Nov.

Number Thirty
(Mrs M Reid), 30 Mountview Rd, BT24 8JR.
☎ (01238) 562956.
B&B s£15 d£36. BB&M s£23 d£52.
Rooms 2, ensuite 1. High tea £6.50. Dinner £8.50.
Last orders 1200 hrs. Open all year.

Pear Tree Farm
(Mrs J Metcalfe), 10 Peartree Rd, BT24 7JY.
☎ & fax (01238) 510437.
B&B s£16 d£32. BB&M s£25 d£50.
Rooms 2, ensuite 2. Dinner £10.
Last orders 1600 hrs. Open all year.

BALLYWALTER

Bed & Breakfast

Ganaway House
(Mrs A Baird), 12 Ganaway Rd, BT22 2LG.
☎ (012477) 57096.
B&B s£23 d£40. BB&M s£35 d£64. Rooms 3.
High tea £8. Dinner £12.
Last orders 2100 hrs. Open all year.

Greenlea Farm
(Mrs E McIvor), 48 Dunover Rd, BT22 2LE.
☎ (012477) 58218.
B&B s£17 d£34. BB&M s£22 d£44. Rooms 5.
High tea £6.50. Dinner £11. Last orders 2000 hrs.
Open all year ex Christmas.
Off A2, ½ m N of Ballywalter

Facilities are liable to change. Check prices when you book. Key to symbols is on inside back flap.

BANBRIDGE

Hotels

Belmont Hotel *
Rathfriland Rd, BT32 3LH.
☎ & fax (018206) 62517.
B&B s£40 d£55. BB&M s£52 d£79.
Rooms 12, ensuite 12. Dinner £12.
Last orders 2130 hrs. Open all year.

🅿 ✿ ♣ 🐾 🍷 🐂 🏛 ⌨ 📞 🗡 ∪ 🍴 🖼

Downshire Arms Hotel *
95 Newry St, BT32 3EF.
☎ (018206) 62638/62343. Fax 26811.
B&B s£30 d£50. Rooms 9, ensuite 6.
Open all year.

🅿 🏨 🍷 🐂 🏛 ⌨ 📞 🗡 🏹 🍴 🖼

Guesthouse

Greenacres (U)
15 Brague Rd, Corbet, BT32 5JZ.
☎ (018206) 23328.
B&B s£17.50 d£35. BB&M s£25.50 d£51.
Rooms 3, ensuite 3. High tea £5. Dinner £8.
Last orders 2030 hrs. Open all year.

🆃 🅿 ✿ ♣ 🐾 🐂 🆗 🏛 ⌨ 🗡 🏹 🌐

Bed & Breakfast

Heathmar
(Mrs J Fleming), 37 Corbet Rd, BT32 3SH.
☎ (018206) 22348.
B&B s£18 d£32. Rooms 2, ensuite 2.
Open all year.
Off B25, 4m N of Banbridge

🆃 🅿 ♣ 🐾 🐂 🏛 ⌨ 🗡 🏹 🏹 ∪ ✓ 🍴 🖾

Meadow View
(Mr & Mrs McAvoy), 26a Monteith Rd, Annaclone,
BT32 5LS.
☎ (018206) 71141.
B&B s£17.50 d£30. Rooms 2. Open all year.

🆃 🅿 🏨 ✿ ♣ 🐾 🐂 🏛 🗡 🏹 🏹 ∪ ✓ 🍴 🖾

Mourneview
(Mrs N Kerr & Mrs E Kerr), 32 Drumnascamph Rd,
Laurencetown, BT63 6DU.
☎ (018206) 26270/24251.
B&B s£20 d£34. Rooms 4, ensuite 4.
Open all year ex Christmas.
2¹/₂m NW of Banbridge

🅿 ✿ ♣ 🐾 🐂 🏛 🗡 🏹 🏹 ∪ ✓ 🍴 🖾 🌐

Springhill
(Mrs D Shanks), 132 Ballygowan Rd, BT32 3QX.
☎ (018206) 23882.
B&B s£20 d£36. Rooms 2, ensuite 2.
Open all year.
1m from Banbridge

🅿 ✿ ♣ 🐾 🐂 🏛 ⌨ 🗡 🏹 🏹 ∪ ✓ 🖾

B&B = bed and breakfast   s = single   d = double   BB&M = bed, breakfast & evening meal

BANGOR

Hotels

Clandeboye Lodge Hotel ***
10 Estate Rd, Clandeboye, BT19 1UR.
☎ (01247) 852500. Fax 852772.
B&B s£95 d£95. BB&M s£110 d£125.
Rooms 43, ensuite 43. Dinner £19.
Last orders 2130 hrs.
Open all year ex Christmas.

Marine Court Hotel ***
18 Quay St, BT20 5ED.
☎ (01247) 451100. Fax 451200.
B&B s£90 d£100. BB&M s£85 d£95.
Rooms 51, ensuite 51. High tea £8. Dinner £20.
Last orders 2200 hrs. Open all year.

Royal Hotel **
26 Quay St, BT20 5ED.
☎ (01247) 271866. Fax 467810.
B&B s£70 d£85. BB&M s£89.50 d£124.
Rooms 50, ensuite 50.
High tea £12.50. Dinner £19.50.
Last orders 2115 hrs. Open all year.

Bangor Bay Inn *
10 Seacliff Rd, BT20 5EY.
☎ (01247) 270696. Fax 271678.
B&B s£60 d£85. Rooms 14, ensuite 14.
High tea £9.50. Dinner £13.95.
Last orders 2115 hrs. Open all year ex Christmas.

Guesthouses

Battersea Guest House (B)
47 Queen's Parade, BT20 3BH.
☎ (01247) 461643.
B&B s£17.50 d£35. Rooms 4. High tea £10.
Open all year.

Beachcroft (B)
5 Princetown Terrace, BT20 3BE.
☎ (01247) 473516.
B&B s£16 d£32. Rooms 3.
Open all year.

Beresford House (A)
5 Queen's Parade, BT20 3BH.
☎ (01247) 452447. Fax 453167.
B&B s£23 d£44. BB&M s£31 d£60.
Rooms 16, ensuite 7. High tea £6. Dinner £8.
Last orders 1800 hrs. Open all year.

Lisnacree (B)
53 Princetown Rd, BT20 3TA.
☎ (01247) 462571.
B&B s£16 d£36. BB&M s£23, d£50.
Rooms 6, ensuite 4. Dinner £7.
Last orders 2130 hrs. Open all year.

Marina Guest House (B)
58 Queen's Parade, BT20 3BH.
☎ (01247) 457733.
B&B s£20 d£30. Rooms 7. Open all year.

Facilities are liable to change. Check prices when you book. Key to symbols is on inside back flap.

Rosewood House (B)
41 Princetown Rd, BT20 3TA.
☎ (01247) 450029.
B&B s£14 d£28. Rooms 5. Dinner £6.
Last orders 1200 hrs. Open all year ex Christmas.

Shelleven House (A)
61 Princetown Rd, BT20 3TA.
☎ & fax (01247) 271777.
B&B s£25 d£40. BB&M s£37.50 d£65.
Rooms 12, ensuite 12. High tea £7.50.
Dinner £12.50. Last orders 1900 hrs. Open all year.

Tara (B)
51 Princetown Rd, BT20 3TA.
☎ (01247) 468924. Fax 469870.
B&B s£23 d£40. BB&M s£29 d£52.
Rooms 10, ensuite 10. Dinner £6.
Open all year.

Bed & Breakfast

Abbeyview Heights
(Mrs R Garbutt), 38 Bryansburn Rd, BT20 3SE.
☎ (01247) 472119.
B&B s£15 d£30. Rooms 4, ensuite 2.
Dinner £5. Last orders 2000 hrs.
Open all year.

Adson House
(Mrs M Adamson), 17 Moira Park, BT20 4RJ.
☎ (01247) 460447.
B&B s£16 d£32. BB&M s£22 d£44.
Rooms 2. High tea £5.50. Dinner £6.
Last orders 1930 hrs. Open all year.

Ambleside
(Mrs E Heaver), 3 Springhill Heights, BT20 3PB.
☎ (01247) 463801.
B&B s£14 d£28. Rooms 2. Open April-Sept.

Anchorage
(Mrs E Erskine), 36 Seacliff Rd, BT20 5EY.
☎ (01247) 461326.
B&B s£15 d£30. Rooms 4. Open all year.

Armell
(Mrs A Armstrong), 30 Donaghadee Rd, BT20 5RU.
☎ (01247) 461903.
B&B s£15 d£28. Rooms 2.
Open April-Sept.

Asda-Keran
(Mrs S Graham), 18 Prospect Rd, BT20 5DA.
☎ (01247) 461309.
B&B s£16 d£30. Rooms 3. Open March-Oct.

Ashley House
(Ms B Walker), 50 Queen's Parade, BT20 3BH.
☎ (01247) 473918.
B&B s£18 d£44. Rooms 6, ensuite 2.
Open all year.

Bayview
(Ms C Unsworth), 140 Seacliff Rd, BT20 5EZ.
☎ (01247) 464545/454726. Fax 454726.
B&B s£15 d£28. BB&M s£25 d£48. Rooms 3.
Dinner £10. Open all year.

B&B = bed and breakfast   s = single   d = double   BB&M = bed, breakfast & evening meal

Bramble Lodge
(Mrs J Hanna), 1 Bryansburn Rd, BT20 3RY.
☎ (01247) 457924.
B&B s£25 d£40. Rooms 3, ensuite 3.
Open all year.

Cairn-Bay-Lodge
(Mr & Mrs Mullen), 278 Seacliff Rd, BT20 5HS.
☎ (01247) 467636. Fax 457728.
B&B s£40 d£70. BB&M s£50 d£98.
Rooms 3, ensuite 3. High tea £8. Dinner £14.
Open all year.

Camelot
(Mrs M Hewitt), 83 Abbey Park, BT20 4BZ.
☎ (01247) 451985.
B&B s£15 d£30. BB&M s£20 d£40.
Rooms 3. Dinner £7.
Last orders 2000 hrs. Open all year.

Carolesta
(Mrs B Spence), 17 Southwell Rd, BT20 3AQ.
☎ (01247) 460640.
B&B s£14 d£28. Rooms 4. Dinner £7.
Open all year.

Emmaus
(Mrs S Campbell), 53 Holborn Avenue, BT20 5ET.
☎ (01247) 456887.
B&B s£13 d£24. Rooms 3. Open all year.

Ennislare House
(Mr & Mrs Ardill), 9 Princetown Rd, BT20 3TA.
☎ (01247) 270858.
B&B s£15 d£30. BB&M s£22 d£44.
Rooms 14, ensuite 2. Dinner £7.
Last orders 1900 hrs. Open all year.

Glenallen House
(Mrs E Patterson), 16 Seacliff Rd, BT20 5EY.
☎ (01247) 473964.
B&B s£16 d£32. Rooms 4, ensuite 2.
Open all year.

Glendale House
(Mrs A Blachford), 77 Southwell Rd, BT20 3AE.
☎ (01247) 468613.
B&B s£14 d£28. BB&M s£20 d£40.
Rooms 3. High tea £4. Dinner £6.
Last orders 1900 hrs. Open all year.

Hebron House
(Mrs I Maddock), 59 Queen's Parade, BT20 3BH.
☎ (01247) 463126.
B&B s£25 d£40. BB&M s£33 d£56.
Rooms 3. High tea £10.
Last orders 2100 hrs. Open all year.

Highfield Country House
(Mrs E Finlay), 531 Belfast Rd, BT19 1UN.
☎ (01247) 853693.
B&B s£18 d£40. Rooms 3, ensuite 1.
Open all year.

Facilities are liable to change. Check prices when you book. Key to symbols is on inside back flap.

119

Kildara
(Mrs T Hughes), 51 Prospect Rd, BT20 5DA.
☎ (01247) 461245.
B&B s£16. Rooms 3, ensuite 2. Open all year.

Leaside
(Mrs C Royle), 22 Southwell Rd, BT20 3AQ.
☎ (01247) 472360.
B&B s£14 d£28. BB&M s£22 d£44.
Rooms 4. Open all year.

Loughview
(Mrs E Jamison), 4 Braemar Park, BT20 5HZ.
☎ (01247) 472479.
B&B s£18 d£36. Rooms 2. Open all year.

Mayfield House
(Mr & Mrs Kempston), 57 Princetown Rd,
BT20 3TA.
☎ (01247) 461000.
B&B s£22 d£38. Rooms 6, ensuite 4.
Open all year.

Mount Pleasant
(Mrs T Forbes), 7 Mount Pleasant, BT20 3TB.
☎ (01247) 456567.
B&B s£20 d£36. Rooms 3. Open all year.

Number 108
(Mrs H Bell), 108 Seacliff Rd, BT20 5EZ.
☎ (01247) 461077.
B&B s£18 d£40. Rooms 2, ensuite 1.
Open all year.

Pier View House
(Mrs J Watts), 28 Seacliff Rd, BT20 5EY.
☎ (01247) 463381.
B&B s£18 d£36. Rooms 5, ensuite 1.
Open all year.

Ramelton House
(Mrs A McAteer), 55 Princetown Rd, BT20 3TA.
☎ (01247) 271813.
B&B s£18 d£36. Rooms 3. Open all year.

Rho-Mar-To Lodge
(Mrs M Davison), 79 Ballycrochan Rd, BT19 6NF.
☎ (01247) 461921.
B&B s£16 d£32. Rooms 3, ensuite 2.
Open all year.

Seacliff House
(Mrs P Foster), 74 Seacliff Rd, BT20 5EZ.
☎ (01247) 453104.
B&B s£14 d£28. BB&M s£24 d£48. Rooms 2.
High tea £10. Dinner £10. Open all year.

Seacrest
(Mrs I Marsden), 98 Seacliff Rd, BT20 5EZ.
☎ (01247) 461935.
B&B s£18 d£30. Rooms 3. Open all year.

Snug Harbour
(Mrs P McKenna), 144 Seacliff Rd, BT20 5EZ.
☎ (01247) 454238.
B&B s£15 d£30. Rooms 4, ensuite 1.
Open all year.

B&B = bed and breakfast   s = single   d = double   BB&M = bed, breakfast & evening meal

BANGOR continued

County DOWN

St Ives
(Mrs T Artt), 58 Seacliff Rd, BT20 5EZ.
☎ (01247) 469444.
B&B s£15 d£29. BB&M s£23 d£45.
Rooms 5, ensuite 1. High tea £7. Dinner £8.
Last orders 1830 hrs. Open all year.

White O'Morn
(Mr & Mrs H Dunlop), 30 Seacliff Rd, BT20 5EY.
☎ (01247) 468400.
B&B s£15 d£30. Rooms 3. Open all year.

138 Seacliff Rd
(Ms N Beadle), BT20 5EZ.
☎ (01247) 461906.
B&B s£15 d£30. Rooms 3. Open all year.

CASTLEWELLAN

Guesthouses

Chestnut Inn (B)
28 Lower Square, BT31 9DW.
☎ (013967) 78247/78344.
B&B s£22 d£40. BB&M s£30 d£56.
Rooms 7, ensuite 7. High tea £7. Dinner £12.
Last orders 2045 hrs. Open all year.

Slieve Croob Inn (A)
119 Clanvaraghan Rd, BT31 9LA.
☎ (013967) 71412. Fax 71162.
B&B s£25 d£55. BB&M s£37.50 d£80.
Rooms 7, ensuite 7. High tea £10. Dinner £15.
Open all year.

Bed & Breakfast

Cleaves House
(Mrs A King), 17 Upper Square, BT31 9DD.
☎ (013967) 71478.
B&B s£15 d£30. Rooms 3. Open all year.

Tonlegee
(Mrs M McAlister), 3 Churchfield Heights,
BT31 9HY.
☎ (013967) 71398.
B&B s£16 d£32. Rooms 2, ensuite 2.
Open Feb-Nov.

Treetops
(Mrs J King), 39 Circular Rd, BT31 9ED.
☎ (013967) 78132.
B&B s£15 d£30. Rooms 3, ensuite 1.
Open all year.

CLOUGHEY

Hotel

Unclassified Hotel
Coastal Lodge Hotel, 204 Main Rd, BT22 1JA.
☎ (012477) 72100.

Facilities are liable to change. Check prices when you book. Key to symbols is on inside back flap.

121

COMBER

Guesthouse

Old Schoolhouse Inn (U)
100 Ballydrain Rd, BT23 6EA.
☎ (01238) 541182. Fax 542583.
B&B s£45 d£65. BB&M s£62 d£99.
Rooms 7, ensuite 7. Dinner £16.95.
Last orders 2200 hrs. Open all year.

Bed & Breakfast

Long Reach
(Mrs M Walker), 140 Belfast Rd, BT23 5JN.
☎ (01247) 871903.
B&B s£20 d£36. Rooms 2, ensuite 2.
Open all year.

Trench Farm
(Mrs M Hamilton), 35 Ringcreevy Rd, BT23 5JR.
☎ & fax (01247) 872558.
B&B s£17.50 d£35. Rooms 3.
Open all year ex Christmas.
Off A21, 3m E of Comber

CRAWFORDSBURN

Hotel

Old Inn ***
15 Main St, BT19 1JH.
☎ (01247) 853255. Fax 852775.
B&B s£85 d£90. BB&M s£107.50 d£135.
Rooms 33, ensuite 33. High tea £15. Dinner £22.50.
Last orders 2130 hrs. Open all year.

CROSSGAR

Guesthouse

Hillhouse (U)
53 Killyleagh Rd, BT30 9EE.
☎ (01396) 830792.
B&B s£25 d£40. Rooms 4, ensuite 4.
Open Jan-Oct.

Bed & Breakfast

Cherith Country House
(Mrs J Matthewson), 30 Raleagh Rd, BT30 9JG.
☎ (01396) 830695.
B&B s£14 d£28. Rooms 3. Open all year.

DONAGHADEE

Hotels

Copelands Hotel **
60 Warren Rd, BT21 0PD.
☎ (01247) 888189. Fax 888344.
B&B s£45 d£60. Rooms 16, ensuite 16.
High tea £12. Dinner £15. Last orders 2130 hrs.
Open all year.

Unclassified Hotel
Dunallan Hotel, 27 Shore St, BT21 0DG.
☎ & fax (01247) 883569.

Bed & Breakfast

Anathoth
(Mrs S McMaster), 9 Edgewater, BT21 0EF.
☎ (01247) 884004.
B&B s£16 d£28. Rooms 1. Open April-Oct.

Facilities are liable to change. Check prices when you book. Key to symbols is on inside back flap.

Bridge House
(Mrs F Logan), 93 Windmill Rd, BT21 0NQ.
☎ (01247) 883348.
B&B s£15 d£28. Rooms 3, ensuite 1.
Open all year.
2 m W of Donaghadee

🅿 ❄ ♣ ☀ ☃ 🛏 ☐ ✂ ✪ 🎵 ▸ ∪

The Deans
(Mrs S Wilson), 52 Northfield Rd, BT21 0BD.
☎ (01247) 882204.
B&B s£19 d£32. Rooms 3. Open all year.

Ⓣ 🅿 ❄ ☃ ♞ 🛏 ☐

Herdstown House
(Mrs C Patterson), 9 Hogstown Rd, BT21 0NL.
☎ (01247) 883773.
B&B s£17 d£30. Rooms 1. Open all year.

🅿 ♻ ❄ ♣ ☃ 🅐🅟 🛏 ☐ ✂ 🎵 ▸ ∪ ♦

Lakeview
(Mrs L Giles), 92a Windmill Rd, BT21 0NQ.
☎ (01247) 883900.
B&B s£17 d£30. Rooms 2. Open all year.

Ⓣ 🅿 ❄ ♣ ☀ ☃ 🛏 ☐ ✂ 🎵 ▸ ∪ ✓ ♦ ⚡

Moor Farm
(Mrs R Gray), 75 High Bangor Rd, BT21 0PP.
☎ & fax (01247) 271840.
B&B s£25 d£40. Rooms 2, ensuite 1.
Open all year.
2 m W of Donaghadee

🅿 ❄ ♣ ☀ ☃ 🛏 ☐ ✂ 🎵 ▸ ∪ ✓ ♦

Waterside
(Mrs A Dalzell), 11 New Rd, BT21 0AH.
☎ (01247) 888305.
B&B s£15.50 d£31. Rooms 2. Open all year.

♻ ❄ ♣ ☀ ☃ 🅐🅟 🛏 ☐ ✂ 🎵 ▸ ∪ ✓ ♦

Waterside Shanaghan
(Mrs M Beattie), 154 Warren Rd, BT21 0PN.
☎ (01247) 888167.
B&B s£15 d£35. Rooms 3, ensuite 3.
Open all year.

🅿 ❄ ♣ ☀ ☃ 🛏 ✂ 🎵 ▸ ∪ ✓ ♦ ⚡

DOWNPATRICK

Hotel

Abbey Lodge Hotel **
Belfast Rd, BT30 9AV.
☎ (01396) 614511. Fax 616415.
B&B s£45 d£60. BB&M s£58 d£86.
Rooms 21, ensuite 21. High tea £9. Dinner £13.
Last orders 2115 hrs. Open all year.

Ⓣ 🅿 ❄ ♣ ☀ ❗ ☃ 🛏 ☐ ☏ ✂ 🎵 ▸ ∪ ✓ ♦ ♟ ✆

Guesthouse

Denvirs (U)
14-16 English St, BT30 6AB.
☎ (01396) 612012.
B&B s£25 d£50. BB&M s£35 d£70.
Rooms 6, ensuite 6. High tea £10. Dinner £15.
Last orders 2100 hrs. Open all year.

🅿 ♻ ❗ ☃ 🛏 ☐ ☏ ▸ ∪ ❗ ✆

Bed & Breakfast

Arolsen
(Mrs E Coburn), 47 Roughal Park, BT30 6HB.
☎ & fax (01396) 612656.
B&B s£16 d£30. BB&M s£26 d£50.
Rooms 2, ensuite 2. Dinner £10.
Last orders 12 noon. Open April-Oct.

Ⓣ 🅿 ❄ ♣ ☀ 🛏 ☐ ✂ 🎵 ▸ ∪ ♦ ⚡ ♟

B&B = bed and breakfast   s = single   d = double   BB&M = bed, breakfast & evening meal

Beachview House

(Mrs M Mackey), 66b Minerstown Rd, Tyrella,
BT30 8LS.
☎ (01396) 851923.
B&B s£20 d£30. Rooms 2. Open Feb-Nov.

Dunleath House

(Mr & Mrs Kerr), 33 St Patrick's Drive, BT30 6NE.
☎ (01396) 613221.
B&B s£21 d£36. Rooms 2, ensuite 2.
Open all year.

Havine Farm

(Mrs M Macauley), 51 Ballydonnell Rd, BT30 8EP.
☎ (01396) 851242.
B&B s£16.50 d£32. BB&M s£28 d£55.
Rooms 3. Dinner £11.50.
Last orders 1500 hrs. Open all year ex Christmas.
Off A25, 4 ¾ m S of Downpatrick
(Tyrella Beach signpost)

Hillcrest

(Mrs F Fitzsimons), 157 Strangford Rd, BT30 7JZ.
☎ (01396) 612583.
B&B s£16 d£30.
Rooms 3, ensuite 1. Open all year ex Christmas

Hillside

(Mr & Mrs Murray), 62 Scotch St, BT30 6AN.
☎ (01396) 613134.
B&B s£15 d£32. Rooms 3, ensuite 1.
Open all year ex Christmas.

Pheasants' Hill

(Mrs J Bailey), 37 Killyleagh Rd, BT30 9BL.
☎ & fax (01396) 617246.
B&B s£22 d£38. Rooms 2. Dinner £16.
Last orders 2100 hrs. Open all year.

Rosebank Country House

(Ms P Forsythe), 108 Ballydugan Rd, BT30 8HF.
☎ (01396) 617021.
B&B s£20 d£34. Rooms 3, ensuite 2.
High tea £7. Dinner £11. Open all year.

Troutbeck

(Mrs R Wright), 38 Cargagh Rd, Annacloy,
BT30 9AG.
☎ (01396) 830894.
B&B s£15 d£30. Rooms 3. Open all year.

Tyrella House

(Mr & Mrs Corbett), Clanmaghery Rd, Tyrella,
BT30 8SU.
☎ & fax (01396) 851422.
B&B s£42.50 d£85. BB&M s£62.50 d£125.
Rooms 3, ensuite 2. Dinner £20.
Last orders 2030 hrs. Open Jan-Nov.

DROMORE

Bed & Breakfast

The Maggiminn

(Mr & Mrs Mark), 11 Bishops Well Rd, BT25 1ST.
☎ (01846) 693520.
B&B s£20 d£40. BB&M s£30 d£60.
Rooms 4, ensuite 1. High tea £6. Dinner £10.50.
Open all year.

Facilities are liable to change. Check prices when you book. Key to symbols is on inside back flap.

Sylvan Hill House
(Mr & Mrs Coburn), 76 Kilntown Rd, BT25 1HS.
☎ & fax (01846) 692321.
B&B s£25 d£48. BB&M s£40 d£70.
Rooms 3, ensuite 2. High tea £10. Dinner £15.
Last orders 1000 hrs. Open all year.

Win-Staff
(Mrs E Erwin), 45 Banbridge Rd, BT25 1NE.
☎ (01846) 692252.
B&B s£20 d£40. BB&M s£30 d£60.
Rooms 6, ensuite 3. Open all year ex Christmas.

DUNDRUM

Bed & Breakfast

Mourneview House
(Mrs S McKeating), off 16 Main St, BT33 0LU.
☎ (013967) 51457.
B&B s£15 d£28. Rooms 4. Open all year.

Roadhouse Inn
(Mr R Scott), 157 Main St, BT33 0LY.
☎ (013967) 51209.
B&B s£25 d£50. BB&M s£35 d£70.
Rooms 7, ensuite 7. High tea £6. Dinner £12.
Last orders 2130 hrs. Open all year.

GILFORD

Bed & Breakfast

Mount Pleasant
(Mrs M Buller), 38 Banbridge Rd, BT63 6DJ.
☎ & fax (01762) 831522.
B&B s£15 d£28. Rooms 4. Open all year.

GREYABBEY

Bed & Breakfast

Brimar
(Mrs M Dixon), 4 Cardy Rd, BT22 2LS.
☎ & fax (012477) 88681.
B&B s£25 d£50. Rooms 5, ensuite 5.
Open all year.

Mervue
(Mrs A Heron), 28 Portaferry Rd, BT22 2RX.
☎ (012477) 88619.
B&B s£17.50 d£35. Rooms 3, ensuite 3.
Open all year.

Woodview Farm
(Mrs A Carson), 8 Ballywalter Rd, BT22 2PD.
☎ (012477) 88242.
B&B s£15 d£28. Rooms 2. Open all year.

B&B = bed and breakfast   s = single   d = double   BB&M = bed, breakfast & evening meal

GROOMSPORT

Hotel

Groomsport House Hotel **
12 Donaghadee Rd, BT19 2LG.
☎ (01247) 270449. Fax 455332.
B&B s£55 d£75. Rooms 16, ensuite 16.
Dinner £14.95. Last orders 2130 hrs.
Open all year.

Bed & Breakfast

Islet Hill
(Mr & Mrs Mayne), 21 Bangor Rd, BT19 6JF.
☎ (01247) 464435.
B&B s£17.50 d£35. Rooms 2, ensuite 2.
Open all year.

HELEN'S BAY

Bed & Breakfast

Carrig-Gorm
(Mrs E Eves), 27 Bridge Rd, BT19 1TS.
☎ (01247) 853680.
B&B s£22 d£54. Rooms 3, ensuite 1.
Open all year ex Christmas.

HILLSBOROUGH

Hotel

White Gables Hotel ***
14 Dromore Rd, BT26 6HS.
☎ (01846) 682755. Fax 689532.
B&B s£79.50 d£100. Rooms 33, ensuite 33.
Dinner £19.75. Last orders 2115 hrs.
Open all year.

Bed & Breakfast

Avoca Lodge
(Mrs M McKeag), 53 Dromore Rd, BT26 6HU.
☎ (01846) 682343.
B&B s£18.50 d£37. Rooms 1. Open all year.

Cashel-Eanen
(Mrs M Shannon), 26 Comber Rd, BT26 6LN.
☎ & fax (01846) 682380.
B&B s£22 d£40. Rooms 2, ensuite 1. Open all year.

Churchview Farm
(Mrs M Hill), 46 Ballyworfy Rd, BT26 6LR.
☎ (01846) 682219. Fax 689820.
B&B s£25 d£40. Rooms 3. Open all year.

Fortwilliam House
(Mrs M Dunlop), 210 Ballynahinch Rd, BT26 6BH.
☎ (01846) 682255/683401. Fax 689608.
B&B s£30 d£50. Rooms 3, ensuite 3.
Open all year.

Facilities are liable to change. Check prices when you book. Key to symbols is on inside back flap.

Growell House

(Mrs E Moorehead), 207 Dromara Rd, BT26 6QW.
☎ (01238) 532271.
B&B s£15 d£30. Rooms 2. Open all year.

🅿 ❄ ♣ 🎦 ✄

HILLTOWN

Guesthouse

Mountain Pass   (U)
(Mrs C Devlin), 49 Sandbank Rd, Leitrim,
BT34 5XS.
☎ & fax (018206) 38002.
B&B s£20 d£34. BB&M s£30 d£54.
Rooms 3, ensuite 2. High tea £7.50. Dinner £10.
Last orders 1900 hrs. Open all year.

🅿 ❄ ♣ 🌿 🐎 🎦 ✄ 🎣 ⚑ ∪ △ 🎿 🏛

HOLYWOOD

Guesthouses

Ardshane Country House   (A)
5 Bangor Rd, BT18 0NU.
☎ (01232) 422044. Fax 427506.
B&B s£60 d£70. Rooms 8, ensuite 8.
Dinner £17.50. Last orders 2000 hrs.
Open all year.

🆃 🅿 🏠 ❄ 🌿 🐎 🅾 🐕 🎦 🖥 🕻 ✄ 🎿 🏛

Rayanne House   (A)
60 Demesne Rd, BT18 9EX.
☎ & fax (01232) 425859.
B&B s£67.50 d£90. Rooms 6, ensuite 6. Dinner £25.
Last orders 2100 hrs. Open all year.

🆃 🅿 🏠 ❄ ♣ 🌿 🐎 🅾 🎦 🖥 ✄ 🎣 ⚑ ∪ △ 🎿 🏛

Bed & Breakfast

Altona House
(Mr & Mrs Donaldson), 69 Church Rd, BT18 9BX.
☎ & fax (01232) 422179.
B&B s£30 d£60. Rooms 9, ensuite 4.
Open all year.

🅿 ❄ 🌿 🐎 🎦 🖥 ✄ 🎣 ⚑ 🎿 🏛

Carnwood House
(Mrs J Foster), 85 Victoria Rd, BT18 9BG.
☎ & fax (01232) 421745.
B&B s£30 d£45. Rooms 2, ensuite 2.
Open Jan-Nov.

🅿 🏠 ❄ 🌿 🐎 🅾 🎦 🖥 ✄ ⚫ 🎣 ⚑ 🎿

Number Two
(Mrs J Walker), 2 Victoria Rd, BT18 6BA.
☎ & fax (01232) 422662.
B&B s£30 d£47. Rooms 3, ensuite 3.
Open all year.

🆃 🅿 🌿 🐎 🎦 🖥 🎿 🏛

KILKEEL

Hotels

Kilmorey Arms Hotel   **
41 Greencastle St, BT34 4BH.
☎ (016937) 62220. Fax 65399.
B&B s£32 d£52. Rooms 26, ensuite 26.
High tea £6. Dinner £6. Last orders 2100 hrs.
Open all year.

🅿 🏠 ❄ 🌿 ‼ 🐎 🔲 🅾 🐕 🎦 🖥 🕻 ✄ 🎣 ⚑
∪ 🎿 🎯 🏛

Unclassified Hotel
Cranfield House Hotel, 57 Cranfield Rd, BT34 4LJ.
☎ *(016937) 62327.*

B&B = bed and breakfast   s = single   d = double   BB&M = bed, breakfast & evening meal

Guesthouses

Morne Abbey   (B)
16 Greencastle Rd, BT34 4DE.
☎ (016937) 62426.
B&B s£17.50 d£35. BB&M s£29 d£58.
Rooms 5, ensuite 3. Dinner £10.50.
Open April-Sept.
Off B27, ½m from Kilkeel

🆃 🅿 ✿ ♣ � ☡ 🎠 ▥ ⊬ ⊦

Wyncrest   (A)
30 Main Rd, BT34 4NU.
☎ & fax (016937) 63012/65988.
B&B d£42. BB&M d£70. Rooms 6, ensuite 4.
Dinner £14. Open April-Oct.
On A2, 3m NE of Kilkeel

🆃 🅿 ✿ ♣ � ☡ 🎠 ▥ 🖵 ⊬ ⊦ ∪ 🈺

Bed & Breakfast

An Caiseal
(Ms M O'Hare), 17A Leestone Rd, BT34 4NW.
☎ (016937) 65211.
B&B s£17 d£34. Rooms 2.
Open April-Oct.

🅿 ✿ ♣ � ☡ ⊙ᴬᴾ ▥ ⊬

Barnescroft
(Mrs H Barnes), 37 Dunaval Rd, Ballyardel,
BT34 4JT.
☎ (016937) 64519.
B&B s£16.50 d£33. BB&M s£26 d£52.
Rooms 3, ensuite 3. Dinner £9.50. Open all year.

🆃 🅿 ✿ ♣ � ☡ ▥ ⊬ ⊦ ☺

Bayview
(Ms S Poland), 92 Benagh Rd, BT34 4SJ.
☎ (016937) 62906.
B&B s£15 d£30. Rooms 2. Open all year.

🅿 ✿ ♣ � ☡ ⊙ᴬᴾ ▥ ⊬ ♪ ⊦ ∪ ⊿ ⚓ 🈺

Carginagh Lodge
(Mrs S McDowell-Veitch), 195 Carginagh Rd,
BT34 4QA.
☎ (016937) 62085.
B&B s£15.50 d£31. Rooms 3. Dinner £5.
Open all year.
Off A2, 3¼m from Kilkeel

🅿 ✿ ♣ � ☡ 🐎 ▥ 🖵 ⊬ ♪ ⊦ ∪ ⚓

Edenville
(Ms M Morris), 77a Benagh Rd, BT34 4SJ.
☎ (016937) 64296.
B&B s£14 d£20. Rooms 2. Open all year.

🅿 ✿ ♣ � ☡ ▥ 🖵 ⊬ ♪ ⊦ ☺

Heath Hall
(Mrs M McGlue), 160 Moyad Rd, BT34 4HJ.
☎ (016937) 62612.
B&B s£17 d£34. Rooms 3, ensuite 1.
Open all year ex Christmas.
On B27, ½m N of Kilkeel

🆃 🅿 ✿ ♣ � ☡ ⊙ᴬᴾ ▥ 🖵 ☏ ⊬ ⚈ ♪ ∪

Hill View House
(Mrs M Trainor), 18 Bog Rd, Attical, BT34 4HT.
☎ (016937) 64269.
B&B s£18 d£32. BB&M s£26 d£40.
Rooms 3, ensuite 2. High tea £7. Dinner £8.
Open all year ex Christmas.
Off B27, 4m NW of Kilkeel

🆃 🅿 ✿ ♣ � ☡ ⊙ᴬᴾ ▥ 🖵 ⊬ ♪ ⊦ ∪ ✓
⚓ ⊿ 🐾 🈺

Homesyde
(Mrs E Haugh), 7 Shandon Drive, BT34 4DF.
☎ (016937) 62676.
B&B s£14 d£28. Rooms 2. Open all year.

🅿 ✿ ♣ � ☡ ⊙ᴬᴾ ▥ 🖵 ⊬ ⊦ ∪

Facilities are liable to change. Check prices when you book. Key to symbols is on inside back flap.

Iona

(Mrs Y Fitzpatrick), 161 Newcastle Rd, BT34 4NN.
☎ (016937) 62586.
B&B s£20 d£33. Rooms 3. Open all year.

Mill Cottage

(Mr & Mrs Donnan), 65 Tullyframe Rd, BT34 1ZY.
☎ (016937) 65204.
B&B s£17 d£28. Rooms 2. Open all year.

Mourne Croft

(Mrs A McConnell), 2 Council Rd, BT34 4ND.
☎ (016937) 62016.
B&B s£14 d£28. Rooms 4. Open all year.

Rozel

(Mrs A Orr), 182 Newry Rd, BT34 4JZ.
☎ (016937) 62132.
B&B s£14 d£28. Rooms 2. Open all year.

Sharon Farm House

(Mrs M Bingham), 6 Ballykeel Rd, Ballymartin,
BT34 4PL.
☎ (016937) 62521.
B&B s£18 d£31. Rooms 3. Open all year.

KILLINCHY

Bed & Breakfast

Barnageeha

(Mr & Mrs Crawford), 90 Ardmillan Rd, BT23 6QN.
☎ (01238) 541011.
B&B s£22.50 d£45. BB&M s£40 d£80.
Rooms 5, ensuite 5. Dinner £20.
Last orders 2000 hrs. Open all year.

Burren Cottage

(Mrs A Gordon), 19 Main St, BT23 6PN.
☎ (01238) 541475.
B&B s£18.50 d£37. Rooms 3, ensuite 2.
Open all year.

Craigeden

(Mrs P Jackson), 33 Craigaruskey Rd, BT23 6QS.
☎ (01238) 541005.
B&B s£18.50 d£37. Rooms 3, ensuite 1.
Open all year.

KILLYLEAGH

Guesthouse

Dufferin Arms Coaching Inn   (A)

35 High St, BT30 9QF.
☎ (01396) 828229. Fax 828755.
B&B s£37.50 d£65. BB&M s£54.50 d£99.
Rooms 7, ensuite 7. High tea £7. Dinner £17.
Last orders 2130 hrs. Open all year.

KIRCUBBIN

Bed & Breakfast

Lough View

(Mrs E McCullough), 31 Rowreagh Rd, BT22 1AS.
☎ (012477) 38324. Fax 38708.
B&B s£20 d£40. Rooms 3, ensuite 2.
Open all year.

B&B = bed and breakfast   s = single   d = double   BB&M = bed, breakfast & evening meal

MILLISLE

Bed & Breakfast

Mount Erin House
(Mr R McBride), 46 Ballywalter Rd, BT22 2HS.
☎ (01247) 861979.
B&B s£15 d£30. Rooms 2. Open all year.

Seaspray
(Mrs H Morrison), 221 Ballywalter Rd, BT22 2LY.
☎ (01247) 862389.
B&B s£16 d£32. Rooms 2.
Open all year ex Christmas.

Wolf Island Farm
(Ms A Robinson), 20 School Rd, BT22 2DZ.
☎ (01247) 861372.
B&B s£17 d£34. Rooms 2.
Open all year.

MOIRA

Bed & Breakfast

Albany House
(Mr & Mrs Irwin), 35 Main St, BT67 0LQ.
☎ (01846) 612211.
B&B s£25 d£40. Rooms 5, ensuite 5.
Open all year.

NEWCASTLE

Hotels

Burrendale Hotel & Country Club   ***
51 Castlewellan Rd, BT33 0JY.
☎ (013967) 22599. Fax 22328.
B&B s£65 d£100. BB&M s£80 d£130.
Rooms 68, ensuite 68. High tea £9. Dinner £19.
Last orders 2130 hrs. Open all year.

Slieve Donard Hotel   ***
Downs Rd, BT33 0AH.
☎ (013967) 23681. Fax 24830.
B&B s£88 d£130. Rooms 130, ensuite 130.
Dinner £19. Last orders 2130 hrs.
Open all year.

Enniskeen House Hotel   **
98 Bryansford Rd, BT33 0LF.
☎ (013967) 22392. Fax 24084.
B&B s£47 d£78. BB&M s£60 d£104.
Rooms 12, ensuite 12. High tea £7. Dinner £15.
Last orders 2030 hrs. Open March-Nov.

Avoca Hotel   *
93 Central Promenade, BT33 0HH.
☎ (013967) 22253.
B&B s£23 d£46. BB&M s£31 d£62.
Rooms 16, ensuite 6. High tea £7. Dinner £8.
Last orders 2100 hrs. Open all year.

Facilities are liable to change. Check prices when you book. Key to symbols is on inside back flap.

Brook Cottage Hotel *
58 Bryansford Rd, BT33 0LD.
☎ (013967) 22204/23508. Fax 22193.
B&B s£42.50 d£68. BB&M d£98.
Rooms 9, ensuite 7. High tea £7.50. Dinner £15.
Last orders 2100 hrs. Open all year.

Donard Hotel *
27 Main St, BT33 0AD.
☎ (013967) 22203/22501. Fax 23970.
B&B s£40 d£60. BB&M s£50 d£80.
Rooms 14, ensuite 14. High tea £7.50. Dinner £12.95.
Last orders 2100 hrs. Open April-Dec.

Unclassified Hotels
Mariner Hotel, 59 Central Promenade,
BT33 0HH. ☎ *(013967) 23473.*
McGlennon's Hotel, 59 Main St, BT33 0AE.
☎ *(013967) 22415.*

Guesthouses

Arundel Guest House (B)
23 Bryansford Rd, BT33 0AX.
☎ (013967) 22232.
B&B s£16 d£32. BB&M s£22.50 d£45. Rooms 4.
Dinner £7. Last orders 1730 hrs. Open all year.

Briers Country House (A)
39 Middle Tollymore Rd, BT33 0JJ.
☎ & fax (013967) 24347.
B&B s£35 d£50. BB&M s£45 d£70.
Rooms 9, ensuite 9. High tea £8. Dinner £12.
Last orders 2100 hrs. Open all year.
Off B180, ¼ m from forest park

Harbour House (B)
4 South Promenade, Kilkeel Rd, BT33 0EX.
☎ (013967) 23445/23535.
B&B s£25 d£40. Rooms 4, ensuite 4.
Last orders 2200 hrs. Open all year.

Bed & Breakfast

Arranmore
(Mrs A Wiggins), 4 Tullybrannigan Rd, BT33 0DU.
☎ (013967) 23525.
B&B d£26. Rooms 2. Open all year.

Ashmount
(Mr & Mrs Biggerstaff), 19 Bryansford Rd, BT33 0HJ.
☎ (013967) 25074.
B&B s£22 d£35. Rooms 3, ensuite 3.
High tea £10. Dinner £10.
Last orders 1800 hrs. Open all year.

Ashvale
(Mrs E Biggerstaff), 27 Bryansford Rd, BT33 0HJ.
☎ (013967) 22689.
B&B s£22 d£35. Rooms 3.
High tea £10. Dinner £10.
Last orders 1800 hrs. Open all year.

Facilities are liable to change. Check prices when you book. Key to symbols is on inside back flap.

Beach House

(Mrs M Macauley), 22 Downs Rd, BT33 0AG.
☎ (013967) 22345.
B&B s£22 d£35. BB&M s£32 d£55.
Rooms 3, ensuite 3. Dinner £10.
Last orders 1900 hrs. Open all year.

Brennans

(Ms H Brennan), 69 Bryansford Ave, BT33 0LG.
☎ (013967) 25198. Mobile 07050 135242.
B&B s£15 d£30. Rooms 3. Open all year.

Castle Corrigs House

(Mr & Mrs Morgan), 41 Castlewellan Rd, BT33 0JY.
☎ & fax (013967) 26986.
B&B s£20 d£30. Rooms 10, ensuite 9.
Open all year.

Castlebridge House

(Mrs K Lynch), 2 Central Promenade, BT33 0AB.
☎ (013967) 23209.
B&B s£14 d£28. Rooms 5. Open all year.

Cherry Villa

(Mrs G Keown), 12 Bryansford Gardens, BT33 0EQ.
☎ (013967) 24128.
B&B s£22 d£36. Rooms 3, ensuite 2. Open all year.

Drumrawn House

(Mrs M Kelly), Central Promenade, BT33 0EU.
☎ (013967) 26847.
B&B s£16.50 d£33. Rooms 2. Open all year.

Fair Winds

(Mr J McCracken), 86 Bryansford Rd, BT33 0LE.
☎ (013967) 26839.
B&B s£16 d£32. Rooms 2. Open April-Sept.

Fern View

(Mrs E O'Hare), 101 Tullybrannigan Rd, BT33 0PW.
☎ (013967) 23949.
B&B s£18 d£30. Rooms 3, ensuite 3.
Open April-Nov.

Fountainville House

(Mr & Mrs Biggerstaff), 103 Central Promenade,
BT33 0HH.
☎ (013967) 25074.
B&B s£22 d£32. High tea £10. Dinner £10.
Rooms 9, ensuite 1. Open all year.

Glenada Holiday & Conference Centre

29 South Promenade, BT33 0EX.
☎ (013967) 22402. Fax 26227.
B&B s£28 d£44. BB&M s£35 d£58.
Rooms 27, ensuite 27. High tea £7. Dinner £10.
Open all year.

Glenside Farmhouse

(Mrs M Murray), 136 Tullybrannigan Rd, BT33 0PW.
☎ (013967) 22628.
B&B s£11 d£22. Rooms 3. Open all year.

Golflinks House

(Mrs E McPolin), 109 Dundrum Rd, BT33 0LN.
☎ (013967) 22054.
B&B s£14 d£28. Rooms 10, ensuite 9.
Dinner £10. Last orders 1800 hrs. Open all year.

B&B = bed and breakfast   s = single   d = double   BB&M = bed, breakfast & evening meal

Grasmere
(Mrs E McCormick), 16 Marguerite Park, BT33 0PE.
☎ (013967) 26801.
B&B s£16 d£32. Rooms 2. Open all year.

Homeleigh
(Mrs M McBride), 7 Slievemoyne Park, BT33 0JD.
☎ (013967) 22305.
B&B s£15 d£28. Rooms 3. Open March-Dec.

Innisfree House
(Mrs M Dornan), 7 Dundrum Rd, BT33 0BG.
☎ (013967) 23303.
B&B s£20 d£30. Rooms 3. Open April-Sept.

Kilbroney
(Miss B McNulty), 7 Braemar Avenue, BT33 0BY.
☎ (013967) 22779.
B&B s£20 d£30. Rooms 2.
Open all year ex Christmas.

Marine Villa
(Mrs E Barr), 151 Central Promenade, BT33 0EU.
☎ (013967) 25030.
B&B s£17 d£34. Rooms 3.
Open all year ex Christmas.

Moneycara
(Mrs N Ritchie), 11 Sunningdale Park, Tullybrannigan Rd, BT33 0GL.
☎ (013967) 22586.
B&B s£15 d£26. Rooms 2. Open April-Sept.

Number Ten
(Mrs K Knight), 10 Westland Avenue, BT33 0BZ .
☎ (013967) 23851.
B&B s£16 d£34. Rooms 2. Open all year.

Oakleigh House
(Mrs P Horrox), 30 Middle Tollymore Rd, BT33 0JJ .
☎ (013967) 23353.
B&B s£18 d£36. Rooms 3. Open all year.

Ocean Breeze
(Mrs C McLoughlin), 5 Cedar Heights, Bryansford, BT33 0PJ.
☎ (013967) 23406.
B&B s£20 d£34. Rooms 2, ensuite 2.
Open April-Sept.

Old Town Farm
(Mrs W Annett), 25 Corrigs Rd, BT33 0JZ.
☎ & fax (013967) 22740.
B&B s£18 d£36. Rooms 3, ensuite 1.
Open May-Sept.

Orchard Brae
(Mrs B Malone), 29 Tollymore Rd, BT33 0JN.
☎ (013967) 25135.
B&B s£20 d£33. Rooms 2, ensuite 2.
Open all year.

Quay Lodge
(Mrs P Deery), 31 South Promenade, BT33 0EX.
☎ (013967) 23054.
B&B s£20 d£30. Rooms 2. Open April-Oct.

Facilities are liable to change. Check prices when you book. Key to symbols is on inside back flap.

135

Rock Cottage
(Mr & Mrs Murphy), 117 Ballagh Rd, BT33 0LB.
☎ (013967) 23661.
B&B s£16 d£32. Rooms 2. Open all year.

Savoy House
(Mr & Mrs Keogh), 20 Downs Rd, BT33 0AG.
☎ & fax (013967) 22513.
B&B s£23 d£34. Rooms 8. Open May-Oct.

Sundial Cottage
(Miss E Wallace), 7 Rowley Meadows, BT33 0RW.
☎ & fax (013967) 26917.
B&B s£15 d£30. Rooms 2. Open all year.

12 Linkside Park
(Mrs M Lavery), Dundrum Rd, BT33 0LR.
☎ (013967) 23638.
B&B s£15 d£28. Rooms 2. Open Jan-Nov.

NEWRY

Hotels

Mourne Country Hotel **
52 Belfast Rd, BT34 1TR.
☎ (01693) 67922. Fax 60896.
B&B s£49.50 d£65. Rooms 43, ensuite 43.
High tea £10.95. Dinner £15.
Last orders 2130 hrs. Open all year.

Unclassified Hotel
Canal Court Hotel, Merchants Quay, BT35.
☎ *(01693) 251234. Fax 251177.*

Guesthouses

Ashton House (B)
37 Omeath Rd, Fathom Line, BT35 8QN.
☎ (01693) 62120.
B&B s£20 d£35. BB&M s£30 d£55.
Rooms 6, ensuite 6. Dinner £10.
Last orders 2130 hrs. Open all year.

Hillside (A)
1 Rock Rd, BT34 1PL.
☎ (01693) 65484/61430. Fax 65484.
B&B s£19 d£34. BB&M s£26 d£48.
Rooms 5, ensuite 3. Dinner £7.
Last orders 2000 hrs. Open all year.

Bed & Breakfast

Ard-Mhuire House
(Mrs M McKeown), 27 Carrickasticken Rd,
Forkhill, BT35 9RJ.
☎ (01693) 888316.
B&B s£13.50 d£27. BB&M s£20 d£40.
Rooms 4. High tea £7. Dinner £8.50.
Open March-Oct.

Barratoore
(Mrs M Campbell), 15 Forkhill Rd, Mullaghbawn.
BT35 9XH.
☎ (01693) 888432.
B&B s£15 d£30. Rooms 1. High tea £8.
Open all year.

B&B = bed and breakfast   s = single   d = double   BB&M = bed, breakfast & evening meal

Black Gap Farm
(Mrs M McIlroy), 26 Divernagh Rd,
Bessbrook, BT35 7BW.
☎ (01693) 830358.
B&B s£17 d£34. Rooms 3. Open all year.

Cara House
(Mrs L Magee), 22 Laurel Grove, BT34 1TP.
☎ (01693) 250587.
B&B s£16 d£32. Rooms 3. Open all year.

Carrow House
(Mrs M Walsh), 22 Newtown Rd,
Belleeks, BT35 7PL.
☎ (01693) 878182.
B&B s£12.50 d£25. Rooms 3. Open all year.

Creag Na N Aitinne
(Mr M Connolly), 56A Upper Fathom Rd,
BT35 8WY.
☎ & fax (01693) 848740.
B&B s£15 d£30. Rooms 2, ensuite 2.
Open all year.

Danesfort
(Mrs L Lonergan), 101 Forkhill Rd, Ayallogue Hill,
BT35 8RA.
☎ (01693) 848311.
B&B d£32. Rooms 2, ensuite 1. Open all year.

Deerpark
(Mrs J Thompson), 177 Tandragee Rd,
Drumbanagher, BT35 6LP.
☎ (01693) 821409.
B&B s£17 d£34. Rooms 3, ensuite 1.
Open all year.

Drumconrath
(Mrs A Magennis), 28 Ballymacdermot Rd,
BT35 8NA.
☎ (01693) 63508.
B&B s£15 d£30. BB&M s£21 d£42. Rooms 3.
High tea £5. Dinner £6.
Last orders 2000 hrs. Open all year.

Fortview Farm
(Mrs R Simpson), 16 Desert Rd, Mayobridge,
BT34 2JQ.
☎ & fax (01693) 851310.
B&B s£15 d£33. BB&M s£24 d£50.
Rooms 2, ensuite 1. High tea £8. Dinner £10.
Last orders 1800 hrs. Open all year.

Green Acre
(Mrs T Guthrie), 8 Church Avenue, BT34 1DY.
☎ & fax (01693) 251479.
B&B s£14 d£30. Rooms 2, ensuite 1.
Dinner £8. Last orders 1800 hrs. Open all year.

Green Vale
(Mrs L McCreesh), 141 Longfield Rd, Forkhill,
BT35 9SD.
☎ (01693) 888314.
B&B s£12.50 d£25. Rooms 2. Open all year.

Lakeview
(Mr & Mrs O'Neill), 34 Church Rd, Forkhill,
BT35 9SX.
☎ (01693) 888382.
B&B s£18 d£36. Rooms 2, ensuite 1.
Open all year.

Facilities are liable to change. Check prices when you book. Key to symbols is on inside back flap.

Lar Na Tuaithe
(Mr & Mrs Rafferty), 89 Maphoner Rd,
Mullaghbawn, BT35 9TR.
☎ (01693) 888897.
B&B s£18 d£36. BB&M s£25 d£50.
Rooms 2, ensuite 2. High tea £6. Dinner £7.
Last orders 2100 hrs. Open all year.

Lavengro
(Mrs A O'Rourke), 5 Liska Rd, Cloughoge, BT35 8NH.
☎ (01693) 63773.
B&B s£16 d£32. Dinner £19. Rooms 3.
Open all year.

Marymount
(Mr & Mrs O'Hare), Windsor Avenue, BT34 1EG.
☎ (01693) 61099.
B&B s£18 d£36. Rooms 3, ensuite 1.
Open all year.

Millvale House
(Mrs C Farrell), 8 Millvale Rd, BT35 7LP.
☎ (01693) 63789. Mobile 0370 728073.
B&B s£18.50 d£34. BB&M s£25 d£46. Rooms 4.
High tea £6.50. Dinner £6.50. Open all year.

Rathcraggan
(Mrs M McVicker), 5 Corgary Rd, BT34 1ST.
☎ (01693) 66133. Fax 250995.
B&B s£15 d£35. Rooms 2, ensuite 1.
Open all year.

Slieve Gullion House
(Mr & Mrs Larkin), 1 Dromintee Rd, Meigh,
Killevy, BT35 8JJ.
☎ (01693) 848225.
B&B s£17 d£34. Rooms 2, ensuite 2.
Open all year.

Woodcroft
(Ms E Baxter), 8 Warren Hill, BT34 2PH.
☎ (01693) 67133.
B&B s£15 d£30. Rooms 3. Open all year.

NEWTOWNARDS

Hotel

Strangford Arms Hotel ***
92 Church St, BT23 4AL.
☎ (01247) 814141. Fax 818846.
B&B s£70 d£80. BB&M s£85 d£110.
Rooms 40, ensuite 40. Dinner £15.
Last orders 2130 hrs. Open all year.

Guesthouse

Greenacres (A)
5 Manse Rd, BT23 4TP.
☎ (01247) 816193.
B&B s£22 d£36. BB&M s£34.50 d£61.
Rooms 3, ensuite 3. Dinner £12.50.
Last orders 1830 hrs. Open all year.
Off A20, ¼ m from Newtownards

B&B = bed and breakfast   s = single   d = double   BB&M = bed, breakfast & evening meal

Bed & Breakfast

Ard Cuan
(Mrs V Kerr), 3 Manse Rd, BT23 4TP.
☎ (01247) 811302.
B&B s£16 d£32. Rooms 2. Open all year.

Ballycastle House
(Mrs M Deering), 20 Mountstewart Rd, BT22 2AL.
☎ & fax (012477) 88357.
B&B s£20 d£40. Rooms 3, ensuite 3.
Open all year ex Christmas.
5m SE of Newtownards

Ballynester House
(Mrs G Bailie), 1a Cardy Rd, Greyabbey,
BT22 2LS.
☎ & fax (012477) 88386.
B&B s£23 d£40. BB&M s£31.50 d£57.
Rooms 3, ensuite 2.
Dinner £8.50. Last orders 1200 hrs. Open all year.

Beech Hill Country House
(Ms V Brann), 23 Ballymoney Rd, Craigantlet,
BT23 4TG.
☎ & fax (01232) 425892.
B&B s£35 d£60. Rooms 3, ensuite 3.
Open all year.

Beechhill Farm
(Mrs J McKee), 10 Loughries Rd, BT23 3RN.
☎ (01247) 818404. Fax 812820.
B&B s£17 d£34. BB&M s£29 d£58.
Rooms 3. High tea £9. Dinner £12.
Last orders 1830 hrs. Open all year.
Off A20, 4m from Newtownards

Cuan Chalet
(Mrs W Cochrane), 41 Milecross Rd, BT23 4SR.
☎ (01247) 812302.
B&B s£15 d£30. BB&M s£25 d£50. Rooms 2.
Dinner £10. Open all year.
Off A20, ¼m W of town centre

Drumcree House
(Mrs E Forde), 18a Ballyblack Rd East, BT22 2AB.
☎ (01247) 862198.
B&B s£19.50 d£39. Rooms 3, ensuite 2.
Open all year.

Edenvale Country House
(Mrs D Whyte), 130 Portaferry Rd, BT22 2AH.
☎ (01247) 814881. Fax 826192.
B&B s£30 d£50. Rooms 3, ensuite 3.
Open all year.

Ernsdale
(Mrs D McCullagh), 120 Mountstewart Rd,
Carrowdore, BT22 2ES.
☎ (01247) 861208.
B&B s£15 d£30. Rooms 3, ensuite 1.
Open March-Nov.
5½m SE of Newtownards

17 Ballyrogan Rd
(Mrs A McKibbin), BT23 4ST.
☎ (01247) 811693.
B&B s£17 d£34. Rooms 2. Open all year.

Facilities are liable to change. Check prices when you book. Key to symbols is on inside back flap.

PORTAFERRY

Hotel

Portaferry Hotel   ***
10 The Strand, BT22 1PE.
☎ (012477) 28231. Fax 28999.
B&B s£55 d£90. BB&M s£80 d£140.
Rooms 14, ensuite 14.
Dinner £25. Last orders 2100 hrs. Open all year.

🇹 🅿 🏠 ♣ 🎿 🍽 🐕 🛏 ⬛ 🔲 📞 ✂ 🧦 🎣 🏠 ∪ ✓
🔺 🚬 🐾 💷

Guesthouse

The Narrows   (U)
8 Shore Rd, BT22 1JY.
☎ (012477) 28148. Fax 28105.
B&B s£34 d£58. BB&M s£49 d£89.
Rooms 13, ensuite 13. High tea £8. Dinner £16.
Last orders 2030 hrs. Open all year.

🇹 🅿 🏠 ✿ 🎿 🐕 🛏 📺 OAP 🛍 🛏 ⬛ 🔲 📞 ✂ ✉ 🎣 🛥
∪ 🔺 🍸 🕐 🐾 💷

Bed & Breakfast

Lough Cowey Lodge
(Mrs F Taggart), 9 Lough Cowey Rd, BT22 1PJ.
☎ (012477) 28263.
B&B s£17.50 d£30. Rooms 2. Open all year.

🇹 🅿 ✿ ♣ 🎿 🐕 🛏 ✂ 🎣 🏠 ∪ ✓ 🔺 🚬

St Clares
(Ms M Ritchie), 8 Marian Way, BT22 1QY.
☎ (012477) 28719. Mobile 0410 600573.
B&B s£20 d£35. Rooms 2. Open all year.

✿ ♣ 🐕 🛏 🔲 ✂ 🎣 🏠 ∪ 🔺 🐾

22 The Square
(Mr & Mrs Adair), BT22 1LW.
☎ (012477) 28412.
B&B s£15 d£29. Rooms 3, ensuite 2.
Open all year.

🐕 🛏 ✂ 🎣 🏠 🔺 🐾

RATHFRILAND

Guesthouse

Rath Glen Villa   (A)
7 Hilltown Rd, BT34 5NA.
☎ (018206) 38090.
B&B s£17 d£30. BB&M s£26 d£46.
Rooms 4, ensuite 1. Open April-Oct.

🇹 🅿 ✿ ♣ 🎿 🐕 OAP 🛍 ✂ 🎣 🛥 🔺 🚬

Bed & Breakfast

Ruellen
(Mrs M Bickerstaff), 59 Dromore St, BT34 5LU.
☎ (018206) 30761.
B&B s£14 d£28. BB&M s£22 d£44. Rooms 2.
Dinner £8. Last orders 1830 hrs. Open all year.

🅿 🏠 ✿ ♣ 🎿 🐕 OAP 🛍 ✂

ROSTREVOR

Bed & Breakfast

Fir Trees
(Mr & Mrs Donnan), 16 Killowen Old Rd,
BT34 3AD.
☎ (016937) 38602.
B&B s£17 d£34. Rooms 3, ensuite 1.
Open all year.

🅿 ✿ ♣ 🎿 🐕 🛍 ✂ 🔍 🎣 ∪ 🚬 🐾

B&B = bed and breakfast   s = single   d = double   BB&M = bed, breakfast & evening meal

Forestbrook House

(Mrs E Henshaw), 11 Forestbrook Rd, BT34 3BT.
☎ (016937) 38105.
B&B s£17 d£34. BB&M s£25 d£50. Rooms 3.
Dinner £8. Last orders 1800 hrs. Open all year.

🅿 🏠 ✿ ♣ 🌣 🍴 🐕 🅳🅰🅿 ▥ 🖵 ✕ 🐾

Hillcrest Farmhouse

(Mrs M Murphy), 12 Kilfeaghan Rd,
Killowen, BT34 3AW.
☎ (016937) 38114.
B&B s£18 d£36. BB&M s£24 d£45.
Rooms 3, ensuite 2. Open March-Oct.

🆃 🅿 ✿ ♣ 🌣 🍴 🅳🅰🅿 ▥ 📞 ✕ 🎣 ⌐ ∪
✓ 🛆 🛫 🐾

SAINTFIELD

Bed & Breakfast

The Hill

(Mrs M Rice), 43 Peartree Rd, BT24 7JY.
☎ (01238) 511330.
B&B s£18 d£36. Rooms 4, ensuite 3.
Open March-Oct.

🅿 ✿ ♣ 🌣 🍴 ▥ ⌐

Marvilla

(Mrs D Ferguson), 162 Crossgar Rd, BT24 7JJ.
☎ & fax (01396) 830414.
B&B s£18 d£36. BB&M s£32 d£64.
Rooms 3, ensuite 1. Dinner £14.
Last orders 1900 hrs. Open all year.

🅿 ✿ ♣ 🌣 🍴 ▥ 🖵 ✕ 🎣 ⌐ ∪ ✓ 🛆 🛫 ⊞

SEAFORDE

Bed & Breakfast

Drumgooland House

(Mr & Mrs McLeigh), 29 Dunnanew Rd, BT30 8PJ.
☎ (01396) 811956. Fax 811265.
B&B s£20.50 d£39. BB&M s£35.50 d£69.
Rooms 3, ensuite 3. Dinner £15.
Last orders 2000 hrs. Open all year.

🆃 🅿 ✿ ♣ 🌣 🍴 🅳🅰🅿 ▥ 🖵 ✕ 🎣 ⌐ ∪
✓ 🛆 🛫 ⊞

STRANGFORD

Bed & Breakfast

Strangford Cottage

(Mrs M Thornton), 41 Castle St, BT30 7NF.
☎ & fax (01396) 881208.
B&B s£37.50 d£75. Rooms 2, ensuite 2.
Dinner £25. Open April-Sept.

🅿 🏠 ✿ ♣ 🌣 ▥ ✕ ⌐ ∪ ✓ 🛆 🐾

WARRENPOINT

Hotel

Unclassified Hotel
Carlingford Bay Hotel, 3 Osborne Promenade,
BT34 3NQ. ☎ *(016937) 73521.*

Guesthouses

Fernhill House   (B)

90 Clonallon Rd, BT34 3HQ.
☎ (016937) 72677.
B&B s£18.50 d£36. BB&M s£30 d£48.
Rooms 4, ensuite 4. Dinner £12. High tea £6.
Open all year.

🅿 ✿ ♣ 🌣 🍴 ▥ 🖵 ✕ 🎣 ⌐ ∪ 🛆 🛫

Facilities are liable to change. Check prices when you book. Key to symbols is on inside back flap.

Whistledown Inn   (U)

6 Seaview, BT34 3NH.
☎ (016937) 52697.
B&B s£20 d£40. BB&M s£30 d£60.
Rooms 5. High tea £15. Dinner £15.
Last orders 2200 hrs. Open all year ex Christmas.

Bed & Breakfast

Cloch Mor

(Mrs N Grant), 7 Cloughmore Terrace, BT34 3HP.
☎ & fax (016937) 53288.
B&B s£20 d£40. Rooms 5. Open all year.

Mariann's Place

(Mr & Mrs Cooper), 18 Upper Dromore Rd,
BT34 3PU.
☎ (016937) 52085. Fax 74306.
B&B d£30. BB&M d£47. Rooms 3. Dinner £8.50.
Last orders 1800 hrs. Open all year.

The Mournes

(Ms M Taaffe), 16 Seaview, BT34 3NJ.
☎ (01693) 772610.
B&B s£17.50 d£35. Rooms 3. Open all year.

Ryan's

(Mrs M Ryan), 19 Milltown St, Burren, BT34 3PS.
☎ & fax (016937) 72506.
B&B s£16 d£32. Rooms 3, ensuite 3. Dinner £8.
Open all year.

Summerhill House

(Mr & Mrs McPolin), 47 Summerhill, BT34 3JB.
☎ (016937) 52065.
B&B s£20 d£30. Rooms 3. Open all year.

The Victoria

(Mr & Mrs Dowdall), The Square, BT34 3LZ.
☎ (016937) 53687/53448.
B&B s£18 d£36. BB&M s£24 d£48. Rooms 4.
Dinner £6. Last orders 2030 hrs. Open all year.

6 Gt George's St

(Mrs J O'Hare), BT34 3NF
☎ (016937) 73265.
B&B s£14 d£28. Rooms 3. Open all year.

B&B = bed and breakfast   s = single   d = double   BB&M = bed, breakfast & evening meal

BALLINAMALLARD

Guesthouse

Jamestown Country House (U)
Magheracross, BT94 2JP.
☎ (01365) 388209. Fax 388322.
B&B s£25 d£50. BB&M s£45 d£90.
Rooms 3, ensuite 3. Dinner £20.
Last orders 1930 hrs. Open Jan-Nov.
1m NE of Ballinamallard

🄿 🏠 ✿ ♣ 🦵 ⌇ 🎑 ✂ 🔍 ⚲ 🔔 ⌒ ∪ ✓ ⚓ ⚡

Bed & Breakfast

The Arches
(Mr & Mrs Duncan), Mill Lane, BT94 2FY.
☎ (01365) 388352.
B&B s£16 d£32. Rooms 1. Open all year.

🄿 ✿ ♣ 🦵 ⎚ 🎑 ▭ 🔔 ∪ ⚓ ⚡

Bremar House
(Mrs M Keown), Whitehill, BT94 2ND.
☎ (01365) 388286.
B&B s£15 d£30. Rooms 2, ensuite 1.
Dinner £10. Last orders 1800 hrs.
Open all year.

🄿 🏠 ✿ ♣ 🦵 ⌇ ⍑ 🎑 ▭ ✂ 🔔 ⌒ ∪ ✓ ⚓ ⚡

Jeanville
(Mrs J McFarland), Goblusk, BT94 2LW.
☎ (01365) 388424.
B&B s£19 d£36. Rooms 2.
High tea £8.50. Dinner £10. Open all year.

🄿 ✿ ♣ 🦵 🎑 ▭ ✂ ⌒ ∪ ⚓

Rossfad House
(Mrs L Williams), Killadeas Rd, BT94 2LS.
☎ (01365) 388505.
B&B s£25 d£40. BB&M s£40 d£70.
Rooms 2, ensuite 2. High tea £10. Dinner £15.
Last orders 1000 hrs. Open March-Nov.

🅃 🄿 🏠 ✿ ♣ 🦵 ⌇ 🎑 ✂ 🔔 ⌒ ∪
✓ ⚐ ⚡ 🄯

Salona
(Mrs C Crooke), Enniskillen Rd, BT94 2ER.
☎ (01365) 388269.
B&B s£15 d£30. BB&M s£27 d£54. Rooms 3.
Dinner £12. Last orders 1900 hrs. Open all year.

🄿 ✿ ♣ 🎑 ▭ ✂ ⌒

BELCOO

Guesthouse

Corralea Forest Lodge (A)
Corralea, BT93 5DZ.
☎ (01365) 386325.
B&B s£24 d£38. BB&M s£36 d£62.
Rooms 4, ensuite 4. Dinner £12.
Open March-Oct.
2½m NW of Belcoo

🄿 ✿ ♣ 🦵 🎑 ▭ 🔔 ☗

Bed & Breakfast

Belcoo House
(Mrs K Sweeney), 31 Main St, BT93 5FB.
☎ (01365) 386304.
B&B s£14 d£28. Rooms 2. Open Jan-Nov.

♣ 🦵 ⌇ 🎑 ▭ ✂ ☗

Facilities are liable to change. Check prices when you book. Key to symbols is on inside back flap.

Bella Vista

(Mrs F Doherty), Cottage Drive, BT93 5EZ.
☎ (01365) 386469.
B&B s£22.50 d£35. Rooms 2, ensuite 2.
Dinner £10.50. Last orders 2100 hrs.
Open all year.

Bush Cottage

(Ms T McGovern), BT93 5EZ.
☎ (01365) 386242.
B&B s£17.50 d£30. Rooms 2. Open April-Sept.

Glann-N House

(Mrs B McGovern), Carrontree Mall, BT93 5GR.
☎ (01365) 386471.
B&B s£15 d£30. BB&M s£22 d£40.
Rooms 3. High tea £7. Dinner £10.
Last orders 2100 hrs. Open all year.

Riverside

(Mrs P Rasdale), Holywell, BT94 5DA.
☎ (01365) 386303.
B&B s£15 d£30. Rooms 2, ensuite 1.
Open all year.

BELLEEK

Hotel

Hotel Carlton   **

2 Main St, BT93 3FX.
☎ (013656) 58282. Fax 59005.
B&B s£45 d£70. BB&M s£59.95 d£99.90.
Rooms 19, ensuite 19. High tea £7. Dinner £14.95.
Last orders 2130 hrs. Open all year.

Guesthouses

Moohan's Fiddlestone   (U)

15 Main St, BT93 5XX.
☎ (013656) 58008.
B&B s£18 d£36. Rooms 5, ensuite 5.
Open all year.

Riverside House   (U)

601 Lough Shore Rd, Drumbadreevagh, BT93 3FT.
☎ & fax (013656) 58649.
B&B s£17 d£34. BB&M s£29 d£58.
Rooms 4, ensuite 4. Dinner £12.
Last orders 1700 hrs. Open April-Oct.

Bed & Breakfast

190 Garrison Rd

(Mrs C Mullin), Corry, BT93 3FU.
☎ (013656) 58588.
B&B s£15 d£30. Rooms 2, ensuite 2.
Open May-Sept.

BROOKEBOROUGH

Guesthouse

Colebrook Park   (U)

BT94 3BW.
☎ (01365) 531402. Fax 531686.
BB&M s£94 d£188. Rooms 10, ensuite 5.
Open all year.

B&B = bed and breakfast   s = single   d = double   BB&M = bed, breakfast & evening meal

Bed & Breakfast

Norfolk House
(Mrs E Norton), Killykeeran, BT94 4AQ.
☎ (013655) 31681.
B&B s£16 d£32. BB&M s£23 d£48.
Rooms 4, ensuite 2. High tea £6. Dinner £8.
Open all year.

P ❀ ♣ ⅍ ⌂ OAP ▥ ⌦ ♪ ▶ ◺

DERRYGONNELLY

Guesthouse

Navar Guest House   (A)
Derryvarey, BT93 6HW.
☎ (013656) 41384.
B&B s£16 d£34. BB&M s£25 d£52.
Rooms 5, ensuite 2. High tea £9. Dinner £9.
Open all year.

P ❀ ♣ ⅍ ⌂ ▥ ⌦ ● ♪ ▶ U ✓ ◷ ≀

Bed & Breakfast

Drumary Farm House
(Mr & Mrs Elliott), Glenasheever Rd,
Drumary North, BT93 6GA.
☎ (013656) 41420. Mobile 0831 579188.
B&B s£18 d£35. Rooms 3, ensuite 3.
Last orders 2130 hrs. Open all year.
Off A46, 9m NW of Enniskillen

P ❀ ♣ ⅍ ⌂ OAP ▥ ▭ ⌦ ♪ ▶ U ✓
◺ ⅃ ≀ ▦

Meadow View
(Mr & Mrs Wray), Sandhill, BT93 6ER.
☎ (013656) 41233.
B&B s£16.50 d£33. BB&M s£31.50 d£63.
Rooms 3, ensuite 2. Dinner £15.
Open April-Oct.

P ❀ ♣ ⅍ ⌂ OAP ▥ ▭ ⌦ ♪ ▶ U ≀

ENNISKILLEN

Hotels

Killyhevlin Hotel   ***
Dublin Rd, BT74 4AU.
☎ (01365) 323481. Fax 324726.
B&B s£55 d90. BB&M s£70 d£120.
Rooms 43, ensuite 43.
High tea £12.50. Dinner £18.50. Open all year.

P ❀ ♣ ⅍ ▼ ⌂ ⊞ OAP ⌕ ▥ ▭ ⌦ ✆ ♪ ▶ U ✓ ◺
⅃ ▼ ◉ ▦

Manor House Country Hotel   ***
Killadeas, BT94 1NY.
☎ (013656) 21561. Fax 21545.
B&B s£55 d£80. Rooms 46, ensuite 46.
Dinner £19.50. Last orders 2130 hrs. Open all year.
5¹/₂ m N of Enniskillen

T P ♠ ❀ ♣ ⅍ ▼ ⌂ ⊞ OAP ▥ ▭ ⌦ ✆ ▤
≀ ♪ ▶ U ◺ ⅃ ▼ ▦

Fort Lodge Hotel   **
72 Forthill St, BT74 6AJ.
☎ & fax (01365) 323275.
B&B s£30 d£60. BB&M s£45 d£90.
Rooms 35, ensuite 35.
High tea £5.95. Dinner £13.95.
Last orders 2130 hrs. Open all year.

P ❀ ▼ ⌂ OAP ▥ ▭ ⌦ ✆ ⌕ ♪ ▶ U ✓
◺ ⅃ ▼ ▦

Railway Hotel   *
34 Forthill St, BT74 6AJ.
☎ (01365) 322084. Fax 327480.
B&B s£35 d£70. Rooms 19, ensuite 18.
Dinner £17. Last orders 2100 hrs.
Open all year ex Christmas.

T ▼ ⌂ ▥ ▭ ⌦ ✆ ⌕ ♪ ▶ U ◺ ▼ ▦

Unclassified Hotel
Ashberry Hotel, Tempo Rd,
BT74 6HR . ☎ *(01365) 320333.*

Facilities are liable to change. Check prices when you book. Key to symbols is on inside back flap.

Guesthouses

Abocurragh Farm Guest House (A)
Abocurragh, Letterbreen, BT74 9AG.
☎ (01365) 348484.
B&B s£25 d£40. BB&M s£37 d£64. Rooms 3, ensuite 3.
High tea £10. Dinner £13. Last orders 2000 hrs.
Open all year.

Ashwood Guest House (A)
Sligo Rd, BT74 7JY.
☎ (01365) 323019.
B&B s£20 d£36. BB&M s£32 d£60.
Rooms 7, ensuite 3. Dinner £12.
Last orders 1400 hrs. Open April-Oct.

Bayview Guest House (A)
Tully, Churchhill, BT93 6HP.
☎ (013656) 41250.
B&B s£18 d£32. BB&M s£28 d£52.
Rooms 4, ensuite 2. High tea £8. Dinner £10.
Last orders 1700 hrs. Open Feb-Nov.
On A46, 11m NE of Enniskillen

Brindley Guest House (A)
Tully, Killadeas, BT94 1RE.
☎ (013656) 28065.
B&B s£22 d£38. BB&M s£34 d£62.
Rooms 8, ensuite 6. High tea £8. Dinner £12.
Last orders 1530 hrs. Open all year.
Off B82, 7m NE of Enniskillen

Corrigans Shore Guest House (B)
Clonatrig, Bellanaleck, BT92 2AR.
☎ (01365) 348572.
B&B s£15 d£30. BB&M s£23 d£46.
Rooms 3, ensuite 3. Dinner £8. Open all year.

Drumcoo House (B)
32 Cherryville, Cornagrade Rd, BT74 4FY.
☎ (01365) 326672.
B&B s£19 d£38. Rooms 4, ensuite 4.
Open all year.

Lackaboy Farm House (A)
Tempo Rd, BT74 6EB.
☎ (01365) 322488. Fax 320440.
B&B s£18 d£32. BB&M s£28 d£52.
Rooms 7, ensuite 4. High tea £8. Dinner £10.
Last orders 1600 hrs. Open all year ex Christmas.
½ m NE of Enniskillen

Lakeview Farm House (A)
Drumcrow, Blaney, BT93 7EY.
☎ (013656) 41263.
B&B s£17 d£31. BB&M s£27 d£51.
Rooms 4, ensuite 1. Dinner £10.
Last orders 1200 hrs. Open March-Nov.
10m NW of Enniskillen

Mountview (A)
61 Irvinestown Rd, Drumclay, BT74 6DN.
☎ (01365) 323147.
B&B s£28.50 d£40. BB&M s£39.50 d£62.
Rooms 3, ensuite 3. Dinner £11.
Last orders 1700 hrs. Open all year.
1m N of Enniskillen

Riverside Farm (B)
Gortadrehid, Culkey Post Office, BT92 2FN.
☎ (01365) 322725.
B&B s£18 d£30. BB&M s£24 d£44.
Rooms 6, ensuite 1. High tea £6. Dinner £10.
Last orders 2000 hrs. Open all year.
1½ m NW of Enniskillen

Facilities are liable to change. Check prices when you book. Key to symbols is on inside back flap.

Rossole House (B)

85 Sligo Rd, BT74 7JZ.
☎ (01365) 323462.
B&B s£18 d£34. Rooms 5, ensuite 2.
Open all year.

🄿 🏨 ✿ ♣ ⛷ ☇ 🕮 ⬛ ✂ ♪ ⌐ ∪ ✓ ⬧ ⚲

Tullyhona House (A)

59 Marble Arch Rd, Florencecourt, BT92 1DE.
☎ (01365) 348452.
B&B s£22.50 d£40. BB&M s£30 d£55.
Rooms 6, ensuite 5. High tea £6. Dinner £7.50.
Last orders 1900 hrs. Open all year.
7 ½ m SW of Enniskillen

🄣 🄿 ✿ ♣ ⛷ ☇ 🕮 ⬛ ✂ ♪ ⌐ ∪ ✓
⬧ ⚲ ⛾ ♞

Willowbank (A)

Bellview Rd, Dolan's Ring, BT74 4JH.
☎ (01365) 328582.
B&B s£21 d£38. BB&M s£32 d£58.
Rooms 5, ensuite 5. Dinner £10.
Open all year.

🄿 ✿ ♣ ⛷ ☇ 🕮 ⬛ ✂ ♪ ⌐ ∪ ⬧ ⚲ 🄵

Bed & Breakfast

Abbeyville

(Mrs M McMahon), 1 Willoughby Court,
Portora, BT74 7EX.
☎ (01365) 327033.
B&B d£33. Rooms 3, ensuite 1. Open all year.

🄿 ✿ ♣ ☇ 🄳🄰🄿 🕮 ⬛ ♪ ⌐ ∪ ✓ ⬧ ⚲

Aleen House

(Mr J Crooke), Cosbystown, BT93 7ER.
☎ (013656) 41472.
B&B s£16 d£32. Rooms 2, ensuite 2.
Dinner £12. Last orders 2000 hrs. Open all year.

🄿 ✿ ♣ ⛷ ☇ 🕮 ⬛ ✂ ♪ ⌐ ∪ ⬧ ⚲

Belmore Court Motel

(Mr R McCartney), Tempo Rd, BT74 6HR.
☎ (01365) 326633. Fax 326362.
Room only d£40. Rooms 30, ensuite 30.
Open all year.

🄿 ✿ ♣ ☇ ⛐ 🕮 ⬛ ✆ ✂ ⌐ ∪ ⬧ ⚲ 🄶 🄔

Blaney House

(Mr & Mrs Robinson), Blaney Post Office, BT93 7ER.
☎ (013656) 41206.
B&B s£16 d£30. Rooms 3, ensuite 2. Open April-Oct

🄿 ✿ ♣ ⛷ ☇ 🄳🄰🄿 🕮 ✂ ⌐ ∪ ✓ ⬧ ⚲ ⚲

Broadmeadows

(Mrs L McKibbin), Cleenish Island Rd,
Bellanaleck, BT92 2AL.
☎ (01365) 348395.
B&B s£16 d£32. BB&M s£26 d£52.
Rooms 2, ensuite 1. High tea £8. Dinner £10.
Last orders 1400 hrs. Open all year.
1 ½ m E of Bellanaleck

🄿 ✿ ♣ 🕮 ✂ ⚫ ⚲

Cloughbally Mill

(Mr M Theedom), Cloughbally Mill, Ballycassidy,
BT94 2LY.
☎ (01365) 324536.
B&B s£16 d£32. Rooms 1. Open all year.

🄿 ✿ ♣ ⛷ ☇ 🕮 ⬛ ✂ ♪ ⌐ ∪ ⬧

Corrakelly House

(Mr & Mrs Cassidy), 14 Drumroosk Rd,
Kinawley, BT92 4DP.
☎ (013657) 48705.
B&B s£15 d£30. Rooms 2. Open all year.

🄿 ♣ ⛷ ☇ 🄳🄰🄿 🕮 ⌐ ∪ ⬧ ♞

Dromard House

(Mrs S Weir), Tamlaght, BT74 4HR.
☎ (01365) 387250.
B&B s£20 d£35. Rooms 4, ensuite 4. Open all year.

🄣 🄿 ✿ ♣ ⛷ ⛐ 🕮 ⬛ ⌐ ✂

B&B = bed and breakfast   s = single   d = double   BB&M = bed, breakfast & evening meal

Dunrovin

(Mrs M McCurry), Skea, Arney, BT92 2DL.
☎ (01365) 348354.
B&B s£15 d£30. BB&M s£25 d£40.
Rooms 5, ensuite 2. Dinner £10.
Last orders 2000 hrs. Open all year.
5m SW of Enniskillen

Dulrush House

(Mrs B Gormley), Leggs PO, BT73 2AF.
☎ (013656) 58066.
B&B s£18 d£36. Rooms 2. Dinner £13.
Open all year.

The Gables

(Mrs F Willis), Toneyloman, Bellanalack,
BT92 2EE.
☎ (01365) 348327.
B&B s£14.50 d£29. BB&M s£22.50 d£45.
Rooms 3. High tea £9. Dinner £8.
Last orders 2000 hrs. Open all year.

Hillcrest

(Mrs J Clements), Bellanaleck, BT92 2BA.
☎ (01365) 348392.
B&B s£14.50 d£29. BB&M s£23 d£45.
Rooms 3. Dinner £8. Open all year.

Hollytree Farm

(Mrs J Whittendale), Drumanybeg,
Knockaraven PO, Derrylin, BT92 9QN.
☎ (013657) 48319.
B&B s£16 d£32. Rooms 3, ensuite 3.
Open all year.

Killyreagh House

(Lord & Lady Hamilton), Tamlaght.
☎ (01365) 387221. Fax 387122.
Terms on application. Rooms 5. Open all year.

Lough Erne House

(Mrs H Bruce), St Catherines, Blaney, BT93 7AY.
☎ (013656) 41216.
B&B s£14 d£28. BB&M s£18 d£36. Rooms 3.
High tea £5. Dinner £10. Last orders 2130 hrs.
Open all year.
Off A46, 9m NW of Enniskillen

Maghera House

(Mr & Mrs Burns), Magherageeragh, BT74 8FB.
☎ (01365) 341662.
B&B s£16 d£32. Rooms 3, ensuite 1.
Open Feb-Sept.

Olde School House

(Mrs J Moore), Tully, Killadeas, BT92 1FN.
☎ (013656) 21688.
B&B s£25 d£36. BB&M s£37 d£60.
Rooms 6, ensuite 5. Dinner £12.
Open all year.

The Point

(Mrs A Schofield), Tempo Rd, BT74 4DS.
☎ (01365) 323595.
B&B s£18 d£32. BB&M s£28 d£52.
Rooms 2. High tea £8. Dinner £10.
Last orders 1900 hrs. Open all year.

Facilities are liable to change. Check prices when you book. Key to symbols is on inside back flap.

Tower View
(Mrs A Graham), 39 The Limes, Drumlyon,
BT74 5NQ.
☎ (01365) 323959.
B&B s£17 d£30. Rooms 2, ensuite 2.
Open all year.

Viewpoint
(Mrs M Love), Garvary, BT94 3BT.
☎ (01365) 327321.
B&B s£15 d£30. BB&M s£25 d£50.
Rooms 2. Dinner £10.
Last orders 2000 hrs. Open all year ex Christmas.

GARRISON

Guesthouse

Heathergrove Guest House   (B)
100 Glenasheevar Rd, Meenacloybane,
BT93 4AT.
☎ (013656) 58362.
B&B s£25 d£35. BB&M s£40 d£50.
Rooms 6, ensuite 6.
Dinner £15. Last orders 1300 hrs.
Open March-Oct.

Bed & Breakfast

Lake View House
(Mr & Mrs Flanagan), Carran West, BT93 4EL.
☎ (013656) 58444.
B&B s£12 d£24. Rooms 3.
Open March-Sept.

Rosskit
(Mrs I Moody), Garrison, BT93 4ET.
☎ (013656) 58231. Fax 58955.
B&B s£30 d£60. BB&M s£45 d£90.
Rooms 5, ensuite 3. Dinner £15.
Last orders 2000 hrs. Open all year.

IRVINESTOWN

Hotel

Mahon's Hotel   **
Mill St, BT94 1GS.
☎ (013656) 21656. Fax 28344.
B&B s£35 d£65. BB&M s£50 d£100.
Rooms 18, ensuite 18. High tea £14.
Dinner £12.50. Last orders 2130 hrs. Open all year.

Guesthouse

The Cedars (A)
301 Killadeas Rd, Castle Archdale, BT94 1PG.
☎ & fax (013656) 21493.
B&B s£25 d£40. Rooms 7, ensuite 7.
High tea £10. Dinner £10.
Last orders 2000 hrs. Open all year ex Christmas.

Facilities are liable to change. Check prices when you book. Key to symbols is on inside back flap.

Bed & Breakfast

Fletchers Farm
(Mrs M Knox), Lisnarick Rd, Drumadravy, BT94 1LQ.
☎ (013656) 21351.
B&B s£15 d£30. Rooms 4, ensuite 4.
Open April-Sept.

🅿 ❀ ♣ ⚘ 🐎 [OAP] ▥ ✄ ♪ ▐ ∪ ✓ △ ⚓ ☺

Fort View Lodge
(Mrs R Armstrong), Coolisk, BT94 1PT.
☎ (013656) 21446.
B&B s£15 d£30. Rooms 1, ensuite 1.
Open all year.

🅿 🏠 ❀ ♣ ⚘ 🐎 [OAP] ▥ ▢ ✄ ♪ ▐ ∪ ✓ △ ⚓

Len-Aire
(Mrs E Allen), Kesh Rd, BT94 1FY.
☎ & fax (013656) 21627.
B&B s£16 d£32. Rooms 3, ensuite 2.
Open March-Oct.

🅿 ❀ ♣ ⚘ 🐎 [OAP] ▥ ✄ ♪ ▐ ∪ △ ☺

Lettermoney House
(Mrs J Kinnear), 51 Mossfield Rd, Lettermoney, BT94 1QU.
☎ (01365) 388347.
B&B s£14 d£28. Rooms 3. Open all year.

🅿 ❀ ♣ ⚘ 🐎 🐕 ▥ ▢ ✄ ♪ ▐ ∪ ✓ △ ⚓

Mountview Cottage
(Mrs P Murphy), 41 Kesh Rd, BT94 1FY.
☎ (013656) 28305.
B&B s£15 d£30. Rooms 2, ensuite 1.
Open all year ex Christmas.

🅿 ❀ ♣ ⚘ 🐎 [OAP] 🐕 ▥ ▢ ♪ ∪ ✓ △ ⚓ 💷

Necarne Castle
Ulster Lakeland Equestrian Park, BT74 7BA.
☎ (013656) 21656. Fax 28344.
B&B s£35 d£50. BB&M s£45 d£70.
Rooms 16, ensuite 16.
High tea £10. Dinner £12.50.
Last orders 2100 hrs. Open all year.

🆃 🅿 🏠 ♣ ⚘ ▢ [OAP] ▥ ✄ ♪ ▐ ∪ ✓
△ ⚓ 🍴 💷

Rookery House
(Mrs J McCanny), 2 Lack Rd, BT94 1FY.
☎ (013656) 28352.
B&B s£15 d£29. BB&M s£25 d£49.
Rooms 3, ensuite 1. Dinner £10.
Last orders 2030 hrs. Open all year.

🅿 🐎 ▥ ▢ ♪ ▐ ∪ ✓ △

Woodhill Farm
(Mrs M Irwin), Derrynanny, BT94 1QA.
☎ (013656) 21795.
B&B s£14 d£28. BB&M s£22 d£42. Rooms 3.
Dinner £8. Last orders 2000 hrs. Open all year.

🆃 🅿 ❀ ♣ ⚘ 🐎 [OAP] ▥ ✄ ▐ ∪ ✓ △ ⚓

KESH

Hotel

Lough Erne Hotel　**
Main St, BT93 1TF.
☎ (013656) 31275. Fax 31921.
B&B s£37 d£64. Rooms 12, ensuite 12.
High tea £13. Last orders 2100 hrs.
Open all year ex Christmas.

🅿 ❀ ♣ ⚘ 🍷 🐎 [OAP] 🐕 ▥ ▢ ☎ ♪ ▐ ∪ ✓
△ ⚓ 🍴 💷

Guesthouses

Ardess Craft Centre   (B)
Ardess House, BT93 1NX.
☎ & fax (013656) 31267.
B&B s£27.50 d£45. BB&M s£40 d£70.
Rooms 4, ensuite 4. Dinner £12.50.
Open all year ex Christmas.

Greenwood Lodge   (B)
Erne Drive, Ederney, BT93 0EF.
☎ (013656) 31366.
B&B s£19 d£34. BB&M s£29 d£54.
Rooms 7, ensuite 5. Dinner £10.
Last orders 1930 hrs. Open all year.

Mullynaval Lodge   (U)
Boa Island, BT93 8AN.
☎ & fax (013656) 31995.
B&B s£20 d£35. BB&M s£30 d£55.
Rooms 11, ensuite 11. High tea £7. Dinner £10.
Last orders 1900 hrs. Open all year.

Bed & Breakfast

Bay View House
(Mr S Armstrong), Drumrush, Boa Island Rd,
BT93 1AD.
☎ (013656) 31578. Fax 32084.
B&B s£20 d£40. BB&M s£30 d£60.
Rooms 12, ensuite 12. High tea £5. Dinner £10.
Last orders 2130 hrs. Open April-Sept.

Clareview
(Mr & Mrs Moore), 85a Crevenish Rd, BT93 1RQ.
☎ (013656) 31455.
B&B d£35. Rooms 3, ensuite 3.
Open all year.
On scenic route

The Courtyard
(Mr A Cadden), Lusty Beg Island, BT93 8AD.
☎ (013656) 32032/31342. Fax 32033.
B&B s£45 d£55. BB&M s£60.95 d£86.90.
Rooms 18, ensuite 18. Dinner £15.95.
Last orders 2100 hrs. Open all year.

Ederney Lodge
(Mrs S Flack), Ederney, BT93 0EF.
☎ (013656) 31261/31975.
B&B s£14.50 d£29. Rooms 2, ensuite 2.
Open all year.

Fairy Tree House
(Mrs A Keys), Glenarn, Lack, BT93 0AT.
☎ (013656) 31015.
B&B s£12 d£24. BB&M s£20 d£40.
Rooms 4, ensuite 1. High tea £6. Dinner £8.
Last orders 2000 hrs. Open all year.

Hollyfield House
(Mr & Mrs Loane), Hollyfield, BT93 1BT.
☎ (013656) 32072.
B&B s£12 d£24. Rooms 2. Open all year.

Facilities are liable to change. Check prices when you book. Key to symbols is on inside back flap.

153

Letterkeen Lodge
(Mr & Mrs Vance), Pettigo Rd, BT93 1QX.
☎ (013656) 31313.
B&B s£17.50 d£31. Rooms 3, ensuite 3.
Open all year.

Manville House
(Mrs M Graham), Aughnablaney, Letter, BT93 2BF.
☎ (013656) 31668.
B&B s£16 d£31. Rooms 3. Open April-Oct.

Montaugh Farm
(Mr & Mrs Loane), Montaughroe,
Drumskinny, BT93 1EL.
☎ (013656) 31385.
B&B s£15 d£30. Rooms 2, ensuite 2.
High tea £5. Dinner £8. Open all year.

Muckross Lodge
(Mrs C Anderson), Muckross Quay, BT74 1TZ.
☎ (013656) 31887/31719.
B&B s£17.50 d£31. Rooms 3, ensuite 3.
Open all year.

Roscolban House
(Mrs N Stronge), Enniskillen Rd, BT93 1TF.
☎ (013656) 31096.
B&B s£17.50 d£30. Rooms 2, ensuite 2.
Open March-Oct.

Rosscah Lodge
(Mrs A Geddes), 11 Crevenish Rd, BT93 1RG.
☎ (013656) 31001.
B&B s£20 d£40. Rooms 3, ensuite 3.
Open March-Sept.

Tudor Farm & Boa Island Activity Centre
(Mr S McCreery), 619 Boa Island Rd,
Portinode, BT93 8AQ.
☎ & fax (013656) 31943.
B&B s£25 d£40. Rooms 5, ensuite 5.
Open April-Oct.

Tulnaglare
(Mrs V Beacon), 16 Fortview Park, BT93 1TD.
☎ (013656) 31293.
B&B s£13 d£25. Rooms 2. Open all year.

Van-Elm
(Messrs J & E Vance), Pettigo Rd, BT93 8DD.
☎ (013656) 31719/31887.
B&B s£17.50 d£31. Rooms 3, ensuite 3.
Open all year.

Willowdale
(Mrs S McCubbin), Drumbarna, BT93 1RR.
☎ (013656) 31596.
B&B s£16 d£32. Rooms 2. Open all year.

B&B = bed and breakfast   s = single   d = double   BB&M = bed, breakfast & evening meal

LISBELLAW

Hotel

Unclassified Hotel
Carrybridge Hotel, Carrybridge,
BT94 5NF. ☎ *(01365) 387148. Fax 387111.*

Guesthouses

Aghnacarra House (A)
Carrybridge, BT94 5NF.
☎ (01365) 387077.
B&B s£23 d£36. BB&M s£31.50 d£53.
Rooms 7, ensuite 7. Dinner £8.50.
Last orders 1900 hrs. Open Feb-Oct.
On B514, S of Lisbellaw

🅣 🅟 ✳ ♣ ⚶ 🛏 ✂ ✎ 🎣 ☝ ∪ ⚓ ⮢ ☺

Tatnamallaght House (A)
39 Farnamullan Rd, Tatnamallaght, BT94 5DY.
☎ (01365) 387174.
B&B s£20 d£34. BB&M s£30 d£54.
Rooms 4, ensuite 2. High tea £8. Dinner £10.
Last orders 1730 hrs. Open April-Oct.

🅣 🅟 ✳ ♣ 🛏 [DAP] 🛏 ▭ ✂ ✎

Bed & Breakfast

Bramley Cottage
(Mr & Mrs Little), Gola Cross, BT94 5ND.
☎ (01365) 387388.
B&B s£15 d£30. Rooms 2. Open all year.

Clitana
(Mrs H Beacom), Leambreslen, BT94 5EX.
☎ & fax (01365) 387310.
B&B s£17 d£32. BB&M s£25.50 d£40.50.
Rooms 4, ensuite 2. Open all year.

🅟 ✳ ⚶ 🛏 🛏 ▭ ✂ ✎ ☝ ∪ ⟋ ⚓ ⮢

Fortmount
(Mrs E Johnston), Mullybritt Rd, BT94 5ER.
☎ (01365) 387026.
B&B s£16.50 d£33. BB&M s£26.50 d£53.
Rooms 2. Dinner £10. Open all year.

🅣 🅟 ✳ ♣ 🛏 🛏 ✂ ✎ ☝ ∪ ⚓ ⮢

Mullaghkippin Farm
(Mrs H Johnston), Derryharney, BT94 5JH.
☎ & fax (01365) 387419.
B&B s£18 d£36. BB&M s£26.50 d£53.
Rooms 2, ensuite 2. High tea £6. Dinner £8.50.
Last orders 2100 hrs. Open May-Sept.
On B514, S of Lisbellaw

🅣 🅟 ♣ ⚶ 🛏 [DAP] 🛏 ▭ ✎ ☝ ⟋ ⚓ ⮢

Wil-Mer Lodge
(Mrs M Mulligan), Carrybridge Rd,
Farnamullan, BT94 5EA.
☎ (01365) 387045.
B&B s£16 d£32. Rooms 3, ensuite 2. Dinner £8.
Open all year.
Off A4, S of Lisbellaw

🅟 ✳ ♣ ⚶ 🛏 🛏 ▭ ✂ ⚄ ✎ ☝ ∪ ⟋ ⚓ ⮢

LISNARICK

Hotel

Drumshane Hotel **
Lisnarick, BT94 1PS.
☎ (013656) 21146. Fax 21311.
B&B s£32.50 d£65. BB&M s£47 d£94.
Rooms 10, ensuite 7. Dinner £14.50.
Last orders 2000 hrs. Open all year.

🅣 🅟 🏮 ✳ ♣ 🍽 🛏 [DAP] 🛏 ▭ ✆ ✂ ✎ ☝ ∪ ⟋
⚓ ⮢ 🍴 🔳

Facilities are liable to change. Check prices when you book. Key to symbols is on inside back flap.

Guesthouse

Rossgweer House (A)
274 Killadeas Rd, BT94 1PE.
☎ (013656) 21924/(01365) 28311.
Fax (013656) 28339.
B&B s£18 d£36. BB&M s£30 d£60. Rooms 8,
ensuite 6. Dinner £12. Last orders 1200 hrs.
Open all year.

Bed & Breakfast

Archdale Lodge
(Mr & Mrs Noble), Drumall, BT94 1PG.
☎ (013656) 28022.
B&B s£17 d£34. Rooms 3, ensuite 3.
Open all year.

Rushindoo House
(Mrs L Anderson), 378 Killadeas Rd, BT94 1PS.
☎ (013656) 21220.
B&B s£18 d£30. Rooms 3, ensuite 3.
Open all year.

LISNASKEA

Hotel

Ortine Hotel *
Main St, BT92 0GD.
☎ & fax (013657) 21206.
B&B s£28.50 d£47. BB&M s£43 d£75.
Rooms 18, ensuite 18. High tea £10.
Dinner £14.50. Last orders 2100 hrs. Open all year.

Guesthouse

Colorado House (A)
102 Lisnagole Rd, BT92 0QF.
☎ & fax (013657) 21486.
Terms on application.
Rooms 8, ensuite 1. Open all year.
On A34, 1m SE of Lisnaskea

Bed & Breakfast

Lea-Ville
(Mr & Mrs Kettyle), Cushwash, BT92 0DW.
☎ (013657) 22800.
B&B s£15 d£30. Rooms 4. Open all year.

MAGUIRESBRIDGE

Bed & Breakfast

Derryvree House
(Mr & Mrs Bothwell), 200 Belfast Rd, BT94 4LD.
☎ (01365) 531251.
B&B s£18 d£32. Rooms 3, ensuite 1.
Open all year.

Sunnybank
(Mrs M Clarke), Littlemount, BT94 4RS.
☎ (013655) 31239.
B&B s£15 d£30. Rooms 2. Open all year.

Facilities are liable to change. Check prices when you book. Key to symbols is on inside back flap.

NEWTOWNBUTLER

Guesthouse

Lanesborough Arms (A)
6-8 High St, BT92 8JD.
☎ (013657) 38488. Fax 38049.
B&B s£20 d£40. Rooms 5, ensuite 5.
Open all year.

Bed & Breakfast

Ports House
(Mr K Mewes), Ports, BT92 8DT.
☎ & fax (013657) 38528.
B&B s£17.50 d£35. Rooms 3, ensuite 2.
Dinner £13. Open all year.

ROSLEA

Bed & Breakfast

Annagulgan House
(Mrs M Callaghan), Roslea, BT92 7FN.
☎ (013657) 51498.
B&B s£14 d£28. BB&M s£23 d£46.
Rooms 2. High tea £8. Dinner £9.
Last orders 2100 hrs. Open all year.

TEMPO

Bed & Breakfast

The Forge
(Mrs C White), 43 Main St, BT94 3LU.
☎ & fax (013655) 41359.
B&B s£15 d£30. BB&M s£25 d£50.
Rooms 3, ensuite 2.
High tea £10. Dinner £10. Last orders 1830 hrs.
Open all year.

Tempo Manor
(Mr & Mrs Langham).
☎ (013655) 41450. Fax 41202.
B&B s£50 d£100. BB&M s£75 d£150.
Rooms 5, ensuite 5.
Dinner £25. Last orders 1200 hrs.
Open March-Oct.

B&B = bed and breakfast   s = single   d = double   BB&M = bed, breakfast & evening meal

AGHADOWEY

Hotel

Brown Trout Golf & Country Inn **
209 Agivey Rd, BT51 4AY.
☎ (01265) 868209. Fax 868878.
B&B s£60 d£85. BB&M s£70 d£110.
Rooms 18, ensuite 18. High tea £12. Dinner £15.
Last orders 2200 hrs. Open all year.

🖵 🛏 ✿ ♣ 🎿 ♟ 🐎 ⊡ 🐕 🕮 ☎ ℅ ✂ 🎵 ▶ ⋃
✓ ⚲ ⚓ ◉ ⌧

Bed & Breakfast

Inchadoghill House
(Mrs M McIlroy), 196 Agivey Rd, BT51 4AD.
☎ (01265) 868250.
B&B s£15 d£30. Rooms 2. Open all year.
9m S of Coleraine

🅿 ✿ ♣ 🎿 🐎 🕮 🎵

BALLYKELLY

Hotel

Unclassified Hotel
Drummond Hotel, 481 Clooney Rd,
BT49 9HP. ☎ *(015047) 22121.*

BELLAGHY

Bed & Breakfast

Bawn Lodge
(Ms M Todd), 10 Castle St, BT45 8LA.
☎ (01648) 386241.
B&B s£15 d£30. BB&M s£25 d£50.
Rooms 2. High tea £7. Dinner £10.
Last orders 2100 hrs. Open all year.

✿ ♣ 🐎 OAP 🐕 🕮 🖵

CASTLEDAWSON

Bed & Breakfast

99 Old Town Rd
(Mr & Mrs Buchanan), BT45 8BZ.
☎ & fax (01648) 468741.
B&B s£16 d£32. Rooms 3. Open all year.

🅿 ✿ ♣ 🐎 🕮 ℅ 🎵 ▶ ⋃ ✓ ⚲ ⚓

Dawson Arms
(Mrs B Garvin), 31 Main St, BT45 8AA.
☎ (01648) 468269.
B&B s£20 d£30. Rooms 3. Open all year.

🅿 🛏 ✿ ♟ 🕮 ℅ 🎵 ▶

CASTLEROCK

Hotel

Golf Hotel *
17 Main St, BT51 4RA.
☎ (01265) 848204. Fax 848295.
B&B s£35 d£60. BB&M s£45 d£85.
Rooms 17, ensuite 15. High tea £7.50.
Dinner £12.50. Last orders 2100 hrs.
Open all year.

🖵 🅿 ✿ ♣ 🎿 ♟ 🐎 OAP 🐕 🕮 🖵 ☎ ℅ ✕ ● 🎵 ▶
⋃ ✓ ⚓ ⚲ ⚭ ⌧

Guesthouse

Marine Inn (B)
9 Main St, BT51 4RA.
☎ (01265) 848456.
B&B s£23 d£40. BB&M s£30.50 d£55.
Rooms 10, ensuite 10. High tea £7.50.
Dinner £9.50. Last orders 2130 hrs.
Open all year.

♟ 🐎 🐕 🕮 🖵 ℅ 🎵 ▶ ⋃ ⚭

Facilities are liable to change. Check prices when you book. Key to symbols is on inside back flap.

Bed & Breakfast

Bannview
(Mrs M Henry), 14 Exorna Lane, BT51 4UA.
☎ (01265) 848033.
B&B s£15 d£30. Rooms 3. Open March-Oct.

Bratwell Farm
(Mrs G Neely), 23 Knocknougher Rd, BT51 4JZ.
☎ (01265) 849088.
B&B s£16 d£35. Rooms 2, ensuite 2.
Open all year.

Carneety House
(Mrs C Henry), 120 Mussenden Rd, BT51 4TX.
☎ (01265) 848640.
B&B s£18 d£34. Rooms 3, ensuite 1. Open all year.
On A2, 5m from Coleraine

Craighead House
(Mrs J McConkey), 8 Circular Rd, BT51 4XA.
☎ (01265) 848273.
B&B s£20 d£36. Rooms 4, ensuite 4. Open all year.

Cranford House
(Mrs M Carr), 11 Circular Rd, BT51 1XA.
☎ (01265) 848669.
B&B s£20 d£33. Rooms 2. Open all year.

Dartries
(Mrs R Butler), 50 Gortycavan Rd, Articlave,
BT51 4JY.
☎ (01265) 848312.
B&B s£22 d£32. Rooms 3, ensuite 1.
Open March-Oct.

Kenmuir House
(Mrs E Norwell), 10 Sea Rd, BT51 4TL.
☎ (01265) 848345.
B&B s£18.50 d£37. Rooms 2. Open all year.

Liskinbwee
(Mrs L Burke), 10 Exorna Lane, Articlave,
BT51 4UA.
☎ (01265) 848909.
B&B s£18 d£36. Rooms 2, ensuite 2.
Open all year.

Maritima House
(Mrs J Caulfield), 43 Main St, BT51 4RA.
☎ (01265) 848388.
B&B s£23 d£39. Rooms 3, ensuite 3.
Open all year.

Sea Breeze
(Mr & Mrs Woods), 1 Liffock Park, BT51 4DG.
☎ (01265) 848946.
B&B s£17 d£34. Rooms 2, ensuite 1.
Open all year.

Guesthouse

Beaufort House   (B)
11 Church St, BT47 4AA.
☎ (01504) 338248.
B&B s£15 d£30. Rooms 4, ensuite 2.
Dinner £6. Last orders 1200 hrs. Open all year.
Centre of village

B&B = bed and breakfast   s = single   d = double   BB&M = bed, breakfast & evening meal

COLERAINE

Hotels

Bohill Hotel & Country Club   ***
69 Cloyfin Rd, BT52 2NY.
☎ (01265) 44406/7. Fax 52424.
B&B s£55 d£80. Rooms 36, ensuite 36.
High tea £10. Dinner £14. Last orders 2115 hrs.
Open all year.

⬛⬛✳♣♟🐎🖼️🖵☎💱🔍🎣🛌∪
✓🎣☕✉

Bushtown House Hotel & Country Club ***
283 Drumcroone Rd, BT51 3QT.
☎ (01265) 58367. Fax 320909.
B&B s£53 d£75. Rooms 39, ensuite 39.
High tea £9.50. Dinner £17.50.
Last orders 2130 hrs. Open all year.

⬛⬛🏮✳♣🔥♟🐎🖼️🖵☎💱🎣🛌∪
✓⬥🏊🎣☕✉

Lodge Hotel & Travelstop ***
Lodge Rd, BT52 1NF.
☎ (01265) 44848. Fax 54555.
B&B s£47.50 d£67.50. BB&M s£62.50 d£97.50.
Rooms 56, ensuite 56. High tea £9.
Dinner £15. Last orders 2100 hrs. Open all year.

⬛⬛✳♣♟🐎🖼️🖵☎🔍🎣🛌∪✓⬥🏊
🎣☕🐕✉

Guesthouse

Greenhill House (A)
24 Greenhill Rd, Aghadowey, BT51 4EU.
☎ (01265) 868241. Fax 868365.
B&B s£29 d£48. BB&M s£45 d£80.
Rooms 6, ensuite 6. Dinner £16.
Last orders 1200 hrs. Open March-Oct.
3m NE of Garvagh

⬛⬛🏮✳♣🔥🐎🖼️🖵☎🔍🎣🛌∪✓✉

Bed & Breakfast

Ballylagan House
(Mrs J Lyons), 31 Ballylagan Rd, BT52 2PQ.
☎ (01265) 822487.
B&B s£20 d£36. Rooms 5, ensuite 5.
Open all year ex Christmas.
Off B17, 2½ m from Coleraine

⬛✳♣🐎🖼️🔍🎣🛌∪⬥

Beardiville Farm Accommodation
(Mrs V McClure), 8 Ballyhome Rd, BT52 2LU.
☎ (012657) 31323.
B&B s£17.50 d£35. Rooms 3, ensuite 2.
Open all year.

⬛✳♣🐎🖼️🔍🎣🛌∪⬥🏊

Beardiville Lodge
(Mr & Mrs Badger), 9 Ballyhome Rd, BT52 2LU.
☎ (012657) 31816.
B&B s£23 d£36. Rooms 3, ensuite 3.
Open March-Oct.
Off B62, off B17, 3m NE of Coleraine

⬛⬛✳♣📠🖼️🔍☕

The Beeches
(Mrs A Blair), 2 Beechfield Drive, BT52 2HX.
☎ (01265) 55331.
B&B s£20 d£34. Rooms 2, ensuite 1.
Open all year.

⬛✳♣🔥🐎🖼️🖵🔍🎣∪⬥🏊🐕

Bellevue Country House
(Mrs E Morrison), 43 Greenhill Rd, BT51 4EU.
☎ & fax (01265) 868797.
B&B s£22 d£36. Rooms 3, ensuite 3.
Open all year.

⬛⬛🏮✳♣🔥🐎📠🖼️🔍🎣🛌∪⬥🐕

Facilities are liable to change. Check prices when you book. Key to symbols is on inside back flap.

Beth-A-Bara
(Mrs S Wells), 1 University Park, BT52 1JU.
☎ (01265) 329279.
B&B s£19 d£40. Rooms 3, ensuite 1.
Open March-Dec.

Cairndhu
(Mr & Mrs Eyre), 4 Cairn Court, Ballycairn Rd,
BT51 3BW.
☎ (01265) 42854.
B&B s£17 d£30. BB&M s£26 d£48. Rooms 2.
Open all year.

Camus House
(Mrs J King), 27 Curragh Rd, BT51 3RY.
☎ (01265) 42982.
B&B s£25 d£45. Rooms 3, ensuite 1.
Open all year.
Off A54, 3m S of Coleraine

Cashel
(Mrs D Marks), 21 Knockaduff Rd, BT51 4DB.
☎ (01265) 868606.
B&B s£17 d£35. Rooms 2. Open all year.

Cherith
(Mrs R Acheson), 9 Waterford Drive, BT52 1NG.
☎ (01265) 55228.
B&B s£15 d£30. Rooms 2.
High tea £6.50. Dinner £8. Last orders 1300 hrs.
Open March-Nov.

Clanwilliam Lodge
(Mrs C McWilliams), 21 Curragh Rd, BT51 3RY.
☎ (01265) 56582.
B&B s£25 d£45. Rooms 3, ensuite 3.
Open all year.

Coolbeg
(Mrs D Chandler), 2e Grange Rd, BT52 1NG.
☎ (01265) 44961.
B&B s£25 d£44. Rooms 5, ensuite 3.
Open all year ex Christmas.

Cranagh Hill
(Mrs A Jack), 52 Cranagh Rd, BT51 3NN.
☎ (01265) 51138.
B&B s£20 d£40. Rooms 3.
Open Easter & June-Sept.

Cranagh Lodge
(Mrs W Gribbon), 50 Cranagh Rd, BT51 3NN.
☎ (01265) 44621.
B&B s£20 d£32. Rooms 1, ensuite 1.
Open March-Sept.

Dunderg Cottage
(Mrs R Armour), 251 Dunhill Rd, BT51 3QJ.
☎ (01265) 43183.
B&B s£20 d£40. Rooms 3, ensuite 1.
Open Feb-Nov.

Heathfield House
(Mrs H Torrens), 31 Drumcroone Rd, Killykergan,
Garvagh, BT51 4EB.
☎ (012665) 58245.
B&B s£23 d£40. Rooms 3, ensuite 3.
Dinner £12.50. Open all year.
On A29, 7m S of Coleraine

Facilities are liable to change. Check prices when you book. Key to symbols is on inside back flap.

Hillview Farm

(Mrs L Neely), 40 Gateside Rd, BT52 2PB.
☎ (01265) 43992.
B&B s£16 d£32. Rooms 3, ensuite 1.
Open April-Oct.

P ❀ ♣ ⚕ ☎ OAP ▥ ❑ ✂ ♪ ⌐ U ◸ ⚖ ☖

Karjul

(Mrs G McConnaghie), 32 Lower Captain St,
BT51 3DT.
☎ (01265) 52038.
B&B s£14 d£32. BB&M s£19 d£42.
Rooms 3. Open all year.

P ❀ ♣ ☎ OAP ▥ ❑ ✂ ♪ ⌐ U ✓ ◸ ⚖ ☖

Killeague Farm Bungalow

(Mrs M Moore), 157 Drumcroone Rd, BT51 4HJ.
☎ (01265) 868229.
B&B s£22 d£40. BB&M s£34 d£64. Rooms 2,
ensuite 2. Dinner £12. Last orders 1600 hrs.
Open all year.

T P ❀ ♣ ☎ OAP ▥ ❑ ✂ U

The Laurels

(Mr & Mrs Guy), 26 Mountsandel Rd, BT52 1JE.
☎ (01265) 51441.
B&B d£35. Rooms 3, ensuite 2. Open all year.

T P ❀ ⚕ ☎ OAP ▥ ❑ ✂ ♪ ⌐ U ◸ ⚖ ☖

Manicoré

(Mrs C Harbinson), 71 Millburn Rd, BT52 1QX.
☎ (01265) 51884.
B&B s£20 d£32. Rooms 3.
Open all year ex Christmas.

P ❀ ⚕ ☎ ▥ ❑ ✂ ⌐ U ☖

Manor Cottage

(Mrs N Roulston), 44 Cranagh Rd, BT51 3NN.
☎ (01265) 44001.
B&B s£15 d£34. Rooms 3, ensuite 1.
Open April-Oct.

P ❀ ♣ ⚕ OAP ⌘ ▥ ☏ ✂ ♪ ⌐ U ✓ ◸ ⚖ ☖

Milesric

(Mr M Pollock), 12 The Boulevard, BT52 1RJ.
☎ (01265) 55674.
B&B s£16 d£32. Rooms 3. Open all year.

P ❀ ☎ ▥ ● ♪ ⌐ U ✓ ◸ ⚖ ☖

Mizpah

(Mrs M Barbour), 44 Carthall Rd, BT51 3PQ.
☎ (01265) 43288.
B&B s£19 d£30. Rooms 3, ensuite 2.
Open all year.

P ❀ ☎ ▥ ❑ ✂ ☖

Oakfield

(Mrs M Richmond), 5 Knockmore Crescent,
Macosquin, BT51 4NY.
☎ (01265) 42118.
B&B s£16 d£32. Rooms 3. Open all year.

P ❀ ☎ ⌘ ▥ ✂

Rathkeel

(Mrs E McCullough), 9 Woodland Pk, BT52 1JG.
☎ (01265) 44755.
B&B s£12 d£24. Rooms 2. Open all year.

P ❀ ☎ OAP ▥ ✂ ☖

Rockmount

(Mrs J Kerr), 241 Windyhill Rd, Ballinrees,
BT51 4JN.
☎ (01265) 42914.
B&B s£14 d£28. Rooms 2. Open April-Oct.
4m SW of Coleraine

P ❀ ♣ ⚕ ☎ ▥ ❑ ✂ U ☖

B&B = bed and breakfast   s = single   d = double   BB&M = bed, breakfast & evening meal

Town House

(Ms D Cuthbert), 45 Millburn Rd, BT52 1QT.
☎ (01265) 44869.
B&B s£28 d£35. Rooms 2, ensuite 1.
Open all year.

Tramalis

(Mrs J Doak), 5 Ballindreen Rd, BT52 2JU.
☎ (01265) 55204.
B&B s£14 d£32. Rooms 3, ensuite 1.
Open all year.

Tullans Farm

(Mrs D McClelland), 46 Newmills Rd, BT52 2JB.
☎ (01265) 42309.
B&B s£17 d£30. Rooms 2, ensuite 1.
Open all year.

University of Ulster at Coleraine

Cromore Rd, BT52 1SA.
☎ (01265) 44141 (ext 4567). Fax 44948.
B&B s£18.68 d£37.36. BB&M s£27.78 d£55.56.
Rooms 400, ensuite 12. Last orders 1800 hrs.
Open July-Sept.

40 Avonbrook Gardens

(Mrs K Gurney), BT52 3SS.
☎ (01265) 57286.
B&B s£12.50 d£25. Rooms 1.
Open all year.

52a Gateside Rd

(Mrs S Neely), BT52 2PB.
☎ (01265) 57185.
B&B s£20 d£34. Rooms 3, ensuite 1.
Open April-Sept.

DRAPERSTOWN

Bed & Breakfast

Moyola View

(Mrs P Flanagan), 35 Tobermore Rd, BT45 7HJ.
☎ (01648) 28495.
B&B s£16 d£32. Rooms 3, ensuite 2.
Open all year.

Neillys

(Mrs M Kelly), 19 Moneyneany Rd, BT45 7DU.
☎ (01648) 28313.
B&B s£16 d£32. Rooms 1.
Dinner £5.50. Last orders 1200 hrs.
Open all year.

Rural College

Derrynoid, BT45 7DW.
☎ (01648) 29100. Fax 27777.
B&B s£40 d£56. BB&M s£48 d£76.
Rooms 30, ensuite 30.
Dinner £16. Last orders 2100 hrs.
Open all year.

DUNGIVEN

Bed & Breakfast

Bradagh

(Ms M McMacken), 132 Main St, BT47 4LG.
☎ (015047) 41346.
B&B s£13.50 d£27. Rooms 3. Open all year.

Facilities are liable to change. Check prices when you book. Key to symbols is on inside back flap.

Cherryview
(Mrs J Haslett), 287 Drumrane Rd, BT47 4NL.
☎ (015047) 41471.
B&B s£20 d£30. Rooms 2. Open all year.

🅿 ✿ ♣ ☀ ♞ 🏛 ☐ ♪ å

Edenroe
(Ms M McCloskey), 5 Lackagh Park, BT47 4ND.
☎ (015047) 42029.
B&B s£15 d£30. Rooms 2. Open all year.

Ⓣ 🅿 ✿ ♞ 🏛 ☐ ✂ ♪ ⌐ U ✓ å

The Grange
(Mr & Mrs O'Connell), 464 Foreglen Rd,
BT47 4PW.
☎ (015047) 42207.
B&B s£18 d£34. Rooms 2. Open all year.

Ⓣ 🅿 ✿ ♣ ☀ ♞ 🏛 ☐ ✂ ♪ ⌐ U ✓

Munreary Lodge
(Mr & Mrs Hayes), 241 Foreglen Rd, BT47 4EE.
☎ (01504) 338803.
B&B s£22 d£35. BB&M s£29 d£42.
Rooms 3, ensuite 2. Dinner £7.50.
Last orders 2100 hrs. Open all year.
On A6, 5m W of Dungiven

Ⓣ 🅿 ✿ ♣ ☀ ♞ OAP 🏛 ☐ ✂ ♪ ⌐ U ✇

Slíabh ná Mon
(Mrs C Sweeney), 918 Glenshane Rd, Carn,
BT47 4SB.
☎ (015047) 41210.
B&B s£20 d£40. Rooms 1. Open all year.

🅿 ✿ ♣ ☀ ♞ OAP 🏛 ✂ ❦ ♪ ⌐ U å

EGLINTON

Hotel

Unclassified Hotel
Glen House Hotel, 9 Main St, Eglinton, BT47 3AA.
☎ (01504) 811777. Fax 812212.

Bed & Breakfast

Greenan Farm
(Mrs E Montgomery), 25 Carmoney Rd, BT47 3JJ.
☎ (01504) 810422.
B&B s£16 d£30. Rooms 2, ensuite 1.
Open all year.

🅿 ✿ ♣ ☀ ♞ 🏛 ☐ ✂

Longfield Farm
(Mrs E Hunter), 132 Clooney Rd, BT47 3DX.
☎ (01504) 810210.
B&B s£18 d£36. Rooms 3. Open April-Oct.
1m W of Eglinton

🅿 ♫ ✿ ♣ ☀ ♞ OAP 🐎 🏛 ☐ ✂ ⌐

Longfield Lodge
(Mr & Mrs Meekin), 122 Clooney Rd, BT47 3PU.
☎ (01504) 810833.
B&B s£16 d£32. Rooms 2, ensuite 2.
Open all year.

🅿 ✿ ♣ ☀ 🏛 ✂ ❦ ♪

Manor House
(Mrs J Davidson), 15 Main St, BT47 3AA.
☎ (01504) 810222.
B&B s£16 d£32. Rooms 2, ensuite 1.
Open April-Oct.

🅿 ♫ ✿ ♣ ☀ OAP 🏛 ☐ ✂ ♪ ⌐ 🖼

Onchan
(Mrs K McCauley), 3 Ballygudden Rd, BT47 3AD.
☎ (01504) 810377.
B&B s£20 d£35. Rooms 3, ensuite 1.
Open all year.
8m NE of Londonderry

🅿 ♫ ✿ ♣ ☀ ♞ 🏛 ✂ ⌐ U ✇

Facilities are liable to change. Check prices when you book. Key to symbols is on inside back flap.

FEENY

Bed & Breakfast

Drumcovitt House
(Mr G Sloan), 704 Feeny Rd, BT47 4SU.
☎ & fax (015047) 81224.
B&B s£20 d£40. Rooms 3. Open all year.

[symbols]

GARVAGH

Hotel

Imperial Hotel *
38 Main St, BT51 5AD.
☎ (012665) 58218. Fax 57078.
B&B s£26 d£42. Rooms 9, ensuite 8.
Last orders 2130 hrs. Open all year.

[symbols]

Bed & Breakfast

Antrim View
(Mrs O Collins), 28a Moneycarrie Rd, BT51 5HX.
☎ (012665) 57264.
B&B s£20 d£35. Rooms 3, ensuite 1.
Open all year.

[symbols]

Bealach Speirin
(Mr & Mrs Mullan), 75 Glen Rd, BT51 5DF.
☎ (012665) 58696.
B&B s£15 d£30. BB&M s£25 d£50.
Rooms 3, ensuite 1. Dinner £10.
Last orders 2200 hrs. Open all year.

[symbols]

Fair View
(Mr & Mrs Stewart), 53 Grove Rd, BT51 5NY.
☎ (012665) 58240.
B&B s£13 d£26. BB&M s£19 d£36. Rooms 2.
High tea £6. Dinner £6. Last orders 1200 hrs.
Open all year.

[symbols]

O'Connor's
(Mr & Mrs O'Connor), 9 Main St, BT51 5AA.
☎ (012665) 58497.
B&B s£20 d£40. Rooms 3, ensuite 3. Open all year.

[symbols]

Tanneymore House
(Mrs P Gordon), 77 Limavady Rd, Tamnymore,
BT51 5ED.
☎ (012665) 58333.
B&B s£13 d£26. Rooms 2. Open June-Sept.

[symbols]

KILREA

Bed & Breakfast

Beechmount
(Mrs A Palmer), 197 Drumagarner Rd, BT51 5TP.
☎ (012665) 40293.
B&B s£17 d£34. BB&M s£26 d£52.
Rooms 3. High tea £6.50. Dinner £9.
Open all year ex Christmas.

[symbols]

Moneygran House
(Mr B Kielt), 59 Moneygran Rd, BT51 5SL.
☎ (012665) 40549.
B&B s£12 d£24. Rooms 2. High tea £10.
Open all year ex Christmas.

[symbols]

Facilities are liable to change. Check prices when you book. Key to symbols is on inside back flap.

Portneal Lodge
(Mr & Mrs McAvinchey), 75 Bann Rd, BT51 5RX.
☎ (012665) 41444. Fax 41424.
B&B s£23 d£40. BB&M s£35 d£64.
Rooms 19, ensuite 19. High tea £6. Dinner £12.
Open all year.

LIMAVADY

Hotels

Radisson Roe Park Hotel
& Golf Resort ****
Roe Park, BT49 9LB.
☎ (015047) 22222. Fax 22313.
B&B s£90 d£130. Rooms 64, ensuite 64.
High tea £5.75. Dinner £23.50.
Last orders 2145 hrs. Open all year.

Gorteen House Hotel *
187 Roe Mill Rd, BT49 9EX.
☎ & fax (015047) 22333.
B&B s£28 d£42. BB&M s£38 d£62.
Rooms 30, ensuite 30. High tea £8. Dinner £11.
Last orders 2200 hrs. Open all year.

Guesthouse

The Poplars (B)
352 Seacoast Rd, BT49 0LA.
☎ (015047) 50360.
B&B s£18 d£32. BB&M s£28 d£52.
Rooms 6, ensuite 5. Dinner £10. Open all year.

Bed & Breakfast

Alexander Arms
(Mr D Morgan), 34 Main St, BT49 0EU.
☎ (015047) 62660/63443. Fax 22327.
B&B s£18 d£36. Rooms 8, ensuite 1.
High tea £10. Dinner £7. Last orders 2200 hrs.
Open all year.

Arden Lodge
(Mrs J McAleese), 18 Gortgarn Rd, BT49 0QW.
☎ (015047) 66934
B&B s£17 d£34. BB&M s£29 d£58. Rooms 4,
ensuite 1. Dinner £12. Last orders 1930 hrs.
Open all year.

Ballyhenry House
(Mrs R Kane), 172 Seacoast Rd, BT49 9EF.
☎ (015047) 22657.
B&B s£18 d£30. BB&M s£30 d£50.
Rooms 3, ensuite 2. High tea £6. Dinner £12.
Last orders 1630 hrs. Open all year.
On B69, 3m N of Limavady

Ballymulholland House
(Mrs D Morrison), 474 Seacoast Rd, BT49 0LF.
☎ (015047) 50227.
B&B s£15 d£30. BB&M s£23 d£46.
Rooms 2. Dinner £8. Last orders 1600 hrs.
Open all year.

Carraig Mor House
(Mrs M McGinn), 17 Duncrun Rd, Milltown,
Bellarena, BT49 0JD.
☎ (015047) 50250.
B&B s£17 d£34. Rooms 2, ensuite 1.
Open April-Sept.

B&B = bed and breakfast　s = single　d = double　BB&M = bed, breakfast & evening meal

Cloghan House
(Mrs J Foster), 8 Cloghan Rd, Drumsurn, BT49 0PJ.
☎ (015047) 62405.
B&B s£13 d£26. Rooms 2. Open May-Sept.

Culmore House
(Mrs J Gilfillan), 131 Seacoast Rd, BT49 9EG.
☎ (015047) 62698.
B&B s£13 d£26. Rooms 3. Open April-Oct.

The Maine
(Mrs M McCartney), 12 Mill Rd, BT49 0NN.
☎ (015047) 22062.
B&B s£13 d£26. Rooms 2. Open April-Sept.

Meadowvale Lodge
(Mrs E Bunting), 5 Meadowvale Park, BT49 0NU.
☎ (015047) 69915.
B&B s£15 d£30. Rooms 3. Open all year.

Mountain Lodge
(Mr & Mrs Tierney), 131 Carnamuff Rd, BT49 9JG.
☎ & fax (015047) 68031.
B&B s£17 d£34. Rooms 2, ensuite 1.
Open all year.

Streeve Hill
(Mr & Mrs Welsh), Drenagh Estate, Dowland Rd,
BT49 0HP.
☎ (015047) 66563. Fax 68285.
B&B d£90. BB&M d£115.
Rooms 3, ensuite 3.
Dinner £25. Last orders 1000 hrs.
Open Jan-Nov.

Old Rectory
(Mrs D Copeland), 4 Duncrun Rd, Bellarena,
BT49 0JD.
☎ (015047) 50477.
B&B s£20 d£40. Rooms 2, ensuite 2.
Open Feb-Nov.

The Palms
(Mrs B McLaughlin), 74 Scroggy Rd, BT49 0NA.
☎ (015047) 64205.
B&B s£16.50 d£33. Rooms 2, ensuite 1.
Open all year.

Whitehill Farm House
(Mrs M McCormick), 70 Ballyquin Rd, BT49 9EY.
☎ (015047) 22306.
B&B s£17 d£34. Rooms 3, ensuite 3.
Open all year.
On B68, 1m S of Limavady.

LONDONDERRY

Hotels

Beech Hill Country House Hotel   ***
32 Ardmore Rd, BT47 3QP.
☎ (01504) 349279. Fax 345366.
B&B s£67.50 d£85. BB&M s£79 d£120.
Rooms 17, ensuite 17. Dinner £23.95.
Last orders 2130 hrs. Open all year.

Facilities are liable to change. Check prices when you book. Key to symbols is on inside back flap.

169

Broomhill Hotel ***
Limavady Rd, BT47 1LT.
☎ (01504) 47995. Fax 49304.
B&B s£45 d£60. BB&M s£60.75 d£75.75.
Rooms 42, ensuite 42.
High tea £12.50. Dinner £15.75.
Last orders 2130 hrs. Open all year.

Everglades ***
Prehen Rd, BT47 2PA.
☎ (01504) 46722. Fax 49200.
B&B s£82 d£98. BB&M s£88 d£110.
Rooms 64, ensuite 64. High tea £10. Dinner £17.
Last orders 2145 hrs. Open all year.

Trinity Hotel ***
22-24 Strand Rd, BT48 7AB.
☎ (01504) 271271. Fax 271277.
B&B s£75 d£95. BB&M s£90 d£120.
Rooms 40, ensuite 40. High tea £7.50. Dinner £15.
Last orders 2230 hrs. Open all year.

Waterfoot Hotel & Country Club ***
Caw Roundabout, 14 Clooney Rd, BT47 1TB.
☎ (01504) 345500. Fax 311006.
B&B s£65 d£78. BB&M s£80 d£95.
Rooms 48, ensuite 48. Dinner £15.
Last orders 2115 hrs. Open all year.

White Horse Hotel ***
68 Clooney Rd, Campsie, BT47 3PA.
☎ (01504) 860606. Fax 860371.
B&B s£50 d£100. Rooms 43, ensuite 43.
High tea £8.25. Dinner £12.50.
Last orders 2215 hrs. Open all year.

Guesthouses

Clarence House (B)
15 Northland Rd, BT48 7HY.
☎ & fax (01504) 265342.
B&B s£18 d£45. Rooms 9, ensuite 7. High tea £10.
Dinner £14. Last orders 1900 hrs. Open all year.

Inn At The Cross
171 Glenshane Rd, BT47 3EN.
☎ (01504) 301480. Fax 301394.
B&B s£45 d£55. BB&M s£55 d£75.
Rooms 19, ensuite 19. High tea £4.95.
Dinner £9.95. Last orders 2130 hrs. Open all year.

Robin Hill
103 Chapel Rd, BT47 2BG.
☎ (01504) 42776. Fax 312776.
B&B s£20 d£36. BB&M s£30 d£56.
Rooms 7, ensuite 6. High tea £6. Dinner £10.
Last orders 1200 hrs. Open all year ex Christmas.

B&B = bed and breakfast   s = single   d = double   BB&M = bed, breakfast & evening meal

Bed & Breakfast

Abode
(Mrs E Dunn), 21 Dunnwood Park, Victoria Rd,
BT47 2NN.
☎ (01504) 44564.
B&B s£12 d£24. Rooms 4. Open all year.

Acorn Cottage
(Mr & Mrs Simpson), 32 Woodside Rd, BT47 2QD.
☎ (01504) 318453.
B&B s£15 d£30. BB&M s£20 d£40. Rooms 2.
High tea £3.50. Dinner £5. Last orders 2100 hrs.
Open all year.

An Móintéan
(Mr D Sweeney), 245 Lone Moor Rd, BT48 9LD.
☎ & fax (01504) 263327.
B&B s£18 d£36. Rooms 2. Open all year.

Ardowen House
(Mrs C Stevin), 13 Northland Rd, BT48 7HY.
☎ (01504) 264950.
B&B s£25 d£40. Rooms 3, ensuite 3.
Open all year.

Banks Of The Faughan Motel
(Mrs M Gourley), 69 Clooney Rd, BT47 3PA.
☎ & fax (01504) 860242.
B&B s£22 d£35. Rooms 12, ensuite 7.
Open all year.

Bayview
(Ms A Hasson), 9 Garden City, BT48 7SL.
☎ (01504) 351818. Fax 354411.
B&B s£16 d£32. Rooms 3, ensuite 1.
Open all year.

Beechwood House
(Mrs P McCallion), 43a Letterkenny Rd, BT48 9KG.
☎ (01504) 261696/271444. Fax 264900.
B&B s£25 d£50. Rooms 3, ensuite 3.
Open all year.

Braehead House
(Mrs M McKean), 22 Braehead Rd, BT48 9XE.
☎ (01504) 263195.
B&B s£16 d£30. Rooms 3, ensuite 1.
Open Feb-Oct.

Castlegregory
(Mrs P Mahon), 90 Gleneagles, Culmore Rd,
BT48 7TF.
☎ & fax (01504) 358087.
B&B s£25 d£50. Rooms 3. Open all year.

Ceol Na Bpáisti
(Ms P Canavan), 8a Northland Rd, BT48 7JD.
☎ (01504) 261167.
B&B s£16.50 d£39. Rooms 3. Open June-Sept.

Country House
(Mrs I Wiley), 153 Culmore Rd, BT48 8JH.
☎ (01504) 352932.
B&B s£12 d£24. Rooms 3. Open all year.

Facilities are liable to change. Check prices when you book. Key to symbols is on inside back flap.

Elagh Hall
(Mrs E Buchanan), Buncrana Rd, BT48 8LU.
☎ (01504) 263116.
B&B s£17.50 d£35. Rooms 3, ensuite 2.
Open April-Oct.
On A2, 2m NW of Londonderry

Ⓣ Ⓟ 🏠 ✿ ♣ ⚘ ⛵ 🖫 ✂ ⚑ ∪

Fairlee House
(Mrs M Cassidy), 86 Duncreggan Rd, BT48 0AA.
☎ (01504) 374551.
B&B s£20 d£34. Rooms 4, ensuite 2.
Open all year.

Ⓣ ⚘ 🖫 ⬜ ✂ ♪ ⚑ ∪ ◊

Florence House
(Mr & Mrs McGinley), 16 Northland Rd, BT48 7JD.
☎ & fax (01504) 268093.
B&B s£17 d£34. Rooms 4. Open all year.

Ⓟ 🏠 ✿ ⚘ 🖫

Gortgranagh Farmhouse
(Mrs M Buchanan), 40 Rushall Rd, BT47 3UG.
☎ (01504) 49291.
B&B s£15 d£30. Rooms 2. Open all year.

Ⓟ ✿ ♣ ⚘ ⚘ 🐎 🖫 ✂

B&B = bed and breakfast   s = single   d = double   BB&M = bed, breakfast & evening meal

Groarty House

(Mrs M Hyndman), 62 Groarty Rd, BT48 0JY.
☎ (01504) 261403.
B&B s£14.50 d£29. Rooms 3. Open all year.

🅣 🅟 🏠 ✿ ♣ ⅍ ⏦ 🕮 ⚊ ✂ ♪ ↑ ∪

Killenan House

(Mrs A Campbell), 40 Killenan Rd, Drumahoe,
BT47 3NG.
☎ (01504) 301710.
B&B s£16 d£32. Rooms 3, ensuite 3.
Open all year.
Off B118, 5m SE of Londonderry

🅟 ✿ ♣ ⅍ ⏦ 🕮 ⚊ ✂ ♪ ↑ 🜄

Laburnum Lodge

(Ms T McCay), 9 Rockfield, Madams Bank Rd,
Steelstown, BT48 8AU.
☎ (01504) 354221.
B&B s£15 d£30. Rooms 2, ensuite 1.
Open all year.

🅟 ✿ ♣ ⅍ ⏦ OAP 🕮 ⚊ ✂ ♪ ↑ ∪

Le Mons

(Ms P O'Donnell), 10 Parklands, Clooney Rd,
BT47 1XS.
☎ (01504) 311356.
B&B s£17 d£34. Rooms 2. Open all year.

🅣 🅟 ✿ ♣ ⏦ ⽊ 🕮 ⚊ ✂ ♪ ↑ ∪ 🜄 🜃

Number 10

(Mr & Mrs McGoldrick), 10 Crawford Square,
BT48 7HR.
☎ (01504) 265000.
B&B s£20 d£34. Rooms 4, ensuite 4.
Open Jan-Nov.

⏦ 🕮 ⚊ ✂ ↑

Oakgrove House

(Mrs M Holmes), 3 Columba Terrace,
Waterside, BT47 1JT.
☎ & fax (01504) 44269.
B&B s£15 d£34. BB&M s£22 d£48.
Rooms 3, ensuite 2. High tea £6. Dinner £7.
Last orders 1800 hrs. Open all year.

🅣 🅟 ⏦ 🕮 ⚊ ↑ ∪

Raspberry Hill Health Farm

(Mr & Mrs Danton), 29 Bond's Glen Rd,
Dunamanagh, BT47 3ST.
☎ & fax (01504) 398000.
Terms on application. B&B s£20. d£35.
Rooms 7, ensuite 7. Open Jan-Nov.

🅟 ✿ ♣ ⅍ OAP 🕮 ✂ 🗲 ♠ 🜚 ♪ ↑ ∪ 🜃

Sunbeam House

(Miss S McNally), 147 Sunbeam Terrace,
Bishop St, BT48 6UJ.
☎ (01504) 263606.
B&B s£18 d£36. Rooms 2. Open all year.

🅣 🅟 ⅍ ⏦ 🕮 ⚊ ✂ ↑

Temple House

(Mrs S McGinley), 1 Temple Rd, Strathfoyle,
BT47 1UA.
☎ (01504) 860960.
B&B s£20 d£40. Rooms 5. Dinner £10.
Last orders 1930 hrs. Open all year.

🅟 ✿ ♣ ⅍ ⏦ 🕮 ⚊ ✂ ♪ ↑ ∪ ✓ 🍷

Thar O'Murachu

(Ms C Millar), 14 Dunhugh Park, BT47 2NL.
☎ (01504) 311059.
B&B s£16.50 d£33. Rooms 3, ensuite 2.
Open all year.

🅣 🅟 ✿ ♣ ⅍ ⏦ OAP ⽊ 🕮 ⚊ ✂ ♪ ↑
∪ ✓ 🜄 🜃

Facilities are liable to change. Check prices when you book. Key to symbols is on inside back flap.

Tor Cuileann
(Mrs I Harkin), 244 Culmore Rd, BT48 8JL.
☎ (01504) 354925.
B&B s£15 d£30. Rooms 2. Dinner £10.
Last orders 2100 hrs. Open all year.

111 Creggan Rd
(Mrs C Sweeney), BT48 9DA.
☎ (01504) 373885.
B&B s£16.50 d£33. Rooms 1. Open all year.

36 Great James St
(Ms J Pyne), BT48 7DB.
☎ (01504) 269691/264223. Fax 266913.
B&B s£18 d£35. Rooms 7, ensuite 1.
Open all year.

MAGHERA

Guesthouse

Ardtara Country House   (A)
8 Gorteade Rd, Upperlands, BT46 5SA.
☎ (01648) 44490. Fax 45080.
Freefone 800 628 4893 (USA).
B&B s£70 d£95. Rooms 8, ensuite 8. Dinner £23.
Last orders 2100 hrs. Open all year.

Bed & Breakfast

Ardcaein
(Mrs A McKenna), 24 Glenshane Rd, BT46 5JZ.
☎ (01648) 43127.
B&B s£18 d£36. Rooms 2, ensuite 1.
Open all year.

Dun Ard
(Mr & Mrs Kelly), 34 Ranaghan Rd, BT46 5PE.
☎ (01648) 43651.
B&B s£15 d£30. Rooms 2, ensuite 1.
Dinner £5. Last orders 1800 hrs. Open all year.

Sperrin-View
(Mrs B Crockett), 110a Drumbolg Rd, Upperlands,
BT46 5UX.
☎ & fax (01266) 822374.
B&B s£17 d£34. BB&M s£26 d£52.
Rooms 3. High tea £6.50. Dinner £9.
Last orders 2000 hrs. Open all year ex Christmas.

MAGHERAFELT

Guesthouse

Laurel Villa   (B)
60 Church St, BT45 6AW.
☎ (01648) 32238. Fax 301459.
B&B s£23.50 d£47. BB&M s£33.50 d£67.
Rooms 5, ensuite 1. Open all year.

Bed & Breakfast

Ardeala
(Mr & Mrs Devlin), 90 Shore Rd, Ballyronan,
BT45 6JG.
☎ (01648) 418444.
B&B s£14 d£28. Rooms 2. Open all year.

Inverlake House
(Mrs M Ryan), 2 Ballyneill Rd, Ballyronan,
BT65 6JE.
☎ (01648) 418500/418452.
B&B s£13 d£36. Rooms 3. Open all year.

B&B = bed and breakfast   s = single   d = double   BB&M = bed, breakfast & evening meal

MONEYMORE

Bed & Breakfast

Fortview
(Mrs J Davison), 36 Tullyboy Rd, BT45 7YE.
☎ (016487) 62640.
B&B s£14 d£26. BB&M s£18 d£36.
Rooms 2, ensuite 1.
Dinner £8. Last orders 1200 hrs.
Open all year.

🅣 🅟 ✿ ♣ ☀ ➳ 🅞🅐🅟 🔟 ⌨ ⚡ ♪ ☝ ∪ ⌂ ⚓ 🔁 🆔

Waterside House
(Mrs T Forsythe), 10 Drumrott Rd, BT45 7QQ.
☎ (016487) 62451.
B&B s£12.50 d£30. BB&M s£17 d£40.
Rooms 2, ensuite 1. High tea £5. Dinner £5.
Open all year.

🅟 ✿ ♣ ☀ ➳ 🔟 ⌨ ⚡ ♪ ☝ ∪ ✓ ⌂ ⚓ 🔁 🆔

Woodview Farm
(Mr & Mrs Forsythe), 51 Cookstown Rd,
BT43 7QF.
☎ (016487) 48417.
B&B s£15 d£30. Rooms 2. Open all year.

🅟 🏠 ✿ ♣ ☀ ➳ 🔟 ⌨ ⚡ ♪ ☝ ∪ ✓ ⌂ ☺

PORTSTEWART

Hotels

Edgewater Hotel　**
88 Strand Rd, BT55 7LZ.
☎ (01265) 833314. Fax 832224.
B&B s£58 d£92. BB&M s£70 d£116.
Rooms 31, ensuite 31. High tea £10. Dinner £20.
Last orders 2130 hrs. Open all year.

🅣 🅟 ☀ 🍴 ➳ 🅞🅐🅟 🔟 ⌨ ☎ ✉ ⚬ ♪ ☝ ∪ ⌂
⚓ 🍴 🔁 🆔

Windsor Hotel　*
8 The Promenade, BT55 7AD.
☎ (01265) 832523. Fax 832649.
B&B s£25 d£45. Rooms 24, ensuite 14.
High tea £6.50. Dinner £9. Last orders 2045 hrs.
Open all year.

🏠 ☀ 🍴 ☺ ➳ 🔟 🅞🅐🅟 🔟 ⌨ ♪ ☝ ∪ ✓ ⌂ ⚓ 🔁 🆔

Guesthouses

Ashleigh House　(A)
164 Station Rd, BT55 7PU.
☎ (01265) 834452.
B&B d£40. BB&M d£64. Rooms 6, ensuite 6.
High tea £9.50. Dinner £12. Last orders 1400 hrs.
Open Feb-Oct.
On B185

🅟 ✿ ♣ ➳ 🅞🅐🅟 🔟 ⌨ ⚡ ♪ ☝ ∪ ⌂ ⚓ 🔁

Lis-Na-Rhin　(U)
6 Victoria Terrace, BT55 7BA.
☎ (01265) 833522.
B&B s£20 d£40. BB&M s£30 d£60.
Rooms 8, ensuite 6. Dinner £10.
Open all year.

🅟 ☀ ➳ 🅞🅐🅟 🔟 ⌨ ⚡ 🍴 🆔

Mulroy Guest House　(U)
8 Atlantic Circle, BT55 7BD.
☎ (01265) 832293.
B&B s£17 d£32. BB&M s£24 d£46. Rooms 6.
Dinner £7. Last orders 1500 hrs. Open all year.

✿ ☀ ➳ 🅞🅐🅟 🔟 ⌨ ⚡ ♪ ☝ ⌂ 🍴 🆔

Facilities are liable to change. Check prices when you book. Key to symbols is on inside back flap.

Oregon (A)

168 Station Rd, BT55 7PU.
☎ (01265) 832826.
B&B s£30 d£45. BB&M s£43 d£71. Rooms 8,
ensuite 8. Dinner £13. Last orders 1400 hrs.
Open Feb-Oct.
On B185, SE of Portstewart

〼 🅿 ❋ ♣ ☎ 🖮 ❑ ✂ 🐟 ♪ ➳ ∪ ◭
🏊 🕭 🅰 🔢

Rockhaven Guest House (A)

17 Portrush Rd, BT55 7DB.
☎ (01265) 833846.
B&B s£25 d£40. Rooms 6, ensuite 6.
High tea £9. Dinner £12. Last orders 1600 hrs.
Open all year.

🅿 ❋ ♣ 🐎 🦢 🖮 ❑ ✂ ♪ ➳ ∪ ◭ 🏊 🕭 🔢

Bed & Breakfast

Akaroa

(Ms D McGarry), 75 The Promenade, BT55 7AF.
☎ (01265) 832067.
B&B s£18 d£36. Rooms 6, ensuite 3.
Open all year.

🦢 🦢 🅰 🖮 ✂ ➳ 🕭

Annamoe

(Mrs M McWilliams), 40 Burnside Rd, BT55 7LB.
☎ (01265) 836306.
B&B s£20 d£40. Rooms 3. Open all year.

〼 🅿 ❋ 🦢 🅰 🖮 ❑ ✂ ♪ ➳ 🕭

Ardbana

(Mr P Donaghy), 23 Portrush Rd, BT55 7DD.
☎ (01265) 834402.
B&B d£44. Rooms 2. Open March-Nov.

🅿 ❋ 🦢 🐎 🅰 🖮 ✂ ➳ 🕭 🔢

Ard Na Tra

(Ms E Brolly), 9 Seaview Drive North, BT55 7JY.
☎ (01265) 832768.
B&B s£19 d£38. Rooms 2. Open March-Oct.

🅿 ❋ 🦢 🦢 🅰 🖮 ❑ ✂ ♪ ➳ ∪ ◭ 🕭

Carnalbanagh House

(Mrs I Moore), 192 Coleraine Rd, BT55 7PL.
☎ (01265) 836294.
B&B s£25 d£36. Rooms 4, ensuite 3.
Open all year.

🅿 ❋ ♣ 🦢 🦢 🐎 🖮 ❑ ✂ ♪ ➳ ∪ ✓ ◭ 🏊 🕭 🔢

Chez Nous

(Mrs T Nicholl), 1 Victoria Terrace, BT55 7BA.
☎ (01265) 832608.
B&B s£14.50 d£29. Rooms 4. Open all year.

❋ 🦢 🐎 🅰 🖮 ✂ ♪ ➳ ∪ ◭ 🏊 🕭

Craigmore

(Mr J Kelly), 26 The Promenade, BT55 7AE.
☎ (01265) 832120.
B&B s£17 d£35. BB&M s£26 d£53.
Rooms 10, ensuite 3. Dinner £9. Open April-Oct.

🦢 🐎 🔢 🖮 ❑ ♪ ➳ ∪ ✓ ◭ 🏊 🕭

Cul-Erg

(Mrs J Maguire), 9 Hillside, BT55 7AZ.
☎ (01265) 836610.
B&B s£17 d£32. Rooms 5, ensuite 2.
Dinner £8.50.
Last orders 1500 hrs. Open March-Oct.

🅿 ❋ 🦢 🐎 🅰 🖮 ❑ ✂ ♪ ➳ ∪ ◭ 🏊 🕭

Elda

(Mr D Reed), 10 Knockancor Drive, BT55 7SP.
☎ (01265) 834192.
B&B s£22.50 d£45. Rooms 2, ensuite 1.
Open all year.

🅿 ❋ 🦢 🐎 🅰 🖮 ❑ ✂ ➳ ∪ 🕭 🔢

B&B = bed and breakfast   s = single   d = double   BB&M = bed, breakfast & evening meal

Forty Winks
(Mr A Beattie), 5 Atlantic Circle, BT55 7DB.
☎ (01265) 834584.
B&B s£20 d£30. BB&M s£26 d£54.
Rooms 8. High tea £6. Dinner £8.
Last orders 1900 hrs. Open April-Sept.

Gorse Bank House
(Mrs M Austin), 36 Station Rd, BT55 7DA.
☎ (01265) 833347.
B&B s£15 d£33. BB&M s£21 d£45.
Rooms 5, ensuite 2.
Dinner £6. Last orders 1200 hrs.
Open all year.

Hebron
(Mrs M Lutton), 37 Coleraine Rd, BT55 7HP.
☎ (01265) 832225.
B&B s£14.50 d£29. BB&M s£20.50 d£41.
Rooms 4. High tea £5.50. Dinner £6.50.
Last orders 1630 hrs. Open all year.

Kelvadene
(Mrs D Rodgers), 42 Agherton Drive, BT55 7JQ.
☎ (01265) 833949.
B&B s£15 d£30. BB&M s£20 d£40.
Rooms 4, ensuite 1. High tea £5.50. Dinner £6.
Open June-Sept.

Kilbarron
(Mr & Mrs O'Cleary), 93 Coleraine Rd, BT55 7HR.
☎ (01265) 836608.
B&B s£16 d£32. Rooms 2. Open all year.

Laura's B&B
(Mrs L McCutcheon), 12 Knockancor Drive, BT55 7SP.
☎ (01265) 836653.
B&B s£15 d£30. Rooms 2.
Open March-Sept.

Mount Oriel
(Mrs B Laughlin), 74 The Promenade, BT55 7AF.
☎ (01265) 832556.
B&B s£15 d£30. Rooms 4, ensuite 1.
Open June-Aug.

Northgate
(Mrs R Beggs), 13 Old Coach Rd, BT55 7BX.
☎ (01265) 832497.
B&B s£14 d£28. BB&M s£24 d£48.
Rooms 3, ensuite 1.
Dinner £10. Last orders 1800 hrs.
Open all year.

Reamuir
(Ms R Houston), 63 Coleraine Rd, BT55 7HP.
☎ (01265) 834983.
B&B s£17 d£34. Rooms 3, ensuite 1.
Open April-Sept.

Facilities are liable to change. Check prices when you book. Key to symbols is on inside back flap.

177

Strandeen

(Mrs E Caskey), 63 Strand Rd, BT55 7LU.
☎ & fax (01265) 833159.
B&B s£30 d£40. Rooms 3, ensuite 3.
Open all year.

Wanderin Heights

(Mr & Mrs Robinson), 12 High Rd, BT55 7BG.
☎ (01265) 833250.
B&B s£25 d£40. Rooms 7, ensuite 2.
Open all year.

Windy Ridge

(Mrs E McKendry), 84 Ballyreagh Rd, BT77 5PT.
☎ (01265) 836008.
B&B s£12.50 d£25. Rooms 2.
Open March-Sept.

B&B = bed and breakfast   s = single   d = double   BB&M = bed, breakfast & evening meal

AUGHER

Guesthouse

Beech Lodge (B)
43 Glenhoy Rd, BT77 0DG.
☎ (016625) 48106.
B&B s£17.50 d£35. BB&M s£26 d£50.
Rooms 4. High tea £8.50. Open all year.

🅿 ✿ ♣ ⚘ ⛵ OAP 🏭 ☐ ✂ ✈ ▶ ✓

AUGHNACLOY

Bed & Breakfast

Garvey Lodge
(Mrs I McClements), 62 Favour Royal Rd,
BT69 6BR.
☎ (016625) 57239.
B&B s£15 d£26. BB&M s£22.50 d£39.
Rooms 2. High tea £6. Dinner £7.
Last orders 1900 hrs. Open all year.

🅿 ✿ ♣ ⛵ 🏭 ✈ ▶ ∪ ✓ ⚓

Rehaghy Lodge
(Mr & Mrs Liggett), 35 Rehaghy Rd, BT69 6EW.
☎ (016625) 57693.
B&B s£18 d£36. BB&M s£26 d£52.
Rooms 1. Dinner £8.
Last orders 2100 hrs. Open all year.

🅿 ✿ ♣ ⚘ ⛵ OAP 🏭 ☐ ✂ ✈ ▶ ∪ ⚓

BALLYGAWLEY

Guesthouse

The Grange (B)
15 Grange Rd, BT70 2HD.
☎ (016625) 68053.
B&B s£17 d£32. Rooms 3, ensuite 3.
Open Jan-Nov.
Ballygawley roundabout

🅿 🏠 ✿ ♣ ⛵ 🏭 ✂ ✈ ▶ ∪

CALEDON

Bed & Breakfast

Model Farm
(Ms C Agnew), 70 Derrycourtney Rd,
Ramakitt, BT68 4UQ.
☎ (01861) 568210.
B&B s£13 d£26. Rooms 2. Dinner £6.50.
Last orders 1200 hrs. Open all year.

🅿 🏠 ✿ ♣ ⛵ OAP 🏭 ✂ ✈ ▶ ∪ ⚓

Tannaghlane House
(Mrs E Reid), 15 Tannaghlane Rd, BT68 4XU.
☎ (01861) 568247. Fax 568153.
B&B s£17 d£30. BB&M s£27 d£40.
Rooms 1, ensuite 1. High tea £8. Dinner £12.
Open all year.
Off B45, 1½ m SW of Caledon

🅿 🏠 ✿ ♣ ⛵ 🏭 ☐ ✈ ▶ ✓ ⚓

Facilities are liable to change. Check prices when you book. Key to symbols is on inside back flap.

CASTLEDERG

Guesthouse

Derg Arms (B)
43 Main St, BT81 7AS.
☎ (016626) 71644. Fax 70202.
B&B s£16 d£32. BB&M s£22.50 d£45.
Rooms 6, ensuite 6. High tea £7.50. Dinner £12.50.
Last orders 2100 hrs. Open all year.

Bed & Breakfast

Ardmourne House & Stables
(Mr & Mrs McElhill), 36 Corgary Rd, Ardarver,
BT81 7YF.
☎ & fax (016626) 70291.
B&B s£14 d£27. BB&M s£23.50 d£47. Rooms 3.
Dinner £10. Last orders 2100 hrs.
Open all year ex Christmas.

Glen House
(Mrs M McHugh), 30 Aghalunny Rd, Killeter,
BT81 7AZ.
☎ (016626) 71983.
B&B s£15 d£26. Rooms 2. Open all year.

Hill House
(Mr C Logue), 9a Pullyteen Rd, Killeter,
BT81 7HO.
☎ (016626) 70318.
B&B s£15 d£28. Rooms 2, ensuite 2.
Open all year.

CLOGHER

Guesthouse

Corick House (A)
20 Corick Rd, BT76 0BZ.
☎ (01662) 548216. Fax 549531.
B&B s£40 d£70. BB&M s£60 d£110.
Rooms 9. High tea £12. Dinner £20.
Last orders 2130 hrs. Open all year.

Bed & Breakfast

River Furey House
(Mr & Mrs Kelly), 24 Monaghan Rd, BT76 0HW.
☎ (01662) 548843.
B&B s£14 d£28. BB&M s£22 d£44.
Rooms 2, ensuite 1. Dinner £8.
Last orders 2000 hrs. Open all year.

Timpany Manor
(Mrs M McFarland), 53 Ballagh Rd, BT76 0LB.
☎ (013655) 21285.
B&B s£16 d£32. BB&M s£27 d£52.50. Rooms 3.
Open all year.

COALISLAND

Guesthouse

McGirr's (U)
11 The Square, BT71 4LN.
☎ (01868) 747559.
B&B s£15 d£30. BB&M s£21 d£42.
Rooms 12, ensuite 11. High tea £3. Dinner £6.
Open all year.

B&B = bed and breakfast   s = single   d = double   BB&M = bed, breakfast & evening meal

Bed & Breakfast

O Ceallaigh oh Aodha (Kathleens)
(Mr & Mrs Hughes), 117 Moor Rd, Shanless,
Stewartstown, BT71 5QD.
☎ (01868) 740403.
B&B s£16 d£30. Rooms 3, ensuite 1.
Open all year.

P ✽ ♣ ⅏ ⌕ 🏠 ⅲ ⌂ ⅃ ✄ ✈ ⌐ ∪ ⟋ ◬ ⚡ ☺

COOKSTOWN

Hotels

Glenavon House Hotel ***
52 Drum Rd, BT80 8JQ.
☎ (016487) 64949. Fax 64396.
B&B s£50 d£80. BB&M s£64 d£108.
Rooms 53, ensuite 53. High tea £7. Dinner £14.
Last orders 2145 hrs. Open all year.

P 🏠 ✽ ♣ ⅏ ☎ ⌕ 🎿 🔲 OAP ⅲ ⌂ ⌐ 🖥 ≋ ⅃ ⌐
∪ ◬ ⚡ ⏻ ☺ ⚏

Royal Hotel **
64 Coagh St, BT80 8NG.
☎ (016487) 62224. Fax 61932.
B&B s£30 d£60. BB&M s£45 d£90.
Rooms 10, ensuite 10. High tea £8.50. Dinner £15.
Last orders 2145 hrs. Open all year.

P ✽ ♣ ⅏ ☎ ⌕ ⅲ ⌂ ⌐ ⅃ ⌐ ∪ ⚏

Tullylagan Country House Hotel **
40b Tullylagan Rd, Sandholes, BT80 8UP.
☎ (016487) 65100. Fax 61715.
B&B s£45 d£90. BB&M s£70 d£140.
Rooms 15, ensuite 15. Dinner £16.95.
Last orders 2130 hrs. Open all year.

✽ ♣ ⅏ ☎ ⅏ ⌕ OAP ⅲ ⌂ ⌐ ✄ ✈ ⌐ ∪ ⟋ ◬
⚡ ⏻ ☺ ⚏

Greenvale Hotel *
57 Drum Rd, BT80 8QS.
☎ (016487) 62243/65196. Fax 65539.
B&B s£35 d£55. BB&M s£52.50 d£90.
Rooms 12, ensuite 12. High tea £8.50. Dinner £15.
Last orders 2130 hrs. Open all year.

T P 🏠 ✽ ♣ ☎ ⌕ 🎿 OAP ⅲ ⌂ ⌐ ✄ ⅃ ✈ ∪ ⟋
◬ ⚡ ☺ ⚏

Guesthouse

Edergole (A)
70 Moneymore Rd, BT80 8RJ.
☎ (016487) 62924. Fax 65572.
B&B s£18 d£36. BB&M s£24 d£48.
Rooms 5, ensuite 3. Dinner £6. Open all year.

T P ✽ ♣ ⌕ 🎿 OAP ⌐ ⅲ ⌂ ✈ ⅃ ⌐
∪ ⟋ ◬ ⚡

Bed & Breakfast

Braeside House
(Mr & Mrs McKeown), 23 Drumconvis Rd, Coagh,
BT80 0HD.
☎ (016487) 37301.
B&B s£15 d£30. BB&M s£18 d£36.
Rooms 4, ensuite 1. High tea £5. Dinner £6.
Last orders 1800 hrs. Open all year.

P 🏠 ✽ ♣ ⅏ ⌕ ⅲ ✈ ⅃ ⟋

Central Inn
(Mr H Quinn), 27 William St, BT80 8AX.
☎ (016487) 62255/62029.
B&B s£16 d£33. Rooms 5, ensuite 4.
Open all year.

P ☎ ⌕ ⅲ ⅃ ⏻

Grandview
(Mrs E Holland), 47 Shivey Rd, BT80 9HB.
☎ (016487) 62286.
B&B s£16 d£32. Rooms 2. Open all year.

T P ✽ ♣ ⅏ ⌕ 🦮 ⅃ ⌐ ∪ ⟋ ◬ ⚡ ⚏

Facilities are liable to change. Check prices when you book. Key to symbols is on inside back flap.

Killycolp House
(Mrs E McGucken), 21 Killycolp Rd, BT80 8UL.
☎ (016487) 63577.
B&B s£16.50 d£33. Rooms 2. Open all year.

Little Thistle
(Mr & Mrs Patterson), 20 Cooke Crescent, BT80 8LD.
☎ (016487) 66717/18.
B&B s£17 d£30. Rooms 1. Open all year.

Meadow Bank
(Mr & Mrs Short), 145 Moneymore Rd, BT80 9UU.
☎ (016487) 61845/63396.
B&B s£18 d£36. Rooms 3, ensuite 1.
Open all year.

Sperrin View
(Ms V McCaughey), 37 Ballynagilly Rd, BT80 9SX.
☎ (016487) 63990.
B&B s£13.50 d£27. Rooms 2. Open March-Oct.

DONAGHMORE

Bed & Breakfast

Clanmór
(Mr & Mrs Grimes), 6 Church View, BT70 3EY.
☎ (018687) 61410.
B&B s£15 d£30. Rooms 2. Open all year.

Ivy Cottage
(Mrs M Thornton), 9 Main St, BT70 3ES.
☎ (018687) 67832.
B&B s£15 d£30. Rooms 3. Open all year.

DROMORE

Bed & Breakfast

Commercial Inn
(Mr F McCaffrey), 48 Main St, BT78 3AB.
☎ (01662) 898219.
B&B s£15 d£25. Rooms 4. Open all year.

Drumconnis House
(Mrs M Teague), 57 Omagh Rd, BT78 3HE.
☎ (01662) 898662.
B&B s£13 d£30. Rooms 2, ensuite 1.
Open April-Sept.

Leaview
(Mr & Mrs Turner), 59 Galbally Rd, BT78 3SN.
☎ (01662) 898301.
B&B s£15 d£30. Rooms 2. Open all year.

DUNGANNON

Hotels

Cohannon Inn Autolodge **
212 Ballynakilly Rd, BT71 6HJ.
☎ & fax (01868) 724488.
B&B d£31.95. Rooms 50, ensuite 50.
High tea £5.95. Dinner £14.95.
Last orders 2200 hrs. Open all year.

Facilities are liable to change. Check prices when you book. Key to symbols is on inside back flap.

Inn On The Park **

Moy Rd, BT71 6BS.
☎ (01868) 725151. Fax 724953.
B&B s£45 d£70. BB&M s£60 d£100.
Rooms 13, ensuite 13. High tea £10. Dinner £16.95.
Last orders 2130 hrs. Open all year.

🅣 🅟 ✿ 🐎 🛏 [OAP] 🐎 🛏 🏛 ⚟ 🌙 🏃 ▶ ∪
✓ 🦎 🍴 🖂

Unclassified Hotel
Glengannon Hotel, Drumgormal, Ballygawley Rd,
BT70 7PT. ☎ *(01868) 727311.*

Guesthouses

Grange Lodge (A)

7 Grange Rd, BT71 1EJ.
☎ (01868) 784212/722458. Fax 723891.
B&B s£49 d£69. BB&M s£69 d£109.
Rooms 5, ensuite 5. Dinner £20.
Last orders 1200 hrs.
Open Feb-Dec ex Christmas.
1m S of M1, junction 15

🅣 🅟 🏠 ✿ ♣ 🍴 🏛 ⚟ 🌙 ⚞ ✗ ● 🏃 ▶ ∪ 🍴 🖂

Stangmore Country House (U)

65 Moy Rd, BT71 7DT.
☎ (01868) 725600. Fax 726644.
B&B s£45 d£70. Rooms 9, ensuite 9.
High tea £10. Dinner £10.
Last orders 2200 hrs. Open all year.

🅟 🏠 ✿ ♣ 🕭 🐎 🛏 🏛 ⚟ ✗ 🏃 ▶ ∪ ✓
⚓ 🦎 🍴 🖂

Tullydowey Country House (U)

51 Tullydowey Rd, BT71 7HF.
☎ (01861) 548230. Fax 548881.
B&B s£35 d£59. BB&M s£45 d£79.
Rooms 9, ensuite 9. High tea £10. Dinner £10.
Last orders 2200 hrs. Open all year.

🅣 🅟 🏠 ✿ ♣ 🕭 🐎 [OAP] 🐎 🏛 ⚟ 🌙 ✗ 🏃 ▶ ∪
⚓ 🦎 🍴 🖂

Bed & Breakfast

Cul Le Lough

(Ms M Lunney), 59 Killycolpy Rd, BT71 5AL.
☎ (01868) 738343.
B&B s£15 d£30. Rooms 2, ensuite 1.
Open all year.

🅟 🏠 ✿ ♣ 🕭 🐎 🏛 ⚟ ✗ 🏃 ▶ ⚓ 🦎 🖂

Farm Bungalow

(Miss M Currie), 225 Ballynakelly Rd, Cohannon,
BT71 6HJ.
☎ (01868) 723156.
B&B s£16 d£32. Rooms 2. Open all year.
On A45, 5m E of Dungannon

🅟 ✿ ♣ 🏛 ✗ 🌙 ▶ ∪

Kilmore Lodge

(Mrs T Donnelly), 28 Lisbofin Rd, Kilmore,
BT71 7JQ.
☎ (01762) 891387.
B&B s£16 d£30. Rooms 2. Open all year.

🅟 ✿ ♣ 🐎 [OAP] 🏛 ✗

Mikora Lodge

(Ms C Barras), 16 Thornhill Rd, Lisnagleer,
BT70 3LJ.
☎ (01868) 767171.
B&B s£18 d£36. BB&M s£26 d£52.
Rooms 2. Dinner £8.
Last orders 2130 hrs. Open all year.

🅟 ✿ ♣ 🐎 🏛 ✗ 🌙 ▶ ⚓

The Town House

(Mr & Mrs Cochrane), 32 Northland Row,
BT71 6AP.
☎ (01868) 723975.
B&B s£15 d£28. Rooms 4. Open all year.

🅟 🏠 ✿ 🕭 🐎 🛏 🏛 ⚟ ✗ ● 🌙 ▶ ∪ ✓ 🦎 🖂

White Gables

(Mrs H Cherry), 18 White Gables, Tullyroan Rd,
BT71 6NF.
☎ (01762) 851242.
B&B s£15 d£30. Rooms 2. Open all year.

P ❀ ♣ ⚶ ⛎ Ⅲ ⅍ ↲ ∪

33 Syerla Rd

(Mrs M Fox), BT71 7EP.
☎ (01868) 722174.
B&B s£13 d£24. Rooms 3, ensuite 1.
Open all year.

P ❀ ♣ ⛎ Ⅲ ⅍ ↲ ↾ ∪ ⚌

FINTONA

Bed & Breakfast

Kilcoutry House

(Mrs M Murray), 150 Tattyreagh Rd, BT78 2HT.
☎ (01662) 841265.
B&B s£15 d£25. Rooms 2. High tea £10. Dinner £10.
Last orders 2100 hrs. Open April-Sept.

P ❀ ♣ ⚶ ⛎ OAP Ⅲ ◻ ↺ ⅍ ↲ ↾ ↗ ⚉

FIVEMILETOWN

Hotels

Valley Hotel   **

60 Main St, BT75 0PW.
☎ (013655) 21505. Fax 21688.
B&B s£30 d£50. BB&M s£42.50 d£75.
Rooms 22, ensuite 22. High tea £7.50. Dinner £12.50.
Last orders 2200 hrs. Open all year.

T P ❀ ⛎ ⊞ ⛏ Ⅲ ◻ ↺ ↾ ∪ ⚉ ⅄ ⊞

Fourways Hotel   *

41 Main St, BT75 0LE.
☎ (013655) 21260/21374. Fax 22061.
B&B s£30 d£54. BB&M s£42 d£78.
Rooms 10, ensuite 10. High tea £8. Dinner £12.
Last orders 2330 hrs. Open all year.

T P ❀ ♣ ⚶ ⅊ ⛎ ⛏ Ⅲ ◻ ↺ ↲ ↾
↗ ⚐ ⅄ ⅄

Guesthouse

Al-Di-Gwyn Lodge   (A)

103 Clabby Rd, BT75 0QY.
☎ (013655) 21298.
B&B s£17 d£34. Rooms 3, ensuite 3.
Open all year.
On B107, 2m N of Fivemiletown

P ❀ ♣ ⚶ ⛎ OAP Ⅲ ↾

Bed & Breakfast

Ashlone House

(Mrs G Malone), 76 Colebrooke Rd, BT75 0SA.
☎ (013655) 21553.
B&B s£16.50 d£33. Rooms 1. Open all year.

P ❀ ♣ ⚶ ⛎ Ⅲ ⅍ ⅄

Blessingbourne

(Capt Lowry), BT75 0QS. ☎ (013655) 21221.
Rooms 4. Open all year.

Church View

(Mrs E Fitzgerald), 2 Murley Rd, BT75 0QS.
☎ (013655) 22059.
B&B s£12 d£24. Rooms 1. Last orders 2230 hrs.
Open all year ex Christmas.

P ❀ ♣ ⚶ ⛎ ⊞ OAP Ⅲ ⅍ ↲ ⅄

Station House

(Ms D McManus), BT75 0QG.
☎ (013655) 21824.
B&B s£12.50 d£25. Rooms 1. Open all year.

P ⌂ ❀ ♣ ⛎ Ⅲ ↲ ⅄

Facilities are liable to change. Check prices when you book. Key to symbols is on inside back flap.

MOY

Guesthouse

Muleany House   (A)
86 Gorestown Rd, BT71 7EX.
☎ (01868) 784183.
B&B s£20 d£32. BB&M s£30 d£52.
Rooms 9, ensuite 9. Dinner £12.50.
Last orders 2000 hrs. Open all year ex Christmas.
1m W of Moy

🅿 ❄ ♣ ☕ 🐎 🎢 ✂ ✈ ♪ ☞ ∪ ♨

Bed & Breakfast

Charlemont House
(Mr & Mrs McNeice), 4 The Square, BT71 7SG.
☎ (01868) 784755/784895.
B&B s£20 d£35. BB&M s£25 d£45.
Rooms 3. High tea £5. Dinner £5.
Open all year.

🅿 🐎 ❄ ♣ 🎢 🐎 OAP 🐕 🎢 ▥ 🗔 ✂ ♪ ☞ ∪ ✓
▵ ♨ ♨ ☆ ♨

Tomney's Inn
(Mr D Tomney), 12 The Square, BT71 7SG.
☎ (01868) 784755.
B&B s£17 d£35. BB&M s£22 d£40.
Rooms 3. Last orders 2030 hrs.
Open all year.

🅿 🐎 ❄ ♣ 🎢 ☕ 🐎 OAP 🐕 ▥ 🗔 ✂ ♪ ☞ ∪ ✓
▵ ♨ ☆ ♨ ♨

Welcome Inn
30 The Square, BT71 7SH.
☎ (01868) 784223.
B&B s£14 d£28. Rooms 2, ensuite 1.
Open April-Oct.

🅿 ❄ ♣ ☕ 🐎 OAP ▥ ✂ ♪ ☞ ∪ ✓ ▵ ♨ ☆ ♨

NEWTOWNSTEWART

Hotel

Hunting Lodge   *
Letterbin Rd, Baronscourt, BT78 4HR.
☎ (016626) 61679. Fax 61900.
B&B s£25 d£50. BB&M s£40 d£80.
Rooms 15, ensuite 15. High tea £9. Dinner £15.
Last orders 2130 hrs. Open all year.

🆃 🅿 🐎 ❄ ♣ 🎢 ☕ 🐎 OAP 🐕 ▥ 🗔 ☎ ✂ ✈ ♪
☞ ∪ ✓ ▵ ♨ ☆ ☆ ♨

Bed & Breakfast

Angler's Rest
(Mr & Mrs Campbell), 12 Killymore Rd, BT78 4DT.
☎ (016626) 61167/61543.
B&B s£14 d£28. BB&M s£22 d£44.
Rooms 2, ensuite 2. High tea £8. Dinner £8.
Last orders 1900 hrs. Open all year.

🅿 ❄ ♣ 🎢 🐎 ▥ ✂ ♪ ☞ ∪ ✓ ▵ ♨

Crosh Lodge
(Mrs E Beattie), 22 Plumbridge Rd, BT78 4DA.
☎ (016626) 61421.
B&B s£15 d£26.
Rooms 2, ensuite 1. Open all year.

🅿 ❄ ♣ 🎢 🐎 ▥ ✂ ♪ ☞ ∪ ✓ ♨

Deer Park House
(Mrs N Gallagher), 14 Baronscourt Rd, BT78 4EX.
☎ (016626) 61083/61565.
B&B s£15 d£30. BB&M s£21 d£42.
Rooms 4, ensuite 1. High tea £7. Dinner £7.
Last orders 2000 hrs. Open all year.

🅿 🐎 ❄ ♣ 🎢 🐎 OAP ▥ 🗔 ✂ ♪ ☞ ∪
✓ ▵ ♨ ♨

Woodbrook Farm
(Mrs I McFarland), 21 Killymore Rd, BT78 4QT.
☎ (016626) 61432.
B&B s£14 d£28. Rooms 3, ensuite 1.
Open all year.

T P ❄ ♠ ⚘ ⛄ DAP ⅏ ✂ ♪ ⌒ ∪ ✓ ⚡

OMAGH

Hotels

Royal Arms Hotel **
51 High St, BT78 1BA.
☎ (01662) 243262/3. Fax 244860.
B&B s£39.50 d£74.95. BB&M s£49.50 d£84.95.
Rooms 21, ensuite 21. High tea £7.50. Dinner £14.95.
Last orders 2200 hrs. Open all year.

T P ♠ ❄ ♟ ⛄ DAP ✠ ⅏ ⎓ ⚲ ♪ ⌒ ∪ ✓
⚘ ⚡ ⚓ ⊞

Silverbirch Hotel **
5 Gortin Rd, BT79 7DH.
☎ (01662) 242520/243360. Fax 249061.
B&B s£37 d£62.50. Rooms 46, ensuite 46.
Dinner £13. Last orders 2130 hrs.
Open all year.

T P ❄ ♠ ♟ ⛄ ⊞ DAP ✠ ⅏ ⎓ ⚲ ⚘ ♪ ⌒ ∪
✓ ∪ ✓ ⚘ ⚡ ⚓ ⊞

Guesthouse

Greenmount Lodge (A)
58 Greenmount Rd, Gortaclare, BT79 0YE.
☎ (01662) 841325. Fax 840019.
B&B s£21 d£36. BB&M s£32 d£58.
Rooms 8, ensuite 8. Open all year.
South off A5 from Omagh

T P ❄ ♠ ⛄ DAP ⅏ ⎓ ⚲ ✂ ⚘ ♪ ⌒
∪ ✓ ⚓ ◐

Bed & Breakfast

Afton House
(Mrs J Donnelly), 32 Tattykeel Rd, Clanabogan,
BT78 5DA.
☎ & fax (01662) 251257.
B&B s£19.50 d£35. BB&M s£31.50 d£59.
Rooms 4, ensuite 4. Dinner £12.
Last orders 1800 hrs. Open all year.

P ❄ ♠ ⚘ ⛄ DAP ⅏ ⎓ ✂ ⚘ ♪ ⌒ ∪ ✓ ⚘ ⚡

Ardmore
(Mrs I McCann), 12 Tamlaght Rd, BT78 5AW.
☎ (01662) 243381.
B&B s£15 d£30. Rooms 3.
Open all year.

P ❄ ♠ ⅏ ✂

Arleston House
(Mrs R Fox), 1 Arleston Park, BT79 7LJ.
☎ (01662) 241719.
B&B s£15 d£30. Rooms 2. Open all year.

P ♠ ⚘ ⛄ DAP ⅏ ✂ ♪

Bankhead
(Mrs S Clements), 9 Lissan Rd, BT78 1TX.
☎ (01662) 245592.
B&B s£13 d£26. Rooms 3. Open all year.

P ❄ ♠ ⚘ ⛄ ⅏

Blessington
(Mrs R McAskie), 35a Dunteige Rd, Mountjoy,
BT78 5PB.
☎ (01662) 243578/251655.
B&B s£15 d£30. Rooms 4.
Open all year ex Christmas

P ❄ ♠ ⚘ ⛄ ⅏ ✂ ♪ ⌒ ∪ ✓ ⚓

Facilities are liable to change. Check prices when you book. Key to symbols is on inside back flap.

Bridies
(Mrs B Cuddihy), 1 Georgian Villas, Hospital Rd,
BT79 0AT.
☎ (01662) 245254.
B&B s£16 d£32. BB&M s£26 d£52. Rooms 3.
High tea £7. Dinner £10. Last orders 1800 hrs.
Open all year.

Clanabogan House
(Mrs J Montgomery), 85 Clanabogan Rd, BT78 1SL.
☎ & fax (01662) 241171.
B&B s£17.50 d£35. BB&M s£26.50 d£53.
Rooms 6, ensuite 3. High tea £9. Dinner £12.
Last orders 2030 hrs. Open all year.

Derrylynn
(Mr & Mrs McAuley), 13 Beltany Rd, BT78 5NA.
☎ (01662) 244256.
B&B s£18 d£36. Rooms 4 ensuite 2.
Dinner £12.50. Last orders 2030 hrs.
Open all year.

Dialinn Country House
(Mrs J Hamilton), 112 Doogary Rd, BT79 0BN.
☎ (01662) 247934.
B&B s£19 d£38. Rooms 3. Open all year.

Drum-na-Gainne
(Mrs B Meenagh), 150 Creggan Rd, Carrickmore,
BT79 9BL.
☎ & fax (016627) 61678.
B&B s£14 d£28. Rooms 2. Open all year.

Dunmore House
(Mrs M McFarland), Mountjoy West, BT78 5WW.
☎ (01662) 242126.
B&B s£16 d£32. Rooms 2. Open April-Oct.

Four Winds
(Mr & Mrs Thomas), 63 Dromore Rd (Old),
BT78 1RB.
☎ (01662) 243554.
B&B s£17 d£34. Rooms 3, ensuite 1.
Open all year.

Heatherlea
(Mr & Mrs Donaghy), 222 Barony Rd, Creggan,
BT79 9AQ.
☎ (016627) 61555.
B&B s£14 d£28. Rooms 2. Open all year.

Hillcrest Farm
(Mrs A McFarland), Lislap, BT79 7UE.
☎ (016626) 48284.
B&B s£13 d£25. BB&M s£18 d£35.
Rooms 2. Dinner £6. Last orders 1800 hrs.
Open all year.
7 m NW of Omagh

Killynure
(Mrs W Sterritt), 95 Castletown Rd, Mountjoy,
BT78 5RG.
☎ (016626) 61482.
B&B s£14 d£28. Rooms 3, ensuite 1.
Open all year.

Letfern
(Miss J Patterson), 118 Letfern Rd, Seskinore,
BT78 1UL.
☎ (01662) 841324.
B&B s£14 d£28. Rooms 4. Open all year.

B&B = bed and breakfast   s = single   d = double   BB&M = bed, breakfast & evening meal

Mon Abri

(Mrs I McLaren), 14 Moylagh Rd, Beragh,
BT79 0RT.
☎ (016627) 58224.
B&B s£15 d£30. BB&M s£22 d£44. Rooms 2.
High tea £5. Dinner £7.
Last orders 2100 hrs. Open all year.

Romona's House

(Mrs C Henry), 96 Circular Rd, BT79 7HA.
☎ & fax (01662) 245084.
B&B s£20 d£40. BB&M s£32 d£64.
Rooms 6, ensuite 6. High tea £8. Dinner £12.
Last orders 2200 hrs. Open all year.

Rylands

(Mrs W Marshall), 31 Loughmuck Rd, BT78 1SE.
☎ (01662) 247318.
B&B s£15 d£30.
Rooms 2. Open all year.

Whiterock House

(Mrs V McKelvey), 47 Cashty Rd, Mountjoy,
BT78 5RL.
☎ (01662) 61144.
B&B s£15 d£24. BB&M s£21 d£36.
Rooms 2. High tea £6. Dinner £6.
Open all year.

218 Drumnakilly Rd

(Mr & Mrs Nugent), BT79 9PN.
☎ (016627) 61219.
B&B s£15 d£30. Rooms 2.
Open all year.

SION MILLS

Bed & Breakfast

Bide-A-Wee
(Mr & Mrs Fletcher), 181 Melmount Rd, BT82 9LA.
☎ (016626) 59571.
B&B s£18 d£36. Rooms 5, ensuite 2.
Open all year.

Marshalls
(Mr C Marshall), 125 Melmount Rd, BT82 9PY.
☎ (016626) 58638. Fax 59793.
B&B s£16.50 d£30. Rooms 4. Dinner £8.
Last orders 2130 hrs. Open all year.

SIXMILECROSS

Bed & Breakfast

The Old School House
(Mrs M Moffitt), 29 Main St, BT79 9NH.
☎ (016627) 58556.
B&B s£15 d£30. BB&M s£23 d£46.
Rooms 2, ensuite 1. High tea £6. Dinner £8.
Open all year.

STRABANE

Hotel

Fir Trees Hotel **
Melmount Rd, BT82 9JT.
☎ (01504) 382382. Fax 383116.
B&B s£35 d£55. BB&M s£45 d£75.
Rooms 24, ensuite 24. Dinner £12.50.
Open all year.

Facilities are liable to change. Check prices when you book. Key to symbols is on inside back flap.

Ballantines
(Mrs J Ballantine), 38 Leckpatrick Rd, Artigarvan,
BT82 0HB.
☎ (01504) 882714.
B&B s£15 d£30. BB&M s£21.50 d£43. Rooms 3.
High tea £6.50. Dinner £6.50.
Last orders 1700 hrs. Open Jan-Nov.
Off B49, 3m NE of Strabane

Beau-vista
(Mrs H Gamble), 19 Barron Rd, Artigarvan,
BT82 0JD.
☎ (01504) 398380.
B&B s£13.50 d£27. BB&M s£23.50 d£50.
Rooms 2, ensuite 1.
Open all year ex Christmas.

Bowling Green House
(Mr & Mrs Casey), 6 Bowling Green, BT82 8AS.
☎ (01504) 884787.
B&B s£13 d£26. Rooms 3. Open all year.

Brook House
(Mrs M O'Connor), 53 Brook Rd, BT82 0RX.
☎ (01504) 398436.
B&B s£14 d£28. Rooms 2, ensuite 1.
Open all year.

Four Seasons
(Mr & Mrs McKane), 28 Ligford Rd, Legforddrum,
BT82 8PN.
☎ (01504) 884249.
B&B s£12.50 d£24. Rooms 2, ensuite 2.
Open April-Oct.

Hollybush
(Mrs J Donnell), 421a Victoria Rd, Ballymagorry,
BT82 0AT.
☎ (01504) 382370.
B&B s£15 d£30. Rooms 2. Open all year.

Mulvin Lodge
(Mr & Mrs Smith), 117 Mulvin Rd, BT82 9JR.
☎ (016626) 58269.
B&B s£15 d£30. Rooms 2.
High tea £8. Dinner £8. Open all year.

Facilities are liable to change. Check prices when you book. Key to symbols is on inside back flap.

Hostels

The hostels listed here offer convenient low-cost accommodation for visitors on a limited budget. The majority of these are likely to be young people under 25 but tourists of any age are welcome.

Entries include the hostels of the Northern Ireland Association of Youth Hostels (YHANI), independent hostels and also some school accommodation. All of them have been inspected by the Northern Ireland Tourist Board under legislation regulating overnight accommodation in Northern Ireland. Facilities at some places are more comprehensive than at others, so check carefully when booking that the hostel meets your requirements.

Hostels which are open all or most of the year for backpackers and individual visitors appear in heavy type.

BELFAST

ARNIE'S BACKPACKERS
63 Fitzwilliam St, Belfast BT9 6AY.
☎ (01232) 242867.

Terraced house close to Queen's University, museum and theatres. Bus station 10 minutes walk and Botanic rail station nearby. 22 beds. Kitchen facilities. From £8. Open all year.

BELFAST INTERNATIONAL YOUTH HOSTEL
22 Donegall Rd, Belfast BT12 5JN.
☎ (01232) 324733. Fax 439699.

Big new central youth hostel (YHANI) near Queen's University, Ulster Museum, Botanic rail station and Europa bus centre. 124 beds. Family rooms. Restaurant. From £10. Open all year 24 hours.

THE ARK
18 University St, Belfast BT7 1FZ.
☎ (01232) 329626.

Terraced house close to Queen's University, museum, theatres and Botanic rail station. Bus station 10 minutes walk. 24 beds. From £9. Open all year.

County ANTRIM

BALLYCASTLE BACKPACKERS
4 North St, Ballycastle BT54 6BN.
☎ (012657) 63612.

Large house on seafront. Kitchen, dining and laundry facilities. Opposite main bus stop. Near Ulster Way. 15 beds. From £7.50. Open all year.

Beds = approx number of bedspaces

CASTLE HOSTEL
62 Quay Rd, Ballycastle BT54 6BH.
☎ (012657) 62337.

Terraced house in resort town. Sea views. Bus stop 50 yd. Horse-riding, golf, boat hire nearby, diving off Rathlin Island. Convenient for Ulster Way walkers. 42 beds. From £6. Open all year.

MONEYVART YOUTH HOSTEL
42 Layde Rd, Cushendall BT44 0NQ.
☎ (012667) 71344. Fax 72042.

Hostel (YHANI) 1 mile north of Cushendall village in the glens. On Cushendall-Ballycastle bus route, bus stop 1/2 mile. Near Ulster Way. Swimming, golf nearby. 54 beds. From £7. Open all year.

FRIENDS SCHOOL
6 Magheralave Rd, Lisburn BT28 3BH.
☎ (01846) 662156. Fax 672134.

Near Lisburn rail station. Town centre/bus station 1/2 mile. Indoor swimming pool, games room. 74 beds. Meals. From £16. Open during school holidays only – July, Aug, Easter, Christmas. *Prebooked groups only.*

GLENDUN COURT
PO Box 14, Glenville Rd, Whiteabbey BT37 0UN.
☎ & fax (01232) 853005.

High quality university accommodation. Bus stop and rail station 200yd. Near Ulster Way. 145 beds. Single and twin rooms and self-catering units. Meals by arrangement. From £10. Open mid-June - mid-Sept.

METROPOLE HOUSE
70 Eglinton St, Portrush BT56 8DY.
☎ (01265) 823511.

Adjacent to Portrush rail station, on Belfast-Londonderry rail and bus routes. 80 beds. Lift to all floors. Near Ulster Way. From £8.50. Open June-Sept.

PORTRUSH INDEPENDENT YOUTH HOSTEL (MACOOL'S)
5 Causeway View Terrace, Portrush BT56 8AT.
☎ (01265) 824845.

House in terrace with views of Causeway. On Belfast-Londonderry bus and rail routes. Portrush bus/rail station nearby. Coastal bus to Belfast, also bus to Dublin. Bus tours from hostel, Giant's Causeway, Carrick-a-rede. Near Ulster Way. 18 beds. From £6. Open all year.

SHEEP ISLAND VIEW
42 Main St, Ballintoy BT54 6LX.
☎ (012657) 69391.

New hostel in centre of village. Belfast-Ballycastle-Coleraine bus stops at door. New hostel in centre of village. Near Giant's Causeway. Ideal for Ulster Way walkers. 38 beds. From £9. Open all year.

ST. MACNISSI'S COLLEGE
Garron Tower, Carnlough BT44 0JJ.
☎ (01574) 885202. Fax 885492.

Residential facility for supervised groups on spacious school campus. 152 beds. 130 single rooms. 4 twin rooms, ensuite, for supervising staff. Conference facilities. Enquiries to Bursar. Open all year.

WHITEPARK BAY YOUTH HOSTEL
157 Whitepark Rd, Ballintoy BT54 6NH.
☎ (012657) 31745.

Hostel (YHANI) 6 miles west of Ballycastle. Bus stop 200 yd. Near Giant's Causeway and Carrick-a-rede rope bridge. Coastal paths. Popular with Ulster Way walkers. 54 beds, ensuite. Laundry room, kitchen, reading room, secure luggage. From £8.50. Open all year.

Beds = approx number of bedspaces

County ARMAGH

ARMAGH CITY HOSTEL

36 Abbey St, Armagh BT61 7EB.
☎ (01232) 324733 for information.

New hostel (YHANI) opening early 1998 in the centre of historic Armagh city, close to St Patrick's Trian. Buses to Navan Fort (Emain Macha) and Gosford Forest Park leave from the Mall (west). Kitchen facilities, TV lounge, foreign currency exchange. 64 beds. From £7. Open all year.

WATERSIDE HOUSE

Oxford Island, Lurgan BT64 1AL.
☎ (01762) 327573.

Detached house on shores of Lough Neagh. Wide range of water-based activities. B&B and half-board available. Also self-catering. 30 beds. From £7. Open all year.

County DOWN

BARHOLM

11 The Strand, Portaferry BT22 1PF.
☎ (012477) 29598.

Detached house overlooking Strangford Lough. Beside Marine Biology Station and Exploris. Ulster Way may be reached by adjacent ferry terminal to Strangford. 45 beds. From £9.95. Open all year.

GREENHILL YMCA

Donard Park, Newcastle BT33 0GR.
☎ (013967) 23172. Fax 26009.

2 chalets adapted for disabled use. Wide range of activities. Convenient for Ulster Way. 48 beds. From £5.30. *Groups only*. Open all year.

CASTLEWELLAN CASTLE CHRISTIAN CONFERENCE CENTRE

Castlewellan BT31 9BU.
☎ & fax (013967) 78733.

In Castlewellan Forest Park. On Newcastle-Castlewellan bus route, bus stop near park gate, ½ mile from Centre. Games room. Pony-trekking nearby. 142 beds. Family rooms. From £12. *Groups only*. Open all year ex Christmas.

HILLYARD HOUSE

1 Castle Avenue, Castlewellan BT31 9DX.
☎ (013967) 70141. Fax 70011.

Situated off main street at the entrance to Castlewellan Forest Park, with its lake and famous arboretum. Outdoor activities, for example mountaineering and canoeing, can be arranged. All meals available. 30 beds. 9 bedrooms, all ensuite. 1 room suitable for disabled visitor. From £15. Open all year ex Christmas.

KNOCKBARRAGH HOSTEL

Lower Knockbarragh Rd, Rostrevor BT34 3DP.
☎ (016937) 39716/74006.

On outskirts of Rostrevor. Water and land-based activities. 28 beds. From £8.50. *Groups only*. Open all year.

NEWCASTLE YOUTH HOSTEL

30 Downs Rd, Newcastle BT33 0AG.
☎ (013967) 22133.

Hostel (YHANI) in resort town in foothills of Mourne mountains. Nature reserve, forest parks and Ulster Way route nearby. Coastal walks. Bus station 50 yd. 42 beds. Meals. From £7. Open all year.

Beds = approx number of bedspaces

ROSTREVOR YOUTH CENTRE
Warrenpoint Rd, Rostrevor BT34 3AY.
☎ (016937) 38536 or (01232) 322284.

Town centre location, convenient to bus stop. Recreation room, table tennis, pool table. Access to forest parks, water sports and mountain climbing. Convenient for Ulster Way. 26 beds. Meals by arrangement. From £5. *Groups only.* Open all year ex Christmas.

ULSTER FOLK & TRANSPORT MUSEUM
Educational Residential Centre,
Cultra, Holywood BT18 0EU.
☎ (01232) 428428. Fax 428728.

In grounds of Ulster Folk & Transport Museum. Price includes entry to all exhibits. On Belfast-Bangor bus/train routes, bus stop nearby, Cultra Halt ½ mile. Near Ulster Way. 76 beds. Meals. From £13. *Groups only.* Open all year.

County FERMANAGH

CASTLE ARCHDALE YOUTH HOSTEL
Lisnarick BT94 1PP.
☎ & fax (013656) 28118.

Converted 18th-century stables in Castle Archdale Country Park, on lough shore (YHANI). 11 miles north of Enniskillen on B82. Nature trails, horse-riding, canoeing, ferry to White Island in summer. Marina 100 yd. On Enniskillen-Kesh bus route (bus stop is 1 mile from hostel). 52 beds. Meals. Family rooms. From £6. Open March-Oct.

LAKELAND CANOE CENTRE
Castle Island, Enniskillen BT74 7BA.
☎ (01365) 324250.

Dormitory accommodation, ½ mile west of Enniskillen town centre and bus station. Archery, canoeing, caving, jet-skiing, windsurfing, sailing, water-biking. Bicycle hire. Summer camps. 42 beds. Meals. From £9 (B&B £10.50). Open all year.

LOUGH MELVIN HOLIDAY CENTRE
Garrison BT93 3FG.
☎ (013656) 58142/58143. Fax 58719.

In Garrison village, 4 miles north of Belleek on shores of Lough Melvin. On Enniskillen-Belleek bus route (bus goes via Garrison Tues & Thur only). Fishing, boating, wind-surfing, bicycle hire. Pony-trekking. Camping/caravan site adjacent. 51 beds. Family rooms. B&B from £8. Accommodation and sporting activities suitable for wheelchair users. Full catering service open to public and residents. Open all year.

Beds = approx number of bedspaces

THE SHARE CENTRE

Smith's Strand, Lisnaskea BT92 0EQ.
☎ (013657) 22122. Fax 21893.

Hostel and self-catering chalets. On Belfast-Enniskillen bus route, 4 miles south of Lisnaskea. Near Ulster Way. Motor sports, water sports, archery, walking, bicycle hire. Viking longship cruises. Tepee campsite. Indoor leisure complex with swimming pool. 170 beds. Meals. Variable rates. Suitable for disabled visitors/groups. Open all year.

TIR NAVAR

Creamery St, Derrygonnelly BT93 6HW.
☎ (01365) 641673. Fax 641771.

In Derrygonnelly village on Enniskillen-Derrygonnelly bus route, near Lower Lough Erne and Ulster Way. Water sports, bicycle hire, fishing, caving and golf. Restaurant, laundry and conference facilities. 60 beds, 18 rooms, ensuite, TV. From £10, B&B £13. Open all year.

WILLOW PATTERN COMPLEX

89 Crevenish Rd, Kesh BT93 1RQ.
☎ (013656) 31012.

Dormitory accommodation, 12 miles north-west of Enniskillen. On Enniskillen-Kesh bus route, bus stop 2¹/₂ miles. Putting green, tennis, fishing, boating, golf nearby. Shop and restaurant on site. 50 beds. Meals by arrangement. From £5. Open all year.

County LONDONDERRY

CAUSEWAY COAST INDEPENDENT HOSTEL

4 Victoria Terrace, Portstewart BT55 7BA.
☎ (01265) 833789.

Terraced house by seafront. On Coleraine-Portstewart bus route. Coleraine rail station 3 miles. Direct bus link to Giant's Causeway from hostel. Near Ulster Way. Golf, pony-trekking, sea-angling, bicycle hire nearby. 28 beds. Family rooms. From £6. Open all year.

THE FLAX MILL

Mill Lane, Gortnaghey Rd, Dungiven BT47 4PY.
☎ (015047) 42655.

Converted stone mill 3 miles from Dungiven. Phone from town centre to arrange pick-up. Traditional music sessions, bicycle hire includes recommended cycle routes, walking (Ben Bradagh nearby). Pub close by, provisions shop within walking distance. 16 beds. From £5, B&B £6.50. Open all year.

GUYSMERE CENTRE

Sea Rd, Castlerock BT51 4RA.
☎ (01265) 848672 or (01232) 768743.

Only 50 yd from beach and within walking distance of a rail link to Belfast. Convenient for Ulster Way walkers. Water-based activities, indoor sports hall, table tennis. 34 beds. Meals by arrangement. From £5. *Groups only.* Open all year.

Beds = approx number of bedspaces

OAKGROVE MANOR
4 Magazine St, Londonderry BT48 6HJ.
☎ (01504) 372273. Fax 372409.

Hostel (YHANI) inside walled city, near museums, galleries, theatres, shops and all services. Close to rail and bus stations. 106 beds. Meals. Family rooms. From £7.50. Open all year.

INDEPENDENT HOSTEL
29 Aberfoyle Terrace, Strand Rd, Londonderry BT48 7NA.
☎ (01504) 370011.

Terraced house close to Magee College 1 mile from Derry city centre. Bus stop 10 yd, bus station 1 mile. 12 beds. From £7.50. Open May-Oct.

ST COLUMB'S PARK HOUSE
4 Limavady Rd, Londonderry BT47 1JA.
☎ (01504) 43080.

Manor house housing reconciliation and activity centre. Convenient to city centre and bus routes. Wide range of activities. 45 beds. From £10. *Groups only.* Open all year.

County TYRONE

BENBURB VALLEY YOUTH HOSTEL
89 Milltown Rd, Tullymore Etra, Benburb BT71 7LZ.
☎ (01861) 549752.

Beside Benburb Valley Heritage Centre. Just outside Benburb village, well signposted. Wildlife, watersports. Convenient for Ulster Way walkers. 23 beds. From £6. Family rooms to suit 3 £18. Open all year.

GORTIN OUTDOOR CENTRE
198 Glenpark Rd, Gortin, Omagh BT79 8PJ.
☎ (01662) 648083 or (01232) 480285.

Old school converted into self-catering hostel. 50 yd from crossroads in Gortin village. Bus to Ulster-American Folk Park. Bike hire, fishing, canoeing, riding nearby. Near Ulster Way. 18 beds. From £6. Open all year for groups, July-Sept for individuals.

OMAGH HOSTEL
9a Waterworks Rd, Omagh BT79 7JS.
☎ (01662) 241973. Fax 241973.

New hostel 2½ miles north-east of Omagh centre and bus station. Backpackers picked up from station by arrangement. 15 minutes' drive/bus from Ulster-American Folk Park, Gortin Forest Park, Fermanagh Lakes. 3 miles off Ulster Way route. 29 beds. From £6.50. Open all year.

ULSTER-AMERICAN FOLK PARK RESIDENTIAL CENTRE
Camphill Road, Omagh BT78 5QY.
☎ (01662) 240918.

Adjacent to folk park, near Gortin Glen Forest Park, Sperrin Heritage Centre and Ulster History Park. Convenient for Ulster Way walkers. 38 beds. Suitable for disabled visitors. From £10. Meals available. *Groups only.* Open all year.

Beds = approx number of bedspaces

Key to self-catering symbols

T Bookable through travel agents
Possibilité de réservation à l'agence de voyage
Reservierung über Reisebüros möglich

P Parking spaces
Parking
Parkmöglichkeit

Building of architectural/ historical interest
Bâtiment d'intérêt architectural/historique
Architecktonisch/ historisch interessantes Gebäude

Garden for guests' use
Jardin à l'usage des résidents
Garten steht den Gästen zur Verfügung

Children welcome
Les enfants sont bienvenus
Kinderfreundlich

Cots and/or high chairs
Lits et/ou chaises d'enfants
Kinderbetten und/oder Hochstühle

Baby sitting/listening service
Service de garde d'enfants/d'écoute
Baby-Sitting/- Lauschdienst

OAP Reduced rates for senior citizens
Réduction pour les retraités
Ermäßigungen für Senioren

Accessible to people with limited mobility
Accessible aux personnes dont la mobilité est limitée
Für gehbehinderte Besucher zugänglich

Dogs accepted
Les chiens sont admis à l'intérieur
Hunde im Haus gestattet

Central heating in unit
Chauffage central dans l'appartement
Wohneinheit mit Zentralheizung

M Gas/electricity charged by meter
Gaz/électricité tariffiés au compteur
Gas- u. Stromabrechnung nach Verbrauch

Clothes washing machine
Machine à laver le linge
Waschmaschine

Clothes drying facilities
Facilités pour le séchage du linge
Möglichkeit zum Wäschetrocknen

Ironing facilities
Facilités pour le repassage
Bügeleinrichtung

Refrigerator
Réfrigérateur
Kühlschrank

Radio

Television
Télévision
Fernsehgerät

Electric shaver point
Prises pour rasoir électrique
Anschluß für Trockenrasierer

Linen available
Linge de maison fourni à la demande
Bettwäsche auf Wunsch

Telephone exclusively for guests' use
Usage du téléphone réservé aux résidents
Telefon nur für Gäste

Food shop
Magasin d'alimentation
Lebensmittelverkauf

Licensed bar
Vente de boissons alcoolisées
Bar mit Ausschanklizenz

Café/restaurant
Café/restaurant
Café/Restaurant

Games room
Salle de jeux
Freizeitraum

Tennis courts
Courts de tennis
Tennisplätze

Indoor heated swimming pool
Piscine couverte chauffée
Beheiztes Hallenbad

Fishing arranged
Pêche
Angelmöglichkeit

Pony trekking/riding arranged
Promenades à poney/ équitation
Pony Trekking -reiten

Not suitable for smokers
Espace non fumeur
Rauchen nicht erlaubt

Credit cards accepted
Cartes de crédit acceptées
Kreditkarten akzeptiert

Self-catering

More people than ever before are enjoying the freedom of a self-catering holiday in Northern Ireland, and there is a wide range of accommodation to choose from. There are chalets and houses on secluded estates, luxury apartments in lively coastal resorts, island cottages and mansion flats in beautiful surroundings, with plenty of leisure activities and places of interest nearby.

All the establishments listed have been inspected by the Northern Ireland Tourist Board (NITB) and are classified by a star system to help you find exactly what you are looking for. Establishments with the most stars have the most facilities.

Please note that units on the same site do not always have the same facilities and so there can be different star ratings. In these cases, the range of units available is shown. Accommodation listed as 'unclassified', includes units that did not meet the criteria of the star rating which had been applied for.

There is every reason to believe that the accommodation you choose will meet your expectations. If there is any kind of problem please tell the owner or manager immediately so that it can be put right without delay. If thereafter you wish to bring the matter to the Tourist Board's attention please write to: Quality Assurance Manager, NITB, 59 North Street, Belfast BT1 1NB.

Self-catering accommodation which may be suitable for wheelchair users but has not yet been inspected under the National Accessible Scheme is indicated by &.

One star *
Clean, comfortable accommodation with adequate facilities and equipment for the number of people accommodated.

Two stars **
Extra facilities include colour television.

Three stars ***
Self-contained. Extra facilities and equipment include the availability of linen.

Four stars ****
Extra facilities include a washing machine and tumble dryer on the site.

Five stars *****
Extra facilities include controlled heating.

Self-catering

Belfast Area

Gleneagles ***
25a Knockbreda Park, Belfast BT6 0HB.
☎ (01232) 693646. Fax 330713.
Mobile 080 275 3126. *(Mrs B McQuillan)*.
Bungalow (sleeps 5), £260 low season,
£300 high season, open Jan-Oct.

P ✿ ⛷ ♿ 🖵 🖩 ⊘ ✦ ⌂ ⬚ 🔔 🖵 ☉ ☎ ⚑ ⛳ ♪ ☂

Glenwhirry Court *
PO Box 14, Glenville Rd, Whiteabbey BT37 0UN.
☎ (01232) 853005. *(Mrs E McNeilly)*.
4 apartments (sleep 5/6). £70 per person per week,
open all year.

P ✿ ⛷ ♿ 🖵 M ⊘ ⌂ ⬚ ♟ ✗ ♪ 🖾

L'Academie *****
14 College Gardens, Belfast BT9 5JQ.
☎ & fax (01232) 666046. *(Ms A Aubrey)*.
2 apartments (sleep 4), £350, open all year.

P ⛪ ⛷ 🖵 ⛴ ✦ ✦ 🖵 ⊘ ✦ ⌂ ⬚ 🔔 🖵 ☉ ☎ ☎
⚑ ♟ ✗ ☂ ☝ 🖾

Malone Mews ***
2 Sandringham St, Belfast BT9 7EG.
☎ (01232) 381606. Fax 381607.
(Mr & Mrs Macklin).
14 5-star apartments (1, 2 & 3 bedrooms, sleep 2-6),
£480, open all year.

T P ⛷ 🖵 ♿ 🖩 ⊘ ✦ ⌂ ⬚ 🔔 🖵 ☉ ☎ ⚑ ☎ ⚑
♟ ✗ ☝ 🖾

Malone View ***
52 Malone Avenue, Belfast BT9 6ER.
☎ (01232) 776889. Mobile 0411 085463.
(Mr & Mrs Cush).
House (3 bedrooms, sleeps 5), £290, open all year.

T ✿ ⛷ 🖵 ⓓⓐⓟ ✦ 🖩 ⊘ ✦ ⌂ ⬚ 🔔 🖵 ☉ ☎ ☎
⚑ ♟ ✗ ☝

5 Brooklands Court ***
1 Annadale Avenue, Belfast BT7 3JH.
☎ (01846) 683131 *evening*. Mobile 0860 338832.
(Dr E MacSorley).
Large s/c apartment (sleeps 4), £290, open all year.

P ⛪ ✿ ⛷ 🖵 🖩 M ⊘ ✦ ⌂ ⬚ 🔔 🖵 ☉ ☎ ☎
⚑ ♟ ✗ 🖾

7 Musgrave Park Court ****
Balmoral, Belfast BT9 7HZ.
☎ & fax (01232) 666046. *(Mrs A Aubrey)*.
Town house (sleeps 4/5), £300, open all year.

P ✿ ⛷ 🖵 ⛴ ⓓⓐⓟ ✦ 🖵 🖩 ⊘ ✦ ⌂ ⬚ 🔔 🖵 ☉ ☎
☎ ⚑ ♟ ✗ ♪ ☝ ☂ 🖾

For rural locations, ask for directions when you book

County Antrim

Antrim

Vale Farm   ***
128 Steeple Rd, Edenvale, Kells, BT42 3NP.
☎ (01266) 898030. *(Mr R Walker).*
Farmhouse (sleeps 5), £245 low season,
£380 high season, open all year.

Ballintoy

Braeside   ***
127 Whitepark Rd, BT54 6LS.
☎ (012657) 62921. *(Mrs M McCullough).*
Cottage (2 bedrooms, sleeps 4), £170 low season,
£220 high season, open March-Nov.

Jura   **
37 Harbour Rd, BT54 6NA.
☎ (01247) 853474. *(Mrs C Belford).*
Bungalow (2 bedrooms, sleeps 4), £280 low
season, £350 high season, open all year.

Ballycastle

Awelon Cottage   ***
22c Ballyvennaght Rd, BT54 6RL.
☎ (01232) 241100. Fax 241198.
(Bookings through Michelle).
Cottage (sleeps 5), £210 low season,
£320 high season, open all year.

Ballinlea Mill   ***
34 Kilmahamogue Rd, BT54 6JJ.
☎ & fax (012657) 62287. *(Mr C Stewart-Moore).*
Restored mill house (3 bedrooms, sleeps 6),
low season by arrangement, £350 high season,
open all year. Paddock.

Capecastle Cottage   ***
68 Hillside Rd, BT54 6HY.
☎ (012657) 62665. Fax (012656) 66129.
(Mr H Taggart).
Cottage type farmhouse (sleeps 4),
£175 low season, £275 high season, open all year.

Marine Apartments   ***
North St, BT54 6BN.
☎ (012657) 62166. Fax 63170. *(Mr C McGinn).*
27 apartments, £150/210 low season, £260/360
high season, open all year.

Murlough Cottage   ***
22 Ballyvennaght Rd, BT54 6RL.
☎ (01232) 241100. Fax 241198.
(Bookings through Michelle).
Cottage (sleeps 5/6), £210 low season, £320 high
season, open all year.

Murlough House   **
10 Murlough Rd, Torr, BT54 6RG.
☎ (012657) 62270/69696. *(Mr P McCarry).*
House (sleeps 6), £250 low season, £330 high
season, open all year.

Self-catering prices given are the weekly rate

Murlough Lodge **
10 Murlough Rd, Torr, BT54 6RG.
☎ (012657) 62270. (*Mr P McCarry*).
Lodge (sleeps 6), £175 low season,
£220 high season, open all year.

Northlands ***
4 Clare Rd, BT54 6DB.
☎ (01232) 427412. (*Mrs K Yoshida*).
Chalet bungalow (sleeps 8), £350 per week,
open July-Aug.

Rathlin View ***
85 Blackpark Rd, Ballyvoy, BT54 6QZ.
☎ (012657) 63497. (*Mr G McCambridge*).
Bungalow (sleeps 5/6), £180 low season,
£250 high season.

Rock Cottage ***
24 Carrickmore Rd, BT54 6QS.
☎ (01232) 241100. Fax 241198.
(*Bookings through Michelle*).
Cottage (sleeps 4), £250 low season,
£365 high season, open all year.

Rowans ***
27 Caman Park, BT54 6LH.
☎ (012657) 63650/63619. (*Mr & Mrs McLister*).
Bungalow (sleeps 6), £270, open April-Sept.

Silvercliffs Holiday Village ***/**
21 Clare Rd, BT54 5DB.
☎ (012657) 62550. Fax 62259. (*Mrs K Hagan*).
25 apartments, 2 chalets: £80/100 low season,
£230/295 high season, open all year.

19 Ballynagard Rd **
BT54 6PW. (*Bookings through: 18 Kensington
Gardens, Belfast BT5 6NP*). ☎ (01232) 795489.
(*Mr A Mullan*). Bungalow (sleeps 4/5), £195 low
season, £230 high season, open May-Sept.

Ballygalley

Ballygalley Holiday Apartments ***
210 Coast Rd, BT40 2QQ.
☎ (01574) 583061. Fax 583100.
(*D & J Enterprises*).
Apartments, (2/3 bedrooms, sleep 4/6), £150/260
low season, £275/400 high season, open all year.

Ballymena

Lisnawhiggle ****
53a Grove Rd, Kells, BT42 3LR.
☎ & fax (01266) 891662.
(*Mr & Mrs Montgomery*).
Cottage (sleeps 6), £120 low season, £250 high
season, open all year.

Lure Cottage at Cleggan Lodge   *
Broughshane, BT43 7JW.
☎ (01266) 862222. Fax 862000.
Remote converted 19th-century shepherd's
cottage (3 bedrooms, sleeps 6), £120 low season,
£200/250 high season, open all year. Open fire,
spring water, pheasant/rough shooting.

Ⓣ Ⓟ ▨ ✿ 🐎 🐴 ⚋ ⬛ 🗄 🖵 ◐ ♩ ∪

Mann's Cottage at Cleggan Lodge   **
Broughshane, BT43 7JW.
☎ (01266) 862222. Fax 862000.
Restored 19th-century farmhouse (3 bedrooms,
sleeps 6), annexe (sleeps 4), £240 low season,
£375/380 high season, open all year. Open fires,
spring water, bicycles, pheasant/rough shooting.

Ⓣ Ⓟ 🏠 ✿ 🐎 🐴 🎞 ⚋ ⬛ 🗄 🖵 ◖ ◑ ♩ ∪

Mews Cottages   ***
Galgorm Manor, 136 Fenaghy Rd, BT42 1EA.
☎ (01266) 881001. Fax 880080.
6 cottages (1/2 bedrooms, sleep 2/5), £400, open
all year except 24/25 Dec.

Ⓣ Ⓟ 🏠 ✿ 🐎 🐴 🎞 🐕 🎞 ⚋ 🗄 ▣ 🖵 ⊙ ◖ ⚑
✕ ♩ ∪ ⊞

Pollock Cottage   ***
19 Old Tullygarley Rd, BT42 2JD.
☎ (01266) 41324. (Mr S Carson).
Cottage (sleeps 2), £180 low season,
£240 high season, open all year.

Ⓟ 🏠 ✿ 🐎 🎞 🄾🄿 🐕 🎞 🗄 ⚋ ⬛ 🗄 ▣
🖵 ⊙ ♩ ∪

Queensway   ***
134a Queen St, BT42 2BQ.
☎ (01266) 656966. (Mr D Lamont).
Apartment (2 bedrooms, sleeps 4/6), £120 low
season, £195 high season.

Ⓟ 🐎 🄾🄿 🎞 🗄 🗄 ▣ 🖵 ⊙ ⚑ ◖ ⚑ ⚑ ✕ ◕ ✂

Conagher Chalets   ***
111a/111b Knock Rd, Conagher, BT53 6NH.
☎ (012657) 41342. (Mrs J Richmond).
2 chalets (sleep 6), £120 low season,
£300 high season, open all year.

Ⓣ Ⓟ ✿ 🐎 🎞 🎞 🄼 🗄 ⚋ ⬛ 🗄 🖵 ⊙ ⚑
◖ ♩ ∪ ✂

O'Harabrook, Old Dairy   ***
Bann Rd, BT53 7PN.
☎ & fax (012656) 66273. (Mr & Mrs Cramsie).
3 apartments (sleep 4/6), £250 low season, £405
high season, open all year.

Ⓟ 🏠 ✿ 🐎 🎞 🚶 ♿ 🐴 🎞 ⚋ 🗄 🖵 ⊙
⚑ ⚑ ◕ ♩

Thornbrook   **
39a Macfin Rd, BT53 6QY.
☎ (012656) 66907. (Mrs D Smith).
House (sleeps 3), £150 low season, £200 high
season, open all year.

Ⓟ ✿ 🐎 🎞 🄾🄿 🎞 🗄 ⚋ ⬛ 🗄 ▣ 🖵 ⊙ ♩ ∪

Achill   ***
21 Bushford, Dunluce Rd, BT57 8AQ.
☎ (01266) 41547. (Mrs M Boyce).
Apartment (ground floor, sleeps 4/6),
£140/175 low season, £280 high season,
open all year.

Ⓟ 🏠 ✿ 🐎 🎞 🄾🄿 🎞 🄼 🗄 ⚋ ⬛ 🗄 ▣ 🖵 ⊙ ◖
⚑ ⚑ ✕ ∪

Acorn Lodge ****
2 Tramway Drive, BT57 8YS.
☎ (01861) 507265. *(Mrs A Wilson).*
Bungalow (4 bedrooms, sleeps 6), £120 low
season, £290/310 high season, open all year.

🅿 ✳ ⛵ ▦ DAP ▥ M ⌨ ⁄ 🛆 🗓 🖥 ⎕ ☉ ☎ ⚓
🍴 ✗ ⚓ ☺

Al Norte Holiday Homes ***
198/200 Causeway Rd, BT57 8SY.
☎ (012656) 63390. *(Mrs F Murdock).*
2 cottages (sleep 7), £160 low season, £275 high
season, open all year.

🆃 🅿 ✳ ⛵ ▦ DAP 🐕 ▥ ⌨ ⁄ 🛆 🗓 ⎕ ☉
🔲 ☺ ☺ ⚓

Ballylinny Holiday Cottages ****
7 Causeway Rd, BT57 8SU.
☎ & fax (012657) 31683. *(Mr & Mrs Laverty).*
6 cottages (sleep 4/7), sea view, £240 low season,
£399 high season, open all year.

🆃 🅿 ✳ ⛵ ▦ ⚷ ▥ M ⌨ ⁄ 🛆 🗓 ⎕ ☉ ☎ ⚓
🍴 ✗ ⚓ ⚲ ⚓ ☺ ☺ ☺

The Cottage ***
184 Ballybogey Rd, BT57 8UQ.
☎ (012657) 32295. *(Mr & Mrs Rankin).*
Cottage (sleeps 4/6), £220 low season,
£280 high season, open all year.

🅿 ✳ ⛵ ▦ ▥ ⁄ 🛆 🗓 ⎕ ☉ ⚓ ✗ ⚓ ☺ ☺

Finch Cottage ****
7 Ballyclough Cottages, Ballyclough Rd, BT57 8TU.
☎ (01846) 682376. *(Mrs J Parks).*
Modern cottage (sleeps 4/5), £200/240 low season,
£320 high season, open April-Sept.

🅿 ✳ ⛵ ▦ ▥ M ⌨ ⁄ 🛆 🗓 ⎕ ☉ 🔲
☺ ⚓ ☺ ☺

Giant's Causeway Holiday Cottages ***
71 Causeway Rd, BT57 8SX.
☎ (012657) 31673. Fax 32533. *(Ms A Millar).*
8 cottages (sleep 6), £190/210 low season,
£350/410 high season, open all year. Bicycle hire.

🆃 🅿 ✳ ⛵ ▦ 🔌 ⚷ ▥ M ⌨ ⁄ 🛆 🗓 ⎕ ☉ 🔲
☎ ⚓ ⚓ ☺ ☺ 🔲

Glebe Lodge ****
3 Cabragh Rd, BT57 8YH. ☎ (012657) 31208.
(Mrs M Page). 1 unit (sleeps 2), £170 low season,
£320 high season, open all year.

🅿 ✳ ⛵ ▦ ▥ ⌨ ⁄ 🛆 🗓 ⎕ ☉ 🔲 ☎ ⚓ ☺

Glenfield Cottage ***
57 Moycraig Rd, Dunseverick, BT57 8YB.
☎ (012657) 31889. *(Mrs A McVicker).*
Cottage (sleeps 5), £180 low season,
£250 high season, open all year.

🅿 ✳ ⛵ ▦ ▥ ⌨ ⁄ 🛆 🗓 ⎕ ☉ 🔲 ⚓ ☺

Hillview **
50 Carnbore Rd, BT57 8YF.
☎ (012657) 31547 after 6 pm. *(Mrs M Dunlop).*
House (3 bedrooms, sleeps 6), £200/225 low
season, £280 high season, open March-Oct.

🅿 ✳ ⛵ ▦ ▥ M ⁄ 🛆 🗓 ⎕ ☉ 🔲 ⚓ ☺ ☺

Jasmine Cottage ****
11 Ballyclough Cottages, Ballyclough Rd, BT57 8XA.
☎ & fax (01225) 837088. *(Mr A Crawford).*
Traditional-style cottage (new, sleeps 4/6),
£160/200 low season, £250/315 high season,
open all year.

🅿 ✳ ⛵ ▦ DAP ▥ ⌨ ⁄ 🛆 🗓 🖥 ⎕ ☉ ☎ ☺

Lavender Cottage ****
9 Ballyclough Cottages, Ballyclough Rd, BT57 8AA.
☎ & fax (012657) 31592. *(Mrs R Campbell).*
Cottage (sleeps 4), £145 low season,
£320 high season, open all year.

🆃 🅿 ✳ ⛵ ▦ 🔌 ▥ M ⌨ ⁄ 🛆 🗓 🖥 ⎕ ☉
☎ ⚓ ☺ ⚓ 🔲

For rural locations, ask for directions when you book

Old Ballyness Cottages ***
38a & 38b Castlecatt Rd, BT57 8TN.
☎ & fax (012657) 31252. *(Mr D Dunlop)*.
2 cottages (a sleeps 8 and b sleeps 7), £140 low
season, £300/320 high season, open all year.

Pebbles ****
49 Bush Gardens, BT57 8AG.
☎ (01232) 851087. *(Mrs I Love)*.
Bungalow (sleeps 6), £200 low season, £320 high
season, open all year.

Quarry Cottage ****
35 Riverside Rd, Ballyloughmore, BT57 8TP.
☎ (012657) 31207. *(Mrs A McKendry)*.
Cottage (sleeps 6), £200 low season, £325 high
season, open March-Nov.

Rose Cottage ****
8 Ballyclough Cottages, Ballyclough Rd, BT57 8XA.
☎ (012657) 31592 after 6 pm. *(Mrs R Campbell)*.
Cottage (2 bedrooms, sleeps 4/6), £145 low season,
£320 high season, open all year.

Scriebe ****
181 Straid Rd, BT57 8XW.
☎ (012657) 31333. *(Mr S Cochrane)*.
Farmhouse (sleeps 8), £140/200 low season,
£260/290 high season, open all year.

Seaview Cottage ****
4 Ballyclough Cottages, Ballyclough Rd, BT57 8AA.
☎ (01232) 649733. Fax 641681. *(Mr M Carlisle)*.
Cottage (sleeps 4/6), £200 low season, £300 high
season, open all year.

Walkmills Holiday Cottage ***
28a Priestland Rd, BT57 8XB.
☎ (012657) 31261. *(Mr D Adams)*.
2 cottages (sleep 4/6), £150 low season,
£280 high season, open all year.

Willow Cottage ****
14 Ballyclough Cottages, BT57 8AA.
☎ & fax (01225) 837088. *(Mr A Crawford)*.
Traditional (new) cottage (sleeps 4/5),
£160/200 low season, £250/315 high season,
open all year.

Carnlough

Kintyre ***
177 Bay Rd, BT44 0HR.
☎ (01266) 653596. *(Mrs K McCullough)*.
Bungalow (sleeps 4/5), £200 low season,
£250 high season, open April-Sept.

Straidkilly ***
Cottage A, 36 Glenarm Rd, Larne BT40 1BP.
☎ (01232) 241100. Fax 241198.
(Bookings through Michelle).
Cottage (sleeps 7), £210 low season,
£320 high season, open all year.

Self-catering prices given are the weekly rate

Straidkilly ***
Cottage B, 38 Glenarm Rd, Larne BT40 1BP.
☎ (01232) 241100. Fax 241198.
(Bookings through Michelle).
Cottage (sleeps 7), £240 low season,
£340 high season, open all year.

🖵 🅿 📠 ✲ 🐴 🎠 🏛 ⬜ ✂ 🛋 🗄 🖥 ☉ 🖵 ☎
🎵 ☕ ✄ 🔲

Straidkilly ***
Cottage C, 31 Glenarm Rd, Larne BT40 1BP.
☎ (01232) 241100. Fax 241198.
(Bookings through Michelle).
Cottage (sleeps 5), £210 low season,
£320 high season, open all year.

🖵 🅿 📠 ✲ 🐴 🎠 🏛 ⬜ ✂ 🛋 🗄 🖥 ☉ 🖵 ☎
🎵 ☕ ✄ 🔲

Carrickfergus

Fairview Terrace Cottages ****
14, 15, 16 Fairview Terrace, Woodburn Rd,
BT38 8PY.
☎ & fax (01960) 363117. *(Mr J Colwell).*
3 cottages (2 bedrooms, sleep 4), £150 low
season, £280 high season, open all year.

🖵 🅿 🎠 🏛 ⬜ Ⓜ 🖥 ✂ 🛋 🗄 🖥 ☉ 🖵 ☎ 🏆
✕ 🎵 ☕ ✄

Clough

Artnacrea House **
107 Ballycregagh Rd, BT44 9RG.
☎ (01960) 353403/4. Fax 353404.
(Mrs M Matthews).
Farmhouse (sleeps 8), £250 low season,
£325 high season, open all year.

🖵 🅿 ✲ 🐴 DAP 🏛 🖥 ✂ 🛋 🗄 🖥 🖥 ☉ 🖵 ☎ 🏆
🏆 ✕ ☕ ✄ 🔲

Cushendall

Glenaan Cottage ***
31 Glenann Rd, BT44 0TG .
☎ (01232) 241100. Fax 241198.
(Bookings through Michelle).
Cottage (sleeps 5), £260 low season,
£360 high season, open all year.

🖵 🅿 📠 ✲ 🐴 🐕 🏛 🖥 ✂ 🛋 🗄 🖥 ☉ 🖵 ☎
🎵 ☕ ✄ 🔲

Portnagolan House ***
17 Layde Rd, BT44 0NQ.
☎ (012667) 71239. *(Mrs L Dobbs).*
Flat (sleeps 4), £200 low season,
£250 high season, open all year.

🖵 🅿 ✲ 🐴 🏛 🐕 🏛 🖥 ✂ 🛋 🗄 🖥 🖥 ☉
🖥 🎵 ☕ ✄

Cushendun

Beachview Cottages ****
185c & 185d Torr Rd, BT44 0PU.
☎ (012667) 61540. *(Mrs P Scally).*
2 bungalows (sleep 6), £250 low season,
£360 high season, open all year.

🅿 ✲ 🐴 🏛 ♿ 🐕 🏛 🖥 ✂ 🛋 🗄 🖥 ☉ 🖥
✕ 🎵 ☕ ✄

Beech Cottage ***
26 Glendun Rd, BT44 0PY.
☎ & fax (012667) 61286. *(Mr D McKenna).*
Cottage (sleeps 7), £150 low season, £350 high
season, open all year.

🖵 🅿 ✲ 🐴 🏛 🐕 🏛 Ⓜ 🖥 ✂ 🛋 🗄 🖥 🖥
☉ 🎵 ☕ ✄

For rural locations, ask for directions when you book

Drumfaskey ****
153 Glendun Rd, BT44 0FT.
☎ (012667) 61239. *(Mrs E McAuley)*.
Cottage (sleeps 5), £100/200 low season,
£300 high season, open all year.

Irragh House ****
8 Irragh Lane, Glendun, BT44 0TB.
☎ (012667) 61400/61264. *(Mrs C Mullan)*.
House (sleeps 8), £230 low season,
£270 high season, open April-Sept.

John O' The Rocks Cottage ****
10 Castlepark, BT44 0PT.
☎ (012667) 61250. Fax 61402. *(Mr P McNeill)*.
Bungalow (sleeps 6), £240 low season, £360 high
season, open all year.

Mullarts Apartments ****
114 Tromra Rd, BT44 0ST.
☎ & fax (012667) 61221. *(Mrs A Blaney)*.
3 apartments (sleep 4/8), £200 low season,
£375 high season, open all year.

Seaside Cottage ***
186 Torr Rd, Ballycleagh, BT44 0PU.
☎ & fax (012667) 61289. *(Mrs M McNeill)*.
Cottage (3 bedrooms, 2 ensuite, sleeps 8),
£230 low season, £360 high season,
open all year.

Strand House ***
2 Bay Rd, BT54 0PS.
☎ (01232) 241100. Fax 241198.
(Bookings through Michelle).
House (sleeps 7), £250 low season,
£405 high season, open all year.

Strand House Annexe ***
2 Bay Rd, BT54 0PS.
☎ (01232) 241100. Fax 241198.
(Bookings through Michelle).
1 unit (sleeps 2), £105 low season,
£180 high season, open all year.

The Turn
130 Knocknacarry Rd, BT44 0NU.
☎ (012677) 61470. *(Ms C Graham)*.
18th-century former roadside inn (sleeps 10),
£300 low season, £400 high season,
open all year.

Tybann House Holiday Homes ***
51 Glendun Rd, BT44 0PY.
☎ & fax (012667) 61289. *(Mrs M McNeill)*.
4 apartments and 2 houses (sleep 8/10), £150/230
low season, £210/300 high season, open all year.

Self-catering prices given are the weekly rate

Glenarm

Bellair Cottage   ****
Tully Rd, BT44 0BJ.
☎ (01232) 241100. Fax 241198.
(Bookings through Michelle).
Traditional farmhouse (3 bedrooms, sleeps 6),
£300 low season, £395 high season,
open all year.

🅣 🅟 🏠 ❄ 🦌 🐎 🐕 🎴 ⬛ ⚋ 🗄 🖬 🖵 ☉ ✂ 🎫

Briarfield   ***
65 Dickeystown Rd, BT44 0BA.
☎ (01574) 841296. *(Mrs C Matthews).*
Cottage-style farmhouse (sleeps 4), £130/175 low
season, £250 high season, open all year.

🅣 🅟 ❄ 🦌 🐎 🐕 🎴 🔌 ⬛ 🖬 🗄 ⚋ 🖬 🖵 ☉
🍴 ✕ 🔍 🥄 ∪ ✂

Rectory Cottage   ***
62 Munie Rd, BT44 0BL.
☎ (01232) 241100. Fax 241198.
(Bookings through Michelle).
Traditional 1880s farmhouse (3 bedrooms,
sleeps 5), £260 low season, £365 high season,
open all year.

🅣 🅟 🏠 ❄ 🦌 🐎 🎴 ⚋ 🗄 🖵 ☉ ✂ 🎫

Tully Cottage   ***
Tully Rd, BT44 0BJ.
☎ (01232) 241100. Fax 241198.
(Bookings through Michelle).
150-year-old farmhouse (2 bedrooms, sleeps 4),
£250 low season, £365 high season, open all year.

🅣 🅟 🏠 ❄ 🦌 🐎 🎴 ⚋ 🗄 🖵 ☉
🖬 🥄 ✂ 🎫

Upper Briarfield   **
59 Dickeystown Rd, BT44 0BA.
☎ (01574) 841413. *(Mrs M Steele).*
Country house (sleeps 5), £170 low season,
£200 high season, open all year.

🅟 ❄ 🦌 🎴 🖬 🖬 ⚋ 🗄 🖵 ☉ 🥄

Islandmagee

Island Cottage   ***
71 Gobbins Rd, BT40 3TY.
☎ (01232) 241100. Fax 241198.
(Bookings through Michelle).
Whitewashed cottage (sleeps 6), £300 low
season, £405 high season, open all year.

🅣 🅟 🏠 ❄ 🦌 🐕 🎴 ⚋ 🗄 🖵 ☉
🖬 🖬 ✂ 🎫

Owl Cottage   ***
146 Gobbins Rd, BT40 3TX.
☎ (01960) 382239. *(Mr & Mrs Hackney).*
200-year-old cottage (sleeps 4), £250 low season,
£350 high season, open all year.

🅟 🏠 ❄ 🎴 🖬 ⚋ 🗄 🖬 🖵 ☉ 🖬 🖬 ∪ ✂

Newtownabbey

Coach House   **
Woodbank, 451 Shore Rd, Whiteabbey, BT37 9SE.
☎ & fax (01232) 863567. *(Mrs R Sherlock).*
Coach house (sleeps 9/10), £250, open June-Sept.
Access to shore, slipway.

🅣 🅟 ❄ 🦌 🎴 🖬 ⚋ 🗄 🖬 🖵 ☉ 🖬
🖬 🥄 ∪

The Cottage   ****
Woodbank, 451 Shore Rd, Whiteabbey, BT37 9SE.
☎ & fax (01232) 863567. *(Mrs R Sherlock).*
House (sleeps 6), access to shore, £250,
open July-Oct.

🅟 🏠 ❄ 🦌 🎴 🐎 🖬 ⚋ 🗄 🖵 ☉ 🖬
🖬 🥄 ∪ ✂

For rural locations, ask for directions when you book

May Lodge ****
Woodbank, 453 Shore Rd, Whiteabbey, BT37 9SE.
☎ & fax (01232) 863567. *(Mrs R Sherlock).*
Gate lodge (sleeps 5/6), £250, open July-Oct.
Access to shore, slipway.

Portballintrae

Apartment 1 ***
Bayhead Apartments, Bayhead House, BT57 8BZ.
☎ (012657) 31441. Fax 31725. *(Mr T Cooke).*
Apartment (sleeps 4), ground floor, £220 low
season, £350 high season, open all year.

Baycrest ****
3 Bayhead Rd, BT57 8RZ.
☎ & fax (01232) 301947. *(Mr B Ferguson).*
Apartment (sleeps 4), spectacular views, £200
low season, £350 high season, open all year.

Causeway View ****
9 Benbane Park, BT57 8BP.
☎ (01846) 699849. *(Mrs G Bamber).*
Cottage (sleeps 4), £250 low season,
£300 high season, open all year.

Fuchsia Cottage ****
38 Benbane Park, BT57 8BP.
☎ & fax (01225) 837088. *(Mr A Crawford).*
Cottage (sleeps 5), £175/220 low season,
£280/330 high season, open all year.

Glenorra ***
3 Bushfoot Avenue, BT57 8XX.
☎ & fax (012657) 31049. *(Mrs J Archibald).*
Bungalow (sleeps 5), £235 low season,
£335 high season, open April-Oct.

Glenville Cottages ***
Bayhead Rd, BT57 8SB.
☎ & fax (012657) 31279. *(Mr S Sweeney).*
6 cottages (sleep 5/6), £200 low season,
£420 high season, open all year.

Kingfisher Cottage ****
9 Gortnee Drive, BT57 8DQ.
☎ (01846) 678533. *(Mrs J Glasgow).*
Cottage (3 bedrooms, sleeps 6), £160 low season,
£360 high season, open all year.

The Port *****
48 Benbane Park, BT57 8BF.
☎ (01232) 644844. *(Mr R Gilmore).*
Cottage style (4 bedrooms, sleeps 8), £195/250
low season, £395 high season, open all year.

Portballintrae Cottages ****
30/32 Benbane Park, BT57 8BP.
☎ (01846) 699849. *(Mr J Bamber).*
2 cottages (sleep 4/5), £200 low season,
£275/332 high season, open all year.

Self-catering prices given are the weekly rate

Seacrest ****
6 Bayhead Apartments, BT57 8RZ.
☎ (01247) 852880. *(Mr D Irwin).*
Apartment, top floor (sleeps 2), £200 low season,
£350 high season, open all year.

🄿 ❋ ▥ 🖬 ⚄ ✄ 🛏 🗂 📠 ⬜ ☉ 🖥 📞 🍴 ✕ 🥾 ∪

Strandview ***
7 Bushfoot Drive, BT57 8YW.
☎ (01265) 43057. *(Mrs A Wilson).*
House (sleeps 5), £150 low season,
£330 high season, open all year.

🄿 ❋ 🐎 ▦ ▥ 🄿 ▥ Ⓜ ✄ 🛏 🗂 📠 ⬜ ☉
🖥 🥾 ∪ ✄

The Summerhouse ****
54 Benbane Park, BT57 8BP.
☎ (01266) 656436. *(Mr & Mrs Millar).*
House (3 bedrooms, sleeps 6), £375 high season,
open June-Oct.

🄿 ❋ 🐎 ▦ 🛶 ▥ ⚄ ✄ 🛏 🗂 📠 ⬜ ☉ 🖥 🥾 ∪

18 Benbane Park ****
BT57 8BP. ☎ (012657) 32603. *(Ms F Nicol).*
Bungalow (2 bedrooms, sleeps 4), £285 low
season, £350 high season, open all year.

🄿 ❋ 🐎 ▦ ▥ ⚄ ✄ 🛏 🗂 📠 ⬜ ☉ 🖥
📞 🥾 ∪ ✄

5 Bushfoot Drive ***
BT57 8YW. ☎ (01266) 659538. *(Mr & Mrs Mills).*
Bungalow (sleeps 4/5), £150 low season,
£295 high season, open all year.

🄣 🄿 ❋ 🐎 ▦ ⚄ ✄ 🛏 🗂 📠 ⬜ ☉ 🐾
✕ 🥾 ∪ ✄

Liscarrick *unclassified*
37 Beach Rd, BT57 8RT.
☎ & fax (01868) 724588. *(Mr J Newtown).*
Cottage (sleeps 5).

Todgre Apartments *unclassified*
12a Seaport Avenue, BT51 8SB.
☎ (012657) 31484. *(Mrs G Morrow).*
2 apartments (sleep 6).

Portrush

Apartment 18 ****
The Links, Bushmills Rd, BT56 8SX.
☎ (01265) 55842. *(Mrs Y Orr).*
Apartment (2 bedrooms, sleeps 4/5), £225 low
season, £285 high season, open all year.

🄣 🄿 🐎 🄿 ▥ ⚄ ✄ 🛏 🗂 📠 ⬜ ☉ 🖥 📞 🐾 🍴
✕ 🥾 ∪ ✄

Ashlea Cottages ****
39 Magheraboy Rd, BT56 8NX.
☎ (01265) 824057/822779. Fax 824057.
(Mr & Mrs Houston).
5 cottages (sleep 4/6), £165/360 low season,
£300/395 high season, open all year. 2 chalets
(sleep 8), £350 low season, £375 high season,
open all year.

🄿 ❋ 🐎 ▦ 🛶 ⚄ 🐕 Ⓜ ⚄ ✄ 🛏 🗂 ⬜ ☉ 🖥 📞
🍴 ✕ 🥾 ∪ ✄

Ballinahone **
160 Causeway St, BT56 8JE.
☎ (016487) 37160. *(Mrs M Wright).*
House (sleeps 5/7), £200 low season,
£220 high season, open June-Sept.

🄿 ❋ 🐎 ▦ 🐕 ▥ Ⓜ ⚄ ✄ 🛏 🗂 📠 ⬜ ☉ 🖥
📞 🥾 ∪ ✄

Ballymacrae Cottage ***
43 Ballymacrae Rd, BT56 8NS.
☎ (01265) 824686. Fax 822364.
(Mrs M Hastings).
Cottage (sleeps 5/6), £160/250 low season,
£250/300 high season, open all year.

🄣 🄿 ❋ 🐎 🐕 ▥ Ⓜ ⚄ ✄ 🛏 🗂 📠 ⬜ ☉
🖥 🥾 ∪ ✄

Beach Head ***
25 Kerr St, BT66 8DG.
☎ & fax (01265) 823666. *(Mr & Mrs McClay).*
Terrace house (sleeps 8), £170/200 low season,
£315 high season, open June-mid-Sept.

🐎 ▥ ✄ 🛏 🗂 📠 ⬜ ☉ 🖥 🐾 🍴 ✕ 🔌 🥾 ∪

For rural locations, ask for directions when you book

Bellemont Cottages   ***

8/8a Islandtasserty Rd, BT52 2PN.

☎ (01265) 823872. *(Mr G Auld).*

2 cottages (sleep 3/6), £160 low season, £330 high season, open all year.

🅿 ❀ ᗢ 🎠 🟫 🖾 ⬛ ▪ 🅼 ◌ ⁄ 🖪 🗄 ◻ ☉ ⬛ 🐾 ⌐ ↺

Carnluce   ***

37 Castleview Park, BT56 8AS.

☎ (01265) 822253. *(Mr J Murray).*

Bungalow (3 bedrooms, sleeps 5/6), £230 low season, £370 high season, open all year.

🅿 ❀ ᗢ 🐕 🟫 ⬛ ▪ ⁄ 🖪 🗄 🖾 ◻ ☉ ⬛
📞 🐾 ↺ ⌕

Claddagh Apartment   ***

4 Dhu Varren Park, BT56 8EL.

☎ & fax (01849) 432741. *(Mrs L Wallace).*

Apartment (sleeps 5/7), £245 low season, £300 high season, open June-Sept.

🆃 🅿 ❀ ᗢ 🟫 🖾 🖾 🅼 ⁄ 🖪 🗄 ◻ ☉ 📞
📞 🐾 ↺ ⌐

Drumgrass   ***

1 Dhu Varren Park South, BT56 8EJ.

☎ & fax (016487) 63617. *(Mrs P Kane).*

Bungalow (sleeps 5), £140 low season, £200 high season, open June-Sept.

🅿 ❀ ᗢ 🟫 🖾 🖾 ⬛ 🖪 🗄 🖾 ◻ 📞 📞

Glendarragh   ***

33 Glen Crescent, BT56 8LL.

☎ (01247) 853869. *(Mr & Mrs Beggs).*

Bungalow (sleeps 6), £160 low season, £250 high season, open June-Sept.

🅿 ❀ ᗢ 🟫 ♿ ⬛ 🅼 ◌ ⁄ 🖪 🗄 ◻ ☉ 📞
📞 🐾 ↺ ⌕

Jacaranda Apartments
& Mermaid Cottages   ***

58/60 Dhu Varren, BT56 8EW.

☎ & fax (012656) 41793, *evening (Mr G Neill).*

Apartments & cottages (2, 3 & 4 bedrooms), £145/200 low season, £315/395 high season, open June-Sept.

🅿 ❀ ᗢ 🟫 ◌ ⁄ 🖪 🗄 ◻ ☉ 📞 🐾 ❗ ✕ 🐾 ↺

Maddybenny Holiday Cottages   ****

18 Maddybenny Park, BT52 2PT.

☎ & fax (01265) 823394. *(Mrs R White).*

6 mews cottages (sleep 6/8), £200/300 low season, £350/400 high season, open all year.

🆃 🅿 ❀ ᗢ 🟫 ♿ 🖾 🅼 ◌ ⁄ 🖪 🗄 ◻ ☉ 📞 📞
📞 🐾 ↺ ⌕ 🅔

Magheramenagh Chalets   ***

57/59 Magheramenagh Drive, BT56 8SP.

☎ (01762) 334943 **or** (01265) 732685.

Fax (01762) 351282. *(Ms S Mortimer).*

2 bungalows (sleep 4/6), £250 low season, £350 high season, open all year.

🅿 ❀ ᗢ 🖾 ◌ ⁄ 🖪 🗄 🖾 ◻ ☉ 📞 🐾 ❗ ✕ 🐾 ↺

Mather's Cottage   **

25 Islandtasserty Rd, BT52 2PW.

☎ (01265) 822254. *(Mr A Owen).*

Cottage (sleeps 5), gas barbecue, £200 low season, £280 high season, open all year.

🅿 ❀ ᗢ 🟫 ♿ 🐕 🖾 🅼 ◌ ⁄ 🖪 🗄 🖾 ◻ ☉ ⬛
📞 🐾 ↺ ⌕

O'Neill's Causeway Coast Apartments   *

36 Ballyreagh Rd, BT56 8LR.

☎ (01265) 822435. Fax 824495.

20 apartments (3 bedrooms, sleep 8), £275 low season, £375 high season, open all year.

🆃 🅿 ᗢ 🟫 ➔ ♿ 🖾 ⁄ 🖪 🗄 ◻ ☉ 📞 ❗ ✕
📞 🐾 ↺ 🅔

Self-catering prices given are the weekly rate

Seaview Cottage **
16b Ballyreagh Rd, BT56 8LR.
☎ (01266) 40003. *(Mrs J Bowens)*.
Cottage (5 bedrooms, sleeps 6), £200 low season,
£300 high season, open all year.

🔲 🅿 🛏 🏠 ♿ 🛋 Ⓜ ✂ 🛢 🗄 ⏹ ☉ 🖥 ♨ ❗ ✕
● 🌙 ∪ ✄

Sunrise Flats **
Flats 3/4, 10 Mount Royal, BT56 8DA.
☎ & fax (01265) 822314. *(Mrs E Stringer)*.
2 flats (sleep 6), £135/170 low season,
£170/240 high season, open June-Sept.

🏚 ✿ ⬜ 🛋 Ⓜ ✂ 🛢 🗄 🖥 ⏹ ☉ 🖥 ♨ ❗ ✕ ● ●

86 Coleraine Rd **
BT56 8HN.
☎ (01265) 823336. *(Ms D Plowman)*.
House (sleeps 6), £250 low season, £300 high
season, open May-Aug.

🅿 ✿ ❄ 🛏 🏠 🛋 🔆 ✂ 🛢 🗄 ⏹ ☉ ♨ ❗ ✕ ∪ ✄

108 Lower Main St   *unclassified*
BT56 8DA.
☎ (01265) 823793. Fax 824625. *(Mr H Clyde)*.
House (5 bedrooms (families only), sleeps 9).

105 Golf Terrace   *unclassified*
BT56 8DZ. ☎ (01265) 848421. *(Mr J Dixon)*.
3 apartments (sleep 4).

Randalstown

Craig-e-Brae ***
22 Tullynamullan Rd, Tannaghmore, BT41 2JZ.
☎ & fax (01266) 898030. *(Mr R Walker)*.
Secluded traditional cottage (sleeps 5), £245 low
season, £380 high season, open all year.

🔲 🅿 🏚 ✿ ❄ 🛏 🏠 Ⓜ 🔆 ✂ 🛢 🗄 🖥 ⏹ ☉ 🖥
● ♨ ❗ ✕ 🌙 ∪

Waterfoot (or Glenariff)

Barraghilly House ***
111 Glen Rd, BT44 0RG.
☎ (012667) 71534. Fax 71440. *(Mrs P O'Boyle)*.
House (sleeps 5/6), £210 low season, £320 high
season, open all year.

🔲 🅿 ✿ ❄ 🛏 🏠 🔆 ✂ 🛢 🗄 ⏹ ☉ 🖥 ● ∪ ✄

Conlee ***
172 Garron Rd, BT44 0RA.
☎ (012667) 71963. *(Mr & Mrs Connolly)*.
Bungalow (sleeps 6), £200 low season,
£300 high season, open all year.

🅿 ✿ ❄ 🛏 🏠 ✈ 🔆 ✂ 🛢 🗄 🖥 ⏹ ☉ ● 🌙 ∪

Glen Cottage ***
39 Glenariff Rd, BT44 0QY.
☎ (01232) 241100. Fax 241198.
(Bookings through Michelle).
Cottage (sleeps 7), £240 low season, £365 high
season, open all year.

🔲 🅿 🏚 ✿ ❄ 🛏 🔆 ✂ 🛢 🗄 ⏹ ☉ ●
🌙 ∪ ✄ 🅱

Red Bay Bungalow ***
233 Garron Rd, BT44 0RB.
☎ (012667) 71396. Fax 71193. *(Mrs K McKillop)*.
Cottage (sleeps 6), £250 low season,
£350 high season, open all year.

🔲 🅿 ✿ ❄ 🛏 🏠 Ⓜ 🔆 ✂ 🛢 🗄 🖥 ⏹ ☉ 🖥 🌙
♨ ❗ ✕ 🌙 ∪

County Armagh

Armagh

The Chalet *
Dean's Hill, 34 College Hill, BT61 9DF.
☎ (01861) 522099. *(Mrs M Armstrong).*
Chalet (sleeps 4), in courtyard of Georgian house,
£90/100 low season, £150 high season,
open all year.

🅿 ❄ 🐃 ♿ �åⅢ Ⓜ 🔲 ⁄ 🛏 🗑 🍽 🖵 ☺ 🔳 🔱
ℚ 🎣 ∪ ⚞

Forkhill

Benbree ***
57 Carrive Rd, BT35 9TE.
☎ (01693) 888394. *(Mrs B Watters).*
House (sleeps 6), £175, open all year.

🆃 🅿 🏠 ❄ 🐃 🎜 🅶🅰🅿 ♿ ⅢⅢ Ⓜ 🔲 ⁄ 🛏 🗑 🍽 🖵
☺ 🎣 ∪

Mullaghbawn

Mountain View ***
11 Cranny Rd, BT35 9XR.
☎ (01693) 888410. *(Mr & Mrs Murphy).*
House (sleeps 4/6), £150, open all year.

🅿 ❄ 🐃 🎜 ♖ 🐕 ⅢⅢ 🔲 ⁄ 🛏 🗑 🍽 🖵
☺ 🎣 ∪ ⚞

County Down

Annalong

Frank's Cottage ****
21 Grove Rd, BT34 4XB.
☎ (01846) 699226. Fax 689984. *(Mr R McKnight).*
Cottage (sleeps 6), £220 low season,
£340 high season, open all year.

P ❄ ⛵ ▥ ▥ ⬚ ∥ ⬛ ⬚ ⛿ ▭ ☉ ☎ ⚹

Jack's Johns Cottage **
30 Old Town Lane, Moneydarraghmore, BT34 4XF.
☎ (01207) 502168. *(Mr Thorpe).*
(013967) 68696. *(Ms Haughian).*
Cottage (sleeps 6), £250, open all year.

P ❄ ⛵ ▥ ▥ ⬚ ∥ ⬛ ⬚ ▭ ☉ ▣ ∪ ⚹

Manx View ***
257 Kilkeel Rd, BT34 4TW.
☎ (016937) 63222. *(Miss M Bingham).*
Cottage (sleeps 3), £185, open June-Sept.

P ❄ ⛵ ▥ ▥ ⬚ ∥ ⬛ ⬚ ⛿ ▭ ☉
⬛ ♫ ∪ ⚹

Ballynahinch

The Sycamores ***
40 Hall Rd, BT24 8XY.
☎ (01238) 562640. *(Mr & Mrs McKay).*
House (4 bedrooms, sleeps 6) £190 low season,
£250 high season, open all year.

⊤ P ❄ ⛵ ▥ ▥ ⬚ ∥ ⬛ ⬚ ⛿ ▭ ☉ ▣ ⬛
☎ ♫ ∪ ⚹

Banbridge

Roadside Bungalow **
21 Knockgorm Rd, BT32 3TE.
☎ (018206) 25261. *(Mr & Mrs Burns).*
Bungalow (3 bedrooms, sleeps 5/6) £100 low
season, £150 high season, open all year.

⊤ P ❄ ⛵ ▥ ▥ Ⓜ ⬚ ∥ ⬛ ⬚ ⛿ ▭ ☉ ▣
⬛ ♫ ∪ ⚹

Bangor

Drumalee **
42 Bellevue, BT20 5QW.
☎ (01247) 465121. *(Mr Brown).*
Bungalow (sleeps 4), £200 low season,
£270 high season, open all year.

P ❄ ⛵ ▥ ♿ ⬛ ▥ ⬚ ⬛ ⬚ ⛿ ▭ ☉ ▣
☎ ⬛ ♫ ∪

Innisfree *
82 Dufferin Avenue, BT20 3AD.
☎ (01247) 472128. *(Mrs J Martin).*
1 flat (sleeps 5/6), £170 low season, £250 high
season; 1 flat (sleeps 3), £160/180, open all year.

P ❄ ⛵ OAP ▥ ⬚ ∥ ⬛ ⬚ ▭ ☉ ▣ ⬛ ♫

Jennies Bungalow ***
8 Station Drive, Carnalea, BT19 1ET.
☎ (01247) 466752. *(Mrs J Jackson).*
Bungalow (sleeps 4/5), £185 low season,
£265 high season, open April-Sept.

P ❄ ⛵ ▥ Ⓜ ⬚ ∥ ⬛ ⬚ ⛿ ▭ ☉ ▣
⬛ ⦿ ✕ ⚹

For rural locations, ask for directions when you book

Magara ***

20 May Avenue, BT20 4JT.
☎ (01247) 462098. (Mrs M Maguire).
Terrace house (sleeps 5/6), £220 low season,
£260 high season, open all year.

Primrose Apartments ***

34b Primrose St, BT20 5NU. (Mrs E Coey).
☎ & fax (01247) 451340 or 469368 after 4.30 pm.
2 units (sleep 4 each), £160 low season,
£200 high season, open all year.

Sea Breeze ***

9 Grays Hill, BT20 3BB.
☎ & fax (01247) 461643. (Mrs S Brann).
House (sleeps 7/8), £250 low season, £340 high
season, open all year.

7 Albert St **

BT20 5ES.
☎ & fax (01247) 461423. (Mrs A Thompson).
Town house (4 bedrooms, sleeps 6/8), £275,
open all year.

1 Alfred St *

BT20 5DH.
☎ & fax (01247) 457078. (Mr D Belton).
House (sleeps 7), £195 low season,
£235 high season, open all year.

Castlewellan

Coast View Cottage **

41 Ballywillwill Rd, BT31 9LF.
☎ (013967) 78006. (Mr D Murray).
Cottage (sleeps 4/5), £150 low season, £215 high
season, open all year.

Slievecroob Self-Catering Holiday Cottages ***

119 Clanvaraghan Rd, BT31 9LA.
☎ (013967) 71412. Fax 71162. (Mr K McGivern).
Cottages (sleep 5/7), £190 low season, £350 high
season, open all year.

Wild Forest Cottage ****

28 Ballyhafrey Rd, BT34 0PS.
☎ (013967) 68451. Fax 67041. (Mrs J Hall).
Cottage (sleeps 8), £350 low season,
£495 high season, open all year.

Comber

Castle Espie Cottages ***

11 Ballyglighorn Rd, BT23 5SX.
☎ (01247) 873011. Fax 820946. (Mrs M Campbell).
2 cottages (sleep 4/6), £170 low season,
£250 high season, open all year.

Self-catering prices given are the weekly rate

Downpatrick

The Barn **
53 Killyleagh Rd, Crossgar, BT30 9LB.
☎ (01396) 830792. *(Mrs M Davison)*.
Flat (sleeps 6), £190, open April-Oct.

▫ ▣ ♠ ✿ ✾ ⊠ ➳ ✿ Ⅲ ⊡ ⁄ ➤ ⬚ ▤ ▭ ⊙
⬚ ✕ ♪ ∪ ⚡

Garden House ***
104 Clanmaghery Rd, Tyrella, BT30 8SU.
☎ & fax (01396) 851422. *(Mrs S Corbett)*.
Cottage (sleeps 6), £300, open all year.

▫ ▣ ♠ ✿ ✾ ⊠ ⬚ Ⓜ ⊡ ⁄ ➤ ⬚ ⊙ ⬚
⬚ ♪ ∪ ⊞

Dromore

Ballykeel **
161 Hillsborough Rd, Dromara, BT25 2AU.
☎ (01238) 532256. *(Miss M Hamilton)*.
Apartment (sleeps 2), £200 low season, £200 high
season, open all year.

▣ ✿ Ⅲ Ⓜ ⁄ ➤ ⬚ ▤ ▭ ⊙ ⬚ ♪ ∪ ⚡

Dundrum

Murlough Holiday Cottages **
Widows Row, South Promenade, BT33 0NG.
(National Trust).
☎ (01238) 510721 or NT Central Reservations
(01225) 791199. 2 cottages (sleep 4), £165 low
season, £315 high season, open all year.

▣ ♠ ✿ ✾ ⊠ Ⅲ ⬚ ✿ Ⅲ ➤ ⬚ ▭ ⊙ ♪ ∪ ⚡ ⊞

Hill House *unclassified*
18 Kilmegan Rd, BT33 0NJ.
☎ (01396) 75464 **or** (01762) 341054.
(Mr J McCauley).
Cottage (sleeps 4).

Groomsport

Evetide **
13 Sandeel Lane, Orlock, BT19 2LP.
☎ (01232) 798247/(01247) 883511.
(Mrs H Crowe).
House (sleeps 6), £120 low season,
£200 high season, open all year.

▣ ✿ ⊠ Ⅲ Ⅲ Ⓜ ⁄ ➤ ⬚ ▤ ▭ ⊙ ⬚ ♪ ∪ ⚡

Hillsborough

Ritchies Courtyard ****/**
Ballynahinch St, BT26 6AW.
☎ (01846) 683601. Fax 689476. *(Mrs P Brown)*.
2 apartments (sleep 4), £275/375, open all year.

▣ ⊠ ✿ Ⅲ ⊡ ⁄ ➤ ⬚ ▤ ▭ ⊙ ⬚ ⚡ ❗ ✕ ♪ ∪ ⊞

Hilltown

Downshire Arms **
Main St, BT34 5UH.
☎ & fax (018206) 38899. *(Mr F O'Hare)*.
7 units (sleep 3/6), £200/300 high season,
open all year.

▣ ♠ ✿ ⊠ Ⅲ ⬚ Ⅲ ⁄ ➤ ⬚ ▭ ⊙ ⬚ ⬚ ⚡ ❗
✕ ♪ ∪ ⚡

Marywood ***
34 Sandbank Rd, BT34 5XU.
☎ (018206) 31206 after 5 pm
or 38733/31063. *(Mrs A O'Hagan)*.
Cottage (3 bedrooms, sleeps 6), £230 low season,
£250 high season, open all year.

▣ ✿ ⊠ Ⅲ ➳ ⑂ ✿ Ⅲ ⊡ ⁄ ➤ ⬚ ▤ ▭
▭ ⊙ ♪ ∪

Kilkeel

Ballymageogh Gate Lodge   ***
Mourne Park, BT34 4LB.
☎ (016937) 62533. Fax 64426. *(Mrs M Anley).*
Traditional cottage (sleeps 6), on private
estate/golf course, £180 low season, £280 high
season, open all year.

🄣 🅟 🏠 ❄ 🛋 🛏 ☷ DAP 🐕 🖥 ⌾ ⁄ 🖨 🗄 🖳 🗔 ⊙ 🗺
💺 ✗ ⌗ ⌂ ⚲

Cranfield Chalets   **
125 Harbour Rd, BT34 4LJ.
☎ (016937) 62745/64518. Fax 63022.
(Mr & Mrs Coulter).
6 bungalows (2 bedrooms), £115 low
season, £190 high season, open April-Sept.

🅟 ❄ 🛋 ☷ 🚿 Ⓜ 🖨 🗄 💺 🏆 ✗ ● ⌗ ⌂ ⚲

Hill View   **
18 Bog Rd, Attical, BT34 4HT.
☎ (016937) 64269. *(Mrs M Trainor).*
Ground floor apartment (2 bedrooms, sleeps 8) in
heart of Mournes, £150 low season, £190 high
season, open all year.

🚿 🄣 🅟 ❄ 🛋 ☷ 🖥 ☷ Ⓜ 🖨 ⁄ 🖨 🗄 🖳 🗔 ⊙
🗺 💺 ⌗ ⌂ ⚲

Mountain View   **
20 Head Rd, Moyad, BT34 4AY.
☎ (013967) 23120. Fax (018206) 38338.
(Mr S Lavery).
Bungalow (sleeps 6), £190 low season, £250 high
season, open all year.

🅟 ❄ 🛋 ☷ DAP ☷ Ⓜ 🖨 ⁄ 🖨 🗄 🖳 🗔
⊙ 💺 ⌗ ⌂

Riverway Cottage   **
31 Ballinran Rd, BT34 4JA.
☎ (016937) 62795. *(Mr D Donnelly).*
Cottage (sleeps 6), £170 low season,
£190 high season, open all year.

🅟 ❄ 🛋 ☷ 🚿 DAP 🖥 🐕 ☷ Ⓜ 🖨 ⁄ 🖨 🗄 🖳 🗔
⊙ ⌗ ⌂ ⊞

Wyncrest Chalet   **
30a Main Rd, Ballymartin, BT34 4NU.
☎ & fax (016937) 63012. *(Mrs J Adair).*
Chalet (sleeps 4), £195, open April-Oct.

🄣 🅟 ❄ 🛋 ☷ Ⓜ 🖨 🖨 🗄 🖳 🗔 ⊙ ● 💺 🏆 ⌗ ⌂ ⊞

Jirah   *unclassified*
91 Greencastle Rd, BT34 4JL.
☎ (01238) 561885. *(Mr B Henderson).*
Bungalow (sleeps 10).

Killinchy

Aulds Close Cottages   ***
17a, 17b Ballymacreely Rd, BT23 6RP.
☎ & fax (01238) 541670. *(Mrs R Morrison).*
2 stone-built cottages, 1 (sleeps 2), 2 (sleeps 4/6),
£175/275, open all year.

🅟 🏠 🛋 ☷ 🖥 ☷ 🖨 ⁄ 🖨 🗄 🗔 ⊙ 🗺 💺 🏆
✗ ⌗ ⌂ ⚲

Rocklin   ***
5 Braddock Reach, Whiterock, BT23 6PY.
☎ & fax (01396) 828901. *(Mrs N Lindsay).*
Bungalow (sleeps 5), £300 low season,
£400 high season, open all year.

🄣 🅟 ❄ 🛋 ☷ Ⓜ 🖨 ⁄ 🖨 🗄 🖳 🗔 ⊙ 🗺 ● 💺
🏆 ✗ ⌗ ⌂

Self-catering prices given are the weekly rate

Killyleagh

Dufferin House ***
38 High St, BT30 9QF.
☎ (01396) 828229. Fax 828755.
(Mr Crawford/Ms Stewart).
3 apartments (sleep 6/7), £225 low season,
£250 high season, open all year. Bicycle hire.

Hill Cottage ***
32 Jericho Rd, BT30 6AF.
☎ (01396) 828245. *(Mr & Mrs Erskine).*
Cottage (sleeps 6), stabling for horses, £280 low
season, £370 high season, open all year.

Killyleagh Castle Towers ****/***
Killyleagh Castle, BT30 9QA.
☎ & fax (01396) 828261.
(Lt Col Rowan Hamilton).
3 towers (sleep 4/5), £200/300 low season,
£250/350 mid/high season, open all year.

Kircubbin

Bloodyburn Cottage ***
108b Shore Rd, Nunsquarter, BT22 2RP.
☎ (012477) 38379. Fax 38099. *(Mrs G Gilmore).*
Cottage (sleeps 2), £225, open all year.

Millisle

Cotcheen ***
61 Donaghadee Rd, BT22 2BZ.
☎ & fax (01247) 823500. *(Mr D McCready).*
Bungalow (3 bedrooms, sleeps 5/6), £175 low
season, £240 high season, open all year.

Newcastle

Ballaghbeg Apartments ***
111 Central Promenade, BT33 0EU.
☎ (013967) 26081. *(Mr & Mrs Calvert).*
Apartment (1 bedroom, sleeps 2/4), £150 low
season, £215 high season, open all year.

Beverley Annex *
72 Tollymore Rd, BT33 0JN.
☎ (013967) 22018. *(Mrs E McNeilly).*
Apartment (sleeps 4), £140 low season,
£160 high season, open all year.

Beverley Cottage *
72 Tollymore Rd, BT33 0JN.
☎ (013967) 22018. *(Mrs E McNeilly).*
Stone-built cottage (sleeps 4), £155 low season,
£175 high season, open all year.

For rural locations, ask for directions when you book

Coast Guard Cottage **
Coastguard Cottages, BT33 0QT.
Mobile 0860 353526 **or** (013967) 22882.
(Mr & Mrs Riley).
Cottage (sleeps 4), £190 low season, £240 high
season, open March-Sept.

Diamond Cottage **
10a Tullybrannigan Rd, BT33 0PW.
& fax (013967) 22687. *(Mr B Downey).*
Flat (sleeps 4), £160 low season,
£240 high season, open all year.

Dispensary Cottage ***
0 Bryansford Village, BT33 0PT.
(01762) 335792. *(Mr A Rooney).*
Cottage (sleeps 6), £100 low season, £200 high
season, open all year.

Mourne Cottages ****
47 Ballyloughlin Rd, Dundrum, BT33 0QG.
(013967) 51251. *(Mrs H Wishart).*
4 traditional stone cottages (sleep 5/7), £250 low
season, £380 high season, open May-Sept.

Retreat **
4 Park Lane, BT33 0AR.
(01238) 562396. *(Mr P King).*
Cottage (sleeps 5), £375, open all year.

Rockville ***
165 Central Promenade, BT33 0EU.
(01232) 642716. *(Mrs M Doherty).*
Apartment (sleeps 6), £200 low season,
£275 high season, open all year.

Roma **
46 Bryansford Gardens, BT33 0EQ.
(013967) 71247. *(Mrs M Morgan).*
House (sleeps 5), £240 low season,
£320 high season, open all year.

Rose Cottage ***
46 Tollymore Rd, BT33 0JN.
(013967) 22018. *(Mrs E McNeilly).*
Stone cottage (3 bedrooms, sleeps 6), £310 low
season, £380 high season, open all year.

Seaview ***
79a Main St, BT33 0AE.
& fax (013967) 26066. *(Mrs M Erwin).*
Apartment (sleeps 4), £190 low season, £275 high
season, open all year.

Strand Apartments ***
58 Main St, BT33 0AE.
(013967) 23472. Fax 26035. *(Mr M Nugent).*
2 units (sleep 4/5), £175 low season,
£280 high season, open all year.

Self-catering prices given are the weekly rate

Tory Bush Cottages ***
79 Tullyree Rd, Bryansford, BT34 5LD.
☎ (013967) 24348. *(Mr D Maginn).*
8 cottages (sleep 5), traditional, £250 low season,
£410 high season, open all year.

The Wee House *
52 Trassey Rd, Bryansford, BT33 0QB.
☎ (013967) 26657. *(Mr & Mrs Patterson).*
House (sleeps 2), £100 low season,
£150 high season, open all year.

White Gate Lodge ***
38 Hilltown Rd, Bryansford, BT33 0PZ.
☎ (013967) 22018. *(Mrs E McNeilly).*
Tudor-style gate lodge (sleeps 6), £350 low
season, £400 high season, open all year.

Wyllie Cottage ***
17 Bryansford Village, BT33 0PT.
☎ (01238) 562800. *(Mr & Mrs Maguire).*
Cottage (sleeps 6), £240 low season,
£300 high season, open all year.

4 Edgewater ***
South Promenade, BT33 0EY.
☎ (013967) 23883. *(Mrs I Sloan).*
Ground floor apartment (2 bedrooms, sleeps 4),
£200 low season, £350 high season,
open May-Sept.

20 Larchfield Park **
BT33 0BB.
☎ (013967) 23851. *(Mr P Knight).*
House (3 bedrooms, sleeps 5), £250/300 low
season, £320 high season, open all year.

161 South Promenade **
Widows Row, BT33 0HA.
☎ (013967) 22642. Fax (013967) 23577.
(Miss P Speedy).
Cottage (sleeps 4), £200 low season,
£275 high season, open all year.

Ivydene Cottage *unclassified*
112 Dundrum Rd, BT33 0LN.
☎ (013967) 22009. *(Mr & Mrs Donnelly).*
Cottage (sleeps 7).

136 Tullybrannigan Rd *unclassified*
BT33 0PW. ☎ (013967) 22628. *(Mrs M Murray).*
Mobile home (sleeps 6).

Newry

Boirean View ***
18a Mullaghans Rd, Mullaghbawn, BT35 9UX.
☎ (01693) 888553. *(Mr M McKeown).*
Unit (sleeps 5), £150, open all year.

Farmhouse Country Cottage *
139 Longfield Rd, Forkhill, BT35 9SD.
☎ (01693) 888314. *(Mrs L McCreesh).*
Cottage (sleeps 5), £100 low season,
£110 high season, open all year.

For rural locations, ask for directions when you book

Grinan Lodge **
49 Grinan Rd, BT34 2PZ.
☎ & fax (01693) 61992. *(Mrs A Farrell).*
House, £200 low season, £250 high season,
open all year.

Parkview ***
4 Shaughan Rd, Belleeks, BT35 7PF.
☎ (01693) 878891. *(Mrs R McKnight).*
Farmhouse (sleeps 6), £200 low season, £250
high season, open all year.

Riverside Cottage ****
67 Forkhill Rd, BT35 8QX.
☎ (01693) 848273. Fax 65050. *(Mrs E Fearon).*
House (sleeps 6), £200 low season, £250 high
season, open all year.

Slieve Gullion Courtyard *
89 Dromintee Rd, Killevy, BT35 8SW.
☎ (01693) 848084. Fax 848028. *(Mr P Agnew).*
5 apartments (sleep 4), £150 low season, £200
high season, open all year.

2 Archview Terrace **
Craigmore, BT35 7AF.
☎ 0181-882 6572. *(Mrs Wright/Mrs Feenan).*
Cottage (sleeps 4), £150, open all year.

Newtownards

Beech Cottage ***
20a Mountstewart Rd, BT22 2AL.
☎ & fax (012477) 88357. *(Mrs M Deering).*
Cottage (sleeps 4), £180 low season,
£240 high season.

Granary Apartments ****
12a Cunningburn Rd, BT22 2AN.
☎ & fax (01247) 812828. *(Mr J Edgar).*
18th-century barn converted into 3 apartments
(sleeps 4/5), £220 low season, £300 high season.

Greba Lodge ***
1a Cardy Rd, Greyabbey, BT22 2LS.
☎ & fax (012477) 88386. *(Mrs G Bailie).*
House (2 bedrooms, sleeps 4/6), £240 low
season, £300 high season, open all year.

Portaferry

Lough Cowey Villa ***
9 Lough Cowey Rd, BT22 1PJ.
☎ (012477) 28263. *(Mrs R Taggart).*
Apartment (sleeps 6), overlooking Lough Cowey,
£250 low season, £350 high season,
open all year.

Self-catering prices given are the weekly rate

South Rock Cottage ***
9 Newcastle Rd, Kearney, BT22 1QQ.
☎ (012477) 28633. *(Mrs A Mulligan).*
Cottage (3 bedrooms, sleeps 6), £130 low season,
£300 high season, open all year.

🅿 ❄ 🐾 🛏 🏠 🛋 🌡 ✂ 🍽 ⊙ 🔌 ✗ 🚗 ⌣ ✂

Rostrevor

Lecale Cottages ***
125 Kilbroney Rd, BT34 3BW.
☎ (016937) 38727. Fax 38965. *(Mr L Baxter).*
Cottages (sleep 6), £250 low season,
£350 high season, open all year.

🆃 🅿 ❄ 🐾 🛏 🛏 ⚓ 🏠 🏠 Ⓜ ✂ 🍽 ⊙ 🔌 📞 ⌕ 🚗 ⌣ ✂

Waring Bank **
107 Shore Rd, BT34 3AB.
☎ (01693) 62034. *(Mrs R Faloon).*
Bungalow (sleeps 6), £200 low season,
£300 high season, open all year.

🅿 ❄ 🐾 🏠 🌡 ✂ 🍽 ⊙ 📞 🚗 ⌣ ✂

Strangford

Number 42 **
42 Downpatrick Rd, BT30 7LZ.
☎ (01232) 403640. Mobile 0402 711730.
(Mrs C Sharvin).
Terrace house (2 bedrooms, sleeps 5/6),
£225 low season, £275 high season,
open all year.

🆃 🅿 🏠 ❄ 🐾 ⚓ 🏠 🌡 ✂ 🍽 🛋 ⊙ 🔌 🍽 ❗ ✗ 🚗 ⌣ ✂

Potter's Cottage **
Castle Ward, BT30 7LS. *(National Trust).*
Stone cottage (1 bedroom, sleeps 4), £165 low
season, £315 high season, open all year.

🅿 🏠 🐾 🛏 🏠 Ⓜ 🍽 🌡 ⊙ ✗ 🚗 ⌣ ✂

Terenichol 1 & 2 ***
Castle Ward, BT30 7LS. *(National Trust).*
2 flats (sleep 8), £185 low season,
£395 high season, open all year.

🅿 🏠 ❄ 🐾 🛏 🏠 Ⓜ 🌡 🍽 🔌 ⊙ ✗ 🚗 ⌣ ✂

*Bookings through ☎ (01396) 881204 or
NT Central Reservations (01225) 791199.
Fax (01396) 881729.*

Warrenpoint

19 Oak Grange ***
Upper Dromore Rd, BT34 3TL.
☎ (01744) 750119. *(Mr & Mrs Atherden).*
Bungalow (sleeps 6), £275, open April-Oct.

🅿 ❄ 🐾 ⚓ 🏠 🌡 ✂ 🍽 🌡 🍽 ⊙ ✂
🍽 🌡 ⌣ ✂

County Fermanagh

Ballinamallard

School House *
31 Rossfad Rd, Whitehill, BT74 8AL.
☎ (01846) 675261/(01232) 614629. *(Mrs M Breen).*
House (5 bedrooms), £180 low season,
£200 high season, open Jan-Nov.

Belcoo

Corralea Activity Centre & Cottages *
Corralea Forest Lodge, Corralea, BT93 5DZ.
☎ & fax (01365) 386668. *(Mr & Mrs Leonard).*
5 bungalows (sleep 4/6), £180 low season,
£260 high season, open all year.

Bellanaleck

Gate Lodge ****
Rushin Farm, BT92 2BA.
☎ (01365) 348221. *(Mrs M Loane).*
Gate lodge (sleeps 5), £150 low season,
£280 high season, open all year.

Belleek

Carlton Cottages ***
Main St, BT93 3FX.
☎ & fax (013656) 58181. *(Mr M McGrath).*
14 cottages (sleep 5), £275 low season, £495 high
season, open all year. Fishing on site, sea fishing
trips, bicycle hire.

Chimney House **
Drumnisaleen, BT94 7FU.
☎ (013656) 58755. *(Mr M McCafferty).*
House (sleeps 6), £150 low season, £300 high
season, open all year. Free use of boat. Pet pony
for children.

Dartry View Cottage ***
Gortnalee, Belleek PO, BT93 3AU.
☎ (013656) 58140. *(Mr & Mrs McNulty).*
Cottage on family farm (sleeps 6), £150 low
season, £275 high season, open all year.

Glenross ***
454 Boa Island Rd, Ross Harbour, Leggs,
BT93 2AD.
☎ (01846) 683656. *(Ms C Hamilton).*
Bungalow (sleeps 8), £300 low season, £400 high
season, open all year. Private jetty, beach.

Lake View Cottage **
Rosscor Bridge Rd, Tawnynoran, Rosscor,
BT93 3GP.
☎ (01923) 265759/(01365) 658351.
(Mr & Mrs Irving).
Bungalow (sleeps 4/5), £180 low season,
£230 high season, open all year.

🎫 🅿 ❄ 🛋 🍴 ➡ 🐕 ▥ Ⓜ ⓞ ⁄ 🛍 🗄 🍽
🖥 ⊙ 🥄 ☉

Lough Erne Cottages **
Bolusty, Rosscor, BT74 7BW.
☎ (01365) 322608. Fax 322967.
(Mr J Richardson).
8 modern bungalows (sleep 2/8), £110 low
season, £190 high season, open all year.

🎫 🅿 🏠 ❄ 🛋 🍴 ▥ ⁄ 🛍 🗄 🖥 ⊙ 🥄 ☉ 🔣

Meadow Brook ****
Laughill, BT93 3DH.
☎ (00 353) 72 51248. *(Mrs B McAuley).*
Bungalow (sleeps 6), £170 low season,
£240 high season, open all year.

🎫 🅿 ❄ 🛋 🍴 ➡ ⱭⱯⱣ 🚻 ▥ Ⓜ ⓞ ⁄ 🛍 🗄 🍽 🖥
⊙ 🔣 🥄 ☉ ✂

Rathmore Cottages ****
Rathmore, BT93 3FX.
☎ & fax (013656) 58181. *(Mr P Clarke).*
11 houses (sleep 4/6), £275 low season,
£495 high season, open all year.

🎫 🅿 ❄ 🛋 🍴 ➡ 🚻 🐕 ▥ Ⓜ ⁄ 🛍 🗄 🍽 🖥 ⊙
⛄ 🏋 ▮ ✗ 🥄 ☉ 🔣

Sandy Vale ***
8 Davog Drive, BT93 3EP.
☎ (013656) 58056/58036. *(Mr R McGough).*
Bungalow (sleeps 6), £250 low season,
£300 high season, open May-Aug.

🅿 ❄ 🛋 🍴 🚻 ▥ Ⓜ ⓞ ⁄ 🛍 🗄 🍽 🖥 ⊙ 🏋 ▮
✗ ⚓ 🥄 ☉

Benmore Courtyard Cottages ***
Churchhill, BT93 6HZ.
☎ & fax (01365) 641450. *(Mr & Mrs Rogers).*
4 cottages (sleep 4/5), £250/300 low season,
£350 high season, open all year.
10 acres woodland.

🅿 🏠 ❄ 🛋 🍴 ➡ ⱭⱯⱣ 🐕 ▥ Ⓜ ⁄ 🛍 🗄 🖥
⊙ ⛄ 🥄 ☉

Blaney Island & Innish Beg Cottages
and Pushen Island Cottage ***/**
Innishbeg, Blaney, BT93 7EP.
☎ & fax (013656) 41525. *(Mrs G Tottenham).*
5 cottages (sleep 10), £130/240 low season,
£220/450 high season, open all year. Rowing
boat, private shore.

🎫 🅿 ❄ 🛋 🍴 ➡ ⱭⱯⱣ 🚻 ▥ Ⓜ 🗄 🖥 ⊙ ⛾
⛄ 🥄 ☉

Alder Cottage **
Glassdrummond, Kinawley, BT92 4DS.
☎ (01232) 583680. *(Mrs B Lenane).*
Cottage (2 bedrooms, sleeps 5), £120 low season,
£200 high season, open all year.

🅿 ❄ 🛋 🍴 🐕 ▥ ⓞ ⁄ 🛍 🗄 🍽 🖥 ⊙
⛄ 🥄 ☉ ✂

The Bungalow **
3 Gola Rd, Tamlaght, BT74 4HJ.
☎ (01365) 387670. *(Mrs J Nixon).*
Bungalow (sleeps 4), £150 low season,
£200 high season, open all year.

🅿 ❄ 🛋 🍴 ➡ ▥ ⓞ ⁄ 🛍 🗄 🍽 🖥 ⊙ ⛾
▮ ✗ 🥄 ☉

Charlie's Place   ***
16 Mullinaskea Rd, Garvary, BT74 4QR.
☎ (01365) 323246. *(Mrs D Rolston).*
Bungalow on farm (sleeps 11), £220 low season,
£250 high season, open all year.

Corrakelly Villa   ***
14 Drumroosk Rd, Kinawley, BT92 4DP.
☎ (013657) 48705. *(Mr & Mrs Cassidy).*
Cottage (sleeps 4/6), £170 low season,
£200 high season, open all year.

Corraquill Country Cottages   ***
Teemore, Derrylin, BT92 9BL.
☎ (013657) 48893. Fax 48493. *(Ms C McManus).*
6 bungalows (sleep 3/6), £200/265 low season,
£265/360 high season, open all year. On the
Shannon-Erne canal link.

Derryallen View   ***
Crocknacrieve, Mackan, BT92 3EB.
☎ (01365) 348559. *(Mr & Mrs Rasdale).*
Bungalow (sleeps 6), £130/150 low season,
£220 high season, open all year.

Diamond House   ***
Derrymacausey, Derrylin, BT92 9NU.
☎ (01365) 748274. *(Ms M McDaid).*
Farmhouse (sleeps 6), £175 low season,
£220 high season, open April-Sept.

Dromard Barn   ****
Dromard House, Tamlaght, BT74 4HS.
☎ (01365) 387250. *(Mrs S Weir).*
Converted barn (1 bedroom, sleeps 2), £170,
open all year.

Gables   *****
Glassmullagh, BT74 4PT.
☎ (01365) 387360. *(Mr C Cooke).*
New house (5 bedrooms, 3 ensuite, sleeps 10),
£350/400 low season, £500 high season,
open all year.

Garden House   ***
Shanmullagh, Ballycassidy, BT94 2LZ.
☎ (01365) 323495. Fax 329428. *(Mrs J Cooke).*
Semi-detached bungalow (sleeps 5/6), £190 low
season, £200/230 high season, open all year.

Gate Lodge   ***
Killyreagh, Tamlaght, BT74 4HA.
☎ (01365) 387221. Fax 387122. *(Lord Hamilton).*
Cottage (sleeps 6), £175 low season, £275 high
season, open all year.

Hill View Apartment   **
Aughindisert, Derrylin, BT92 9LA.
☎ (013657) 48879. *(Mr & Mrs Drumm).*
Apartment (sleeps 4/5), £160, open April-Oct.

Self-catering prices given are the weekly rate

Holiday Bungalow ***
3 Devenish Crescent, Silverhill, BT74 5JP.
☎ (01365) 324339. *(Mr T Callan).*
Bungalow (4 bedrooms, sleeps 8), £40, open all
year. Adapted for disabled visitors.

Kate's Cottage ***
Corramonaghan, Derrylin, BT92 9BB.
☎ (013657) 48188. Fax 48876. *(Mrs R Clarkson).*
Cottage (sleeps 6), £150 low season,
£230 high season, open all year.

Killee Old School *
2 Lough Scale Rd, Topped Mountain, BT94 5BN.
☎ (01365) 323017. *(Mr & Mrs Barbour).*
Cottage (sleeps 4/5), £100/120 low season, £140
high season, open April-Sept. Lake shore setting.

Killyhevlin Chalets **
Dublin Rd, BT74 4AU. ☎ (01365) 323481.
Fax 324726. 13 chalets (2 bedrooms), £275 low
season, £375 high season, open all year.

Knockninney View ****
Corragole, Thompson's Bridge, BT92 9DW.
☎ (01365) 748285. *(Mrs M McBarron).*
House (sleeps 6), £180 low season,
£250 high season, open all year.

Manor House Chalets ***
Killadeas, BT94 1NY.
☎ (013656) 28100. Fax 28000. *(Mr T Noble).*
12 chalets (2 bedrooms), £275 low season,
£395 high season, open all year. Boats, cruisers,
bicycles for hire. Pitch & putt, barbecue site.

Old School ***
Ballycassidy, BT94 2LY.
☎ (01365) 323030. *(Mr A Johnston).*
Cottage (sleeps 4/5), £160 low season,
£180 high season, open all year.

Pine Cottage ***
Tonywall, Kinawley, BT92 4AU.
☎ (013657) 48518 *evening. (Mr P Finlay).*
Thatched cottage, £200 low season,
£280 high season, open all year.

Riverside Farm **
Gortadrehid, Culkey, BT92 2FN.
☎ (01365) 322725. *(Mr M Fawcett).*
Bungalow (3 ensuite bedrooms, sleeps 6),
£300 low season, £350 high season, open all year.

Riverside Suite **
Ballycassidy, BT94 2FN.
☎ (01365) 323013. *(Mr M Kent).*
Apartment (sleeps 5), £180 low season,
£220 high season, open all year.

For rural locations, ask for directions when you book

Roche's Cottage ***
Clontymullan, Mackan, BT92 3BX.
☎ & fax (01365) 348285. *(Mr L Roche)*.
Cottage (sleeps 4/5), £220 low season, £260 high season, open all year.

Shallany Lodge ***
Lisnarick, BT94 1PX.
☎ (013656) 21083. *(Mrs A Maguire)*.
Lodge (sleeps 5), £130 low season,
£220 high season, open June-Oct.

Thompsons Bridge House ***
Laragh, Kinawley PO, BT92 4DB.
☎ (01365) 748205. *(Mr & Mrs Cathcart)*.
House (sleeps 6), £150 low season,
£200 high season, open all year.

Tully Bay Holiday Homes *****/***
Blaney, BT93 7EG.
☎ (01365) 641507. Fax 641734. *(Mr C Park)*.
8 units (sleep 6), £400/600 low season
£500/700 high season, open all year.

Tully Cottages **
383 Loughshore Rd, Tully, Churchhill, BT94 3HP.
☎ (013656) 41656. *(Mr & Mrs McManus)*.
2 cottages (sleep 2/4 & 5/7), £75/100 low season,
£150/200 high season, open all year.

Florencecourt

Heather Lodge ***
Derriens East, BT79 9AN.
☎ (01365) 348812. *(Mrs R Millar)*.
Apartment (sleeps 2/3), £80 low season,
£110 high season, open all year.

Laurel Leaf House ****
Marlbank, BT92 1FB.
☎ (01365) 348917. *(Mrs U Fitzpatrick)*.
House (sleeps 9), £300, open all year.

Marlbank Apartment ***
BT92 1FB.
☎ (01365) 348904. *(Mrs J Elliott)*.
Apartment (sleeps 4/5), £130 low season,
£180 high season, open all year.

Rose Cottage ***
Florence Court Demesne, BT92 1DB.
(National Trust).
☎ (01365) 348249/348788. Fax 348873.
Or NT Central Reservations ☎ (01225) 791199.
Walled garden cottage (sleeps 5), £185 low season, £430 high season, open all year.

Garrison

Devenish Villa Holiday Homes ***
Garrison, BT93 4ER.
☎ (013656) 58743. *(Mr P Ferguson)*.
3 houses (sleep 6), £200/220 low season,
£325/350 high season, open March-Sept.

Self-catering prices given are the weekly rate

Melvin Cottages ***
Garrison, BT93 4ET.
☎ (01365) 326747. Fax 326145. *(Mrs R Treacy)*.
4 cottages (sleep 6/7), £200 low season,
£325 high season, open all year.

Rossmore Country House **
Muckenagh, BT93 4FA.
☎ (013656) 58476. *(Mr B Flanagan)*.
House (sleeps 8), £330 low season, £370 high
season, open all year. Boat.

7 Loughside Rd **
Knockraven, BT93 4ET.
☎ (01504) 884646. *(Ms M McGarrigle)*.
Bungalow, near Garrison (sleeps 5/6), £150 low
season, £250 high season, open all year.

Kesh

Ashgrove House ***
1 Ardess Villas, BT93 1NX.
☎ (013656) 51932. *(Mr K Leslie)*.
House (3 bedrooms, sleeps 5), £160 low season,
£235 high season, open all year.

The Bungalow **
Agharainy, BT93 1QP.
☎ (013656) 31327. *(Mrs V Hamilton)*.
Bungalow (sleeps 6), £150/180 low season,
£220 high season, open all year.

Erne See ***
Clonaweel, BT93 8DD.
☎ (013656) 31771. *(Mrs H Johnston)*.
(On A35, 3m W of Kesh).
Bungalow (3 bedrooms), £175 low season,
£250 high season, open all year.

Fermanagh Lakeland Lodges ****
Muckross Wood, Letter, BT93 2BF.
☎ & fax (013656) 31957. *(Mr R Beare)*.
12 houses (sleep 6), £290/460 low
season, £485/505 high season, open all year.
Boat, bicycles, beside lake.

Innish Lodges ****
Lusty Beg Island, Boa Island, BT93 8AD.
☎ (013656) 32032/31342. Fax 32033.
(Mr & Mrs Cadden).
10 Finnish lodges (sleep 6), £495 low season,
£620 high season, open all year. Sauna, fitness
room, lake view.

Lusty Beg Chalets ***
Lusty Beg Island, Boa Island, BT93 8AD.
☎ (013656) 32032/31342. Fax 32033.
(Mr & Mrs Cadden).
10 chalets (sleep 4/6), £280/460 low season,
£340/480 high season, open all year.

For rural locations, ask for directions when you book

Railway Cottage **

Ederney Rd, BT93 1TF.
☎ (013656) 31096. *(Mrs N Stronge).*
Cottage (sleeps 4/6), £175 low season,
£200 high season, open all year.

Riverview Holiday Homes **

High St, Tullyhommon, BT93 8BD.
☎ (013656) 31224. *(Mrs M Gallagher).*
2 town houses, (3&4 bedrooms, sleep 4/5),
£175 low season, £220 high season, open all year.

Swan's Reach ***

Mullynaval, 609 Boa Island Rd, BT93 8AQ.
☎ (01365) 561228. *(Mrs S Johnston).*
Modern house (3 bedrooms, sleeps 6), £180/250
low season, £350 high season, open all year.

The Villa & The Annexe *

89 Crevenish Rd, Clareview, BT93 1RB.
☎ (013656) 31012. *(Mrs E Baxter).*
2 chalets (sleep 4/5), £150 low season,
£250 high season, open all year.

Lisbellaw

Bridge Cottage ***

Belle Isle Estate, BT94 5HG.
☎ (01365) 387231. Fax 387261. *(Mr C Plunket).*
Cottage (3 bedrooms, sleeps 5/6), £200 low
season, £400 high season, open all year.

Bridge House ***

Belle Isle Estate, BT94 5HG.
☎ (01365) 387231. Fax 387261. *(Mr C Plunket).*
House (3 bedrooms), £220 low season,
£420 high season, open all year.

Carry Lodge **

Carry, Inishmore, BT74 4LW.
☎ (01365) 387270. *(Mr & Mrs Johnston).*
House (sleeps 4), £200 low season, £275 high
season, open all year. Use of 19ft rowing boat &
engine.

Coach House ****

Belle Isle Estate, BT94 5HG.
☎ (01365) 387231. Fax 387261. *(Mr C Plunket).*
Coach house built 1836, 2 units (each sleeps 4),
£180 low season, £350 high season,
open all year.

Coolbuck Cottage ***

Coolbuck, BT94 5BJ.
☎ (01365) 387162. *(Ms K Waterson).*
Cottage (sleeps 6), £150 low season,
£250 high season, open all year.

The Cottage ****

Bunnahesco, BT94 5HJ.
☎ (01365) 387717. *(Mr & Mrs Rogers).*
Cottage (sleeps 6), £150 low season,
£260 high season, open all year.

Self-catering prices given are the weekly rate

Drumbadmore Lodge ***
Derryharney, BT94 5JW.
☎ (013657) 21837. *(Mrs F Wright).*
Lodge (sleeps 5), £175 low season, £250 high season, open all year.

Farm Cottage ***
Tattygar, BT94 5GQ.
☎ (01365) 387415. *(Mr J Bannon).*
Cottage (sleeps 7), £150 low season, £250 high season, open all year.

Garden House ***
Belle Isle Estate, BT94 5HG.
☎ (01365) 387231. Fax 387261. *(Mr C Plunket).*
Modern bungalow (3 bedrooms, sleeps 6), £200 low season, £400 high season, open all year.

Glen Cottage **
Belle Isle Estate, BT94 5HG.
☎ (01365) 387231. Fax 387261. *(Mr C Plunket).*
Cottage (sleeps 4), £140 low season, £275 high season, open all year.

Hamilton Wing *****
Belle Isle Estate, BT94 5HG.
☎ (01365) 387231. Fax 387261. *(Mr C Plunket).*
Self-contained wing of listed mansion (5 bedrooms, sleeps 14), £1000/1200 low season, £1200/1600 high season, open all year.

Millwood Cottage ***
Millwood, Beagho, BT94 5FY.
☎ & fax (01365) 387417. *(Mr D Elton).*
Cottage (sleeps 5), £150 low season, £250 high season, open all year.

Walled Garden Cottage ***
Belle Isle Estate, BT94 5HG.
☎ (01365) 387231. Fax 387261. *(Mr C Plunket).*
Traditional cottage (sleeps 4), £220 low season, £420 high season, open all year.

Lisnaskea

Corradillar *
Corradillar Quay, BT92 0ES.
☎ (013657) 21165. *(Mr & Mrs Clifford).*
Bungalow (2 bedrooms, sleeps 4/8), £185 low season, £375 high season, open all year.

Cygnet Lodge ****
208 Newbridge Rd, Smith's Strand, BT92 0EQ.
☎ (013657) 22122. Fax 21893.
(Mr & Mrs Livingstone).
Lodge (sleeps 8), private lough shore site, £185 low season, £375 high season, open all year.

For rural locations, ask for directions when you book

Idlewild Villa ***
Derryad, BT92 0BX.
☎ & fax 0181-567 4487. *(Mr E Dawson).*
Lakeside villa (sleeps 8), £220 low season,
£450 high season, open all year. Free use of boat,
private jetty. Restaurant discounts.

[icons]

Innisfree Cottage ***
Derryad, BT92 0BX.
☎ & fax 0181-567 4487. *(Dr W Dawson).*
Lakeside cottage (sleeps 5), £160 low season,
£350 high season, open all year. Free use of
boat, private jetty. Restaurant discounts.

[icons]

Kilmore Chalets *
Kilmore South, BT92 0DT.
☎ (01247) 472118. *(Mr G Hopes).*
5 chalets (sleep 4), £140 low season, £250 high
season, open April-Oct. Fishing boat for hire.
Café, restaurant.

[icons]

Kilmore Cottage *
17 Kilmore South, BT92 0DT.
☎ (013655) 31726/31808. *(Mr M Maguire).*
Cottage (sleeps 5), £225 low season,
£350 high season, open all year.

[icons]

Ross Lodge ***
Rossmacaffry, BT92 0LB.
☎ (013657) 21565 after 6 pm. *(Mr J Haire).*
Bungalow (sleeps 5), £175 low season,
£275 high season, open all year.

[icons]

Share Holiday Village **
Smith's Strand, Shanaghy, BT92 0EQ.
☎ (013657) 22122. Fax 21893. *(Ms D Latimer).*
15 chalets (sleep 4/12), £280 low season, £320
high season (for 8 berth), open all year. Sports
instruction for disabled visitors.

[icons]

Sunbeam **
Drummack, Ballindarragh, BT92 0PG.
☎ (013657) 21775. *(Mr & Mrs Wallace).*
Bungalow (sleeps 6), £175 low season,
£200 high season, open all year.

[icons]

Newtownbutler

Bellagrall Cottage ***
Killard, BT92 8DS.
☎ (013657) 38269. *(Mr H Fleming).*
Cottage (sleeps 4/5), £110 low season,
£180 high season, open all year.

[icons]

Crom Cottages ****
Crom Estate, BT92 8AP.
(National Trust).
☎ (013657) 38118. Fax 38174. Or NT Central
Reservations ☎ (01225) 791199.
7 cottages (sleep 2/6) £185 low season, £435 high
season, open all year. One unit suitable for
disabled visitors.

[icons]

Three Oaks Country House **
Ports, BT92 8DT.
☎ (013657) 38456. *(Mr P Clarke).*
House (5 bedrooms, sleeps 9), £150 low season,
£250 high season, open all year.

[icons]

Self-catering prices given are the weekly rate

Tempo

The Barn ****
Sunnybank Farm, Pubble, BT94 3NB.
☎ (01365) 541431. *(Mrs J Little)*.
Converted barn (sleeps 4), £100 low season,
£200 high season, open all year.

Doon Lodge ***
Windyridge, Doon, BT94 3GQ.
☎ (01365) 541282. *(Mr & Mrs Campbell)*.
2 houses (2/3 bedrooms), £200 low season,
£240 high season, open April-Oct.
Barbecue site.

Greendale House ***
Mullyknock, BT94 3AZ.
☎ (01365) 541522. *(Mr T Phair)*.
Cottage (sleeps 6), £150 low season,
£225 high season, open all year.

Hillside **
6 Dooneen Rd, Tonyglaskan, BT94 3GT.
☎ (01365) 541346. *(Mr & Mrs Breen)*.
House (sleeps 7), £225, open April-Sept.

The Loft ***
Mountview, Ballyreagh, BT94 3EH.
☎ (01365) 541217. *(Ms K Murphy)*.
Converted barn (sleeps 3), £110 low season,
£150 high season, open all year.

For rural locations, ask for directions when you book

County Londonderry

Bellaghy

Lough Beg Coach Houses ****
Ballyscullion Park, BT45 8NA.
☎ (01648) 386235. Fax 386416. *(Mr R Mulholland)*.
6 houses (3 bedrooms, sleep 8), in courtyard of
estate. £200 low season, £380 high season,
open all year.

🛈 🅿 🏧 ❋ 🐎 🐕 🛏 🖼 ⬛ Ⓜ ✂ 🛢 📻 🖵 ☺ 🔋
📞 🔍 🎣 ∪ ✂

Castlerock

Heather View **
229b Mussenden Rd, BT51 4TY.
☎ (01265) 848234. *(Mr & Mrs Moody)*.
Bungalow (sleeps 6/7), £250 low season,
£270 high season, open May-Sept.

🛈 🅿 ❋ 🐎 OAP ⬛ Ⓜ 🛢 ✂ 🛢 📻 🖵 ☺ 🔋
🎣 🎣 ∪ ✂

Honeysuckle Cottage ****
10 Belvedere Park, Sea Rd, BT51 4XW.
☎ & fax (01225) 837088. *(Mr A Crawford)*.
Detached bungalow (sleeps 6), £200 low season,
£375 high season, open all year.

🅿 ❋ 🐎 🛏 OAP ⬛ 🛢 ✂ 🛢 📻 🖵 ☺ 🔋 📞 🎣
🎣 ✕ 🎣 ∪

The Rock *****
8 Belvedere Park, Sea Road, BT51 4XW.
☎ (01265) 849143. *(Mr R Gilmore)*.
Bungalow (4 bedrooms, sleeps 8), £195/250 low
season, £395 high season, open all year.

🛈 🅿 🏧 ❋ 🐎 🛏 ⬛ Ⓜ 🛢 ✂ 🛢 📻 🖵 ☺ 🔋
📞 🎣 🎣 ✕ 🔍 🎣 ∪

7 Cliff Terrace **
BT51 4RQ.
☎ (01265) 53083. *(Mrs S Dwyer)*.
Cottage (3 bedrooms, sleeps 4/5), £150 low
season, £300 high season, open all year.

🅿 🏧 ❋ 🐎 🛏 ♿ ⬛ 🛢 ✂ 🛢 📻 🖵 ☺
🔋 🎣 ∪ ✂

Claudy

Rio Grande **
207 Learmount Rd, Park, BT47 4BA.
☎ (015047) 81210. Fax 81801.
(Mr & Mrs McElhinney).
2 apartments (sleep 5/9), terms on application,
open all year.

🅿 🏧 🐎 🛏 OAP ⬛ ✂ 🛢 📻 🖵 ☺ 📞 🎣 🍴
🔍 🎣 ∪ ✂

Coleraine

Drumslade Holiday Apartments ***
88 Portstewart Rd, BT52 1SD.
☎ (01265) 833684. *(Mr M Conn)*.
Apartment (sleeps 6), £100 low season,
£250 high season, open all year.

🅿 ❋ 🐎 🛏 OAP ⬛ Ⓜ 🛢 ✂ 🛢 📻 🖵 ☺
📞 🎣 ∪ 💷

King's Country Cottages ***/**/*
66 Ringrash Rd, Macosquin, BT51 4LJ.
☎ (01265) 51367. *(Mr & Mrs King).*
3 cottages (sleep 4/6), £150 low season,
£185 high season, open all year.

Breezemount House *unclassified*
26 Castlerock Rd, BT51 3HP.
☎ (01265) 44615. Fax 43641. *(Mr W Wallace).*
2 apartments (sleep 3).

Eglinton

Longfield Farm Cottages ***
140 Clooney Rd, BT47 3DX.
☎ & fax (01504) 810952. *(Mr S Hunter).*
4 cottages (sleep 5), £200 low season,
£320 high season, open all year.
Panoramic views.

Feeny

Drumcovitt Barn ****
704 Feeny Rd, BT47 4SU.
☎ & fax (015047) 81224. *(Mrs F Sloan).*
2 cottages & 1 converted barn (sleep 5/6),
£260 low season, £350 high season, open all year.

Market House ***
2 Mullaghmesh Road, BT47 4JD.
☎ (015047) 81328. *(Mrs A Devine).*
Bungalow (sleeps 6), £150 low season,
£230 high season, open all year.

Garvagh

Halcyon **
3 Killykergan Rd, BT51 4EA.
☎ (012665) 58012 or (01762) 332854.
(Rev. Wilson).
Bungalow (sleeps 6), £150 low season,
£250 high season, open all year.

Limavady

Barnmill West ****
57 Seacoast Rd, BT49 9DW. *(Mr E Boyle).*
☎ (015047) 62105. Fax 63321.
Cottage (sleeps 4), £180 low season,
£220 high season, open all year.

Keepers Cottage ***
57 Seacoast Rd, BT49 9DW.
☎ (015047) 62105. Fax 63321. *(Mr E Boyle).*
Cottage (sleeps 7), £220 low season,
£280 high season, open all year.

Old Railway Station ***
459 Seacoast Rd, BT49 0LL.
☎ (015047) 50437. *(Mr & Mrs Lestas).*
Renovated railway station (1 bedroom, sleeps 4),
£190 low season, £230 high season,
open all year.

Golden Sands *unclassified*
26a Benone Avenue, Magilligan, BT49 0LQ.
☎ (015047) 50324. Fax 50405.
(Messrs J & S Walls).
6 caravans (8 berths).

For rural locations, ask for directions when you book

Londonderry

Foxfield Accommodation ***
2 Ballynacraig Gardens, Kingsfort Park,
Culmore Rd, BT48 7SX.
☎ (01504) 351618. *(Mrs M McDermott).*
House (sleeps 6), £270, open all year.

Maghera

Moneysharvan ***
89 Moneysharvan Rd, BT46 5PT.
☎ (01648) 401259. *(Mr P Quigg).*
Farmhouse (sleeps 7), £190 low season,
£210 high season, open all year.

Portstewart

Burren View ***
27 Millbrook Park, BT52 7DU.
☎ (01266) 862435. *(Mrs D McMullan).*
Bungalow (3 bedrooms, sleeps 5), £260/320 low
season, £360 high season, open all year.

Cornerstone **
1 Flowerfield Rd, BT55 7JG.
☎ (01762) 326040. *(Mrs T Cadden).*
Bungalow (sleeps 5), £170 low season, £220 high
season, open end June-Sept.

The Mews ***
6a & 6b Central Avenue, BT55 7BP.
☎ (01265) 833214. *(Mrs J Coulter).*
2 town houses in private mews (5 bedrooms),
£250 low season, £350 high season,
open June-Sept.

Rock Castle Cottages ***
Rock Castle, Berne Rd, BT55 7PB.
☎ & fax (01265) 832271. *(S Pollock).*
8 apartments (2 bedrooms), £130/380 low season,
£250/485 high season, open all year.

Spires ***
32 Church St, BT55 7AH.
☎ (01247) 466132. *(Mr J Logan).*
Town house (sleeps 5/6), £200 low season,
£350 high season, open all year.

Wavecrest **
2 Queenora Avenue, BT55 7BU.
☎ (01846) 682376. *(Mrs J Parks).*
Terrace (4 bedrooms, sleeps 5/6), £200 low
season, £240 high season, open July-Sept.

York ***
2 Station Rd, BT55 7DA.
☎ (01265) 833594/834973.
(Mr & Mrs Henderson).
8 apartments (sleep 3), £230 low season,
£350 high season, open all year.

Self-catering prices given are the weekly rate

9 Inishowen Park ***
BT55 7BQ.
☎ (01266) 871283. *(Mrs J Clarke)*.
Detached house (3 bedrooms, sleeps 5/6), £220
low season, £330 high season, open Easter-Sept.

7 Lever Rd ***
BT55 7BN.
☎ (01648) 32582. *(Mr & Mrs McKeever)*.
Semi-detached house (sleeps 6), £250,
open May-Oct.

17 Lever Rd ***
BT55 7BN.
☎ (01648) 44736. *(Mrs M Mullen)*.
House (5 bedrooms, sleeps 9), £200 low season,
£250 high season, open all year.

3 Meadow Gardens ***
BT55 7SS.
☎ (01232) 401271. Fax 471535. *(Mr A Rodgers)*.
Bungalow (4 bedrooms, sleeps 6), £200/250 low
season, £300/350 high season, open May-Oct.

5 Mill Court ***
BT55 7SJ.
☎ (01232) 486699. *(Mr & Mrs McCormick)*.
Chalet (sleeps 6), £175 low season,
£325 high season, open all year.

6 Mill Court **
BT55 7SJ.
☎ (01232) 837447. *(Mr J Dickson)*.
Bungalow (sleeps 6), terms on application,
open July-Aug.

7 Mill Court ***
BT55 7SJ.
☎ (01232) 486699. *(Mr J McCormick)*.
Bungalow (sleeps 6), £175 low season,
£325 high season, open May-Sept.

18 Seahaven Court ***
BT55 7DS.
☎ (01232) 486699. *(Mr & Mrs McCormick)*.
Apartment (sleeps 4), £140 low season,
£250 high season, open May-Sept.

20 Strandview Avenue ****
BT55 7LL.
☎ (01232) 486699. *(Mr & Mrs McCormick)*.
Bungalow (3 bedrooms, sleeps 6), £175 low
season, £320 high season, open May-Sept.

80 Mill Rd   *unclassified*
☎ & fax (01846) 601686. *(Mr C Millar)*.
Mobile home (sleeps 6).

County Tyrone

Clogher

Ashfield Park **
8 Ashfield Rd, BT76 0HF.
☎ (016625) 48684. Mobile 0850 820379.
(Mr & Mrs Beatty).
2 flats (ground floor, sleep 6/8), £175 low
season, £200 high season, open all year.

Kirks Home **
36 Fardross Rd, BT76 0HH.
☎ (01365) 387490. *(Mr M Kirkpatrick).*
Cottage (sleeps 4), £130 low season, £170 high
season, open all year.

Dungannon

Curragh Cottage ***
164 Killycolpy Rd, Ardboe, BT71 5AP.
☎ (016487) 37328. *(Mrs M Quinn).*
Cottage (sleeps 5), £175 low season, £250 high
season, open all year.

Fivemiletown

Blessingbourne Apartments *
Blessingbourne, BT75 0QS.
☎ (013655) 21221. *(Capt Lowry).*
2 apartments (2 bedrooms, sleeps 6), £150 low
season, £200 high season, open all year. Coarse
fishing on private lake.

Porter's Cottage **
Blessingbourne, BT75 0QS.
☎ (013655) 21221. *(Capt Lowry).*
Farm cottage (sleeps 6), £200 low season,
£250 high season, open all year.

Gortin

Rose Cottage **
11 Leardin Rd, BT79 8QD.
☎ (01762) 326857. *(Mrs R Mitchell).*
Cottage (sleeps 5), £75/150 low season,
£200 high season, open all year.
Close to folk park.

Newtownstewart

The Barn ****
15 Brocklis Rd, Ardstraw, BT78 4LS.
☎ & fax (016626) 58531. *(Mr & Mrs Magee).*
Converted barn (sleeps 6), £150 low season,
£250 high season, open all year.

Self-catering prices given are the weekly rate

Baronscourt Country Cottages **

Golf Course Rd, BT78 4LF.
☎ (016626) 58602. *(Mr D Forbes)*.
8 cottages (2 and 3 bedrooms), £180 low season,
£240 high season, open all year. Private lake.
Golf, windsurfing, water skiing, clay pigeon
shooting.

[symbols]

Grange Court ****/***

21/27 Moyle Rd, BT78 4AP.
☎ & fax (016626) 61877. *(Mrs F McFarland)*.
6 units (sleep 6), £200 low season,
£300 high season, open all year.

[symbols]

Omagh

An Clachan ***/**

Creggan, BT79 9AE.
☎ (016627) 61112. Fax 61116. *(Mr J Donaghy)*.
8 cottages, £110/220 low season, £180/330 high
season, open all year. Visitor centre.

[symbols]

Aughalane Clachan ****

Glenelly Rd, Plumbridge, BT79 8AA
☎ (01232) 241100. Fax 241198.
(Bookings through Michelle).
2 houses (sleep 3 & 5), £180 low season,
£330 high season, open all year.

[symbols]

Bridge View **

18 Relagh Rd, Trillick, BT94 2GJ.
☎ (01365) 388735. *(Mrs E McElhinney)*.
Bungalow (sleeps 5), £110 low season, £200 high
season, open all year.

[symbols]

Gortin Glen Cottage **

186 Glen Park Rd, Gortin, BT79 8PT.
☎ (01662) 249242. *(Mrs D Brogan)*.
Forester's cottage (sleeps 6), £150 low season,
£250 high season, open all year.

[symbols]

Lislap Cottages ***

Lisnaharney Rd, Lislap, BT79 7UG.
☎ & fax (016626) 48108. *(Mr J Allen)*.
10 cottages (1/3 bedrooms, sleep 2/6), some
suitable for disabled visitors, £90/160 low season,
£180/270 high season, open all year.

[symbols]

Loughview House ***

Loughmacrory, BT79 9LU.
☎ (016627) 61888. *(Mrs K McCullagh)*.
House (sleeps 12), £100 low season,
£150 high season, open all year.

[symbols]

Riverside ***

4 Holmview Court, Holmview Avenue, BT79 0BD.
☎ (01203) 381942. *(Mr & Mrs McGale)*.
Flat (sleeps 3), £110 low season, £220 high
season, open all year.

[symbols]

For rural locations, ask for directions when you book

Sperrin Clachan ****

272 Glenelly Rd, Cranagh, BT79 8AA.
☎ (01232) 241100. Fax 241198.
(Bookings through Michelle).
4 houses (sleep 3/5), £180 low season, £330 high season, open all year.

⊤ P 🏠 ❄ ➳ OAP ❌ 🐕 Ⅲ ⧉ ⁄ 🛆 ⬚ ⬛ ⊙ ⬚
📞 ✕ 🧦 ∪ ✄

Stewartstown

The Bungalow ****

Kingsmills, 62a Ballynargan Rd, BT71 5NF.
☎ & fax (016487) 37106. *(Mrs N McReynolds).*
Thatched bungalow (5 bedrooms, sleeps 9), £350 low season, £380 high season, open all year.

⊤ P 🏠 ❄ ➳ ▦ 🛒 OAP ⧉ Ⅲ ⧉ ⁄ 🛆 ⬚ ⬛ ⬚
⊙ 🎵 ∪ ⊞

Erin Dene ***

98 Knockinroe Rd, Ardtrea, BT71 5NA.
☎ (016487) 62606. *(Mr & Mrs Gibson).*
Modern bungalow (sleeps 6), £250 low season.
£325 high season, open all year.

⊤ P ❄ ➳ ▦ ⧉ Ⅲ ⧉ ⁄ 🛆 ⬚ ⬛ ⬚
⊙ 🎵 ∪ ✄

Strabane

Woodend Cottage **

42 Woodend Rd, BT82 0BN.
☎ (01504) 382817. *(Mr P Hegarty).*
Thatched cottage (sleeps 5/6), £125 low season, £230 high season, open all year.

P 🏠 ❄ ➳ OAP 🐕 Ⅲ ⧉ ⁄ 🛆 ⬚ ⬛ ⬚ ⊙ 🎵

Trillick

Corkhill **

31 Old Junction Rd, BT78 3RN.
☎ (01365) 61865. *(Mrs T Brunt).*
Newly renovated 2 storey farmhouse (sleeps 5/6), £130 low season, £220 high season,
open all year.

⊤ P ❄ ➳ ▦ OAP Ⅲ ⧉ ⁄ 🛆 ⬚ ⬛ ⬚ ⊙ ⬚ 📞
⬛ 🎵 ∪ ✄

Key to camping & caravan symbols

Spaces for touring caravans
Les caravanes sont admises
Aufnahme von Wohnwagen

Spaces for motor caravans
Les camping-cars sont admis
Aufnahme von Wohnmobilen

Spaces for tents
Les tentes sont admises
Aufnahme von Zelten

Dogs admitted on lead
Les chiens sont admis en laisse
Hunde nur an der Leine

Showers
Douches
Duschen

Electric points for shavers
Prises électriques pour rasoirs
Elektroanschlüsse für Rasierapparate

Electricity supply to pitches
Prises électriques conjugués pour caravanes
Elektro-Gemein-schaftsanschluß für Wohnwagen

Gas cylinders for hire
Cartouches de gaz à louer
Austausch von Gaszylindern

Booking recommended in summer
Il est prudent de réserver l'été
Im sommer empfiehlt sich Voranmeldung

Café/restaurant
Café/restaurant
Café/Restaurant

Food shop/mobile shop
Magasin ou camion épicerie
Lebensmittelladen

Public telephone
Téléphone public
Öffentlicher Fernsprecher

Laundry facilities
Machine à laver
Waschmaschine

Lounge/television room
Salle de télévision
Fernsehraum

Games/sports area
Terrain réservé aux jeux et sports
Sportplatz

Children's playground
Terrain de jeux pour enfants
Kinderspielplatz

Facilities nearby

Indoor swimming pool
Piscine couverte
Hallenbad

Tennis courts
Courts de tennis
Tennisplätze

Golf

Riding/pony trekking
Equitation ou poney
Reiten/Pony-Trekking

Boating
Bateau ou voile
Bootfahren/Segeln

Convenient to Ulster Way
Pratique pour faire l'Ulster Way
Idealer Ausgangspunkt für den Ulster Way

Sites graded by British Holiday & Home Parks Association/National Caravan Council
The more ticks the better!

Sites classés par la BHHPA/NCC. Le nombre de coches est proportionnel à la qualité des services et équipements offerts.

Von der BHHPA/NCC eingestufte Plätze. Je mehr Häkchen, desto besser!

The maximum speed limit for cars towing caravans or trailers on single carriageways in Northern Ireland is 50 mph, and on dual carriageways and motorways 60 mph.

Camping & Caravan Parks

The province is well provided with camping parks near points of entry. For visitors coming by ferry from Britain sites around Larne and Belfast ports are convenient for overnight stops. Kilbroney park in Rostrevor forest is popular with tourists travelling north from the Republic via Newry. Over in the west, the Fermanagh Lakeland has attractive parks easily accessible from south of the border, and caravanners entering from Donegal have a wide choice all along the Causeway Coast.

All the parks listed are suitable for touring visitors. However, not all of them are manned 24 hours. You are therefore strongly advised to use the telephone numbers to get information in advance of your arrival. In addition some parks may be better signposted than others and you are advised to ask for route directions when you telephone.

Popular parks like Tollymore Forest Park tend to fill up quickly in peak periods so check availability. Nearly all have mains water supply and flush toilets. Overnight charges are based on two persons, car, and caravan or tent.

Details of amenities and prices, where given, have been supplied by the owners and are subject to alteration. Not all site owners have supplied prices. The Northern Ireland Tourist Board has no control over caravan sites.

Belfast Area

Jordanstown Lough Shore Park
Shore Rd, Newtownabbey. ☎ (01232) 868751 (Newtownabbey Borough Council).
Overlooking Belfast Lough. Adapted toilets for wheelchair users. Close to leisure centre.
On A2, 5 miles north of Belfast.
Open all year (booking essential October-March).

6 🚐🚑 1🛆 @ £6.50 per night, hook-up £1 per night. Maximum stay 2 consecutive nights.

🐕 🏠 ☉ 🚐 (16amps) 🛆 🗘 🖍 🌂 🔍 🏴 ∪ 🛆

Lorne House & Estate
30 Station Rd, Craigavad, Holywood.
☎ (01232) 423180 (The Guide Association).
On A2, 8 miles east of Belfast. Open all year.
50 🛆 @ £10 per night.

🐕 🏠 ☉ 🛆 🗘 🖃 🌀 🗘 🔍 🏴 🛆 🐕

Dundonald Leisure Park
111 Old Dundonald Rd, Belfast.
☎ (01232) 482611. *Opens summer 1998.*

County Antrim

Antrim

Sixmilewater Marina & Caravan Park
Antrim Forum, Lough Rd. ☎ (01849) 464131/ 463113 (Antrim Borough Council). On shore of Lough Neagh, watersports, slipway. Adapted toilet and shower for wheelchair users. Picnic and barbecue areas. Antrim town 3/4 mile.
Open 1 May-30 September.

16 🚐🚑 @ £4.50 per night, hook-up £1.50 per night   24 🛆 @ £4 per night.
Refundable key deposit £5.

🐕 🏠 ☉ 🚐 (13amps) 🛆 🗘 🖃 🌀 🗘 🔍 🏴 ∪ 🛆 ✓4

Ballintoy

Larrybane Campsite
121a Whitepark Rd.
☎ (012657) 62178/31582 (National Trust).
Interpretive centre, small aquarium, tea room.
½ mile from Carrick-a-rede rope bridge,
8 miles east of Giant's Causeway.
Open all year.

6 🚐 🚎 6 ▲ @ £3. One night only (dusk to
10 am). Minimal facilities.

🛌🐕☉♿✕🛒♨️⚡🚿ⵣ☂️⛱▲♨️

Sheep Island View Campsite
42 Main St. ☎ (012657) 69391.
Open all year.

30 ▲ @ £6 per night.

🅿☉🐕♿✕🛒☎⚡♨️ⵣ☂️⛱▲♨️

Ballycastle

Fair Head Caravan Park
13 Whitepark Rd. ☎ (012657) 62077.
Open 17 March-31 October.

8 🚐 4 🚎 10 ▲ @ £9 per night,
hook-up £1 per night.

🛌🐕☉🚐(16amps) ☂️🛒☎⚡♨️🏍 ♨️ⵣ
☂️⛱▲♨️

Maguire's Strand Caravan Park
32 Carrickmore Rd. ☎ (012657) 63294.
South of Ballycastle, ¾ mile off A2 road.
Rock climbing, walking, fishing.
Open 17 March-31 October.

20 🚐 🚎 @ £10 per night, hook-up £1.50,
awning £1 per night   10 ▲ @ £8 per night.

🛌🐕🚐(6amps) ☂️♿☎⚡♨️🏍 ♨️ⵣ
☂️⛱▲♨️

Silvercliffs Holiday Village
21 Clare Rd. ☎ (012657) 62550.
Overlooking sea. Heated indoor swimming pool,
water slide, sauna. Bar, lounge facilities.
Open all year.

60 🚐 🚎 @ £12 per night, hook-up £2 per night.

🛌🐕☉🚐(16amps) ☂️✕🛒☎⚡♨️🏍 ♨️
ⵣ☂️⛱▲✓4

Watertop Open Farm
188 Cushendall Rd. ☎ (012657) 62576.
Working farm, museum, tours, pony trekking,
boating, fishing, walks. On A2, 6 miles
south-east of Ballycastle, opposite Ballypatrick
Forest entrance.
Open all year.

14 🚐 🚎 @ £10 per night (includes hook-up
and awning)   10 ▲ @ £6 per night.

🛌🐕☉🚐(13amps) ☂️♿✕☎⚡♨️🖵♨️🏍 ♨️
ⵣ☂️⛱▲♨️

Ballymoney

Drumaheglis Marina & Caravan Park
36 Glenstall Rd. ☎ (012656) 66466/62280
(Ballymoney Borough Council).
On Lower Bann, water sports, fishing, walks.
Off A26, signposted 3 miles north of Ballymoney.
Open 1 April-30 September.

52 🚐 🚎 @ £10 per night, hook-up £1 per night
12 ▲ @ £9 per night.

🛌🐕☉🚐(5amps) ☂️♿✕🛒☎⚡♨️🏍 ♨️
ⵣ☂️⛱▲✓5

Bushmills

Bush Caravan Park
95 Priestland Rd. ☎ (012657) 31678/(01265) 54240.
Adapted toilet and shower for wheelchair users.
Off B62, Bushmills 3 miles, Portrush 3 miles,
Coleraine 4 miles.
Open 1 March-31 October.

25 ⛺ 🚐 @ £9 per night, hook-up £1, awning £1
per night   10 ▲ @£5 per night.

🐕 🏠 ☉ 🔌 (15amps) ⛽ ⚲ 🏪 🕭 🗑 ✪ 🏔 ⚲
♨ ▶ ∪ ⌂

Carnlough

Bay View Caravan Park
39 Largy Rd. ☎ (01574) 885685.
Open 1 April-10 October.

4 ⛺ 2 🚐 @ £5 per night, awning £3 per night
5 ▲ @ £4 per night.

🐕 ⛽ ✪ ⌂ ⚲

Ruby Hill Caravan Park
46 Largy Rd. ☎ (01574) 885692.
Open 17 March-31 October.

4 ⛺ 🚐 @ £6 per night, hook-up £1 per night
5 ▲ @ £4 per night.

🐕 🏠 ☉ 🔌 (6amps) ⛽ ⚲ 🗑 ⌂ ⚲

Whitehill Caravan Park
30a Whitehill Rd. ☎ (01574) 885233.
Open 1 April-31 October.

2 ⛺ 🚐 @ £5 per night.

🐕 🏠 ☉ ⛽ ⚲ ✖ 🏪 🗑 ✪ 🏔 ⌂

Cushendall

Cushendall Caravan Park
62 Coast Rd. ☎ (012667) 71699 (Moyle D. C.).
Open 10 April-30 September.

22 ⛺ 🚐 @ £7.90 per night, awning £2 per night
4 ▲ @ £4.65 per night.

🐕 ☉ ⚲ ✖ 🏪 🕭 🗑 ▶ ⌂ ⚲ ✓[4]

Glenville Caravan Park
22 Layde Rd. ☎ (012667) 71520
or (01265) 832442.
Open 1 March-31 October.

2 ⛺ 🚐 @ £7 per night (includes hook-up and
awning) 4 ▲ @ £3 per night.

🐕 🏠 ☉ 🔌 (5amps) ⛽ ⚲ 🗑 ✪ 🏔 ▶ ⌂ ⚲

Cushendun

Cushendun Caravan Park
14 Glendun Rd. ☎ (012667) 61254
(Moyle District Council). Adjacent to beach.
Open 10 April-30 September.

14 ⛺ 🚐 @ £7.90 per night, awning £2 per night
10 ▲ @ £4.65 per night.

🐕 🏠 ☉ ⚲ ✖ 🏪 🕭 🗑 ▭ ✪ ▶ ⌂ ⚲ ✓[3]

Glenariff (or Waterfoot)

Glenariff Forest Park
98 Glenariff Rd, Ballymena BT44 0QX.
☎ (012667) 58232 or (01266) 662873.
The forest park's foremost attraction is the
spectacular glen walk with three waterfalls.
A scenic path runs round the sheer sides of the
gorge and there are waymarked walks and trails
to mountain viewpoints. In spring and early
summer the upper glen is bright with wild
flowers. Visitor centre, café. Picnic and barbecue
areas. On A43, Waterfoot 4 miles, Cushendall
6 miles.
Open all year.

20 ⛺ 🚐   50 ▲ @ £5.50/8 per night,
hook-up £1.50 per night.

🐕 🏠 ☉ 🔌 (6amps) ⛽ ⚲ ✖ ✪ ▶ ⌂

Caravan & Camping in the

 Borough of **Larne**

Our popular sites include

★ Carnfunnock Country Park

Advanced caravan site facilities. Unique collection of sundials in a time garden, a labyrinth, gift and coffee shop. Children's activity centre with crazy golf, target ball, and exciting play area, a 9 hole par 3 golf course, also seasonal outdoor events.

★ Curran Caravan Park

Ideal location for those on the move, close to harbour and busy shopping town of Larne. Leisure centre and multi-screen cinema nearby. Bowling, putting, picnic areas and children's playground on site. All sites have hard stands and electric hook-up is available.

★ Brown's Bay Caravan Park

Picturesque setting in Islandmagee close to an excellent sandy beach. Riding centre, two open farms, abundant bird life, and many interesting historical features. Perfect for family holidays.

For further information please contact:

Tourist Information Centre
Narrow Gauge Road
Larne, County Antrim
BT40 1XB

LARNE
Tourist Information
C E N T R E ☎ (01574) 260088

Don't fly through,
There's so much to do!

Islandmagee

Brown's Bay Caravan Park

Brown's Bay. ☎ (01960) 382497 or
(01574) 260088 (Larne Borough Council).
At head of Islandmagee peninsula, overlooking
sea. Long sandy beach. Barbecue, picnic area.
Open 10 April-30 September.

29 🚐🚚 @ £7 per night   40 ▲ @ £4.50 per night.
Prices under review.

Ranch Caravan Park

93 Mullaghboy Rd. ☎ (01960) 382441.
Follow signs for Mullaghboy/Portmuck.
Open 1 April-31 October.

4 🚐🚚 @ £8 per night, hook-up £1.50,
awning 50p per night.

🐕 🐾 ☉ 🚐 (6amps) 🔥 🛒 📞 🗑 ☻ ⚙ ☂
☕ ┏ ∪ 💧

Larne

Carnfunnock Country Park

Coast Rd. ☎ (01574) 260088/270541
(Larne Borough Council).
Maze, walled garden, wildlife, walks, picnicking,
coffee shop, gift shop. Children's adventure
playground. Nine-hole par 3 golf course, putting.
Barbecue area.
On A2, 3½ miles north of Larne.
Open 10 April-30 September.

28 🚐🚚 @ £12 per night (includes electric,
water and waste hook-up)   20 ▲ @ £6 per night.
Prices under review.

🐕 🐾 ☉ 🚐 (5amps) 🔥 ✕ 📞 ⚙ ☂ ☕
┏ ∪ 💧 ✓⁵

Curran Caravan Park

131 Curran Rd. ☎ (01574) 260088/273797
(Larne Borough Council). Follow signs for
leisure centre. Putting, barbecue, picnic area.
Convenient for cross-channel ferries.
Leisure centre, parks, bowling nearby.
Open 10 April-30 September.

29 🚐🚚 @ £7 per night, hook-up £1.50
per night   40 ▲ @ £4.50 per night.
Prices under review.

🐕 🐾 ☉ 🚐 (5amps) 🔥 ✕ 🛒 📞 ☻ ⚙ ☂ ☕
┏ ∪ 💧 ✓⁴

Portballintrae

Portballintrae Caravan Park

Ballaghmore Avenue. ☎ (012657) 31478.
On B145, 1 mile north-west of Bushmills.
Open 3 April-2 November.

43 🚐🚚 @ £11 per night, hook-up £1,
awning £1 per night   10 ▲ @ £6 per night.
Prices under review.

🐕 🐾 ☉ 🚐 (6amps) 🔥 ✕ 📞 🗑 ☻ ⚙ ☂ ┏
∪ 💧 ♨ ✓⁴

Portglenone

Kingfisher Angling Centre & Caravan Park

54 Gortgole Rd. ☎ (01266) 821630.
On banks of Bann river, coarse fishing,
forest walks.
Open 1 April-31 October.

24 🚐🚚 @ £8 per night, hook-up £1, awning 50p
per night   20 ▲ @ £5 per night.

🐕 🐾 ☉ 🚐 (16amps) 🔥 ✕ 🛒 ☂ ┏ ∪ 💧

Check availability before you travel

Portrush

Ballymacrea Touring Caravan Park
220 Ballybogy Rd. ☎ (01265) 824507.
On B62, ¼ mile from junction of A2 coast road at
White Rocks, signposted at junction with
Ballyhome Rd. Portrush 1½ miles.
Open all year.

40 ⛺🚐 @ £9 per night, hook-up £1.50, awning
£1 per night   2 ▲ (family) @ £6 per night.

🐕 🏪 ☉ 🍴 (16amps) ⊕ ♨ ✕ 🧺 ☎ 🗄 ✪ ♨ 🎣 ⚲
🏹 ∪ ⚓ 🛝

Bellemont Caravan Park
10 Islandtasserty Rd. ☎ (01265) 823872.
Signposted off A29, mid-way between Portrush
and Coleraine. Portrush 1½ miles.
Open 1 April-31 October.

24 ⛺🚐 @ £10 per night (includes electric,
water and hook-up), awning £1 per night
6 ▲ @ £7 per night.

🏪 ☉ 🍴 (15amps) ♨ 🗄 ✪ ♨ 🎣 ⚲ 🏹 ∪ ⚓ 🛝

Blair's Caravan Park
29 Dhu Varren, Portstewart Rd.
☎ (01265) 822760. Close to beach, walks.
On A2, 1 mile west of Portrush.
Open 17 March-31 October.

35 ⛺🚐 @ £9 per night, hook-up £1 per night
4 ▲ @ £7 per night.

🐕 🏪 ☉ 🍴 (10amps) ⊕ ♨ ✕ 🧺 ☎ 🗄 ♨ ⚲ 🏹 ∪ ⚓ 🛝

Carrick Dhu Caravan Park
12 Ballyreagh Rd. ☎ (01265) 823712
(Coleraine Borough Council).
One mile west of Portrush, off A2 coast road.
Open 6 April-12 October.

45 ⛺🚐 @ £10 per night (includes hook-up
and awning) 20 ▲ @ £5 per night.

🐕 🏪 ☉ 🍴 (15amps) ⊕ ♨ ✕ 🧺 ☎ 🗄 🖵 ✪ ♨ 🎣
⚲ 🏹 ∪ ⚓ 🛝 ✓4

Golf Links Holiday Home Park
Bushmills Rd. ☎ (01265) 822288.
Bars, entertainment on site.
Open 17 March-31 October.

15 ⛺🚐 @ £9 per night (hook-up included),
awning £2 per night.

🐕 🏪 ☉ 🍴 (5amps) ⊕ ♨ ✕ 🧺 ☎ 🗄 ♨ 🎣 ⚲ 🏹
∪ ⚓ 🛝 ✓5

Margoth Caravan Park
126 Dunluce Rd. ☎ (01265) 822531/822853.
Open 1 April-30 September.

84 ⛺🚐 20 ▲ @ £9 per night (includes awning),
hook-up £1 per night.

🐕 🏪 ☉ 🍴 (16amps) ⊕ ♨ 🧺 ☎ 🗄 ✪ ♨ 🎣 ⚲
🏹 ∪ ⚓ 🛝

Portrush Caravan Park
60 Loguestown Rd. ☎ (01265) 823537.
Open 28 March-30 September.

78 ⛺🚐 20 ▲ @ £9 per night (includes awning),
hook-up £1 per night.

🐕 🏪 ☉ 🍴 (16amps) ⊕ ♨ 🧺 ☎ 🗄 ✪ ♨ 🎣 ⚲
🏹 ∪ ⚓ 🛝

Rathlin Island

▲ free at east side of Church Bay.

County Armagh

Lurgan

Kinnego Marina Caravan Park

Kinnego Marina, Oxford Island. ☎ (01762) 327573
(Craigavon Borough Council).
At Oxford Island National Nature Reserve. RYA
sailing and powerboat courses, waterskiing. Five
miles of walks, bird-watching. Lough Neagh
Discovery Centre features history and geography
of Lough Neagh, café. Cruises on Lough Neagh.
Open 1 April-1 October.

10 🚐🚛 @ £6 per night   30 🛆 @ £5 per night.

🐕 🎣 ☉ ♨ 📞 🔲 🌀 ⚠ 🍴 🔍 ⛽ ∪ ⛽ ✓³

Maghery

Maghery Caravan Park

Thirty acre country park on southern shore of
Lough Neagh at Maghery Country Park.
☎ (01762) 322205 (Craigavon Borough Council).
On B196, 3 miles from junction 12 of M1.
Shipway and jetty on site. Boat trips to Coney
Island. Fishing.
Open 1 April-30 September.

9 🚐🚛 @ £6 per night, hook-up £1.50 per night
20 🛆 @ £5 per night.

🐕 🎣 ☉ 🚐 (16amps) ♨ ✕ 📞 🌀 ⚠ ⚡ ✓⁴

Markethill

Gosford Forest Park

54 Gosford Rd, Markethill BT60 1UG.
☎ (01861) 551277.
Some of the broadleaved and coniferous trees in
the forest park are over 200 years old. Gosford
Castle belongs to a rare architectural style –
Norman revival. Estate has associations with
Dean Swift. Walled garden, red deer park, poultry
collection, ornamental pigeons in dovecote.
Nature trail, barbecue site, café. Off A28, near
Markethill. Armagh 7 miles, Newry 12 miles.
Open all year.

34 🚐🚛   36 🛆 @ £5.50/8.50 per night,
hook-up £1.50 per night.

🐕 🎣 ☉ 🚐 (6amps) 🅿 ♨ ✕ 📞 🔲 🌀 🍴
⛽ 🔍 ∪ ✓⁴

County Down

Annalong

Annalong Caravan Park
38 Kilkeel Rd. ☎ (013967) 68248.
Open 17 March-30 October.

15 🚐 🚏 @ £10 per night (includes electric, water and water waste hook-up), awning £1 per night.

🐾 🏠 ☉ 🍴 (6amps) 🕭 ♨ ✕ 🔌 📞 🔲 🌀 ⚠ ✎
🏁 ∪ 🛆 ✓5

Annalong Marine Park
Marine Park, Main St.
☎ (013967) 68736 or (01693) 68877
(Newry & Mourne District Council).
Cornmill and herb garden.
Open all year.

25 🚐 🚏 @ £5.50 per night
25 ⚐ @ £3.80 per night. Prices under review.

🐾 🏠 ☉ ♨ ✕ 🔌 🌀 ⚠ ✎ 🏁 ∪ 🛆

Ardglass

Coney Island Caravan Park
75 Killough Rd. ☎ (01396) 841448/841210.
Open 10 April-24 November.

30 🚐 🚏 @ £8 per night (includes hook-up).
50 ⚐ @ £5 per night.

🐾 🏠 🍴 (6amps) 🕭 ♨ 🔌 📞 🔲 🔲 🌀 ⚠ ✎
🏁 ∪ 🛆 🐕

Ballywalter

Ballyferris Caravan Park
211 Whitechurch Rd. ☎ (012477) 58244.
Millisle side of the town. Access to sandy beach.
Open 17 March-15 November.

15 🚐 🚏 @ £8 per night, hook-up £1, awning £1 per night.

🐾 ☉ 🍴 (5amps) 🕭 ♨ 🔌 📞 🔲 🌀 ⚠ ✎
🏁 ∪ 🛆 ✓4

Ganaway Caravan Park
10 Ganaway Rd. ☎ (012477) 58422.
Off A2 coast road.
Open 1 April-31 October.

12 🚐 🚏 @ £9 per night (includes hook-up).

🐾 🏠 ☉ 🍴 (10amps) 🕭 ♨ 🔌 🔲 🌀 ⚠
✎ 🏁 ∪ 🛆

Rockmore Caravan Park
69 Whitechurch Rd. ☎ (01247) 861428, or write to: H J Warnock, 6 Ballydoonan Rd, Carrowdore, Newtownards BT22 2HE.
Open 1 April-31 October.

10 🚐 🚏 @ £7 per night, hook-up 50p per night.

🐾 🏠 ☉ 🍴 (15amps) 🕭 ♨ 🔲 🌀 ⚠ ✎ 🏁 ∪ 🛆

Rockmore Caravan Park
150 Whitechurch Rd (shore side).
☎ (012477) 58342.
Note: caravans must be equipped with a chemical toilet.
Open 17 March-31 October.

6 🚐 🚏 @ £5 per night (includes hook-up).

🐾 🍴 (5amps) 🕭 🔲 🌀 ⚠ ✎ 🏁 ∪ 🛆

Rosebank Caravan Park
199 Whitechurch Rd. ☎ (012477) 58211.
Open 1 April-31 October.

3 🚐 🚏 @ £7 per night (includes hook-up), awning 50p per night.

🐾 🏠 ☉ 🍴 (5amps) ♨ 🔌 📞 🔲 🌀 ⚠ ✎ 🏁 ∪ 🛆

Sandycove Caravan Park
191 Whitechurch Rd. ☎ (012477) 58062.
Millisle side of the town. Access to sandy beach.
Open 17 March-15 November.

40 🚐 🚏 @ £8 per night, hook-up £1,
awning £1 per night.

🐕 📷 ☺ 🍴 (5amps) 🚻 ⚑ 🛒 📞 🗑 ♿ 🏧 ⚲
🚩 ∪ ⚓ ✓⁵

Banbridge

Banbridge Gateway
Tourist Information Centre
200 Newry Rd. ☎ (018206) 23322
(Banbridge District Council).
Off A26, 1 mile south of Banbridge, at junction
with A1. Restaurant. Note: arrival on site before
5pm (7pm July-August) please.
Open daily June-Sept, Mon-Sat October-May.

8 🚐 🚏 @ £8 per night (includes hook-up)
6 ⚑ @ £4 per night. Maximum stay 3 consecutive
nights. Refundable key deposit £20.

🐕 📷 ☺ 🍴 (6amps) ⚑ ✗ 📞 🏧 ⚲ 🚩 ✓⁵

Old Mill Caravan Park
Ballydown Rd. ☎ (018206) 22226/22842.
Open all year.

16 🚐 🚏 @ £3 per night, hook-up £1 per night
10 ⚑ @ £2 per night.

🐕 📷 ☺ 🍴 (15amps) 🚻 ⚑ 🗑 ⚲ 🚩

Castlewellan

Castlewellan Forest Park
The Grange, Castlewellan BT31 9BU.
☎ (013967) 78664.
Outstanding feature of the forest park is the
national arboretum, begun about 1740 with trees,
shrubs and exotic plants from all over the world.
The Scottish Baronial style castle is now a
conference centre. The lake is stocked with trout
(fishing permit required). The early 18th-century
farmstead is a fine example of Queen Anne style
courtyards. Tropical birds in glasshouse.
Sculpture trail, orienteering course, picnic and
barbecue areas. Visitor centre has café.
Entrance in Main St.
Open all year.

81 🚐 🚏 20 ⚑ @ £6/9.50 per night,
hook-up £1.50 per night.

🐕 📷 ☺ 🍴 (6amps) 🚻 ⚑ ✗ 🛒 📞 🗑 ⚲ ♿
🚩 ∪ ⚓ ✓⁴

Cloughey

Kirkistown Caravan Park
55 Main Rd. ☎ (012477) 71183.
Sandy beach, windsurfing. Adapted toilet and
shower for wheelchair users. Off A2, 2 miles
south of Portavogie.
Open 17 March-31 October.

62 🚐 🚏 12 ⚑ @ £7.50 per night, hook-up £1.50
per night.

🐕 📷 ☺ 🍴 (5amps) ⚑ ✗ 🛒 📞 🗑 ⚲ 🏧
⚲ 🚩 ∪ ⚓

Silver Bay Caravan Park

15 Ardminnan Rd, Portaferry. ☎ (012477) 71321.
On Kearney coast road, ¹/₂ mile south of Cloughey.
Adjacent to White House Inn. Portaferry 4¹/₂ miles.
Open 3 April-31 October.

10 ⊟ ⊞ @ £5 per night (includes hook-up),
awning £1 per night   3 ▲ @ £4 per night.

🐕 🏕 ☉ ⊞ (5amps) ⊕ ✗ 🔋 ☎ ⊟ ⊞ ⊛
⚲ ⏚ ∪ ⬦

Donaghadee

Donaghadee Caravan Park

Edgewater, 183 Millisle Rd. ☎ (01247) 882369.
Open 3 April-31 October.

10 ⊟ ⊞ 10 ▲ @ £6 per night.

🐕 🏕 ☉ ⊕ ⊕ ⊛ ⚲ ⏚ ∪ ⬦

Hillsborough

Lakeside View Caravan Park

71 Magheraconluce Rd, Annahilt.
☎ (01846) 682098.
Off B177, 3 miles from Hillsborough, signposted
at Annahilt. Waterskiing, jet skiing, fishing,
birdwatching.
Open 1 March-31 October.

20 ⊟ ⊞ @ £5 per night, hook-up £1, awning £2
per night   100 ▲ @ £4 per night

🐕 🏕 ☉ ⊕ (16amps) ⊕ ⊛ ☎ ⊟ ⊛ ⚲ ⏚ ∪

Kilkeel

Chestnutt Caravan Park

3 Grange Rd, Cranfield West. ☎ (016937) 62653.
Off A2, signposted. Kilkeel 4 miles. Adjacent to
beach.
Open 17 March-30 October.

20 ⊟ ⊞ 10 ▲ @ £9.50 per night (includes
electric, water and water waste hook-up),
awning £1 per night.

🐕 🏕 ☉ ⊕ (6amps) ⊕ ✗ 🔋 ☎ ⊟ ⊛ ⚠ ⚲
⏚ ∪ ⬦ ✓⁵

Cranfield Caravan Park

123 Cranfield Rd. ☎ (016937) 62572.
Open 10 April-31 October.

50 ⊟ ⊞ @ £11 per night (includes
hook-up), awning £1.50 per night

🐕 🏕 ☉ ⊕ (10amps) ✗ 🔋 ☎ ⊟ ⊛ ⚠ ⚲
⏚ ∪ ⬦ ✓⁵

Leestone Caravan Park

60 Leestone Rd. ☎ (016937) 62567.
Tennis courts. Off A2, 1¹/₂ miles north of Kilkeel.
Open 1 March-31 October.

16 ⊟ ⊞ @ £9 per night, hook-up £1 per night
10 ⊟ (family) @ £7 per night

🐕 🏕 ☉ ⊕ (15amps) ⊕ ⊛ ☎ ⊟ ⊛ ⚠
⚲ ⏚ ∪ ⬦

Sandilands Caravan Park

30 Cranfield Rd, Cranfield East.
☎ (016937) 63634.
Off A2, signposted. Kilkeel 3 miles. Private beach.
Open 17 March-30 October.

27 ⊟ ⊞ 5 ▲ @ £9.50 per night (includes electric,
water and water waste hook-up),
awning £1 per night.

🐕 🏕 ☉ ⊕ (6amps) ⊕ ⊛ ✗ 🔋 ☎ ⊟ ⊛ ⚠ ⚲
⏚ ∪ ⬦ ✓⁵

Shanlieve Caravan Park

69a Cranfield Rd. ☎ (016937) 64344.
Open 3 April-20 October.

8 ⛺🚐 @ £8.50 per night (includes hook-up and awning).

🐕 🏠 ☉ 🚐 (10amps) ⌂ ⚡ ✕ 🚿 🔌 📦 ⊕ ⚠ ⚲ ☛ ∪ ⛿

Silvercove Caravan Park

98a Leestone Rd. ☎ (016937) 63136.
Open 10 April-31 October.

5 ⛺🚐 @ £7.50 per night, hook-up £1 per night.

🐕 🏠 ☉ 🚐 (6amps) ⌂ ⚡ 🚿 🔌 📦 ⊕ ⚠ ⚲ ☛ ∪ ⛿

Killough

Minerstown Caravan Park

50 Minerstown Rd, Killough, Downpatrick.
☎ (01396) 851527.
On A2, 3 miles west of Killough. Private beach.
Open 17 March-31 October.

9 ⛺ 2 🚐 5 ⚠ @ £6 per night, hook-up £2 per night.

🐕 ☉ 🚐 (5amps) ⌂ 🚿 🔌 📦 ⊕ ⚠ ☛ ⛿ 🦮

Millisle

Ballywhiskin Caravan & Camping Park

216 Ballywalter Rd. ☎ (01247) 862262.
Small livestock farm, nature walks.
Open all year.

30 ⛺🚐 @ £5.50 per night, hook-up £1, awning £1 per night   25 ⚠ @ £5 per night.

🐕 🏠 ☉ 🚐 (5amps) ⌂ ⚡ 🚿 🔌 📦 ⊕ ⚠ ⚲ ☛ ∪ ⛿

Ganaway Activity Centre

Ballywalter Rd.
☎ (01232) 324853 (Boys' Brigade).
Open all year.

12 ⛺🚐 @ £7 per night   30 ⚠ @ £2 per person per night (groups only).

🐕 🏠 ☉ ⚡ 🔌 ⊕ ⚲ ⚲ ☛ ∪ ⛿

Happyvale Caravan Park

108 Ballywalter Rd. ☎ (01247) 861457.
Open 10 April-31 October.

6 ⛺🚐 @ £3.50 per night.

🐕 ⌂ ⊕ ⚲ ⚲ ☛ ∪ ⛿

Rathlin Caravan Park

45 Moss Rd. ☎ (01247) 861386.
Open 28 April-1 November.

5 ⛺ 5 🚐 @ £5 per night, hook-up £1 per night.

🐕 ☉ 🚐 (5amps) ⌂ ⚡ 🔌 ⬜ ⊕ ⚲ ⚲ ☛ ∪ ⛿ ✓3

Seaview Caravan Park

1 Donaghadee Rd. ☎ (01247) 861248.
Open 1 April-30 October.

15 ⛺🚐 @ £9 per night, hook-up £1 per night.

🐕 🏠 ☉ 🚐 (5amps) ⌂ ⚡ ✕ 🚿 🔌 📦 ⊕ ⚠ ⚲ ⚲ ☛ ∪ ⛿

Walker's Caravan Park

88 Ballywalter Rd. ☎ (01247) 861181.
Open 1 April-31 October.

Phone for details.

Moira

Moira Demesne Caravan Park
Main St. ☎ (01846) 619974/682477
(Lisburn Borough Council).
Open all year.

15 🚐 🚎 @ £4 per night   10 ▲ @ £2 per night.

🐕 🏠 ☉ ♨ ✕ 🔌 ⊕ ⚠ ⌐ ∪

Newcastle

Bonny's Newcastle Trailer Park
82 Tullybrannigan Rd. ☎ (013967) 22351.
Open 17 March-31 October.

30 🚐 🚎 @ £6 per night, hook-up £2 per night.

🐕 🏠 ☉ 🔌 (5amps) ☯ 🔌 ☎ 🗑 ⊕ ⚠ ⚡
⌐ ∪ ♨ ✓5

Bonny's Sunnyholme Caravan Park
33 Castlewellan Rd. ☎ (013967) 22739.
Open 17 March-31 October.

30 🚐 🚎 @ £6 per night, hook-up £2 per night.

🐕 🏠 ☉ 🔌 (5amps) ☯ 🔌 ☎ 🗑 ⊕ ⚠ ⚡
⌐ ∪ ♨ ✓5

Boulevard Caravan Park
114 Dundrum Rd. ☎ (013967) 22130
or (01846) 638336.
Putting green. Donkey rides.
Open 3 April-31 October.

15 🚐 🚎 @ £6 per night (includes hook-up),
awning £1 per night.

🐕 🏠 ☉ 🔌 (5amps) ☯ ♨ 🔌 ☎ 🗑 ⊕ ⚠ ⚡
⌐ ∪ ♨ ✓5

Bryansford Caravan Park
1 Bryansford Village. ☎ (013967) 24017.
Open 1 April-31 October.

11 🚐 🚎 @ £10 per night (includes hook-up).
Prices under review.

🐕 🏠 ☉ 🔌 (15amps) ☯ ♨ 🔌 ☎ 🗑 ⊕ ⚠
⚡ ⌐ ∪ ♨

Mourneview Caravan Park
195 Dundrum Rd. ☎ (013967) 23327
or (01232) 454566.
Heated indoor swimming pool.
Open 1 April-30 September.

50 🚐 🚎 @ £12 per night (includes hook-up and
awning).

🐕 🏠 ☉ 🔌 (5amps) ✕ 🔌 ☎ 🗑 ⊡ ⊕ ⚠ ⚡
⚡ ⌐ ∪ ♨

Murlough Cottage Farm Caravan Park
180 Dundrum Rd. ☎ (013967) 23184/22906.
One mile north of Newcastle.
Adjacent to Murlough Bay National Nature
Reserve, and beach. Fishing, walking.
Open 17 March-17 October.

38 🚐 🚎 @ £9 per night (includes hook-up),
awning £1 per night.

🐕 🏠 ☉ 🔌 (5amps) ☯ ♨ 🔌 ☎ 🗑 ⊡ ⊕ ⚠ ⚡
⌐ ∪ ♨ ✓5

Check availability before you travel

Tollymore Forest Park

176 Tullybrannigan Rd, BT33 0PW.
☎ (013967) 22428.
At the foot of the Mournes, the 2,000-acre forest park has some magnificent Himalayan cedars and, in the arboretum, a sequoia tree over 100 ft tall. An 18th-century barn contains exhibits, lecture theatre and a café. Pony trekking, game fishing (permit required), fallow deer, wildfowl collection, hill climbs and walks. On B180, 3 miles from Newcastle. Tollymore Mountain Centre is nearby, on the Hilltown road.
Open all year.

70 🚐 🚎   30 ▲ @ £6/9.50 per night, hook-up £1.50 per night.

🐕 🏕 ☺ 🚰 (6amps) 🕭 ♨ ✕ 📞 🔲 🔌 ⚲ ⚑
⛱ ∪ ♿ ✓4

Windsor Caravan Park

138 Dundrum Rd. ☎ (013967) 23367.
Open 17 March-31 October.

40 🚐 🚎 @ £10 per night, hook-up £2, awning £1 per night.

🐕 🏕 🚰 (16amps) 🕭 ♨ 📞 🔲 🔌 /瓜 ⚲
⚑ ∪ ♿ ✓4

Woodcroft Caravan Park

104 Dundrum Rd. ☎ (013967) 22284.
On coast road, ½ mile north-east of town.
Open 17 March-12 October.

35 🚐 🚎 @ £8 per night, hook-up £1 per night.

🐕 🏕 ☺ 🚰 (15amps) 🕭 ♨ ✕ 📞 🔲 🔌 🔲 /瓜
⚲ ⚑ ∪ ♿

Portaferry

Exploris Touring Caravan Park

Exploris Aquarium, The Rope Walk, Castle St.
☎ (012477) 28610 (Ards Borough Council).

Phone for details.

Tara Caravan Park

4 Ballyquintin Rd, Tara.
☎ (012477) 28459.
Scenic location overlooking Irish Sea, slipway. Long sandy beach, rock fishing. Three miles south-east of Portaferry.
Open 1 April-31 October.

10 🚐 🚎 @ £5 per night, hook-up £2 per night
2 ▲ @ £4 per night.

☺ 🚰 (16amps) 🕭 ♨ /瓜 ⚲ ⚑ ∪ ♿

Rostrevor

Kilbroney Caravan Park

Kilbroney Park, Shore Rd.
☎ (016937) 38134
(Newry & Mourne District Council).
Off A2, south of Rostrevor, in parkland overlooking Carlingford Lough. Forest walks, barbecue site.
Open 10 April-31 October.

36 🚐 🚎 @ £7.70 per night, hook-up £1.05 per night   40 ▲ @ £5.10 per night.

🐕 🏕 ☺ 🚰 (15amps) ♨ ✕ 📞 🔲 🔌 /瓜 ⚲ ⚑
∪ ♿ ✓4

Strangford

Castle Ward Caravan Park
Castle Ward Estate (1½ miles west of
village, on A25).
☎ (01396) 881680 (National Trust).
The mansion is open to the public. Restaurant,
shop. Victorian laundry, Victorian pastimes for
children, many acres of wood and lake, walks,
formal gardens and a wildfowl collection.
Restored cornmill. A bird hide 250 yards from the
park overlooks the wildfowl reserve on Strangford
Lough. Exhibition in Strangford Lough Wildlife
Centre.
Open 17 March-30 September.

30 🚐🚎 15 ⚊ @ £7.50 per night.

🐕 📻 ☉ ⚐ ✕ ⚠ ⚑ ⚴ ⚬ ✓³

Strangford Caravan Park
87 Shore Rd. ☎ (01396) 881888.
Fishing, walking, parachuting, cycle hire.
Open all year.

12 🚐🚎 @ £7 per night, hook-up £1 per night
30 ⚊ @ £6 per night.

🐕 📻 ☉ ⚐ (5amps) ⚐ ⚴ ⚬ ☎ ⚬ ⚬ ⚴
⚑ ⚴ ⚬ ✓³

County Fermanagh

Blaney

Blaney Caravan & Camping Park
8 miles north-west of Enniskillen on A46.
Adjacent to service station. ☎ (013656) 41634.
Open all year.

20 🚐 🚚 @ £10 per night, hook-up £1 per night
10 ▲ @ £6 per night.

🐕 🅿 ☉ ⊕ (5amps) 🗓 ♨ ✕ 🔌 📞 🗟
🔂 ⚠ ⚓ 🛆

Enniskillen

Lakeland Canoe Centre
Castle Island. ☎ (01365) 324250.
Tents, water sports equipment and bikes for hire,
archery. Qualified instructors. Free ferry service to
Castle Island operates daily 9 am-midnight from
jetty beside Fermanagh Lakeland Forum (leisure
centre).
Open all year.

20 ▲ @ £8 per night.

🐕 🅿 ☉ ♨ ✕ 🔌 📞 🗟 🖵 🔂 🔔 ⚓ ⚓ ⚓ 🛆

Garrison

Lough Melvin Holiday Centre
Main St. ☎ (013656) 58142
(Fermanagh District Council).
Fishing, canoeing, sailing, cycling. Restaurant.
Enniskillen 4 miles.
Open all year.

20 🚐 🚚 @ £10 per night, hook-up £2 per night
25 ▲ @ £6 per night.

🐕 🅿 ☉ 🚗 (16amps) ♨ ✕ 🔌 📞 🗟 🖵 🔂 ⚠
⚓ ⚓ ⚓ 🛆 ✓4

Irvinestown

Castle Archdale Caravan Park
☎ (013656) 21333/32159.
Good centre for visitors to Lower Lough Erne. The
marina in the country park has full servicing for
cruisers and water-based sports and a public ferry
to White Island. Once an RAF base, the
outhouses contain a WWII exhibition on the
Battle of the Atlantic. Pony-trekking through park,
bikes for hire. Off B82 Enniskillen/Kesh road,
signposted. Irvinestown 3 miles. Enniskillen
10 miles.
Open 1 April-31 October.

60 🚐 10 🚚 @ £12 per night, hook-up £1 per
night 50 ▲ @ £10 per night.

🐕 🅿 ☉ 🚗 (10amps) ♨ ✕ 🔌 📞 🔂 ⚠
⚓ ⚓ 🛆 ✓5

Gublusk Bay Caravan Park
Killadeas. ☎ (01365) 388111.
Near shore of Lough Erne. Sailing. Pleasure flights
from nearby airport. Enniskillen 6 miles.
Open 17 March-31 October.

10 🚐 🚚 @ £8.50 per night, hook-up £1.50,
awning £1.50 per night.

🐕 🅿 ☉ 🚗 (16amps) 🗓 ♨ ✕ 🔌 📞 🗟 🔂 ⚠ ⚓
⚓ ⚓ 🛆

Check availability before you travel

Kesh

Clareview Caravan Park
89 Crevenish Rd. ☎ (013656) 31012.
Open all year.

12 🚐 🚙 @ £9 per night, hook-up £1,
awning £2 per night   12 ▲ @ £6 per night.

🐕 ⛺ ☉ 🚿 (15amps) 🚰 ⚡ ✕ 📞 🔲 🖵
🌀 ♨ ∪ 💧

Lakeland Caravan Park
Boa Island Rd, Drumrush.
☎ (013656) 31578.
Watersports, licensed restaurant.
Open all year.

50 🚐 🚙 20 ▲ @ £10 per night (includes
hook-up).

🐕 ⛺ ☉ 🚿 (14amps) 🚰 ⚡ ✕ 📞 🔲 🖵 🌀 🏔
♨ ⏏ ∪ 💧

LoanEden Caravan Park
Highgrove, Muckross Bay.
☎ (013656) 31603.
Near shores of Lough Erne. 5 minutes' walk to
beach, jetty, marina and Kesh village.
Watersports.
Open all year.

20 🚐 🚙 @ £11 per night (includes hook-up and
awning)   10 ▲ @ £6 per night.

🐕 ⛺ ☉ 🚿 (16amps) 🚰 ⚡ ✕ 📞 🔲 🌀
🏔 ♨ ∪ 💧

Lisnaskea

Mullynascarthy Caravan Park
☎ (013657) 21040 (Fermanagh District Council).
On Colebrooke River. On B514, 1½ miles north
west of Lisnaskea.
Open 1 April-31 October.

43 🚐 🚙 @ £9 per night, hook-up £1 per night
25 ▲ @ £5.50 per night.

🐕 ⛺ ☉ 🚿 (16amps) ⚡ 🌀 🏔 ∪ 💧 ✓5

Telephone for route directions

Share Holiday Village
Smith's Strand, Shanaghy.
☎ (013657) 22122/21892.
Purpose-built facilities for disabled visitors. Indoor
swimming pool, sauna, steam room, fitness suite.
Marina, cruises on Lough Erne, watersports,
archery, bicycles, go-karts. Three miles south of
Lisnaskea on B127 Derrylin road, signposted.
Open 10 April-30 September.

26 🚐 🚙 from £10 per night (includes hook-up
and awning)   21 ▲ @ £7.50 per night.

🐕 ⛺ ☉ 🚿 (10amps) ⚡ ✕ ⏏ 📞 🔲 🖵 🌐 🏔 〰
♨ ∪ 💧 ⚓ ✓5

County Londonderry

Ballyronan

Ballyronan Marina & Caravan Park
99 Shore Rd. ☎ (016487) 62205
(Cookstown District Council).
Watersports, walks, picnic area.
Magherafelt 5 miles. Cookstown 12 miles.
Open 1 April-30 September.

12 🚐 🚏 @ £8 per night, hook-up £1 per night
3 ▲ @ £3.50 per night.

🐕 🏕 ☉ 🔌 (30amps) ✕ 🕽 🗑 ⚠ ⚘ ⚲ 🏳 ∪ ⚓

Benone

Benone Complex
53 Benone Avenue. ☎ (015047) 50555
(Limavady Borough Council).
Adjacent to Benone beach. Outdoor heated pool,
children's pool, bowling green. Off A2, 12 miles
north of Limavady. Roe Valley Country Park
12 miles, Coleraine 9 miles. Binevenagh
Mountain 1 mile.
Open all year.

70 🚐 🚏 @ £7.50 per night, hook-up £1.50,
awning £1 per night   12 ▲ @ £5.50 per night.
Prices under review.

🐕 🏕 ☉ 🔌 (5amps) ⊕ ⚘ ✕ 🕽 🗑 ⊕ ⚠ ⚲
🏳 ∪ ⚓ ✓[4]

Deighan Caravans/Benone Caravan Park
5 Benone Avenue. ☎ (015047) 50284.
Open 15 March-31 October.

42 🚐 🚏 @ £7 per night, hook-up £1.50,
awning £1 per night.

🐕 🏕 ☉ 🔌 (5amps) ⊕ ⚘ ✕ 🕽 🗑 ⊕ ⚠
⚲ 🏳 ∪ ⚓

Golden Sands Caravan Parks
26a Benone Avenue. ☎ (015047) 50324.
Adjacent to seven-mile stretch of beach. Gliding.
Open 1 April-31 October.

52 🚐 🚏 12 ▲ (family) @ £7.50 per night,
hook-up £1, awning £1 per night.

🐕 🏕 ☉ 🔌 (5amps) ⚘ ✕ 🕽 🕽 🗑 ⊕ ⚠ ⚲
🏳 ∪ ⚓ ✓[5]

Castlerock

Castlerock Holiday Park
24 Sea Rd. ☎ (01265) 848381.
Open 21 March-31 October.

20 🚐 🚏 @ £10 per night, awning £1.50 per night
3 ▲ @ £8 per night (includes hook-up).

🐕 🏕 ☉ 🔌 (10amps) ⊕ ⚘ ✕ 🕽 🗑 ⊡ ⊕ ⚠
⚲ ⚲ 🏳 ∪ ⚓ ⚱ ✓[5]

Downhill Campsite
☎ (01265) 848728/848567 (National Trust).
In the grounds of Downhill Castle, on A2, 1 mile
west of Castlerock. Coleraine 5 miles.
Open all year.

20 🚐 🚏 20 ▲ one night only (dusk to 10 am).
Donation £3 to National Trust. Minimal facilities.

🐕 ⚲ ⚲ 🏳 ∪ ⚓ ⚱

WHEREVER YOU ARE

CALOR
That's Life

Coleraine

Loughan Marina
197 Loughan Rd. ☎ (01265) 55700.
Waterskiing, canoeing, banana boat rides.
Volleyball, barbecue, picnic areas.
Lodge Rd roundabout 3 miles.
Open all year.

9 ⊕ ⏰ @ £10 per night, hook-up £1 per night
3 ⚑ @ £5 per night.

🐕 🏕 ☉ ⚡(16amps) ⛺ ♿ ✕ ⛽ ☎ ▣ ⌷ ⊕ ⚠
⚐ ⚲ ☂ ∪ ⬦

Tullans Farm Caravan Park
46 Newmills Rd. ☎ (01265) 42309.
Working farm, pet lambs in season, sheep
shearing. Barbecue, barn dances. Off A29,
one mile from Coleraine. Follow signposts for
Windyhall.
Open 1 March-31 October.

30 ⊕ ⏰ @ £8 per night, hook-up £1,
awning £1 per night   4 ⚑ @ £6 per night.

🐕 🏕 ☉ ⚡(16amps) ♿ ☎ ▣ ⌷ ⊕ ⚠ ⚐ ⚲ ☂
∪ ⬦ ⚘ ✓5

Moneymore

Springhill Caravan Park
20 Springhill Rd. ☎ (016487) 48210
(National Trust).
The caravan park is in the farmyard of Springhill,
a 17th-century whitewashed manor house in
National Trust care. There are splendid woodland
walks, a formal garden and a costume museum at
the house. One mile south of Moneymore on the
Coagh road (B18). Cookstown 5 miles.
Open all year.

20 ⊕ ⏰ @ £3 per night. Minimal facilities.

🐕 ♿ ⚐ ☂ ∪ ⬦

Portstewart

Juniper Hill Caravan Park
70 Ballyreagh Rd. ☎ (01265) 832023
(Coleraine Borough Council).
One mile east of Portstewart on A2 coast road.
Open 6 April-12 October.

80 ⊕ ⏰ @ £10 per night (includes hook-up
and awning) 6 ⚑ @ £5 per night.

🐕 🏕 ☉ ⚡(15amps) ⛺ ♿ ✕ ⛽ ☎ ▣ ⌷ ⊕ ⚠
⚐ ⚲ ☂ ∪ ⬦ ⚘ ✓4

Portstewart Holiday Park
80 Mill Rd. ☎ (01265) 833308.
Off A2 Coleraine-Portstewart road, signposted
from first roundabout, 1 mile south of Portstewart.
Beach 1 mile.
Open all year.

36 ⊕ ⏰ 12 ⚑ @ £9 per night, hook-up £1,
awning £1 per night.

🐕 🏕 ☉ ⚡(5amps) ⛺ ♿ ☎ ▣ ⚠ ⚐ ⚲ ☂
∪ ⬦ ⚘ ✓4

County Tyrone

Drum Manor Forest Park
Oaklands. ☎ (016487) 62774.
The park has two lakes and a walled butterfly garden. The demonstration garden is well worth a visit. Arboretum, interpretive centre, heronry. Nature trails have wheelchair access. On A505, 4 miles west of Cookstown.
Open all year.

30 🚐 🚗 @ £5.50/8 per night, hook-up £1.50 per night.

🐕 🏠 ☺ 🔌 (6amps) ☐ ⚡ ✕ 🗑 🔄 ⚒ 🏴 ∪

Clogher

Clogher Valley Country Caravan Park
Fardross Forest (signpost 1 mile west of Clogher on A4). ☎ (016625) 48932.
Forest walks, crazy golf, bikes for hire.
Open 17 March-31 October.

20 🚐 🚗 @ £8 per night, hook-up £1.50, awning £1 per night   20 ⛺ @ £5 per night.

🐕 🏠 ☺ 🔌 (16amps) ☐ ⚡ 🔋 📞 🗑 🔄 ⚠ 🏴 ⚓

Dungannon

Dungannon Park
Moy Rd. ☎ (01868) 727327
(Dungannon District Council).
Fishing, putting green, target golf, scenic walks.
Barbecue sites. Off A29, 1 mile from Dungannon.
Open all year.

25 ⊕ ⇌ @ £8 per night   15 ▲ @ £6 per night.

Killymaddy Centre
Ballygawley Rd. ☎ (01868) 767259
(Dungannon District Council).
Picnic site. Tourist office. On A4, 6 miles west of
Dungannon. Parkanaur Forest Park 2 miles.
Open all year.

5 ⊕ ⇌ @ £8 per night   12 ▲ @ £6 per night.

Fivemiletown

Round Lake Caravan Park
Murley Rd (signposted). ☎ (01868) 767259
(Dungannon District Council).
Children's paddling pool.
Open all year.

12 ⊕ ⇌ @ £8 per night (includes hook-up and
awning)   6 ▲ @ £6 per night.

Gortin

Gortin Glen Caravan Park
Lisnaharney Rd, Lislap, Omagh.
☎ (016626) 48108
(Omagh District Council).
Opposite Gortin Glen Forest Park and adjacent to
Ulster History Park. Ulster-American Folk Park
6 miles, Omagh 7 miles.
Open all year.

24 ⊕ ⇌ @ £7.50 per night, hook-up £1.50,
awning 50p per night   36 ▲ @ £4/7 per night.

Newtownstewart

Harrigan Caravan Park
Old Bridge, Gortin Rd. ☎ (016626) 62414
(Strabane District Council).
Note: arrival on site before 5 pm please.
Open all year.

3 ⊕ ⇌ @ £3.50 per night   3 ▲ @ £2 per night.

Pomeroy

Altmore Fisheries & Open Farm
32 Altmore Rd. ☎ (01868) 758977/758992.
Off B4, 3½ miles north-east of Pomeroy
Open all year.

20 ⊕ ⇌ @ £6 per night, hook-up £2 per night
50 ▲ @ £5 per night.

Index to hotels and guesthouses

HOTELS

Abbey Lodge
  Downpatrick   124
Adair Arms Ballymena   *18*   69
Aldergrove Airport
  Belfast International
  Airport   53
Ashberry Enniskillen   145
Ashburn Lurgan   109
Avoca Newcastle   131

Ballygally Castle
  Ballygalley   69
Balmoral Belfast   54
Bangor Bay Inn   Bangor   117
Bay Cushendun   83
Bayview
  Portballintrae   93
Beach House
  Portballintrae   93
Beech Hill Country House
  Londonderry   169
Beechlawn House
  Belfast   53
Belmont Banbridge   116
Bohill Coleraine   *40*   161
Brook Cottage
  Newcastle   133
Broomhill Londonderry   170
Brown Trout
  Aghadowey   159
Burrendale Newcastle   *28*   131
Bushmills Inn Bushmills   *19*   75
Bushtown House
  Coleraine   *40*   161

Canal Court; Newry   136
Carlingford Bay
  Warrenpoint   141

Hotels

Carlton Belleek   144
Carngrove Portadown   109
Carnwood Lodge Keady   108
Carrybridge Lisbellaw   *35*   155
Causeway Coast Portrush   94
Causeway Hotel
  Giant's Causeway   84
Charlemont Arms
  Armagh   107
Chimney Corner
  Newtownabbey   92
Clandeboye Lodge
  Bangor   117
Coast Road
  Carrickfergus   79
Coastal Lodge
  Cloughey   121
Cohannon Inn Autolodge
  Dungannon   183
Copelands Donaghadee   123
Corr's Corner
  Newtownabbey   92
Country House
  Kells, Ballymena   69
Cranfield House
  Kilkeel   128
Culloden Belfast   53
Curran Court Larne   87

Deerpark Antrim   63
Dobbins Inn
  Carrickfergus   79
Donard Newcastle   133
Downshire Arms
  Banbridge   116
Drummond Ballykelly   159
Drumnagreagh
  Glenarm   85

Hotels

Drumshane Lisnarick   155
Drumsill Armagh   107
Dukes Belfast   53
Dunadry Dunadry   84
Dunallan Donaghadee   123

Edgewater Portstewart   *41*   175
Eglinton Portrush   94
Enniskeen Newcastle   131
Europa Belfast   53
Everglades
  Londonderry   170

Fir Trees Strabane   189
Fort Lodge Enniskillen   145
Forte Posthouse Belfast   53
Fourways Fivemiletown   185

Galgorm Manor
  Ballymena   69
Glenavna Belfast   53
Glenavon House
  Cookstown   *45*   181
Glengannon Dungannon   184
Glen House Eglinton   166
Golf Castlerock   *42*   159
Golf Links Portrush   94
Gorteen House Limavady   168
Gosford House Markethill   109
Greenvale Cookstown   181
Groomsport House
  Groomsport   127

Halfway House Ballygalley   69
Highways Larne   *20*   87

Index to hotels and guesthouses

Hotels

Holiday Inn Express Belfast 53
Holiday Inn Garden Court
 Belfast 53
Hunting Lodge
 Newtownstewart 186

Imperial Garvagh 167
Inn On The Park
 Dungannon 184
Ivanhoe Inn Belfast 54

Jurys Inn Belfast 54

Killyhevlin Enniskillen 34 145
Kilmorey Arms
 Kilkeel 128
Kilwaughter House
 Larne 87

La Mon Belfast 55
Lansdowne Court
 Belfast 54
Leighinmohr Ballymena 19 69
Lodge Hotel Coleraine 41 161
Londonderry Arms
 Carnlough 77
Lough Erne Kesh 152

McGlennon's Newcastle 133
Madison's Belfast 54
Magherabuoy Portrush 94
Magheramorne Larne 87
Mahon's Irvinestown 35 151
Malone Lodge Belfast 54

Hotels

Manor Ballymoney 72
Manor House
 Enniskillen 145
Marine Ballycastle 64
Marine Court Bangor 117
Mariner Newcastle 133
Millbrook Lodge
 Ballynahinch 114
Mourne Country Newry 136

Old Inn Crawfordsburn 28 123
O'Neill Arms
 Toomebridge 103
Ortine Lisnaskea 157

Parador Belfast 55
Park Avenue Belfast 54
Port Portrush 94
Portaferry Hotel
 Portaferry 29 140

Quality Carrickfergus 79

Radisson Roe Park
 Limavady 40 168
Railway Enniskillen 145
Regency Belfast 54
Renshaws Belfast 55
Royal Bangor 117
Royal Cookstown 46 181
Royal Arms Omagh 187
Royal Court Portrush 94

Seagoe Portadown 109
Silverbirch Omagh 46 187

Hotels

Silverwood Craigavon 108
Shaftesbury Plaza Belfast 55
Slieve Donard Newcastle 131
Stormont Belfast 53
Strangford Arms
 Newtownards 138

Templeton
 Templepatrick 19 103
Thornlea Cushendall 82
Trinity Hotel Londonderry 170
Tullyglass House Ballymena 70
Tullylagan Country House
 Cookstown 181

Valley Fivemiletown 185

Waterfoot Londonderry 41 170
Wellington Park Belfast 54
White Gables
 Hillsborough 127
White Horse
 Ballynahinch 29 114
White Horse Londonderry 170
Windsor Portstewart 175

GUESTHOUSES

Abbeydean Portrush 94
Abocurragh Farm
 Enniskillen 147
Aghnacarra House
 Lisbellaw 155
Al-Di-Gwyn Lodge
 Fivemiletown 185

Guesthouses

Alexandra Portrush		95
Anvershiel Portrush		95
Ardess Craft Centre		
Kesh		153
Ardshane Holywood	29	128
Ardtara Maghera		174
Arundel Newcastle		133
Asher Cottage Portrush		95
Ash-Rowan Belfast		55
Ashleigh House		
Portstewart		175
Ashton House Newry		136
Ashwood Enniskillen		147
Athdara Ballymoney		72

Ballinahinch House		
Richhill		110
Ballymagarry House		
Portrush		95
Battersea Bangor		117
Bayview Enniskillen		147
Beaufort House Claudy		160
Beachcroft Bangor		117
Beeches Antrim	20	63
Beechfield Ballymena		70
Beech Lodge Augher		179
Belvedere Portrush		95
Beresford House Bangor		117
Bethany Carnlough		77
Bienvenue Belfast		55
Blakely Lodge Belfast		55
Bridge Inn Carnlough		77
Briers Newcastle		133
Brindley Enniskillen		147
Brook Lodge Lisburn		89
Brookvale Portrush		95
Brown's Portrush		95
Burford Lodge Ardglass		114

Guesthouses

Caireal Manor		
Cushendall	21	82
Caldhame House		
Crumlin	21	80
Caldhame Lodge		
Crumlin		80
Camera Belfast		55
Carnside		
Giant's Causeway		84
Carrick-Dhu Portrush		95
Casa-A-La-Mar Portrush		95
Castle Erin Portrush	21	95
Cedars Irvinestown	35	151
Chestnut Inn		
Castlewellan		121
Clarence House		
Londonderry		170
Clarmont Portrush		97
Colebrook Park		
Brookeborough		144
Colorado House		
Lisnaskea		157
Cooleen Ballymoney		72
Corick House Clogher		180
Corralea Forest Lodge		
Belcoo		143
Corrigans Shore		
Enniskillen	37	147
Creeve House Randalstown		102
The Cushendun		
Cushendun		83

Dan Campbell's Larne	22	87
De-Averell Armagh		107
Denvirs Downpatrick		124
Derg Arms Castlederg	46	180
Derrin House Larne		87
Drumcoo House		
Enniskillen		147

Guesthouses

Drumcree House		
Portadown		110
Dufferin Arms		
Killyleagh	30	130

Edergole Cookstown		181
Eglantine Belfast		55

Fernhill House		
Warrenpoint		141
Fullerton Arms Ballintoy		64

Glassdrumman Lodge		
Annalong		113
Glencroft Portrush		97
Glenkeen Portrush		97
Glenluce Ballycastle		64
Grange Ballygawley		179
Grange Lodge		
Dungannon		184
Greenacres Banbridge		116
Greenacres		
Newtownards		138
Greenhill House		
Coleraine		161
Greenmount Lodge		
Omagh		187
Greenwood Belfast		55
Greenwood Lodge		
Kesh		153

Harbour House Newcastle		133
Hayesbank Kantara		
Portrush		97
Heathergrove Garrison		151

Index to hotels and guesthouses

Guesthouses

Hillhouse Crossgar	123
Hillside Newry	136
Hob Green Ballymoney	72

Inn at the Cross	
Londonderry	170

Jamestown House	
Ballinamallard	143

Keef Halla Crumlin	22 81
Kilnamar Belfast	55
Knockanboy Dervock	84

Laburnum Lodge Belfast	13 55
Lackaboy Farm House	
Enniskillen	147
Lakeview Enniskillen	147
Lanesborough Arms	
Newtownbutler	158
Laurel Inn Lisburn	89
Laurel Villa Magherafelt	174
Lisdara Belfast	14 57
Liserin Belfast	57
Lismore Lodge Belfast	57
Lis-na-Rhin Portstewart	42 175
Lisnacree Bangor	117

McGirr's Coalisland	180
Ma-Ring Portrush	97
Malone Belfast	57
Manor Larne	87
Marina Bangor	117
Marine Inn Castlerock	159

Guesthouses

Millbay Inn Islandmagee	86
Moohan's Fiddlestone	
Belleek	144
Morne Abbey Kilkeel	129
Mount Royal Portrush	97
Mountain Pass Hilltown	128
Mountview Enniskillen	147
Muleany House Moy	186
Mullynaval Lodge Kesh	37 153
Mulroy Portstewart	175

Narrows Portaferry	140
Navar Derrygonnelly	145

Oakdene Lodge Belfast	14 57
Old Manse Portrush	97
Old Rectory Belfast	14 57
Old Schoolhouse	
Comber	123
Oregon Portstewart	176

Pearl Court House Belfast	57
Planters Tavern	
Waringstown	111
Poplars Limavady	42 168
Prospect House Portrush	97

Rath Glen Villa Rathfriland	140
Rathlin Rathlin Island	103
Rayanne House	
Holywood	128
Riverside Farm	
Enniskillen	147
Riverside House Belleek	144
Robin Hill Londonderry	170

Guesthouses

Rockhaven Portstewart	176
Roseleigh House Belfast	15 57
Rosewood House Bangor	118
Rossgweer House	
Lisnarick	157
Rossole House Enniskillen	148

Seacon Hall Ballymoney	72
Seaview Larne	87
Shelleven House Bangor	118
Slieve Croob Inn	
Castlewellan	121
Stangmore Dungannon	47 184

Tara Bangor	118
Tatnamallaght House	
Lisbellaw	155
Tullydowey Country House	
Dungannon	184
Tullyhona House	
Enniskillen	37 148
Tullymore House	
Ballymena	22 70

Villa Cushendun	83

West Bay View Portrush	97
West Strand Portrush	97
Whistledown Inn	
Warrenpoint	142
Willowbank Enniskillen	148
Windermere House	
Belfast	57
Windsor Portrush	23 98
Wyncrest Kilkeel	129

Index to towns and villages

Aghadowey LONDONDERRY 159
(see also Coleraine &
Garvagh)

Agharainy : see Kesh

Ahoghill : see Ballymena

Aldergrove : see Crumlin &
Belfast

Annaclone : see Banbridge

Annacloy : see Downpatrick

Annahilt : see Hillsborough

Annalong DOWN 113 214 248

Antrim ANTRIM 63 201 241

Ardarver : see Castlederg

Ardboe : see Dungannon

Ardglass DOWN 114 248

Ardress : see Portadown

Ardstraw : see Newtownstewart

Armagh ARMAGH 107 194 213

Armoy : see Ballymoney

Arney : see Enniskillen

Articlave : see Castlerock

Artigarvan : see Strabane

Attical : see Kilkeel

Augher TYRONE 179

Aughnablaney : see Kesh

Aughnacloy TYRONE 179

Ballinamallard FERMANAGH 143
223

Ballindarragh : see Lisnaskea

Ballinrees : see Coleraine

Ballintoy ANTRIM 64 193 201
242

Ballyardel : see Kilkeel

Ballybogey : see Ballymoney

Ballycarry : see Carrickfergus

Ballycassidy : see Enniskillen

Ballycastle ANTRIM 64 192 201
242

Ballyclare ANTRIM 68

Ballycleagh : see Cushendun

Ballygalley ANTRIM 69 202
(see also Larne)

Ballygawley TYRONE 179

Ballyhalbert DOWN 114

Ballykelly LONDONDERRY 159

Ballyloran : see Larne

Ballyloughmore : see Bushmills

Ballymagorry : see Strabane

Ballymartin : see Kilkeel

Ballymena ANTRIM 69 202

Ballymoney ANTRIM 72 203
242

Ballynahinch DOWN 114 214

Ballynure : see Ballyclare

Ballyreagh : see Tempo

Ballyronan LONDONDERRY 259
(see also Magherafelt)

Ballyscullion : see Bellaghy

Ballyvoy : see Ballycastle

Ballywalter DOWN 115 248

Ballywatt : see Portrush

Balmoral : see Belfast

Banbridge DOWN 116 214 249

Bangor DOWN 117 214

Baronscourt : see
Newtownstewart

Beagho : see Lisbellaw

Belcoo FERMANAGH 143 223

Belfast 53 192 200 241

Bellaghy LONDONDERRY 159 233

Bellanaleck FERMANAGH 223
(see also Enniskillen)

Bellarena : see Limavady

Belle Isle : see Lisbellaw

Belleek FERMANAGH 144 223

Belleeks : see Newry

Benburb TYRONE 197

Benone LONDONDERRY 259
(see also Limavady)

Beragh : see Omagh

Bessbrook : see Newry

Birches : see Portadown

Blaney FERMANAGH 257
(see also Derrygonnelly &
Enniskillen)

Blessingbourne : see
Fivemiletown

Boa Island : see Kesh

Boardmills : see Lisburn

Brookeborough FERMANAGH 144

Broughshane ANTRIM 74
(see also Ballymena)

Bryansford : see Newcastle

Bunnahesco : see Lisbellaw

Burren : see Warrenpoint

Bushmills ANTRIM 75 203 243
(see also Coleraine, Giant's
Causeway, Portballintrae
& Portrush)

Caledon TYRONE 179
(see also Killylea)

Campsie : see Londonderry

Carn : see Dungiven

Carnalea : see Bangor

Carnlough ANTRIM 77 193 205 243

Carran West : see Garrison

Carrickfergus ANTRIM 79 206

Carrickmore : see Omagh

Carrowdore : see Newtownards

Carrybridge : see Lisbellaw

Carryduff : see Belfast & Lisburn

Castle Archdale : see Irvinestown & Lisnarick

Castle Ward : see Strangford

Castlecatt : see Bushmills

Castledawson LONDONDERRY 159

Castlederg TYRONE 180

Castlereagh : see Belfast

Castlerock LONDONDERRY 159 196 233 259

Castlewellan DOWN 121 194 215 249

Churchhill : see Derrygonnelly & Enniskillen

Clanabogan : see Omagh

Clandeboye : see Bangor

Clareview : see Kesh

Claudy LONDONDERRY 160 233

Clogher TYRONE 180 237 262

Clonaweel : see Kesh

Clough ANTRIM 206 (see also Ballymena)

Cloughey DOWN 121 249

Cloughmills ANTRIM 80

Cloughoge : see Newry

Coagh : see Cookstown

Coalisland TYRONE 180

Cohannon : see Dungannon

Coleraine LONDONDERRY 161 233 261

Comber DOWN 123 215

Conagher : see Ballymoney

Cookstown TYRONE 181 262

Coolbuck : see Lisbellaw

Coolisk : see Irvinestown & Lisnarick

Corbet : see Banbridge

Corradillar Quay : see Lisnaskea

Corralea : see Belcoo

Corry : see Belleek

Cosbystown : see Enniskillen

Craigantlet : see Newtownards

Craigavon ARMAGH 108 (see also Lurgan & Portadown)

Cranagh : see Omagh

Cranfield : see Kilkeel

Crawfordsburn DOWN 123

Creggan : see Omagh

Crom : see Newtownbutler

Crossgar DOWN 123 (see also Downpatrick)

Crossmaglen ARMAGH 108

Crumlin ANTRIM 80

Culkey : see Enniskillen

Cullybackey : see Ballymena

Cullyhanna : see Crossmaglen

Cultra : see Belfast & Holywood

Cushendall ANTRIM 82 193 206 243 (see also Glenariff)

Cushendun ANTRIM 83 206 243

Cushwash : see Lisnaskea

Derry : see Londonderry

Derryad : see Lisnaskea

Derrygonnelly FERMANAGH 145 196 224 (see also Enniskillen)

Derryharney : see Lisbellaw

Derrylin : see Enniskillen

Derrynanny : see Irvinestown

Derrynoid : see Draperstown

Derryvarey : see Derrygonnelly

Dervock ANTRIM 84 (see also Ballymoney)

Dolan's Ring : see Enniskillen

Donaghadee DOWN 123 251

Donaghmore TYRONE 183

Donegore : see Templepatrick

Doon : see Tempo

Downhill : see Castlerock

Downpatrick DOWN 124 216

Draperstown LONDONDERRY 165

Droagh : see Larne

Dromara : see Dromore DOWN

Dromore DOWN 125 216

Dromore TYRONE 183

Drumadravy : see Irvinestown

Drumahoe : see Londonderry

Drumary : see Derrygonnelly

Drumbadreevagh : see Belleek

Drumbanagher : see Newry

Drumbarna : see Kesh

Drumbo : see Lisburn

Drumclay : see Enniskillen

Drumlyon : see Enniskillen

Index to towns and villages

Drumskinny : see Kesh

Drumsurn : see Limavady

Dunadry ANTRIM 84

Dunamanagh : see Londonderry

Dundonald : see Belfast

Dundrum DOWN 126 216
. (see also Newcastle)

Dungannon TYRONE 183 237
263

Dungiven LONDONDERRY 165
196

Dunloy : see Ballymena &
Cloughmills

Dunmurry : see Belfast

Dunseverick : see Bushmills

Ederney : see Kesh

Eglinton LONDONDERRY 166 234

Enniskillen FERMANAGH 145 195
224 257

Farnamullan : see Lisbellaw

Feeny LONDONDERRY 167 234

Ferniskey : see Ballymena

Fintona TYRONE 185

Fivemiletown TYRONE 185 237
263

Florencecourt FERMANAGH 227
(see also Enniskillen)

Forkhill ARMAGH 213
(see also Newry)

Garrison FERMANAGH 151 195
227 257

Garvagh LONDONDERRY 167 234
(see also Coleraine)

Garvary : see Enniskillen

Giant's Causeway ANTRIM 84

Gilford DOWN 126

Glarryford : see Ballymena

Glassdrumman : see Annalong

Glasmullagh : see Enniskillen

Glenariff ANTRIM 243
(see also Waterfoot)

Glenarm ANTRIM 85 208

Glenavy : see Crumlin

Glendun : see Cushendun

Goblusk : see Ballinamallard &
Irvinestown

Gola : see Lisbellaw

Gortaclare : see Omagh

Gortin TYRONE 197 237 263
(see also Omagh)

Gosford : see Markethill

Gracehill : see Ballymena

Greenisland : see Carrickfergus &
Newtownabbey

Greyabbey DOWN 126
(see also Newtownards)

Groomsport DOWN 127 216

Helen's Bay DOWN 127

Hillsborough DOWN 127 216
251

Hilltown DOWN 128 216
(see also Newry)

Hollyfield : see Kesh

Holywell : see Belcoo

Holywood DOWN 128 195
(see also Belfast &
Newtownards)

Inishmore : see Lisbellaw

Irvinestown FERMANAGH 151 257
(see also Enniskillen)

Island Flackey : see Portrush

Islandmagee ANTRIM 86 208
245

Jordanstown : see
Newtownabbey

Keady ARMAGH 108

Kearney : see Portaferry

Kells : see Ballymena

Kesh FERMANAGH 152 196 228
258

Kilbroney : see Rostrevor

Kilkeel DOWN 128 217 251

Killadeas : see Enniskillen &
Irvinestown

Killard : see Newtownbutler

Killeter : see Castlederg

Killevy : see Newry

Killinchy DOWN 130 217

Killough DOWN 252

Killowen : see Rostrevor

Killykeeran : see Brookeborough

Killylea ARMAGH 108

Killyleagh DOWN 130 218

Killymaddy : see Dungannon

Kilmore : see Dungannon

Kilmore South : see Lisnaskea

Kilrea LONDONDERRY 167

Kinawley : see Enniskillen

Kircubbin DOWN 130 218

Index to towns and villages

Lack : see Kesh

Larne ANTRIM 87 245
(see also Carnlough)

Laughill : see Belleek

Laurencetown : see Banbridge

Leambreslen : see Lisbellaw

Leggs : see Belleek & Enniskillen

Leitrim : see Hilltown

Letter : see Kesh

Letterbreen : see Enniskillen

Lettermoney : see Irvinestown

Limavady LONDONDERRY 168
234

Lisbellaw FERMANAGH 155 229

Lisburn ANTRIM 89 193

Lislap : see Gortin & Omagh

Lisnagleer : see Dungannon

Lisnarick FERMANAGH 155 195
(see also Enniskillen)

Lisnaskea FERMANAGH 157 196
230 258

Littlemount : see Maguiresbridge

Loanends : see Crumlin

Londonderry LONDONDERRY 169
197 235

Lough Melvin : see Garrison

Loughgall ARMAGH 109

Loughmacrory : see Omagh

Lower Ballinderry : see Lisburn

Lurgan ARMAGH 109 194 247
(see also Craigavon)

Lusty Beg Island : see Kesh

Mackan : see Enniskillen

Macosquin : see Coleraine

Maghera LONDONDERRY 174 235

Magheracross : see
Ballinamallard

Magherafelt LONDONDERRY 174

Magherageeragh : see Enniskillen

Maghery ARMAGH 247
(see also Dungannon)

Magilligan : see Limavady

Maguiresbridge FERMANAGH 157

Markethill ARMAGH 109 247
(see also Armagh)

Marlbank : see Florencecourt

Martinstown : see Cushendall

Mayobridge : see Newry

Maze : see Lisburn

Meenacloybane : see Garrison

Millbrook : see Larne

Millisle DOWN 131 218 252

Moira DOWN 131 253

Moneydarraghmore : see
Annalong

Moneymore LONDONDERRY 175
261 (see also Cookstown)

Moorfields : see Ballymena

Moss-side : see Ballymoney

Mountjoy : see Omagh

Mountnorris : see Armagh

Moy TYRONE 186 (see also
Dungannon)

Moyad : see Kilkeel

Muckamore : see Antrim

Muckenagh : see Garrison

Muckross : see Kesh

Mullaghbawn ARMAGH 213
(see also Newry)

Mullyknock : see Tempo

Newcastle DOWN 131 194 218
253

Newry DOWN 136 220

Newtownabbey ANTRIM 92 208
(see also Belfast)

Newtownards DOWN 138 221
(see also Holywood)

Newtownbutler FERMANAGH 158
231

Newtownhamilton ARMAGH 109

Newtownstewart TYRONE 186
237 263

Nunsquarter : see Kircubbin

Nutts Corner : see Crumlin

Omagh TYRONE 187 197 238

Orlock : see Groomsport

Oxford Island : see Craigavon &
Lurgan

Park : see Claudy

Plumbridge : see Omagh

Pomeroy TYRONE 263

Portadown ARMAGH 109
(see also Craigavon)

Portaferry DOWN 140 194 221
255
(see also Cloughey)

Portballintrae ANTRIM 93 209
245

Portglenone ANTRIM 93 245

Portinode : see Kesh

Portora : see Enniskillen

Portrush ANTRIM 94 193 210
246

Ports: see Newtownbutler

Index to towns and villages

Portstewart LONDONDERRY 175 196 235 261

Pubble : *see Tempo*

Ramakitt : *see Caledon*

Randalstown ANTRIM 102 212

Rathmore : *see Belleek*

Rathfriland DOWN 140

Rathlin Island ANTRIM 103 246

Richhill ARMAGH 110

Roe Park : *see Limavady*

Roslea FERMANAGH 158

Rosscor : *see Belleek*

Rossmacaffry : *see Lisnaskea*

Rostrevor DOWN 140 194 195 222 255

Saintfield DOWN 141

Sandhill : *see Derrygonnelly*

Sandholes : *see Cookstown*

Seaforde DOWN 141

Seskinore : *see Omagh*

Shanaghy : *see Lisnaskea*

Shanless : *see Coalisland*

Silverbridge : *see Crossmaglen*

Silverhill : *see Enniskillen*

Silverwood : *see Craigavon*

Sion Mills TYRONE 189 (*see also Strabane*)

Sixmilecross TYRONE 189

Smith's Strand : *see Lisnaskea*

Spa : *see Ballynahinch*

Steelstown : *see Londonderry*

Stewartstown TYRONE 239 (*see also Coalisland*)

Stormont : *see Belfast*

Strabane TYRONE 189 239

Stranocum : *see Ballymoney*

Strangford DOWN 141 222 256

Strathfoyle : *see Londonderry*

Tamlaght : *see Enniskillen*

Tamnymore : *see Garvagh*

Tannaghmore : *see Randalstown*

Tara : *see Portaferry*

Tatnamallaght : *see Lisbellaw*

Tattygar : *see Lisbellaw*

Temple : *see Lisburn*

Templepatrick ANTRIM 103

Tempo FERMANAGH 158 232

Tollymore : *see Newcastle*

Tonyglaskan : *see Tempo*

Toomebridge ANTRIM 103

Topped Mountain : *see Enniskillen*

Torr : *see Ballycastle*

Trillick TYRONE 239 (*see also Omagh*)

Tullyhommon : *see Kesh*

Tyrella : *see Downpatrick*

Upperlands : *see Maghera*

Upper Ballinderry : *see Lisburn*

Waringstown ARMAGH 111

Warrenpoint DOWN 141 222

Waterfoot ANTRIM 104 212 (*see also Glenariff*)

Waterside : *see Londonderry*

Whiteabbey ANTRIM 193 200 (*see also Belfast & Newtownabbey*)

Whitehead ANTRIM 105

Whitehill : *see Ballinamallard*

Whitepark Bay : *see Ballintoy*

Whiterock : *see Killinchy*

Whiterocks : *see Portrush*

Reminder
This book is intended only as a convenient reference guide to accommodation in the province. Care has been taken to ensure the information is correct at the time of going to press, but the Northern Ireland Tourist Board does not accept responsibility for errors or omissions. While each establishment listed, except camping/caravan parks, is inspected annually, changes will inevitably occur after this book goes to press. In addition, before confirming your booking you should make your own enquiries.